Reprints of Economic Classics

PRINCIPLES OF POLITICAL ECONOMY

PRINCIPLES

OF

POLITICAL ECONOMY

Considered with a View to Their Practical Application

BY

THOMAS ROBERT MALTHUS

With an Introduction
By Morton Paglin

AUGUSTUS M. KELLEY · PUBLISHERS

First edition 1820
Second edition 1836
(London: W. Pickering, 1836)

Reprinted 1986 by
Augustus M. Kelley, Publishers
Fairfield, NJ 07006

Library of Congress Cataloging-in-Publication Data

Malthus, T. R. (Thomas Robert), 1766-1834.
Principles of political economy.

(Reprints of economic classics)
Reprint. Originally published: 2nd ed. with additions. London : W. Pickering, 1836.
Includes bibliographical references.
1. Economics. 2. Classical school of economics. I. Title. II. Series.
HB161.M25 1986 330.15 3 86-10606
ISBN 0-678-00038-7

Manufactured in the United States of America

MALTHUS'S *Principles* AND THE CLASSICAL TRADITION

Malthus's *Principles of Political Economy* is now recognized as one of the great books in classical economics, but when the first edition was issued in 1820, the public response was not encouraging. The *Edinburgh Review,* perhaps the most influential English journal of the period, which had enthusiastically endorsed Ricardo's *Principles,* quietly ignored Malthus's book. Likewise, no reviews appeared in the *Quarterly Review, Blackwoods Magazine,* the *Analectic Magazine* or the *London Magazine,* all of which (other than the *Quarterly)* had devoted one or more articles to a discussion of Ricardo's work.[1] The indifference of the journals is all the more surprising since Malthus had earlier acquired a considerable reputation as the author of the *Essay on Population.* One reason for this poor reception may be found in the effective opposition offered by Ricardo's disciples: McCulloch exercised exclusive control over the economics department of the *Edinburgh Review,* and in addition published his own newspaper, the *Scotsman,* in which Ricardian economics was regularly explained and extolled while Malthus was usually described as the apologist of the

[1] A significant exception to the poor press which Malthus received was a favorable two-part review in the *British Critic.* This journal further supported Malthus vis-à-vis J. B. Say when it subsequently reviewed Say's *Letters to Malthus.* (*British Critic,* Vol. XIV, 1820, pp. 177 ff., 285 ff., and 617 ff.) A few years later the *British Critic* became an exclusively theological journal.

landlords, and frequently in worse terms.[2] Torrens, gravitating toward Ricardian ideas, gave Malthus a very critical review in his newspaper, the *Traveller.*[3] James Mill and DeQuincey were also effective popularizers of the Ricardian doctrine who showed little sympathy for rival systems.[4] Malthus was quite aware of his exclusion from certain influential publications because of the dedication of Ricardo's followers. In a letter to Sismondi he notes:

> The *Edinburgh Review* has so entirely adopted Mr. Ricardo's system of Political Economy that it is probable neither you nor I shall be mentioned in it. I know indeed that a review of your work was written and sent, but it appears to have been rejected through the influence of the gentlemen who is the principal writer in the department of Political Economy, and who is known to have adopted fully and entirely all Mr. Ricardo's views.[5]

A few years later, (1823) Ricardian doctrine was given added authority and status as the new eco-

[2] Cf. the *Scotsman* of 10 March 1827. Quotes from this review are given in my Introduction to Malthus's *Definitions in Political Economy,* (New York: Augustus M. Kelley, 1963), p. xiii. Malthus was a friend of Francis Jeffrey, the editor of the *Edinburgh.* Jeffrey, knowing the kind of review Malthus would get at the hands of McCulloch, probably avoided a clash by not reviewing the book at all. McCulloch's exclusive dominion over the economics articles published in the *Edinburgh* is revealed in his correspondence with MacVey Napier who followed Jeffreys as editor. (*Selections from the Correspondence of the Late MacVey Napier, Esq.*, edited by his son, MacVey Napier, London, 1879, pp. 73-76.) A list of McCulloch's extensive contributions to the *Edinburgh*, approximately 78 articles, are given in Frank W. Fetter, "The Authorship of Economic Articles in the *Edinburgh Review*, 1802-47." (*Journal of Political Economy*, June 1953, pp. 232-59).

[3] In a letter of Ricardo to Malthus: "Torrens . . . has some remarks on your book . . . and as his arguments are on my side I of course think his criticism just." (Ricardo, *Works and Correspondence*, edited P. Sraffa, Vol. VIII, pp. 185-86n.)

[4] For a discussion of James Mill and the utilitarians, and the impetus they gave to Ricardian economics—to the disadvantage of Malthus—see Morton Paglin: *Malthus and Lauderdale, the Anti-Ricardian Tradition*, Chapter V, (New York: Augustus M. Kelley, 1961).

[5] Ricardo, *Works and Correspondence*, Vol. VIII, pp. 376-77.

nomics of the age by the *Encyclopedia Britannica* which for its 5th edition commissioned Ricardo, McCulloch and James Mill to write all the articles on economics. Malthus reviewed these contributions in an article written for the leading Tory Journal, the *Quarterly Review* and conceded that the new economics represented by the *Britannica* articles had in England attracted a very large proportion of the able men inclined to the subject.[6] Finally in 1828, Ricardian economics became the quasi-official doctrine of the utilitarians in their new publication, the *Westminster Review*.

When the 2nd edition of Malthus's *Principles* was issued posthumously in 1836, public interest was even less than in 1820. Malthus's controversy with Ricardo was no longer central to the current economic dialogue, for a new criticism of classical economics was developing along lines indicated by Bailey and Nassau Senior. However, Malthus at last received favorable mention in the *Edinburgh Review*, a long and laudatory obituary notice by Empson![7]

Some important insights into Malthus's *Principles* may be gained by comparing it with his own earlier work as well as with Ricardo's *Principles*. Malthus's *Principles of Political Economy* represents a marked shift in theory and policy from the contents of the *Essay on Population*. The economic-demographic model suggested in the *Essay* ran in terms of long cycles produced by variations in the ratio of population to resources: a sudden improvement in agricultural output would make for comfortable living, induce earlier marriages and lower child mortality; the resulting increase in population would eventually push the level of living down to the subsistence line or below. This population pressure would generate the positive checks—famine, disease, and related fac-

[6] *Quarterly Review*, Jan. 1824, pp. 333-34.

[7] "Life, Writings, and Character of Mr. Malthus", *Edinburgh Review*, Jan. 1837.

tors which raise mortality rates and again bring population into a more favorable relationship to agricultural resources. The only positive policy conclusions drawn from the theory were suggestions to the working classes that they lift themselves by their own bootstraps through postponement of marriage and the accumulation of savings. On the negative side, Malthus proposed a stringent revision of the poor laws with a view to their gradual elimination. Equally unpopular was the suggestion that emigration of agricultural workers should be encouraged as a means of reducing population, but only if the cottages of the departing workers were torn down. By maintaining a severe housing shortage, Malthus reasoned, the marriage rate might be reduced.[8] The argument of the *Essay* made nugatory any program for reform or economic improvement which did not act directly to reduce the birth rate of the lower classes.

The analysis and policy proposals of the *Principles of Political Economy* are in sharp contrast with those of the *Essay:* Instead of population relentlessly pressing on the means of subsistence, Malthus in the *Principles* sees vast powers of production lying fallow, with existing resources adequate for ten times the present population.[9] In place of exhortations to the working class to save and to establish banks to encourage thrift, he vigorously argues against those who declare thrift and parsimony to be a virtue and national benefit, and suggests devices to encourage consumption.[10] In the *Essay* advocates of poor employment schemes are treated with condescension; in

[8] Cf. *Essay on Population*, Everyman's edition, Vol. II, pp. 30-37, and C. R. Fay quoting Malthus's testimony before the Emigration Committee in 1827, *(Economic Journal*, June 1935, pp. 227-28.)

[9] *Principles of Political Economy*, p. 311. "The increased productiveness of the powers of labor . . . [offsets] the effect of taking poorer land into cultivation . . . for some centuries to come . . ." (p. 288).

[10] *Principles*, pp. 433-34. The economic importance of menial servants and luxury expenditures is stated on p. 408.

the *Principles*, Malthus advocates public works programs. Yet no formal revision of the arguments in the *Essay* were made even though Malthus brought out a 6th edition in 1826, seven years after he wrote the *Principles*.[11]

While the reasoning of the *Essay* fits in perfectly with the classical Ricardian approach, and was incorporated into Ricardo's long run theory of distribution and development, Malthus's *Principles* represents a new line of thinking which, as indicated above, was sometimes at odds with the earlier Malthus. Ricardo fully approved of the *Essay* and the basic theory of rent presented in the *Inquiry*, but as the *Notes on Malthus* clearly shows, he regarded many sections of the *Principles* as being on a par with Malthus's "dangerous heresy on the corn laws" which made him question whether Malthus's "abilities as a political economist have not been overrated."[12] Malthus in turn wrote the *Principles* with Ricardo looking over his shoulder. In the Introduction he notes that his book was written in large part as a reaction to Ricardo's work which "specifically engaged a considerable portion of my attention"—and he was at times almost "staggered" by Ricardo's authority even when unconvinced by his reasoning *(Principles*, 2nd ed., p. 18). A few of the main areas of disagreement will now be briefly reviewed.

Malthus, anticipating later developments, refused to limit real costs to the sacrifice of labor, but broadened the concept to include the real cost of saving which he pointed out might be quite high in poor and primitive countries (pp. 85-86). Accordingly, Malthus was not sympathetic to Ricardo's search for a measure of value which would minimize the deviation of exchange values from labor inputs, because

[11] I have discussed this further in my *Malthus and Lauderdale: the Anti-Ricardian Tradition*, pp. 137-50.

[12] Cf. Letters exchanged with McCulloch, Ricardo, *Works*, Vol. VIII, pp. 139-142.

he fully recognized the legitimacy of non-labor costs as a fundamental constituent of value. Malthus was looking for a measure of value which would function as a price index deflator, and thus facilitate the comparison of real value over time, free of the disturbing effects produced by changes in the value of money. For this purpose he used a labor-command measure of value—the amount of common day-labor which a commodity could be exchanged for, given the prevailing market prices. Assuming a fairly constant real wage, a unit of common labor would represent a fixed basket of wage-goods and in this way Malthus's measure of value would short-circuit changes in money wages and prices, enabling him to make real value comparisons over time. Finally, whereas Ricardo sought to minimize or eliminate the effects of supply and demand on long run equilibrium prices by assuming constant costs as the typical condition of supply, Malthus integrated cost of production with the long run supply and demand determination of prices. [13]

On the static theory of rent, Malthus and Ricardo started out from a common ground—they both developed essentially the same differential rent doctrine. [14] But in applying the classical rent formula to the historical analysis of the trend of the distributive income shares, the two men sharply diverged. The main theoretical disagreement arose over the issue of improvements in agriculture and their effort on rent as a distributive share. The broader social issue centered on the relation of the landed class to the rest of society. Did the landlords have a vested interest in the status quo or were they likely to share in the benefits

[13] Malthus, *Principles*, pp. 65-69, 78.

[14] Ricardo, in the *Essay on Profits:* "In all that I have said concerning the origin and progress of rent, I have briefly repeated and endeavored to elucidate the principles which Mr. Malthus has so ably laid down, on the same subject, in his 'Inquiry into the Nature and Progress of Rent', a work abounding in original ideas . . ." *(Works*, Vol. IV, p. 15n.) But a few years later, Ricardo was more aware of differences with Malthus. Cf. Ricardo, *Principles*, ch. 32.

of technological progress? Was the policy of agricultural protection merely a device to redistribute income from the "productive classes" to the landowners; or would the Corn Laws induce permanent improvements in agriculture which would benefit all classes of society?

In order to prove that the landlords were the enemies of progress, Ricardo employed a model in which all change ceased except for technology in agriculture. Population was static, demand for food was inelastic, and hence output-increasing innovations in agriculture would lead to the abandonment of marginal lands, less intensive cultivation of intramarginal land, and a decline in total rents. Malthus challenged this reasoning by pointing out that agricultural innovations occurred slowly in a context of growing population, capital accumulation, and an increasing demand for food—therefore, historically rents did not decline with improvements, and would not do so in the future.[15]

Malthus was justified in criticising Ricardo for abstracting from population change and capital accumulation in a model which was offered as a realistic projection of the effects of technical progress in agriculture. But Malthus was wrong when he attempted to prove that although agricultural protection leads to a rise in rents, this increase in rents is a net addition to the surplus of society rather than a transfer from consumers to landlords.[16]

Much of the recent literature on Malthus has been concerned with the question of whether Malthus's theory of aggregate demand, and his concepts of saving and investment, truly anticipate Keynes, or whether they belong mainly with the classical tradition.[17] There is still considerable room for various

[15] *Principles*, pp. 194-97, 210.

[16] Malthus, *Principles*, pp. 207-10. Ricardo's criticism is in the *Notes on Malthus* (*Works*, Vol. II, pp. 210-13).

[17] *E. g.*, S. Hollander, "Malthus and Keynes", *Economic Journal*, June 1962, pp. 355-59 and references therein.

interpretations of Malthus, but the facts concerning his theory of aggregate output are now clearly emerging: Malthus's theory of the cycle stresses the damaging consequence of restricted consumption and a high level of saving (investment); this imbalance produces a glut of commodities and a drop in the rate of profit; the meager return on investments then leads to hoarding ("owners of floating capital vainly seeking outlets") and a partial switch from investment to unproductive consumption (menial servants). But the switch from investment to consumption (in the form of greater expenditure on menial servants) is not regarded as a sufficient economic stabilizer. Malthus felt it necessary to recommend public works and a large government budget. Contrary to the classical aversion to taxation and government expenditure, Malthus justified a large budget—not because he regarded the government services as desirable—but exclusively in terms of its stabilizing effect on demand and employment.[18]

In the Malthusian sequence of the cycle, hoarding is secondary to under-consumption and over-investment which seem to be the strategic factors. Hoarding follows the over-investment phase and worsens the crisis. But this is not adequate justification for asserting that Malthus "maintained the classical savings-investment doctrine".[19] Malthus was clearly not a believer in the typical classical doctrine that all savings are automatically spent (invested). The fact that he considers hoarding a distinct possibility is itself a significant departure from the classical tradition. For example, in a discussion of fiscal policy, Malthus points out that tax reductions may lead to hoarding and therefore undesirable effects on demand and em-

[18] *Principles*, pp. 418-27, 429-30, ". . . I feel very little doubt that instances have practically occurred of national wealth being decidedly stimulated by the consumption of those who have been supported by taxes." (p. 410.)

[19] Hollander, *op. cit.*, p. 359.

ployment.[20] For similar reasons he opposed the redemption of the public debt. Ricardo considered these conclusions almost beyond the pale of respectable opinion and reacted with quiet exasperation. Equally incomprehensible to him was the notion that restricted consumption and high investment could produce a crisis.[21]

It is probably unwise to put a simple label on the Malthusian analysis of total output and call it either Keynesian or classical. However, it is clear that Malthus went far beyond the Ricardians (including John Stuart Mill) both in his macro-theory and in his willingness to recommend highly unorthodox fiscal policy measures. Malthus, in his attack on Say's Law, in his limited but definite role assigned to hoarding, in his sharp differentiation of the effects of consumption expenditure versus investment expenditure, and in his advanced approach to debt and fiscal policies, travelled a good part of the road from typical classical doctrine to Keynesian and post-Keynesian thinking.

[20] *Principles*, pp. 421, 423, 426.

[21] Ricardo, *Works*, Vol. II, pp. 307, 433-36, 441, 449, 451-52.

MORTON PAGLIN

International Population and Urban Research
University of California, Berkeley

CONTENTS.

BOOK II.

ADVERTISEMENT

TO THE

SECOND EDITION.

Not many years had elapsed after the first edition of this work, when it became known to all with whom Mr. Malthus had the opportunity of communicating on the subject, or who were acquainted with his last publications, that his opinions on the subject of value had undergone some change.

Having formerly assumed, in common with most other Economists, that there was no perfectly accurate and unvarying measure of value, he had proposed a mean between corn and labour, as being the nearest approximation to it, which could be found.

But maturer reflection led him to a different view; and he subsequently became convinced that the standard of which he had been in search must necessarily reside in some *one* unalterable object, which had a fixed and permanent existence; rightly judging, that it would be impossible to establish any satisfactory conclusions respecting the rise or fall in the value of commodities, unless there existed a real test, which could, at all times, be practically referred to.

It was not, however, till after long meditation, and the most careful consideration of the subject, that he finally adopted the measure proposed by the author of the *Inquiry into the Wealth of Nations*, and became a convert to the doctrine, that as "Labour was the first price, the original purchase money that was paid for all things,"* the *value* of every thing must be greater or less in proportion "as it is worth more or less of this original purchase money."

That many eminent writers since the time of Adam Smith, should have rejected this measure, has probably arisen from their having given to the term *value*, a sense different from that which he gave to it, and which it is usually meant to express. According to their notion of value, it consists in the *general power of purchasing*,† or expresses the *relation* which commodities bear to *each other*, from which it would necessarily follow, that if the cost of producing all things were either increased or diminished, their value would nevertheless remain unaltered, provided they continued to exchange with each other in the same proportion as before; and by the same rule, that when a *rise or fall* takes place in any commodity or commodities, all other commodities must experience a corresponding *fall or rise*, or that, when some become cheaper, the rest must *necessarily* become dearer, and *vice versa*.

Now this definition makes the value of a commodity to depend as much upon the causes affecting all others which may be exchanged for

* Wealth of Nations, Book I. ch. v.

† It is true that Adam Smith has also defined value (Book I. ch. iv.) as *the power of purchasing;* but it is clear from the context, and from the whole tenor of his work, that he meant the power of purchasing which a commodity derives from causes *peculiar to itself*, and which depend upon the cost of procuring it. This limitation is most essential; but it has not been generally made.

it, as upon those which may affect itself; and of value so understood, it is perfectly obvious that there can be no standard, since there is no one object which can at all times purchase or exchange for an uniform quantity of all others; and if there were any such object, it would not be a better measure of others, than they would be of it.

But *value* in its popular signification, and in the sense in which it has been for the most part used by Adam Smith, expresses a very different sort of *relation*, namely, that which subsists between commodities and their *cost*, (including profit) or *the sacrifice* that must be made in order to procure them;* and if the quantity of labour which they are worth, or which must be given in exchange for them, be the proper measure of that sacrifice, it becomes the very standard sought for.

So thought latterly Mr. Malthus, and his coincidence with Adam Smith, on so important a point, founded as it appears to have been upon entirely distinct grounds, was first made known by him in a pamphlet, entitled ***The Measure of Value, stated and illustrated with an application of it to the alterations in the value of the English***

* That this is what is commonly meant by *value*, every practical man perfectly well knows. If, for instance, the question is asked what is the value of corn, no one ever supposes it to mean, what is the relation or proportion which it bears to oil, or wine, or hides, or cloth, or linen, or to other commodities generally, but what will it *cost* to any one desirous of purchasing it, or giving an equivalent for it. Now of this, the quantity of other commodities which it will exchange for, can give no idea, unless *their* cost happens to be previously known; but the cost of obtaining money, or its value, is always known, or at least easily ascertained, being clearly indicated by the *money price* of labour in each country. It is on this account, that the object of the question is, in almost every instance, sufficiently answered by a reference to the money price of the article concerning which the inquiry is made. (*See three lectures on the cost of obtaining money, by N. W. Senior, Esq.*)

currency since 1790, which he published in the year 1823.

But the subject, notwithstanding the Author's practical application of it was, at the time, regarded chiefly as a theoretical one; and it consequently attracted but little attention, being seldom alluded to, except in the immediate circles where such questions were discussed.

The more, however, Mr. Malthus reflected upon it, the more did it acquire importance in his eyes; and in 1827, he took another opportunity of enforcing his views respecting it in a small volume, which he published. *On Definitions in Political Economy*, in which some of the leading principles of the science are likewise to be found, admirably explained, in a concentrated form.

The intervention of these minor publications and Mr. Malthus's other pursuits prevented him from sooner devoting himself to the second edition of his *Political Economy*. The first edition had been long out of print, and the work could not of course again make its appearance, until the author had remodelled it, so as to adapt it to his new opinions on value.

In doing this, if he had contented himself (as he at one time intended) with making such alterations only as were strictly necessary, the task would have been comparatively easy. His new views, so far from interfering with his general train of reasoning, or affecting any of his main conclusions, served only to confirm and establish them. A fresh section in the chapter on value, in place of the sixth and seventh sections of the former edition, together with a few slight changes in other parts of the book, chiefly of a verbal kind, would have been all that was absolutely required to preserve the unity and consistency of the work.

But this did not satisfy Mr. Malthus. He

conceived that to pass over so main a doctrine thus slightly, would not be treating it in a way, which its importance seemed to demand. Being persuaded that it was not a mere matter of nomenclature, but a most fundamental principle, which affected more or less all other parts of the subject, he was desirous of imparting to others, the like conviction of its utility and importance. In this new Edition, therefore, he has gone more largely into the question of value than before, having preferred to incur the charge of tediousness and prolixity, rather than omit saying anything that might render it more clear and intelligible to his readers, or meet the objections which had been urged against it by those whose opinions differed from his own. But before he had completed the whole of the alterations which he had in contemplation, and while he was yet occupied in correcting and improving the latter parts of the work, his mortal career was suddenly closed, and an end for ever put to his earthly labours.

What other changes he might have made, had his days been prolonged, it is of course not possible to say; but from the state in which his manuscripts were found, there is reason to believe that he had done all, or nearly all, that he considered essential.

Very little indeed has been required to put the work in a state fit for publication. The text has in some places been slightly varied, where a regard to perfect clearness or precision seemed to require it, some passages have been omitted, where the sense of them appears to have been better expressed in other parts of the work, and a few notes have been interspersed here and there, which if they add nothing to the force of the Author's reasonings, may serve still further to elucidate the several subjects to which they refer.

If, notwithstanding, the care which has been taken to free the present copy from imperfection, some discrepancies should be found to exist, and some needless repetitions and verbal inaccuracies to occur, which have escaped the Editor's notice, (and which, considering the insertion of so much new matter, is far from being improbable,) the Reader will bear in mind, that he is perusing a work, to which, the last touches have not been given by the hand of the Master.

MEMOIR

OF

ROBERT MALTHUS.

It is matter of general observation that the lives of literary men, especially of the good and virtuous, are rarely fruitful in that class of incidents which are wont to be most attractive in the public eye. With the minds of such persons, however, it may be far otherwise: of these the march is often varied and eventful; and to describe faithfully their state and condition at the different stages of their being, the steps by which they have advanced, the helps and hindrances they have experienced, and the influences which have most contributed to form or to fix their character, would be a task not less interesting than instructive; but the misfortune is that it is one which can only be performed adequately by the subject himself, and, as great merit is usually accompanied with great modesty, they who are best qualified to execute the office, are generally the least disposed to undertake it. In neither of these respects can Mr. Malthus be considered as an exception: the tenor of his life was one of the most even serene and peaceful that can be well imagined; and such was his diffidence and habitual disregard of self, that he has left nothing upon record intended directly as a memorial of his life, and little else which can be made subservient to such a purpose by others. But this reserve, so becoming and characteristic in himself, would be almost culpable in his friends. They are well aware that such a man could not depart from a scene, in which as an author he had borne so conspicuous a part, without exciting much curiosity respecting the principles and the conduct of his private life; and as they have nothing to communicate but what is honourable to himself and edifying to the public, there is no reason why they should be silent. It happens too, fortunately, that the materials at their disposal are quite sufficient in this respect; for as the recollections of his friends, still fresh and vivid, are fully competent to exhibit his character and manners in his later years, so also his own filial piety, by treasuring up every record of his father, has undesignedly furnished more particulars for the history of his early youth than are usually found in the annals of literary men.

Nor will the task of recording these memorials be an unprofitable one. No one could have been intimate with Mr. Malthus without deriving much instruction as well as pleasure from his conversation, and many salutary lessons from the contemplation of his character under the trials he underwent. To review therefore the course of his life is to bring back these influences to the memory, and, impressed as they must be now with the sad reflection that the spirit which imparted them is gone, they will return with more force than when they first came from the living man.

But higher interests than these are concerned in this memorial. The character of Mr. Malthus has been so industriously mixed up with his writings, and for so long a time; and the writings themselves have been so egregiously misinterpreted and misunderstood, that it becomes an act of common justice to rescue his name from the obloquy in which it has been involved.

To the Author himself, who is now far beyond the reach of earthly praise or blame, it is matter of no importance what the world may judge; but to his family it is otherwise. To them the memory of his virtues is much more precious than that of his literary fame; it is connected with more tender recollections, and cheered with nobler prospects; besides it is an inheritance more especially their own; and it would be matter of future shame and sorrow to those who shared in his regard, if, while so much has been said by others to whom he was little known, no friendly voice should be raised to speak of him as he really was, and to lessen the weight of those calumnies, which, though they passed lightly over his family while he was alive, are calculated to aggravate their grief now they are deprived of him. Their own conviction of his worth, is indeed the most unfailing source of comfort under his loss, but next to this is the assurance that others will partake of it; and, under this impression, it will be pleasing to them to know, that, in whatever age or country his works may hereafter be studied, they will carry with them a memorial of the spirit in which they were composed, and of the objects they were intended to accomplish.

But there is another and a far more important purpose which the diffusion of this memoir may be made to serve, and one still more congenial to the mind of the author himself, if yet cognizant of earthly things; and that is the vindication of truth itself, by procuring for his writings a calmer and more impartial hearing than they have hitherto received. No intelligent and well-educated person can have observed what has been passing in the civil economy of this country for the last forty years without being convinced that a great change has been gradually wrought into the public mind respecting the poor laws, and their administration, and that the works of

Mr. Malthus have been exceedingly influential in bringing it about. To this pre-eminence, whether it be good or evil, neither friends nor enemies will be disposed to dispute his claim; and though the natural course of events in our domestic history has singularly concurred in illustrating the principles of the "Essay on Population," and daily experience has practically exhibited its conclusions, it is to Mr. Malthus chiefly we are to attribute the improved knowledge we now possess, and the advanced position in which we stand. His was the warning voice which first roused the public attention to the errors which prevailed upon the subject; his the sagacious and patient mind which reduced the various and perplexing phenomena of social life to the law he had laid down; and from his works was derived the light which has given value to the experience and confidence to the lessons which have been drawn from it. For some time, indeed, he may be said to have stood alone upon the ground he had taken; nor is it too much to affirm, that there is scarcely any other instance in the history of the world of so important a revolution effected in public opinion, within the compass of a single life and by a single mind. It was not likely, however, that a victory like this could be achieved without a contest; still less that a contest of such a nature, against opinions venerable by age and usage, and backed by a formidable host of prejudices, interests, and feelings, could possibly be carried on for so long a period without exciting a great degree of irritation and abuse, of which a large portion would naturally be poured out upon the leader.

Accordingly, we find that while, even by the intelligent and candid, every step was yielded slowly, and reluctantly, the tide of public opinion ran obstinately against him; the Malthusian code and the Malthusian doctrines became by-words of ominous import in the people's mouths, and thousands were ready to join in the cry, who knew nothing of Mr. Malthus, and had never read a line of his works. But this was not the worst feature of the case: many estimable and pious men there were, whose concurrence and approbation he would have been delighted to obtain, who read his work, and were at once convinced and offended by it. Misled by the turn the controversy had at first unfortunately taken, and too intent upon the evil involved in the "principle of population" to discern or even to enquire after the many blessings which are bound up with it, and overbalance it, they could not be in charity with a work which at once shook their confidence in the Divine Benevolence, and dissipated those visions of perfectibility in which they had indulged. Their faith was weak, because it was founded upon a narrow basis, and instead of enquiring how far they were in fault themselves, they laid the whole blame upon the author: irritated and suspicious they turned away impatiently from the truth because its first aspect was forbidding to them; and while some obstinately closed their eyes against the facts, and others eagerly caught at any empyrical solution of them which was offered, they all came hastily to the conclusion that Mr. Malthus was a cold and heartless, if not an impious man. From these first impressions, notwithstanding the light which has been lately thrown upon the subject from various quarters, many have found it impossible to recover; hence it has happened, that though the cause has triumphed, the author is still odious in their eyes, and instances may be pointed out even at the present day, where in the same work, and even in the same page, the fruits of Mr. Malthus' labours are recorded with entire approbation, while the man and his works are treated with unqualified abuse.

Now nothing, it is believed, can serve more effectually to soften these feelings, and to remove these prejudices, in whatever quarter they may exist, than to exhibit the author himself as he really was, and to prove what manner of spirit he was of. "A good tree can not bring forth evil fruit;" and to shew indisputably that Mr. Malthus was an enlightened, and benevolent man, is to furnish a strong argument a priori in favour of the principle, and the tendency of the work; at all events it will be an irresistible reason with all candid minds for not rejecting it at once. And if under this impression, proceeding one step further, they would fairly examine the principle of population laid down by him under all its aspects, and in all its influences, direct and indirect, upon the moral conduct of man in social life, there is reason to hope that every thing would appear different to them; they would find their sense of the Divine Goodness improved and strengthened rather than diminished by their acquiescence in his views, and they would be thankful to an author, who, while he has developed at so much cost and pains a law of deep practical importance to the welfare of mankind, has brought into view a fresh and striking instance of the Divine Economy, in perfect harmony with that state of discipline and trial by which the scripture teaches us we are to be improved and purified for a higher and happier state hereafter. Hence, then, the great advantage which the diffusion of this memoir may produce; imperfect notions of Mr. Malthus' writings have been the means of casting a shade over his name, and it is reasonable to hope that a better knowledge of his character may bring about a fairer estimate of his work.

But the benefit by no means stops here. Were this a question of a speculative nature, and referring only to some imaginary constitution of things, we might safely commit it to that tribunal which, sooner or later, never fails to do justice to the truth; but this is not the case, it is in reality identified with a subject now occupying a great share of the public mind, and coming home to every man's business and bosom, and under this view it is quite essential that no unnecessary delay should intervene in the removal of all errors respecting it. The struggle about the Poor Laws has ended as most political struggles happily do in England, not by the subversion of an institution which, however corrupted by abuse, or injured by time, is yet congenial to the institutions of the country, and founded upon christian principles; but by the renewal of its spirit, the correction of its errors, and the supply of its defects. With these views the Poor Laws Amendment Bill has been framed and passed into a law; and a great experiment is now making throughout the country under its authority, upon the result of which, the due and harmonious adjustment of the relations between the rich and the poor will hereafter mainly depend. But this act is founded upon the basis of Mr. Malthus' work. The Essay on Population and the Poor Laws Amendment Bill, will stand or fall together. They have the same friends and the same enemies, and the relations they bear to each other, of theory and practice, are admirably calculated to afford mutual illumination and support. Nor can it be said that this cooperation is not needed. Notwithstanding the favourable auspices under which the working of the bill has commenced, it is still a question with many how much of this advantage is owing to the intrinsic merits of the act, and how much to the unexampled state of prosperity we now enjoy, and the increasing demand for labour which accompanies it: at all events a strong and lively opposition is still daily carried on against it, as well in the metropolis as in the country; and so long as any influential persons are found disposed to dispute the truth of Mr. Malthus' principles, or the force of his conclusions, so long must the Poor Laws Amendment Bill expect hostility and mistrust. It is true, indeed, that the best testimony to the soundness of the measure will be a general experience of its blessings throughout the country under a wise, a moderate, and, above all, a Christian administration of its provisions—blessings, indeed, not such simply or mainly as result to the wealthier classes of society, from the diminution of their burdens, and the assignment of parochial odium to others, but such as the poor themselves will derive and eventually be conscious of, in the elevation of their minds, the bettering of their condition, the improvement of their morals and habits, and especially the softening of that harsh temper and disposition towards the other classes of society, at present one of the worst features of the times, and of which the flatterers and disturbers of the people are always ready to take advantage. Such are the ends which must finally consecrate this measure in the hearts of the British public, as well as in the sight of God, and of such were the visions which cheered the labours of Mr. Malthus, and consoled him for the ingratitude with which they were received. Nor is the day far distant, we trust, when these visions will, humanly speaking, be realized; meanwhile, it cannot be denied that a juster appreciation of the author and his works cannot fail of being of the greatest service, as well in the actual operation of the bill, as in facilitating its favour and acceptance with the public.

It remains for us to say a few words respecting the authority on which this Memoir rests. It was written, for the most part, immediately after his death, by an early and intimate friend of Mr. Malthus, thoroughly acquainted with his character and views, and, what is more, familiar with the rise and progress of those opinions which have so often brought his name before the world; and though many months have elapsed since this event, and calmer reflexion has succeeded to the excitement under which it was drawn up, there is nothing in it which the writer is disposed either to abandon or to change. On the contrary, the more he considers and reflects, the more he is convinced that all that is here personal to Mr. Malthus is simply just, and nothing else. Nor is there wanting to this conviction the testimony of others, less liable to suspicion than his own. Defective as the sketch may be, there has been no question respecting its fidelity and truth. The general form and character and the leading features of his mind are there: they have been recognized by his friends, and have not been disputed by his adversaries; and whatever difference of opinion may arise respecting the judgment here pronounced upon Mr. Malthus as an author, from which, however, his friend is by no means willing to recede, there is reason to hope that this statement may go forth as an undoubted and authentic testimony to his character as a man.

Thomas Robert Malthus was born in 1766, at the Rookery, in the county of Surrey, a small but beautiful estate at that time in the possession of his family, and now well known throughout the neighbourhood of Guildford and Dorking. His father was Daniel Malthus, a gentleman of good family and independent fortune, attached to a country life, but much occupied in classical and philosophic pursuits, and with a strong bias towards foreign literature. He was the friend and correspondent of Rousseau, and one of his executors, and in some of his tastes, especially that of botany, is said to have resembled him. His habits and manners were retired, and his character so unostentatious, that though he was the author of several works which seem to have succeeded in their day, he never could be persuaded to put his name to any of them. In the obituary of the Monthly Magazine for 1800, in which his death is noticed, he is described as the translator of some pieces from the French and German; an error which was visited by the subject of this memoir with more indignation than he ever shewed towards his own persecutors.* Of this gentleman, Robert Malthus was the second son, and in early life seems to have displayed so fine a promise of character and abilities, as to have excited a strong interest in his father's mind; insomuch, that he undertook the conduct of his education in a great measure himself, directing his youthful studies, and entering with him into the details of his pleasures and amusements for the purpose of forming his habits and disposition. At what school the first years of his youth were passed, does not appear, but whether from the changes which took place about this time in the residence of his family, or from some peculiar opinions which his father seems to have entertained respecting edu-

* TO THE EDITOR OF THE MONTHLY MAGAZINE.

SIR, Feb. 19.

I SHALL esteem it as a particular favour if you will allow me to correct an erroneous paragraph which appeared in your obituary for last month. Daniel Malthus, Esq. is there mentioned as the translator of some pieces from the French and German. I can say, from certain knowledge, that he did not translate them; nor was he born to copy the works of others.—Whatever he wrote was drawn from the original and copious source of his own fine understanding and genius; but, from his character, which was so singularly unostentatious, as to shun everything that might attract notice, it will probably never be known as his.

I am, Sir, yours, &c.
ROBERT MALTHUS.

cation, he was never sent to any public school; and in this respect, is one, amongst many other remarkable instances in the present time, of men who have risen into eminence under the disadvantage of an irregular and desultory education.

From the age of nine or ten, until the time of his admission at Cambridge, with the exception of a short period which he spent at the academy at Warrington, he remained always under private tuition, and was sometimes a solitary pupil in his tutor's house. It must be allowed, however, that his instructors were men of no common minds; for besides his father, whose watchful care never deserted him, one of them was Richard Graves, and another, Gilbert Wakefield—the first, the author of the Spiritual Quixote, a gentleman of considerable learning and humour; the last, a person very prominent in his day, in several departments of literature—a scholar, a politician, and a divine; a classical correspondent also of Charles Fox; but wild, restless, and paradoxical in many of his opinions, a prompt and hardy disputant, and, unhappily for himself, deeply engaged in several of those violent controversies, to which the French Revolution had given birth.

It is difficult to believe that a youth like Robert Malthus, naturally sensitive and intelligent, could be brought in frequent contact with men of such qualities and attainments without deriving great advantages, and incurring some danger. From the last, however, his natural good sense, and his early habits of observation, happily protected him. He was not born, indeed, as he himself said of his father, readily to mould his own character and opinions upon those of the first person under whose influence he might be accidentally thrown. On the contrary, he began very early to judge for himself, even in matters relating to his education, and in this respect as well as others, was a proof in how short a time, and at what an early period of life, a fund of useful experience may be laid up by an intelligent and observing mind, thrown upon its own resources, and disposed to make the most of them.

It is curious to observe in looking back upon this period of his life, with what singular discretion he seems to have steered his course amid the critical circumstances which surrounded him—how much he owed in the formation of his character to influences which were never taken into the account, and how few marks and signs it bore when grown into maturity of the scenes and persons to which he had been entrusted for the specific purpose of education. More than one instance occurred, as appears from his correspondence of this date, in which, without any injury to their mutual affection, the advice of the father was successfully combated by the superior discretion of the son. Nor was the moral influence of his official instructors in any respect more decisive; he left the house of Mr. Graves, indeed, at an early period, before any lasting impressions from sympathy or antipathy were likely to have been made, and though he remained with Gilbert Wakefield till his admission at college, and always upon the kindest terms, and by his own acknowledgement derived great benefit from the course of study which he pursued with him, there seems to have been no great community of sentiment or opinion between them upon the graver subjects connected with the conduct of human life. In truth their characters were altogether very different, nor was there ever anything in the truly catholic spirit of Mr. Malthus which could be traced to his training in that school.

It would be unjust, however, to the kindness of an excellent parent, to deny that to him he was more indebted than to any other person who had mingled in his education for the form and condition of his mind, and this, not so much from any instructions directly conveyed, as from the opportunities which their intimacy afforded of stimulating the faculties of the son, of encouraging him to think for himself, and of first implanting in his mind that love of truth and independence of spirit, which were ever afterwards so remarkable in him. If the nature of this memoir would permit, it might be pleasing to lay before the reader many specimens of that happy intercourse of mutual good feeling, and of amicable and frank discussion between the father and the son to which we have referred; but we may venture to insert extracts from two or three letters, which will serve to confirm what has been said. The first was written just after the father had removed from his former residence in Surry to Albury, where a new one was preparing:

June 16, 1787.

"You must find your way to us over bricks and tiles, and meet with five in a bed, and some of us under hedges; but every body says, they will make room for Robert. May I take the liberty of sending my compliments to Mr. Frend, with my most grateful thanks for the attention he has been so kind as to shew you. You will guess the pleasure I have in returning thanks for that notice which you would not have had without deserving it.

"Everything I have heard of you has given me the most heart-felt satisfaction. I have always wished, my dear boy, that you should have a love of letters, that you should be made independent of mean and trifling amusements, and feel a better support than that of the next man who is idle enough to offer you his company. I have no doubt that you will be able to procure any distinction from them you please. I am far from repressing your ambition; but I shall content myself with their adding to your happiness. Every kind of knowledge, every acquaintance with nature and art, will amuse and strengthen your mind, and I am perfectly pleased that cricket should do the same by your legs and arms. I love to see you excel in exercises of the body, and I think myself that the better half, and much the most agreeable one, of the pleasures of the mind is best enjoyed while one is upon one's legs;—this is pretty well for me to say, who have little else left but my bed and my arm-chair. May you long enjoy all the delights of youth and youthful spirits, of an improving mind, and of a healthful body,—but ever and above all, my dear boy, with virtue and its best affections in your heart.

"Adieu! "DANIEL MALTHUS."

It is pleasing to observe in what a prophetic spirit this prayer of an affectionate father in the close of his letter was drawn up; for such, in all these particulars, was Mr. Malthus, and such he remained to the last moment of his life.

To illustrate still farther the remark we have made of the manner in which the graver instruction of his father was mingled with lighter matters intended for the same purpose, it may be interesting to add another extract from one of his letters to him at Cambridge:

"MY DEAR BOB,

"I find you are not yet in your new rooms. I heartily hope they will prove agreeable to you. We should have been truly glad to have seen you here in the leisure of Christmas, and would have subscribed to your journey; not that I used to think Oxford the less pleasant, and certainly not the less useful for being disburthened of some of its society: I imagine you will say the same of Cambridge.

"I have always found that one of my greatest comforts in life was the delight I have ever taken in solitude—if, indeed, one can give that name to anything which is likely to happen to you or me. A true hermitage for any length of time is, I believe, an unnatural state; it would be a cruel deprivation of what we have both experienced to be the heart's dearest happiness. But even this at certain seasons will always strengthen and refresh the mind, and suffer her wings to grow, which

In the various bustle of resort,
Were all too ruffled and sometimes impair'd.

The skating has been good this year. Did you go to Ely? By the way have you learnt the heart and cross roll? All the other tricks, such as skating backwards, &c. are absurd; but I like these as they amuse one upon a small piece of ice, and they are very clever in society either for two or four; four make this figure, ꝏ. The frost was harder than is usual in England. January 2, at sunrise, 14 Fahr. January 3, at 9½ post merid. 14 again. Ask Mr. —— how it was at Cambridge. My thermometer was upon a north wall at a distance from the house. Did not I ask you whether you had got my Theocritus with you? Have you got Rutherford's Philosophy, 2 vols. quarto? I would advise you to read something of that kind, while you are engaged in mathematical studies; and constantly to use yourself to apply your tools. I hate to see a girl working curious stitches upon a piece of rag. I recommend Sanderson's Optics to you, and Emerson's Mechanics; Long's Astronomy you certainly have. There are papers of the mathematical kind in the Royal Society transactions which are generally worth reading. How do you manage about books? What good book on mensuration have you met with? Have you seen Bougner's mensuration of the degree in South America? I suppose Sir I's Principia to be your chief classical book after the elementary ones.

"We are all pretty well; but Charlotte will write in a day or two. All send love. Adieu, my dear boy!

"D. M."

It was this eagerness of the father to engage his son in the practical application of mathematics, expressed in other places as well as this, which produced the following sensible observations in reply.

"The plan of mathematical and philosophical reading pursued at Cambridge is perhaps too much confined to speculation; the intention seems to be to ground you well in the principles supposing you to apply them at leisure after your degree. In going through this course of study if I read popular treatises upon every branch, it will take up my whole time, and absolutely exclude all other kinds of reading whatever, which I should by no means wish. I think therefore it will be better for me to pursue the general courses adopted by the university, seeing the general application of everything I read without always descending to particulars.

"When I mentioned popular treatises I did not mean to refer to the books you recommended in your last letter, but to what you said in a former one, expressing a wish to see me a practical surveyor, mechanic, and navigator; a knowledge of which kind would be difficult to obtain before I took my degree, while engaged in the plan of mathematical reading adopted by the university.

"I am by no means, however, inclined to get forward without wishing to see the use and application of what I read. On the contrary I am rather remarked in college for talking of what actually exists in nature, or may be put to real practical use. With regard to the books you mentioned in your last, as it is absolutely necessary to read those which our lecturer makes use of, it is difficult to find time to apply to other tracts of the same nature, in the regular manner they deserve: particularly as many other books are required to be read during our course of lectures to be able to understand them as we ought. For instance, we have had no lectures of any consequence in algebra and fluxions, and yet a man would find himself very deficient in going through the branches of natural philosophy and Newton's Principia, without a decent knowledge of both. As I attended lectures with the year above me, and the course only continues three years, I shall be entirely my own master after the next summer vacation, and then will be my time to read different authors, make comparisons, and properly digest the knowledge I have taken in.

"I believe from what I have let fall at different times, you have conceived the Senate House examination to be more confined to mathematical speculations than it really is. The greatest stress is laid on a thorough knowledge of the branches of natural philosophy, and problems of every kind in these as well as in mathematics are set during the examination; such a one as the ascertaining the distance of the Sun by a transit of Venus is not unlikely sometimes to be among the number.

"If you will giveme leave to proceed in my own plans of reading for the next two years, (I speak with submission to your judgment,) I promise you at the expiration of that time to be a decent natural philosopher, and not only to know a few principles, but to be able to apply those principles in a variety of useful problems. I hope you will excuse me for detaining you so long upon this subject, but I thought I had not sufficiently explained myself in my last letter, and that you might possibly conclude from what I there said, that I intended to go on in the beaten track, without once reflecting on the use and application of the study in which I was engaged."

The last extract we shall give is from a letter written we believe on the election of Mr. Malthus to a fellowship:

"I heartily congratulate upon your success; it gives me a sort of pleasure which arises from my own regrets. The things which I have missed in life, I should the more sensibly wish for you.

"Alas! my dear Bob, I have no right to talk to you of idleness, but when I wrote that letter to you with which you were displeased, I was deeply impressed with my own broken purposes and imperfect pursuits; I thought I foresaw in you, from the memory of my own youth, the same tendency to lose the steps you had gained, with the same disposition to self-reproach, and I wished to make my unfortunate experience of some use to you. It was, indeed, but little that you wanted it, which made me the more eager to give it you, and I wrote to you with more tenderness of heart than I would in general pretend to, and committed myself in a certain manner which made your answer a rough disappointment to me, and it drove me back into myself. You have, as you say, worn out that impression, and you have a good right to have done it; for I have seen in you the most unexceptionable character, the sweetest manners, the most sensible and the kindest conduct, always above *throwing little stones into my garden*, which you know I don't easily forgive, and uniformly making every body easy and amused about you. Nothing can have been wanting to what, if I were the most fretful and fastidious, I could have required in a companion; and nothing even to my wishes for your happiness, but where they were either whimsical, or unreasonable, or most likely mistaken. I have often been on the point of taking hold of your hand and bursting into tears at the time that I was refusing you my affections: my approbation I was precipitate to give you.

"Write to me, if I could do any thing about your church, and you want any thing to be done for you, such as I am, believe me, dear Bob, yours most affectionately,

"DANIEL MALTHUS."

There is a strain of tender remonstrance, singularly mingled with diffidence and self-accusation throughout this letter which exhibits in a strong and very amiable light the character of the father, nor is it less interesting as an encouragement to youthful instruction, by shewing how early those virtues were planted in the son, to which his character remained faithful ever afterwards.

Changes there were in him, indeed, as there generally have been in all persons whose minds have laboured with great questions of moral interest; and some of them certainly remarkable. They who had seen him only in his later years, and had been accustomed to the calm and peaceful tenor of his life, his kind and gentle manners, and the earnest and serious tone of his general conversation, would scarcely credit that the two features most remarkable in his boyhood were a pugnacious spirit and a keen perception of the ludicrous. And yet such was the report made to his father by his earliest tutor, Mr. Graves: the former being evinced in his unconquerable love of fighting for fighting's sake, the latter in the ease and delight with which he entered into many refined and unexpected strokes of wit in classic poets, which were entirely lost upon the minds of others much older than himself. "Don Roberto," says this gentleman in one of his letters, speaking of the first quality, "though most peaceably inclined, and seeming even to give up his just rights, rather than to dispute with any man, yet, paradox as it may seem, loves fighting for fighting's sake, and delights in bruising; he has but barely recovered his eye-sight, and yet I have much ado to keep him from trying again the chance of war; and yet he and his antagonist are the best friends in the world, learn together, assist each other, and I believe, love each other, better than any two boys in the school." It would not be difficult, indeed, to trace this unyielding spirit through different changes of his being, under the guidance of christian discipline, till it reached its maturity in the moral courage which enabled him to contend patiently and manfully for the truth, in defiance of a virulent opposition which ceased not even with his life; but it may suffice to say here, that in every stage of the progress it was entirely exempt from all malice and ill will, that no man living was ever less disposed to give a provocation, or more prone to overlook one, and that as far as the physical part of the quality was concerned, the only remnant of it, even in his youth, was a calm fortitude which inspired respect, and a desirable presence of mind, in all the difficulties and emergencies of life.

Of his taste for humour, however, which has been truly said to be almost always allied to genius, something more deserves to be said. Mr. Graves, who must be considered as no mean judge of these matters, thus speaks of the dawn of this quality in his pupil's mind: "He has finished Horace, and has read five satires in Juvenal with apparent taste, and I never saw a boy of his age enter more instantaneously into the humour of the fifth satire, which describes so feelingly the affronts and mortifications which a parasite meets with at a great man's table."

"I never saw a boy shew a quicker sense of

the beauties of an author, or at least of any humorous and unexpected strokes. They are reading the Hecyra of Terence, and I was willing to see whether any one in the class was struck with that characteristic stroke of humour which Dr. Hurd lays so great stress upon, 'Tum tu igitur nihil adduxisti huc plus unâ sententiâ,' and though there were two boys of 15 years old, Bob was the only one that discovered a smile of approbation, as he did at Phidippus' reproach in the same scene, 'Quia paululum vobis accessit pecuniæ sublati animi sunt;' though it is not clear I think whether Phidippus intended a sneer upon their disappointment, or envied their fancied good luck."

Such were the early indications of this quality as observed by Mr. Graves, but it did not end here; it was prevalent throughout his youth, and even survived a portion of his manhood, and at Cambridge in particular, set off as it used to be by a very comic expression of features, and a most peculiar intonation of voice when he was in the vein, was often a source of infinite delight and pleasantry to his companions. In his riper years however this taste gradually faded away, and at last had so entirely disappeared, as to induce his later friends to say, that if any thing were wanting to his mind, it was a more expansive play of the imagination, and a more vivid exercise of the memory. But the reason is obvious. From the moment the principle of population had been struck out from his mind, and had taken hold of the public attention, it became to him the predominant and absorbing subject of his thoughts, constraining him to grave reflection, and causing every other tendency to yield to it. From this time too, most of his writings took of necessity a controversial turn: and as the constant exercise of the reasoning faculty, which this required, could not be carried on but at the expense of those lighter graces which have their origin in the fancy, it is no wonder that the taste for humour became less and less influential in his mind. But there was nothing in all this to regret; the change was gradual and even graceful, every step of it being suited to his advancing years, and in harmony with the new relations he had contracted in the progress of his life; and while the world at large, and this country in particular, was greatly benefited by the concentration of his faculties upon a subject of such deep interest to the public welfare, for the accomplishment of which he seemed almost to have been destined by his very nature, the kindly source of his innocent and cheerful humour (for such it always was) remained as fresh and as abundant as ever. Its spirit, indeed, was somewhat subdued, and its course became more steady in proportion as its aims and objects were enlarged; and instead of appearing in fitful bursts of fancy, which were wont to set the table in a roar, it flowed on in a perpetual stream of cheerfulness and benevolence, gladdening the walks of domestic life, and diffusing itself over all his conduct as well as his conversation. To return, however, to the progress of his life.

In 1784 he removed from Mr. Wakefield's house to Jesus College, Cambridge, where he was admitted at the recommendation of that gentleman, formerly a fellow of the society. At this time, he was generally distinguished for gentlemanlike deportment and feelings, a polished humanity which remained with him through life, and a degree of temperance and prudence, very rare at that period, and carried by him even into his academical pursuits. In these he was always more remarkable for the steadiness than for the ardour of his application, preferring to exert his mind equably in the various departments of literature then cultivated in the college, rather than to devote it exclusively or eminently to any one, and evidently actuated more by the love of excellence than by the desire of excelling. For this happy disposition he seems to have been indebted next to his own gracious nature to the peculiar character of his education, which while it had employed higher motives with good effect, had rarely brought into action the principle of competition, so generally resorted to in colleges and schools; and the consequence was, that he read in a better spirit, reflected more freely and more usefully and acquired more general information than any of his contemporaries. Under this view, it is difficult to suppress a wish that the persons appointed to the important task of superintending education, could be induced to apply this stimulus of emulation with more caution and restraint: at all events, that they would exercise some discrimination in its use, and especially that they would accompany it with frequent and cogent memorials, that there are other things in the world in store for diligence and virtue, and of higher value, than worldly emolument or applause.

To exclude emulation indeed altogether from our means and instruments would be as impracticable as the attempt would be unwise; it is a natural remedy for the natural evils of our youth, indolence and the love of pleasure, and the advantages are as obvious and immediate as they are comprehensive; nor can it be denied that an impulse upwards is often given by it to sluggish minds which afterwards continued under better auspices, leads to great acquirements, and enables them to look down with indifference upon the vantage ground from which the spring was taken. But generally speaking it is otherwise: the course of a youth chiefly actuated by this stimulus, is irregular and uneven, and at the best liable to frequent crosses and disappointments;

there is more of passion than of habit in his efforts, and when the object of competition is obtained, the ardour for study abates; on the other hand, the unchristian principles of envy, jealousy, and ambition, which it tends to foster, and to which our nature is already prone, are powerful and durable, and rarely lose their grasp of the youthful mind on which they have once seized. These evils which are not always apparent to others, are sometimes a secret even to the men themselves, and generally the discipline of life, and the influence of religion are sufficient to control every outward symptom or effect; but the fire is often smouldering within, and is one of the worst foes to virtue and tranquillity of mind. Not so, however, with the love of knowledge, especially when informed by the wisdom which is from above. When this principle once takes the lead in the formation of the youthful mind, it generally goes on increasing, and is little liable to disorder or decay. It never can be satiated, for its objects are continually expanding, multiplied and varied; and instead of the low born passions with which the other is united, it constantly allies itself to some of the noblest principles and qualities of our nature, especially generosity, justice, and benevolence; giving to all their due, aiding and rejoicing in the success of others who are running the same career, and sympathising with all that is good and honourable around. It is probable, indeed, that a youth stimulated chiefly by the former may rise through almost unnatural exertions to a greater height of distinction in some particular branch; but upon the whole the effect is rarely or ever satisfactory; and whether we look to worldly happiness and tranquillity, to the advantage of a compact and well proportioned mind, or what is much more important to the formation of the christian character, there can be no comparison between the two. However this may be, such in this case was the education of Mr. Malthus, and such was the result; it would be impossible to point out in the present age any distinguished person more moderate and contented, more exempt from jealousy and ambition, more disposed to rejoice with those who rejoice, or with more of the charity that envieth not, seeketh not its own.

Notwithstanding this moderation, there was nothing he attempted in which he did not arrive at some distinction. He obtained prizes for declamations both in Latin and English. He was always esteemed amongst the foremost in the classical lecture room, and on taking his degree in 1788, his name appeared in the Tripos as the ninth wrangler. Besides all this he found sufficient time for the cultivation of history and general literature, particularly of poetry, of which he was always a great admirer and a discerning judge. In 1797, he proceeded to his master's degree, and was made fellow of his college, and having taken orders about the same time, he undertook the care of a small parish in Surrey, near his father's house, occasionally residing in Cambridge upon his fellowship, for the purpose of pursuing with more advantage that course of study to which he was attached.

His first essay, as a writer, was a pamphlet called the Crisis, which he left in MS. and refrained from printing it at his father's request. It betrays some marks of a youthful taste both in the matter and in the style; but it is a work of great reflexion for so young a man, and shews considerable political sagacity and observation. It is further interesting at present on account of the many curious notices it contains of the temper and character of the times, and especially as exhibiting his early views and opinions respecting the condition of the poor. It was written about the year 1797, and its chief object was to impugn the measures and general government of Mr. Pitt. We have made extracts of one or two passages from this little work, which will be acceptable to those who can compare the opinions here delivered, respecting the treatment of the poor, with the conclusions of his maturer years.*

In 1798 appeared his first printed work, an octavo volume, upon Population, under the following title, " An Essay on the Principle of Population as it affects the future improvement of Society, with remarks on the speculations of Mr. Godwin, M. Condorcet, and other writers ;" in which the general principle was laid down and explained, and some very important consequences deduced from it ; but his documents and illustrations were imperfect, and he himself perhaps at that time scarcely aware of the whole extent and bearings of the subject. The book was received with some surprise, and excited considerable attention, and while the minds of the generality were in suspense, the author left the country in search of materials to complete it. In 1799 he sailed for Hamburg with three other members of his college, of whom Dr. Edward Clarke was

*" But though it is by no means to be wished that any dependent situation should be made so agreeable, as to tempt those who might otherwise support themselves in independence ; yet as it is the duty of society to maintain such of its members as are absolutely unable to maintain themselves, it is certainly desirable that the assistance in this case should be given in the way that is most agreeable to the persons who are to receive it. An industrious woman who is left a widow with four or five children that she has hitherto brought up decently, would often gladly accept of a much less sum, than the family would cost in the work-house, and with this assistance added to her own exertions, might in all probability succeed in keeping herself and her children from the contamination of a society that she has surely just reason to dread. And it seems peculiarly hard upon old people, who perhaps have been useful and respectable members of society, and in their day, "have done the state some service," that as soon as they are past their work, they should be obliged to quit the village where they have always lived, the cottage to which time has attached them, the circle of their friends, their children and their grand-children, and be forced to

one: the party separated in Sweden, and Dr. Clarke and Mr. Cripps having proceeded rapidly to the north, Mr. Malthus with Mr. Otter continued leisurely their tour through Sweden, Norway, Finland, and a part of Russia, these being the only countries at the time open to English travellers. Of this tour he has left other memorials besides those embodied in his own work; amongst which may be mentioned many valuable notes which have since served to enrich the last volume of Dr. Clarke's Travels. During the short peace of 1802 he again left England, and visited with some of his relations, France and Switzerland; exploring with them, all that was most interesting in nature or art in those countries, but always continuing, wherever he went, to collect facts and documents for the illustration of the principle he had announced and for the completion of his work. In 1805, he married Harriet, the eldest daughter of Mr. Eckersall, a gentleman now resident at Bath, and soon after was appointed to the professorship of Modern History and Political Economy, at Haileybury, in which situation he remained till his death. In 1825, he

spend the evening of their days in noise and unquietness among strangers, and wait their last moments forlorn and separated from all they hold dear."

"It is an old saying that home is home, be it ever so homely; and this sentiment certainly operates very strongly upon the poor. Out of the reach of most of those enjoyments that amuse the higher ranks of society, what is there that can attach them to life, but their evening fire-side with their families in a house of their own; joined to the consciousness that the more they exert themselves the better they shall support the objects of their affection. What is it but a sentiment of this kind that tempts many who have lived in the ease and luxury of service, to forego these advantages, to marry, and submit to the labour, the difficulties, the humbler condition and hard fare, that inevitably attend the change of situation? And surely no wise legislature would discourage these sentiments, and endeavour to weaken this attachment to home, unless indeed it were intended to destroy all thought and feeling among the common people, to break their spirit, and prepare them to submit patiently to any yoke that might be imposed upon them."

lost a beloved and affectionate daughter in the bloom of youth, who was carried off by a rapid decline, "a sad break in," as he said, "upon their small and happy family circle;" he bore it, however, with his usual resignation, but for the sake of Mrs. Malthus, who felt her loss most acutely, and in the hope of bringing more composure to all their minds, he made a tour upon the continent with his family, but returned in the autumn to his ordinary duties at Haileybury, and his usual domestic habits.

It has been sometimes insinuated by persons who have been desirous to depreciate the merits of Mr. Malthus as an original writer, that he was indebted to his father for those new views of population which appeared in his first essay and have since excited so much attention in the world. There is no foundation whatever for this report; but it is not difficult to explain in what manner it took its rise. The mind of Mr. Malthus was certainly set to work upon the subject of population, in consequence of frequent discussions between his father and himself respecting another question, in which they differed entirely from each other. The former, a man of romantic and somewhat sanguine temper, had warmly adopted the opinions of Condorcet and Godwin respecting the perfectibility of man, to which the sound and practical sense of the latter was always opposed; and when the question had been often the subject of animated discussion between them, and the son had rested his cause, principally upon the obstacles which the tendency of population to increase faster than the means of subsistence, would always throw in the way; he was desired to put down in writing, for maturer consideration, the substance of his argument, the consequence of which was, the Essay on Population. Whether the father was converted or not we do not know, but certain it is that he was strongly impressed with the importance of the views and the ingenuity of the argument contained in the MS., and recommended his son to submit his labours to the public. This is the substance of the story as it was related by the author himself to the writer of this memoir; and if any confirmation were wanting of the fact, there is sufficient in the internal evidence of the works themselves. The main object of the octavo volume, being the refutation of Godwin and Condorcet, it is against them that his arguments are throughout chiefly directed; while the chapter on the poor laws occupies a very minor portion of the work, and was in truth only a branch of the subject into which he was involuntarily led. Upon reflexion, however, he soon found that the field into which he had now entered was of infinitely more interest than that on which he had at first set out. In this therefore he wisely continued his researches, and finding the subject grow upon him both in extent and importance as he advanced, he insensibly assigned to it the ascendancy which it deserved. Accordingly it will be found that in his quarto volume which he published upon his return from the continent, the order as well as the proportions of the matter is reversed. The state and prospects of the poor become the prominent feature, and occupy the principal portion of his book, while Mr. Godwin, and the perfectibility of man, are treated as matters of less moment, and are restricted to a much smaller space. These facts will furnish an interesting key to many passages in these works as well as to the forms and order in which they are put. They shew how curiously one thought was pushed out from another, till the whole grew together into the goodly system in which it now appears.

Qual ramicel a ramo
Tal da pensier pensiero
In lui germogliava.

And they illustrate still more strongly a profound observation of Dr. Butler, in which, speaking of Christianity as a scheme not yet entirely understood, and only likely now to be further developed in the same way that natural knowledge is come at, he remarks, " For this is the way that all improvements are made, by thoughtful men tracing out obscure hints as it were dropped us by nature accidentally, or which seemed to come into our minds by chance. For all the same phenomena, and the same faculties of investigation from which such great discoveries in natural knowledge have been made in the present and last age, were equally in the possession of mankind several thousand years before,"

The latter years of his life were passed with little variety in the society of his family and friends, in his ministerial and official duties at the college, and in the cultivation of studies more immediately connected with them. Amidst these employments, and the satisfaction derived from a contented, pious, and conscientious mind, he awaited patiently and confidently the sequel of his labours, in that improvement of society to which they were dedicated; mean while, he had many compensations and encouragements calculated to reward his perseverance, and to support his hopes. In proportion as the principle of population became better known, his reputation as an author increased. Most of the great statesmen of his time, and all the most eminent political economists, embraced his opinions, and in their several departments paved the way for the application of them to the public welfare; and as his estimation as an author was amply supported by his character, conversation, and manners, his society was much sought after by able men of all parties, and few, if any, were ever disappointed in him. His own home also was frequently the resort of men of cultivated minds in every department of literature, and the warm but simple and unpretending hospitality that reigned there was not more pleasing than it was remarkable to all who partook of it. But the high estimation in which he was held was not confined to this country; his writings were framed not for Great Britain only, which he most loved, but for the world at large, and as such they were received by it. In truth, the principle he had laid down found fewer prejudices to encounter in other countries than in this; principally, because the situation of the poor was almost everywhere less critical: its importance, however, in a prospective view could not be concealed from any, and the consequence was, that the attention he had awakened was largely propagated by many distinguished authors through every part of Europe; as well philosophers as men of science; and under their auspices a great variety of facts and documents has been collected, which has contributed not only to confirm his views, but also to diffuse the benefit of his labours in various parts of the continent. Upon the same grounds he was honoured with distinctions from several sovereigns of Europe, and elected a member of many of the most eminent literary societies, especially the French Institute, and the Royal Academy at Berlin. He was one of the founders of the Political Economy club in this country, and also of the more recent institution, the Statistical Society, of both which he attended regularly the meetings, and partook largely of their discussions. He kept up a frequent correspondence with the most eminent political economists of the day, both at home and abroad, especially Ricardo; by all of these he was esteemed, and by some affectionately regarded and beloved.

Mr. Malthus had, we believe, just entered his 70th year, when attacked by the disorder of which he died, but he was in the full enjoyment of all his faculties, and his death was totally unexpected by his friends. He left London a few days before his death, on a visit to his father-in-law at Bath, in good spirits, and apparently in strong health, anticipating a cheerful Christmas with his children and other members of his family, who were invited to meet him; but Providence had ordained otherwise—the meeting took place, but the joy was not there; Mr. Malthus was taken ill soon after his arrival, with a disorder of the heart, of which it is believed he was never conscious, and which in a few days hurried him to the grave. He has left a widow, and a son and daughter both grown up.

Below is subjoined a list of his works in the order in which they were published.* A slight attention to the subjects of these works, in connection with the occasions on which they were written, will suffice to shew how anxious the author always was to make a practical application of his labours, for the public good, and how readily he came forward on every national emergency that arose.

* An Essay on the Principle of Population, as it affects the Future Improvement of Society: with Remarks on the Speculations of Mr. Godwin, M. Condorcet, and other Writers. 1798. (Anon.)

An Investigation of the Cause of the Present High Price of Provisions, containing an Illustration of the Nature and Limits of Fair Price in Time of Scarcity, and its Application to the particular Circumstances of this country. (3rd Edit.) 1800.

An Essay on the Principle of Population, or a View of its past and present effects on human happiness, with an Enquiry into our prospects respecting the future removal or mitigation of the evils which it occasions. (A new Edit. very much enlarged,) 1803.

A Letter to Samuel Whitbread, on his proposed Bill for the Amendment of the Poor Laws. 1807.

A Letter to Lord Grenville, occasioned by some Observations of his Lordship on the East India Company's Establishment for the Education of their Civil Servants. (1813.)

Upon his character as an author, in which he stands most prominent, our observations will be brief; his principal work has been long known, not only in this country, but in every civilized portion of the globe, and the judgment generally pronounced upon it by intelligent men has been such as to satisfy the warmest and most admiring of his friends. One or two remarks only we shall venture to make, and these chiefly with a view of placing his literary claims upon a proper basis, and of throwing a clearer light upon the motives with which his labours were undertaken.

It was one consequence of his professional engagement at the East India College, that, for many of his later years, the studies of Mr. Malthus were chiefly directed to Political Economy, and especially in accordance with the turn the subject took to the discussion of certain subtle and controverted points of the science, in which an unavoidable ambiguity of language had added greatly to the natural obscurity of the subject, and increased the difficulty of arriving at a clear

Observations on the Effects of the Corn Laws, and of a Rise or Fall in the Price of Corn on the Agriculture and General Wealth of the Country. 1814. (3rd Edit. 1815.)

The Grounds of an Opinion on the Policy of restricting the Importation of Foreign Corn; intended as an Appendix to the "Observations on the Corn Laws." 1815.

An Inquiry into the Nature and Progress of Rent, and the Principles by which it is regulated. 1815.

Statements respecting the East India College, with an Appeal to Facts in Refutation of the Charges lately brought against it in the Court of Proprietors. 1817.

Principles of Political Economy considered, with a view to their practicable application, 1820. (2nd. Edit. 1836.)

The Measure of Value Stated and Illustrated, with an Application of it to the Alteration in the Value of the English Currency since 1790. 1823.

Definitions in Political Economy, preceded by an Enquiry into the Rules which ought to guide Political Economists in the Definition and Use of their Terms. 1827.

A Summary View of the Principle of Population. 1830. (From the Supplement to the Encyclopedia Britannica.)

understanding; such as the measure of value, the excess of commodities, &c. In this field Mr. Malthus will be always classed with the most distinguished of his fellow-labourers; and we may venture to add, that his "Theory of Rent," a discovery of the greatest importance, and always spoken of in the highest terms by Mr. Ricardo, is of itself sufficient to place him in the foremost rank. It is not, however, upon his success in this department, in which he shares the palm with many, but upon his "Essay on Population," that his reputation ought to rest. In this work he stands alone as the expounder and illustrator of a branch of knowledge, heretofore little thought of or cultivated in any country, but now, by his labours, raised to a degree of eminence in men's minds, corresponding with its vast importance, and brought with great efficacy to bear upon the morals and welfare of mankind. To inquire, as many have done, whether he were really the discoverer of the principle of population, on which the Essay rests, is something worse than idle, especially as the author himself never laid claim to such a title: undoubtedly many scattered notices of it may be found in other works, particularly in the "Travels of Mr. Townshend in Spain," which Mr. Malthus was ever ready to acknowledge; but the practical use, and the full developement and application of the principle, are entirely his own. Of the time in which this work first appeared, and of the circumstances which led to it, an account has been already given, but it is well worthy of observation, that the system then came from him in so complete and perfect a form, so guarded on every side, so clearly explained, and so correctly and carefully exhibited under all its aspects and in all its consequences, as to require little or no alteration afterwards, either from himself or any other person. It went rapidly through a great number of editions in this country, and has been translated into almost every language of the civilized world.

We are well aware, indeed, of the different judgments which have been formed of this Essay, and of the calumnies with which the author has been assailed. We know that coldness, harshness, and even cruelty, have been frequently imputed to the most humane and considerate of men, and that a design of degrading the poor has been charged upon a work whose sole motive and tendency was to increase their comforts, and to raise their moral and intellectual condition;—it is a consolation, however, to remember that the most reflecting and cultivated minds in this, as well as in every other country, have almost unanimously adopted and approved both the principle and the reasoning of his work, whilst its most violent opponents and vilifiers have been, with one or two exceptions, either persons who have not read it at all, or who have grossly misunderstood or misrepresented it. Its greatest triumph, indeed, has been reserved for our own times, in which it has been solemnly adopted as a principle of legislation; nor can we hesitate to believe, that at no distant period, when the cloud of prejudice and passion in which the subject is involved shall have been dispersed, the humanity of the Essay will be as apparent to all mankind as its usefulness and truth.

It has been sometimes said and repeated publicly, since the author's death, that the view Mr. Malthus himself took of the principle of population, was a gloomy one. The remark is true, though somewhat uncharitable, for the fault was in the position of the author, not in his mind. It would be easy, no doubt, to separate certain propositions from his work, and construing them strictly to make out a case of cheerlessness and gloom against the author. But this is not dealing fairly with him; it is a maxim in philosophy to interpret the positions of a work not only in connection with other parts of it, but also with a special reference to the circumstances of the times, and the opinions which prevailed in them, or preceded them. These circumstances and opinions do, in point of fact, constitute a portion of the positions themselves, or rather they are the conditions on which their truth depends, and if the former are changed, the latter must change with them, or be no longer true. Why then should we deny to Mr. Malthus, a writer upon a new and difficult subject, that indulgence which is so freely granted to the moralist and the divine? Let it be remembered that at the time when the Essay on Population was published, now more than thirty years ago, there were two great dangers threatening the peace of society, with which he had to deal; on the one hand, Mr. Godwin and his followers were striking at the reverence for all social institutions, by holding out delusive visions of perfectibility which could never be realized, and on the other a real and practical pauperism was diffusing itself widely and rapidly over the land, and undermining more surely the basis both of property and law, by an ignorant and indolent reliance upon their omnipotence—that foresight and frugality, the special virtues of their station, were fast losing ground in the estimation of the poor, and that they were recklessly sinking into a state of entire dependence on the parish rate; while the conduct and opinions of those above them, so far from repressing their error, rather tended to encourage it. With these facts before him, and the consequences strongly impressed on his mind, we cannot wonder that Mr. Malthus, having laid down and demonstrated the great law of nature respecting population, should have thought it necessary in the first instance to point out, in all their naked deformity, the dangers it would always involve, and the sin and misery which would inevitably attend an habitual disregard of it; and that under this aspect he himself should have chiefly regarded it. That there is a bright side to this law of nature, is most true; and they who have read the work of Bishop Sumner upon the "Records of the Creation," will remember how ingeniously and beautifully he has shown that, in the hands of a gracious Providence, this principle is made subservient to the most beneficial and improving ends; being the great moving cause, which, by the necessities it creates, and the fears and hopes it suggests, excites the best energies of mankind into action, overcomes their natural indolence, and gives spirit and perseverance to their most valuable labours. But this view of the subject, however favourable to the argument of Dr. Sumner, was not adapted to the adversary which Mr. Malthus had to encounter. Finally it is necessary to remember, that whatever might have been the author's view of the evils incident to the principle, temperance, frugality, foresight, and especially self-control—virtues strictly scriptural and evangelical—were the sole remedies recommended by him. Nor can it be said at present that these gloomy views, and these strong statements, were unnecessary; notwithstanding all the warnings of the "Essay on Population," the evil it contemplated had lately risen to so great a height as to threaten the most serious mischief to society, and to call for the strongest measures; and we believe, firmly, that had it not been for this book of Mr. Malthus, and all the wise and salutary parochial regulations which have sprung from it, the danger would have been infinitely greater, and our way out of it much more obscure and difficult,—if any way could have been found at all, short of a convulsion of society.

It must always however be a matter of regret

that Mr. Malthus was led to the important conclusions of his essay, through the avenue of such a controversy; had he been at liberty to select his own path it would have been a more cheerful and consolatory one, more bright with the rays of divine benevolence,* more congenial in truth to his own mind. The goodness of the Deity was a theme on which he loved to dwell, and if any thing were wanting to testify to his piety and humanity it might be drawn from that very work which has been the subject of so much animadversion. After all it must be allowed that the great, we had almost said the only, fault of Mr. Malthus with the public was that his opinions were in advance of his age. Nor should it be forgotten that in this respect his reputation has in many instances suffered more from the headlong zeal of his followers and imitators than from the mistakes and even malice of his enemies; by the former his propositions have not only been affirmed more generally than he himself intended, but they have been pushed, contrary to his own practice, to extremes, and applied indifferently without any modification or reserve. Hence it has happened that the author has been made responsible for consequences which he never contemplated, and for opinions which we know he reprobated and abjured.†

* "Life is, generally speaking, a blessing independent of a future state. It is a gift which the vicious would not always be ready to throw away, even if they had no fear of death. The partial pain, therefore, that is inflicted by the Supreme Creator, while he is forming numberless beings to a capacity of the highest enjoyments, is but as the dust of the balance in comparison of the happiness that is communicated; and we have every reason to think, that there is no more evil in the world than what is absolutely necessary as one of the ingredients in the mighty process." 8vo. edit. *Essay on Population*, page 391.

† "The sorrows and distresses of life form another class of excitements, which seem to be necessary by a peculiar train of impressions, to soften and humanize the heart, to awaken social sym-

Of his character in a social and domestic view, it would be difficult to speak in terms which would be thought extravagant by those who knew him intimately, and who, after all, are the only judges of it. Although much conversant with the world, and engaged in important labours, his life was, more than any other we have ever witnessed, a perpetual flow of enlightened benevolence, contentment, and peace; it was the best and purest philosophy, heightened by Christian views, and softened by Christian charity. His temper was so mild and placid, his allowances for others so large and so considerate, his desires so moderate, and his command over his own passions so complete, that the writer of this article, who has known him intimately for nearly fifty years, scarcely ever saw him ruffled, never angry, never above measure elated or depressed. Nor were

pathy, to generate all the Christian virtues, and to afford scope for the ample exertion of benevolence. The general tendency of an uniform course of prosperity is rather to degrade, than exalt the character. The heart that has never known sorrow itself will seldom be feelingly alive to the pains and pleasures, the wants and wishes of its fellow beings. It will seldom be overflowing with that warmth of brotherly love, those kind and amiable affections, which dignify the human character, even more than the possession of the highest talents. Talents, indeed, though undoubtedly a very prominent and fine feature of mind, can by no means be considered as constituting the whole of it. There are many minds which have not been exposed to those excitements that usually form talents, that have yet been vivified to a high degree by the excitements of social sympathy. In every rank of life, in the lowest as frequently as in the highest, characters are to be found, overflowing with the milk of human kindness, breathing love towards God and man; and though without those peculiar powers of mind called talents, evidently holding a higher rank in the scale of beings than many who possess them. Evangelical charity, meekness, piety, and all that class of virtues, distinguished particularly by the name of Christian virtues, do not seem necessarily to include abilities; yet a soul possessed of these amiable qualities, a soul awakened and vivified by these delightful sympathies, seems to hold a nearer commerce with the skies than mere acuteness of intellect." *Essay on Population*, 8vo. edit. chap. xix. p. 372.

his patience and forbearance less remarkable—no unkind word or uncharitable expression respecting any one, either present or absent, ever fell from his lips; and though doomed to pass through more censure and calumny than any author of this or perhaps of any other age, he was little disposed to advert to this species of injury, still less to complain of it, and least of all to retort it. Indeed, he had this felicity of mind, in a degree almost peculiar to himself, that, being singularly alive to the approbation of the wise and good, and anxious generally for the regard of his fellow-creatures, he was impassive to abuse—so conscious was he of his integrity of purpose, so firmly convinced of the truth of the principles he advocated, and so thoroughly prepared for the repugnance with which, in some quarters, they would be heard. But never was his equanimity so striking as when towards the close of his life, in the plenitude of his success, he saw his doctrines adopted and propagated in every part of Europe, and heard himself called the greatest benefactor to mankind since the days of Adam Smith; then to his honour be it spoken, he was never known to betray, even to his most intimate friends, the slightest symptom of vanity, triumph or self-applause.

The most remarkable feature of his mind was the love of truth, and it was also the most influential: it was this which enabled him patiently to investigate, and fearlessly to expose, an inveterate and popular error; and it was this which, in his private life, was the parent or the nurse of many other virtues conspicuous in him—justice, prudence, temperance, and simplicity. It is almost unnecessary to add, that in his domestic relations, all these qualities appeared under their fairest form, and with their sweetest influence. All the members of his family loved and honoured him; his servants lived with him till their marriage or settlement in life, and the humble and poor within his influence always found him disposed, not only to assist and improve them, but to treat them with kindness and respect.

His conversation naturally turned upon those important subjects connected with the welfare of society which were his peculiar study; in them he was always earnest, serious, and impressive, producing his opinions in such a clear and intelligible way, as to show that they were the fruit of considerable thought and reflection, and always impressing you with the notion that he was speaking in sincerity and truth; apart from these he was habitually cheerful and playful, and as ready to engage in all the innocent pursuits and pleasures of the young, as to encourage them in their studies. By his intelligent colleagues at Haileybury, his loss will be long and sincerely felt—few persons knew so well as they how to appreciate his worth, and none had so many opportunities of observing its influence. His good-breeding, candour, and gentlemanly conduct were felt in everything; and his sound judgment and conciliatory spirit, were not less remarkable in the councils of the college, than his manners and attainments were delightful and improving in their social intercourse and relations. To his intimate friends his place will rarely, if ever, be supplied; there was in him an union of truth, judgment, and warmth of heart, which at once invited confidence, and set at nought all fear of being ridiculed or betrayed. You were always certain of his sympathy, and wherever the case allowed it, his assistance was as prompt and effective as his advice was sound and good. In politics he was a firm, consistent, and decided Whig, the earnest advocate of salutary improvement and reform, but strongly and sincerely attached to the institutions of his country, and fearful of all wanton experiment and innovations.

In controversy which he never invited, nor

ever shunned when the truth was likely to be elicited, he was calm, clear and logical, fertile in argument, and though sufficiently tenacious, just and open to conviction; and being always deliberate in composition, and habitually disposed to weigh well every opinion before he submitted it to the public, he was rarely called upon to retract, but whenever the case required it, no one could do it with more candour, or with a better grace. He expunged two whole chapters from his first work, in deference to the opinions of some distinguished persons in our church; and after the publication of Dr. Sumner's work, On the Records of the Creation, he did not hesitate in a subsequent Edition of his Essay, to modify, correct, and even to omit several expressions, at the suggestion of the author for whom he had a profound respect; and all this, in a tone and spirit which proved that it was not victory, but truth for which he was contending.*

The same spirit was shewn in the correspondence between Mr. Malthus and Mr. Ricardo, which would form, if laid before the public, a perfect model of benevolent and enlightened controversy, and though at last each retired with

* "It is probable, that having found the bow bent too much one way, I was induced to bend it too much the other, in order to make it straight. But I shall always be quite ready to blot out any part of the work which is considered, by a competent tribunal as having a tendency to prevent the bow from becoming finally straight, and to impede the progress of truth. In deference to this tribunal I have already expunged the passages which have been most objected to, and I have made some few further corrections, of the same kind, in the present Edition. By these alterations, I hope, and believe, that the work has been improved, without impairing its principles. But I still trust, that whether it is read with or without these alterations, every reader of candour must acknowledge that the practical design uppermost in the mind of the writer, with whatever want of judgment it may have been executed, is to improve the condition, and increase the happiness of the lower classes of society." Vol. iii. p. 428. 5th Edition of an Essay on Population.

his own opinion, the effect of the whole was rather to improve than to diminish the respect and affection which each bore to the other. The discussion between the author and Mr. Senior was brief, and rather concerning words than things; it ended, however, as few controversies do, in mutual agreement, and was creditable to both; and in no part of his works has Mr. Malthus expressed himself with more clearness, or reasoned with more sagacity and strength than in this.

Mr. Malthus was a clergyman of the Church of England, and during a large portion of his life read prayers and preached regularly in turn with the other professors in the chapel of the East India College at Haileybury: in these services, and, indeed, in every other ordinance of religion, his manner was uniformly serious and devout; nor could he ever say grace at his own table, without inspiring those present with a sense of his piety. Of his sermons, it may be said, that they were calculated to make a strong impression on the minds of the young men, for whose edification they were chiefly intended; and it is now particularly pleasing to record, that they became more earnest and more edifying every year he lived. In religion, indeed, as well as in other things, he was always unobtrusive and unostentatious, but it was easy to perceive that the spirit of the Gospel had shared largely in forming his character, and that both the precepts and doctrines of Christianity had made a deep impression upon his mind.

In the latter period of his life, his temper and character were subjected to a peculiar trial: the government, by adopting the principles of his work, as the basis of their Poor Laws Amendment Bill, recalled in a remarkable manner the public attention towards him, which had before begun to decline; and the praise lavished upon him during the discussion in parliament, only served to connect him more intimately with the measure. The consequence was, that from all quarters a fresh flood of calumny and abuse was poured upon him, which has continued without intermission to the present day; and though he was never consulted about any of the provisions or enactments of the bill, yet every real or supposed defect which was discovered in the construction of it, every rub or difficulty which was found in the working of it, were without ceremony attributed to him. We verily believe that if the late ministry* had remained longer in power, some solid mark of favour or encouragement would have been bestowed upon him or his, as well to vindicate their adoption of his views, as to express their sense of the support he had so long and consistently given to the principles upon which their administration was founded; and further, that it is a subject of deep regret to them now, that, as far as he himself is concerned, the opportunity is lost for ever. At all events, we know well, Mr. Malthus himself was never heard to utter the slightest murmur or complaint: with his usual equanimity he bore the neglect of one party and the abuse of the other; and, whatever might have been his apprehensions and feelings respecting the change of the ministry, as far as regarded the country, he never for a moment spoke of it as affecting, or likely to affect, himself.

* The first ministry of Lord Melbourne.

PRINCIPLES

OF

POLITICAL ECONOMY.

INTRODUCTION.

It has been said, and perhaps with truth, that the conclusions of Political Economy partake more of the certainty of the stricter sciences than those of most of the other branches of human knowledge. Yet we should fall into a serious error if we were to suppose that any propositions, the practical results of which depend upon the agency of so variable a being as man, and the qualities of so variable a compound as the soil, can ever admit of the same kinds of proof, or lead to the same certain conclusions, as those which relate to figure and number. There are indeed in political economy great general principles, to which exceptions are of the most rare occurrence, and prominent land-marks which may almost always be depended upon as safe guides; but even these, when examined, will be found to resemble in most particulars the great general rules in morals and politics founded upon the known passions and propensities of human nature: and whether we advert to the qualities of man, or of the earth he is destined to cultivate, we shall be compelled to acknowledge, that the science of political economy bears a nearer resemblance to the science of morals and politics than to that of mathematics.

This conclusion, which could hardly fail to be formed merely from a view of the subjects about which political economy is conversant, is further strengthened by the differences of opinion which have prevailed among those who have directed a large share of talent and attention to this study.

During the prevalence of the mercantile system, the interest which the subject excited was confined almost exclusively to those who were engaged in the details of commerce, or expected immediate benefit from its results. The differences which prevailed among merchants and statesmen, which were differences rather in practice than principle, were not calculated to attract much attention. But no sooner was the subject raised into a science by the works of the French Economists and of Adam Smith, than a memorable schism divided, for a considerable time, the students of this new branch of knowledge, on the fundamental questions—What is wealth? and from what source or sources is it derived?

Happily for the interests of the science and its usefulness to society, the Economists and Adam Smith entirely agreed on some of those great general principles which lead to the most important practical conclusions; such as the freedom of trade, and the leaving every person, while he adheres to the rules of justice, to pursue his own interest his own way, together with some others: and unquestionably their agreement on these principles affords the strongest presumption of their truth. Yet the differences of the Economists and Adam Smith were not mere differences in theory; they were not different interpretations of the same phenomena, which would have no influence on practice; but they involved such views of the nature and origin of wealth, as, if adopted, would lead, in almost every country, to great practical changes particularly on the very important subject of taxation.

Since the æra of these distinguished writers, the subject has gradually attracted the attention of a greater number of persons, particularly during the last twenty or thirty years. All the main propositions of the science have been examined, and the events which have since occurred, tending either to illustrate or confute them, have been repeatedly discussed. The result of this examination and discussion seems to be, that on some very important points there are still great differences of opinion. Among these, perhaps, may be reckoned—The definitions of wealth and of productive labour—The nature and measures of value—The nature and extent of the principles of demand and supply—The origin and progress of rent—The causes which determine the wages of labour and the profits of stock—The causes which practically retard and limit the progress of wealth—The level of the precious metals in different countries—The principles of taxation, &c. On all these points, and many others among the numerous subjects which belong to political economy, differences have prevailed among persons whose opinions are entitled to attention. Some of these questions are to a certain degree theoretical; and the solution of them, though obviously necessary to the improvement of the science, might not essentially affect its practical rules; but others are of such a nature, that the determination of them one way or the other will necessarily influence the conduct both of individuals and of governments; and their correct determination therefore must be a matter of the highest practical importance.

In a science such as that of political economy, it is not to be expected that an *universal* assent should be obtained to all its important propositions; but, in order to give them their proper weight and justify their being acted upon, it is extremely desirable, indeed almost necessary, that a considerable *majority* of those who, from their attention to the subject, are considered by the public as likely to be the most competent judges, should agree in the truth of them.

Among those writers who have treated the subject

scientifically, there is not perhaps, at the present moment, so general an agreement as would be desirable to give effect to their conclusions; and the writers who peculiarly call themselves practical, either draw no general inferences, or are so much influenced by narrow, partial, and sometimes interested views, that no reliance can be placed on them for the establishment of general rules. The last twenty or thirty years have besides been marked by a train of events of a most extraordinary kind; and there has hardly yet been time so to arrange and examine them as to see to what extent they confirm or invalidate the received principles of the science to which they relate.

The present period, therefore, seems to be unpropitious to the publication of a new systematic treatise on political economy. The treatise which we already possess is still of the very highest value; and till a more general agreement shall be found to take place, both with respect to the controverted points of Adam Smith's work, and the nature and extent of the additions to it, which the more advanced stage of the science has rendered necessary, it is obviously more advisable that the different subjects which admit of doubt should be treated separately. When these discussions have been for some time before the public, and a sufficient opportunity has been given, by the collision of different opinions and an appeal to experience, to separate what is true from what is false, the different parts may then be combined into a consistent whole, and may be expected to carry with it such weight and authority as to produce the most useful practical results.

The principal cause of error, and of the differences which prevail at present among the scientific writers on political economy, appears to me to be a precipitate attempt to simplify and generalize. While their more practical opponents draw too hasty inferences from a frequent appeal to partial facts, these writers run into a contrary extreme, and do not sufficiently try their theories by a reference to that enlarged and comprehensive experience which, on so complicated a subject, can alone establish their truth and utility.

To minds of a certain cast there is nothing so captivating as simplification and generalization. It is indeed the desirable and legitimate object of genuine philosophy, whenever it can be effected consistently with truth; and for this very reason, the natural tendency towards it has, in almost every science with which we are acquainted, led to crude and premature theories.

In political economy the desire to simplify has occasioned an unwillingness to acknowledge the operation of more causes than one in the production of particular effects; and if one cause would account for a considerable portion of a certain class of phenomena, the whole has been ascribed to it without sufficient attention to the facts, which would not admit of being so solved. I have always thought that the late controversy on the bullion question presented a signal instance of this kind of error. Each party being possessed of a theory which would account for an unfavourable exchange, and an excess of the market price above the mint price of bullion, adhered to that single view of the question, which it had been accustomed to consider as correct; and scarcely one writer seemed willing to admit of the operation of both theories, the combination of which, sometimes acting in conjunction and sometimes in opposition, could alone adequately account for the variable and complicated phenomena observable.*

It is certain that we cannot too highly respect and venerate that admirable rule of Newton, not to admit more causes than are necessary to the solution of the phenomena we are considering; but the rule itself implies, that those which really are necessary must be

* It must be allowed, however, that the theory of the Bullionists, though too exclusive, accounted for much the largest proportion of the phenomena in question; and perhaps it may be said with truth that the Bullion Report itself was more free from the error I have adverted to than any other work that appeared.

admitted. Before the shrine of truth, as discovered by facts and experience, the fairest theories and the most beautiful classifications must fall. The chemist of thirty years ago may be allowed to regret, that new discoveries in the science should disturb and confound his previous systems and arrangements; but he is not entitled to the rank of philosopher, if he does not give them up without a struggle, as soon as the experiments which refute them are fully established.

The same tendency to simplify and generalize, produces a still greater disinclination to allow of modifications, limitations, and exceptions to any rule or proposition, than to admit the operation of more causes than one. Nothing indeed is so unsatisfactory, and gives so unscientific and unmasterly an air to a proposition as to be obliged to make admissions of this kind; yet there is no truth of which I feel a stronger conviction than that there are many important propositions in political economy which absolutely require limitations and exceptions; and it may be confidently stated that the frequent combination of complicated causes, the action and reaction of cause and effect on each other, and the necessity of limitations and exceptions in a considerable number of important propositions, form the main difficulties of the science, and occasion those frequent mistakes which it must be allowed are made in the prediction of results.

To explain myself by an instance. Adam Smith has stated, that capitals are increased by parsimony, that every frugal man is a public benefactor,* and that the increase of wealth depends upon the balance of produce above consumption.† That these propositions are true to a great extent is perfectly unquestionable. No considerable and continued increase of wealth could possibly take place without that degree of frugality which occasions, annually, the conversion of some revenue into capital, and creates a balance of produce above consumption; but it is quite obvious

* Wealth of Nations, Book II. c. iii. pp. 15—18, 6th edit.

† Book IV. c. iii. p. 250.

that they are not true to an indefinite extent, and that the principle of saving, pushed to excess, would destroy the motive to production. If every person were satisfied with the simplest food, the poorest clothing, and the meanest houses, it is certain that no other sort of food, clothing, and lodging would be in existence; and as there would be no adequate motive to the proprietors of land to cultivate well, not only the wealth derived from conveniences and luxuries would be quite at an end, but if the same divisions of land continued, the production of food would be prematurely checked, and population would come to a stand long before the soil had been well cultivated. If consumption exceed production, the capital of the country must be diminished, and its wealth must be gradually destroyed from its want of power to produce; if production be in a great excess above consumption, the motive to accumulate and produce must cease from the want of an effectual demand in those who have the principal means of purchasing. The two extremes are obvious; and it follows that there must be some intermediate point, though the resources of political economy may not be able to ascertain it, where, taking into consideration both the power to produce and the will to consume, the encouragement to the increase of wealth is the greatest.

The division of landed property presents another obvious instance of the same kind. No person has ever for a moment doubted that the division of such immense tracts of land as were formerly in possession of the great feudal proprietors must be favourable to industry and production. It is equally difficult to doubt that a division of landed property may be carried to such an extent as to destroy all the benefits to be derived from the accumulation of capital and the division of labour, and to occasion the most extended poverty. There is here then a point as well as in the other instance, though we may not know how to place it, where the division of property is best suited to the actual circumstances of the society, and calculated to give the best stimulus to production and to the increase of wealth and population. It follows clearly that no general rule can be laid down respecting the advantage to be derived from saving, or the division of property, without limitations and exceptions; and it is particularly worthy of attention that in cases of this kind, where the extremes are obvious and striking, but the most advantageous mean cannot be marked, that in the progress of society effects may be produced by an unnoticed approximation to this middle point, which are attributed to other causes, and lead to false conclusions.

The tendency to premature generalization occasions also, in some of the principal writers on political economy, an unwillingness to bring their theories to the test of experience. I should be the last person to lay an undue stress upon isolated facts, or to think that a consistent theory, which would account for the great mass of phenomena observable, was immediately invalidated by a few discordant appearances, the reality and the bearings of which there might not have been an opportunity of fully examining. But certainly no theory can have any pretension to be accepted as correct, which is inconsistent with general experience. Such inconsistency appears to me at once a full and sufficient reason for its rejection. Under such circumstances it must be either radically false, or essentially incomplete; and in either case, it can neither be adopted as a satisfactory solution of existing phenomena, nor acted upon with any degree of safety for the future.

The first business of philosophy is to account for things as they are; and till our theories will do this, they ought not to be the ground of any practical conclusion. I should never have had that steady and unshaken confidence in the theory of population which I have invariably felt, if it had not appeared to me to be confirmed, in the most remarkable manner, by the state of society as it actually exists in every country with which we are acquainted. To this test

I appealed in laying it down; and a frequent appeal to this sort of experience is pre-eminently necessary in most of the subjects of political economy, where various and complicated causes are often in operation, the presence of which can only be ascertained in this way. A theory may appear to be correct, and may really be correct under given premises; it may further *appear* that these premises are the same as those under which the theory is about to be applied; but a difference which might before have been unobserved, may shew itself in the difference of the results from those which were expected; and the theory may justly be considered as failing, whether this failure arises from an original error in its formation, or from its general inapplicability, or specific misapplication, to actual circumstances.

Where unforeseen causes may possibly be in operation, and the causes that are foreseen are liable to great variations in their strength and efficacy, an accurate yet comprehensive attention to facts is necessary, both to prevent the multiplication of erroneous theories, and to confirm and sanction those that are just.

The science of political economy is essentially practical, and applicable to the common business of human life. There are few branches of human knowledge where false views may do more harm, or just views more good. I cannot agree, therefore, with a writer in one of our most popular critical journals, who considers the subjects of population, bullion, and corn laws in the same light as the scholastic questions of the middle ages, and puts marks of admiration to them expressive of his utter astonishment that such perishable stuff should engage any portion of the public attention.*

In the very practical science of political economy perhaps it might be difficult to mention three subjects more practical than those unfortunately selected for a comparison with scholastic questions. But in fact, most of the subjects which belong to it are peculiarly

* Quarterly Review, No. xxix. Art. viii.

applicable to the common concerns of mankind. What shall we say of all the questions relating to taxation, various and extensive as they are? It will hardly be denied that they come home to the business and bosoms of mankind. What shall we say of the laws which regulate exchangeable value, or every act of purchase and exchange which takes place in our markets? What of the laws which regulate the profits of stock, the interest of money, the rent of land, the value of the precious metals in different countries, the rates of exchange, &c. &c.?

The study of the laws of nature is, in all its branches, interesting. Even those physical laws by which the more distant parts of the universe are governed, and over which, of course, it is impossible for man to have the slightest influence, are yet noble and rational objects of curiosity; but the laws which regulate the movements of human society have an infinitely stronger claim to our attention, both because they relate to objects about which we are daily and hourly conversant, and because their effects are continually modified by human interference.

There are some eminent persons so strongly attached to the general rules of political economy, that, though they are aware that in practice some exceptions to them may occasionally occur; yet they do not think it wise and politic to notice them, for fear of directing the public attention too much and too frequently to exceptions, and thus weakening the force and utility of the general rules. In this conclusion, however, I cannot agree with them. If the consequences of not attending to such exceptions were of sufficient magnitude and frequency to be conspicuous to the public, I should be decidedly of opinion that the cause of general principles was much more likely to lose than to gain by concealment.

It is, for instance, a just and general rule in political economy, that the wealth of a particular nation is increased by the increasing wealth and prosperity of surrounding states; and unquestionably there cannot be a more obvious truth than that, if these states are not successful competitors in those branches of trade in which the particular nation had excelled, their increasing wealth must tend to increase the demand for its products, and call forth more effectively its resources. But if this rule be repeatedly insisted upon without noticing the above most important limitation, how is the student in political economy to account for some of the most prominent and best attested facts in the history of commerce. How is he to account for the rapid failure of the resources of Venice under the increasing wealth of Portugal and the rest of Europe, after the discovery of a passage to India by the Cape of Good Hope; the stagnation of the industry of Holland, when the surrounding nations grew sufficiently rich to undertake their own carrying trades, the increasing trade and wealth of Great Britain, during the war of the French Revolution, under the diminishing trade and increasing poverty of the greatest part of Europe, and the comparative distress of America, when other states were enabled to participate in those trades, which as a neutral she had carried on during a great part of the late war with such signal success. It is not favourable to the science of political economy, that the same persons who have been laying down a rule as universal should be obliged to found their explanations of most important existing phenomena on the exceptions to it. It is surely much better that such a rule should be laid down at first with its limitations. Nothing can tend so strongly to bring theories and general principles into discredit as the occurrence of consequences, from particular premises, which have not been foreseen. Though in reality such an event forms no just objection to theory, in the general and proper sense of the term; yet it forms a most valid objection to the specific theory in question, as proving it in some way or other wrong; and with the mass of mankind this will pass for an impeachment of general principles, and of the knowledge or good faith of those who are in the habit of inculcating them. It appears to me, I confess, that the most perfect sincerity, together with the greatest degree of accuracy attainable, founded upon the most comprehensive view of all the circumstances of the case, are necessary to give that credit and circulation to general principles which is so desirable. And no views of temporary advantage, nor, what is more likely to operate, the fear of destroying the simplicity of a general rule, should ever tempt us to deviate from the strict line of truth, or to conceal or overlook any circumstances that may interfere with the universality of the principle.

There is another class of persons who set a very high value upon the received general rules of political economy, as of the most extensive practical use. They have seen the errors of the mercantile system refuted and replaced by a more philosophical and correct view of the subject; and having made themselves masters of the question so far, they seem to be satisfied with what they have got, and do not look with a favorable eye on new and further inquiries, particularly if they do not see at once clearly and distinctly to what beneficial effects they lead.

This indisposition to innovation, even in science, may possibly have its use, by tending to check crude and premature theories; but it is obvious that, if carried too far, it strikes at the root of all improvement. It is impossible to observe the great events of the last twenty-five years in their relation to subjects belonging to political economy, and sit down satisfied with what has been already done in the science. But if the science be manifestly incomplete, and yet of the highest importance, it would surely be most unwise to restrain inquiry, conducted upon just principles, even where the immediate practical utility of it was not visible. In mathematics, chemistry, and every branch of natural philosophy, how many are the inquiries necessary to their improvement and completion, which, taken separately, do not appear to lead to any specifically advantageous purpose! How many useful inventions, and how much valuable and improving knowledge would have been lost, if a rational curiosity and a mere love of information had not generally been allowed to be a sufficient motive for the search after truth!

I should not, therefore, consider it as by any means conclusive against further inquiries in political economy, if they would not always bear the rigid application of the test of *cui bono?* But such, in fact, is the nature of the science, so intimately is it connected with the business of mankind, that I really believe more of its propositions will bear this test than those of any other department of human knowledge.

To trace distinctly the operations of that circle of causes and effects in political economy which are acting and re-acting on each other, so as to foresee their results, and lay down general rules accordingly, is, in many cases, a task of very great difficulty. But there is scarcely a single inquiry belonging to these subjects, however abstruse and remote it may at first sight appear, which in some point or other does not bear directly upon practice. It is unquestionably desirable, therefore, both with a view to the improvement and completion of the science, and the practical advantages which may be expected from it, that such inquiries should be pursued; and no common difficulty or obscurity should be allowed to deter those who have leisure and ability for such researches.

In many cases, indeed, it may not be possible to predict results with certainty, on account of the complication of the causes in action, the different degrees of strength and efficacy with which they may operate, and the number of unforeseen circumstances which are likely to interfere; but it is surely knowledge of the highest importance to be able to draw a line, with tolerable precision, between those cases where the expected results are certain, and those where they are doubtful; and further to be able satisfactorily to explain, in the latter case, the reasons of such uncertainty.

To know what can be done, and how to do it, is

beyond a doubt, the most valuable species of information. The next to it is, to know what cannot be done, and why we cannot do it. The first enables us to attain a positive good, to increase our powers, and augment our happiness: the second saves us from the evil of fruitless attempts, and the loss and misery occasioned by perpetual failure.

But these inquiries demand more time and application than the practical statesman, whom of all others they most nearly concern, can give to them. In the public measures of every state all are, no doubt, interested; but a peculiar responsibility, as well as interest, must be felt by those who are the principal advisers of them, and have the greatest influence in their enactment; and if they have not leisure for such researches themselves, they should not be unwilling, under the guidance of a sound discretion, to make use of the advantages which may be afforded by the leisure of others. They will not indeed be justified in taking any decided steps, if they do not themselves see, or at least think they see, the way they are going; but they may be fairly expected to make use of all the lights which are best calculated to illumine their way, and enable them to reach the object which they have in view.

It may perhaps be thought that, if the great principle so ably maintained by Adam Smith be true, namely, that the best way of advancing a people towards wealth and prosperity is *not* to interfere with them, the business of government, in matters relating to political economy, must be most simple and easy.

But it is to be recollected, in the first place, that there is a class of duties connected with these subjects, which, it is universally acknowledged, belongs to the Sovereign; and though the line appears to be drawn with tolerable precision, when it is considered generally; yet when we come to particulars, doubts may arise, and certainly in many instances have arisen, as to the subjects to be included in this classification. To what extent education and the support of the poor should be public concerns? What share the Government should take in the construction and maintenance of roads, canals, public docks? What course it should adopt with regard to colonization and emigration, and in the support of forts and establishments in foreign countries? On all these questions, and many others, there may be differences of opinion; and on all these questions the sovereign and his ministers are called upon to decide.

Secondly, every actual government has to administer a body of laws relating to agriculture, manufactures, and commerce, which was formed at a period comparatively unenlightened, and many of which, therefore, it must be very desirable to repeal. To remain inactive in such a state of things, can only be justified by a conviction, founded on the best grounds, that in any specific change contemplated, taken in all its consequences, the balance of evil will preponderate; while to proceed straight forward in the rigid application of general principles without any reference to the difficulties created by the existing laws of the country, and its actual situation and circumstances, might plunge it into such complicated distress, as not only to excite the public indignation against the authors of such measures, but to bring permanent discredit upon the principles which had prompted them.*

Thirdly, there is one cause in every state which absolutely impels the government to action, and puts an end to the possibility of letting things alone. This is the necessity of taxation; and as taxes cannot, in the nature of things, be imposed without interfering with individual industry and wealth, it becomes a matter of the very highest importance to know how they may take place with the least possible prejudice to the prosperity of the state, and the happiness of individuals.

* Measures calculated to terminate in a rise in the value of money might be little felt in a country without a national debt; but with a large money amount to be paid annually to public creditors, they might occasion a distribution of property most unfavourable to production.

With regard to this latter subject indeed, it bears on so many points, that the truth or falsehood of the theories on all the principal questions in political economy would occasion, or at least ought to occasion, a practical difference in the mode of raising some of the actual taxes. It is well known that, if the theory of the Economists were true, all taxes should be laid on the land; and it depends entirely upon the general laws which regulate the wages of labour, the profits of stock, the rent of land, exchangeable value, the currencies of different countries, the production and distribution of wealth, &c. &c. whether any existing system of taxation be the best, or whether it might be altered for the better.

It is obviously, therefore, impossible for a government strictly to let things take their natural course; and to recommend such a line of conduct, without limitations and exceptions, could not fail to bring disgrace upon general principles, as totally inapplicable to practice.

It may, however, safely be asserted, that a propensity to govern too much is a certain indication of ignorance and rashness. The ablest physicians are the most sparing in the use of medicine, and the most inclined to trust to the healing power of nature. The statesman, in like manner, who knows the most of his business, will be the most unwilling to interrupt the natural direction of industry and capital. But both are occasionally called upon to interfere, and the more science they respectively possess, the more judiciously will they do it; nor will the acknowledged propriety of interfering but little supersede, in any degree, the use of the most extensive professional knowledge in both cases.

One of the specific objects of the present work is to prepare some of the most important rules of political economy for practical application, by a frequent reference to experience, and by endeavouring to take a comprehensive view of all the causes that concur in the production of particular phenomena.

In this mode of conducting inquiry, there is, no doubt, a chance of falling into errors of an opposite kind to those which arise from a tendency to simplification. Certain appearances, which are merely co-existent and incidental, may be mistaken for causes; and a theory formed upon this mistake will unite the double disadvantage of being both complex and incorrect. Adam Smith has occasionally fallen into this error, and drawn inferences from actual appearances, not warranted by general principles. From the low price of wheat, for instance, during the first half of the last century, he seems to have inferred that wheat is generally cheaper in rich than in poor countries; and from the small quantity of corn actually imported during that period, even in the scarcest years, he has inferred generally, that the quantity imported can never be such as to interfere with the home growth. The actual state of things at a subsequent period, and particularly during the last twenty-five years, has sufficiently shewn that these appearances were merely incidental; that a very rich country may have its corn extremely dear, as we should naturally expect; and that importation in England has amounted to more than $\frac{1}{10}$ instead of $\frac{1}{571}$* part of the crop raised in the country; and may, therefore, to a considerable extent, interfere with the home growth.

Aware, however, of my liability to this error on the one side, and to the error of not referring sufficiently to experience on the other, my aim will be to pursue, as far as I am able, a just mean between the two extremes, and to approach, as near as I can, to the great object of my research—the truth.

Many of the doctrines of Adam Smith, which had been considered as settled, have lately been called in question by writers entitled to great attention; but they have often failed, as it appears to me, to make good their objections; and in all such cases I have

* Wealth of Nations, B. IV. c. ii. p. 190. 6th edit.

thought it desirable to examine anew, with reference to such objections, the grounds on which his doctrines are founded.

It has been my wish to avoid giving to my work a controversial air. Yet to free it entirely from controversy, while one of my professed objects is to discuss controverted opinions, and to try their truth by a reference to an enlarged experience, is obviously not possible. There is one modern work, in particular, of very high reputation, some of the fundamental principles of which have appeared to me, after the most mature deliberation, to be erroneous; and I should not have done justice to the ability with which it is written, to the high authority of the writer, and the interests of the science of which it treats, if it had not specifically engaged a considerable portion of my attention. I allude to Mr. Ricardo's work, "*On the Principles of Political Economy and Taxation.*"

I have so very high an opinion of Mr. Ricardo's talents as a political economist, and so entire a conviction of his perfect sincerity and love of truth, that I frankly own I have sometimes felt almost staggered by his authority, while I have remained unconvinced by his reasonings. I have thought that I must unaccountably have overlooked some essential points, either in my own view of the subject, or in his; and this kind of doubt has been the principal reason of my delay in publishing the present volume. But I shall hardly be suspected of not thinking for myself on these subjects, or of not feeling such a degree of confidence in my own conclusions, after having taken full time to form them, as to be afraid of submitting them to the decision of the public.

To those who are not acquainted with Mr. Ricardo's work, and do not properly appreciate the ingenuity and consistency of the system which it maintains and developes with so much ability, I am apprehensive that I shall appear to have dwelt too long upon some of the points on which we differ. But as they are, for the most part, of great importance both theoretically and practically, and as it appeared to me extremely desirable, with a view to the interests of the science, that they should, if possible, be settled, I did not feel myself justified in giving less time to the consideration of them.

I am far from saying that I may not be wrong in the conclusions at which I have arrived, in opposition to those of Mr. Ricardo. But I am conscious that I have taken all the means to be right, which patient investigation and a sincere desire to get at the truth can give to the actual powers of my understanding. And with this consciousness, both with respect to the opinions I have opposed, and those which I have attempted to establish, I feel no reluctance in committing the results to the decision of the public.

T. R. MALTHUS.

East India College,
Dec. 1, 1819.

CHAPTER I.

OF THE DEFINITIONS OF WEALTH AND OF PRODUCTIVE LABOUR.

SECTION I.—*On the Definitions of Wealth.*

Of the subjects which have given rise to differences of opinion among political economists, the *definition* of wealth is not the least remarkable. Such differences could hardly have taken place, if the definition had been obvious and easy; but in reality, the more the subject is considered, the more it will appear difficult, if not impossible to fix on one not liable to some objection. In a work, however, on a science, the great object of which is, to inquire into the causes which influence the progress of wealth, it must be of use to describe as distinctly as the nature of the subject will admit, what is meant by that wealth the increase or decrease of which we are about to estimate: and if we cannot arrive at perfect accuracy, so as to embrace all we wish, and to exclude all we wish in some short definition, it seems desirable to approach as near to it as we can. It is known not to be very easy to draw a distinct line between the animal, vegetable, and mineral kingdoms; yet the advantages of such a classification are universally acknowledged; and no one on account of a difficulty, in a few cases of little importance would refuse to make use of so convenient an arrangement.

It has sometimes been said, that every writer is at liberty to define his terms as he pleases, provided he always uses them strictly in the sense proposed. Such a liberty however may be fairly questioned; at least, it must be allowed that if a person chooses to give a very unusual and inadequate definition in reference to the subject on which he proposes to treat, he may at once render his inquiries completely futile. If for instance, a writer professing to treat of the wealth of nations were to define wealth as consisting exclusively of broad cloth, it is obvious that however consistent he might be in the use of his terms, or however valuable a treatise he might produce on this one article, he would have given very little information to those who were looking for a treatise on wealth according to any common or useful acceptation of the term.

So important indeed is an appropriate definition, that perhaps it is not going too far to say, that the comparative merits of the system of the *Economists*,* and of that of Adam Smith depend upon their different definitions of wealth, and of productive labour. If the definitions which the economists have given of wealth and of productive labour, be the most useful and correct, their *system*, which is founded on them, is the correct one. If the definitions which Adam Smith has given of these terms accord best with the sense in which they are usually applied, and embrace more of the objects, the increase or decrease of which we wish to make the subject of our inquiry, his system must be considered as superior both in utility and correctness.

Of those writers who have either given a regular definition of wealth, or have left the sense in which they understand the term to be collected from their works, some appear to have confined it within too narrow limits, and others to have extended it greatly too far. In the former class *the Economists* stand pre-

* The reader will understand that when the term *the Economists* is used, it is intended to apply to the French economists, of the school of Quesnay. In order the better to mark the distinction from other economists, without circumlocution, italics are used.

eminent. They have confined wealth or riches to the neat produce derived from the land, and in so doing they have greatly diminished the value of their inquiries in reference to the most familiar and accustomed sense in which the term wealth is understood.

Among the definitions which have extended the meaning of the term wealth too far, Lord Lauderdale's may be taken as an example. He defines wealth to be, "All that man desires as useful and delightful to him."

This definition obviously includes every thing whether material or intellectual, whether tangible or otherwise, which contributes to the advantage or pleasure of mankind, and of course includes the benefits and gratifications derived from religion, from morals, from political and civil liberty, from oratory, from instructive and agreeable conversation, from music, dancing, acting, and all personal qualities and services. It is certain, however, that an inquiry into the nature and causes of all these kinds of wealth, would not only extend beyond the bounds of any single science, but would occasion so great a change in the use of common terms as to introduce the utmost confusion into the language of political economists. It would be impossible to form any judgment of the state of a country from the use of the terms rich or richer. A nation might be said to be increasing in wealth, when to all common eyes, and in all common language, it might be growing poorer. This would be the case, according to the definition, if a diminution of the manufacturing and mercantile products had been balanced in the opinions of some persons by the gratifications derived from the intellectual attainments, and the various personal qualities and services of the inhabitants. But how is this balance to be ascertained? how is it possible to estimate the degree of wealth derived from these sources? Yet it is quite obvious that we cannot practically apply any discussions respecting the relative increase in the wealth of different nations, without having some means, however rough, of estimating the amount of such increase.

Some modern writers who do not choose to adopt the language of Adam Smith, and yet see the confusion which would arise from including under the head of wealth, every kind of benefit or gratification of which man is susceptible, have confined the definition to those objects alone, whether material or immaterial, which have value in exchange.

This definition is certainly preferable to the more comprehensive one just noticed, but by no means to the extent which might at first be supposed. When it is considered attentively, it will be found to be open to a very great portion of the objections to which the more general one is liable, and to draw the line of demarcation between what ought, and what ought not to be considered as wealth, in the most indistinct and unsatisfactory manner.

Passing over the incorrectness of introducing a term open to so much controversy as *value* into a definition of wealth, it may be observed,

1st. That if by an object which has value in exchange, be understood its susceptibility of being purchased or hired, then there is scarcely any quality or accomplishment of the mind or body that would not come under the category of wealth. The possessor of the lowest species of literary knowledge, that of reading and writing, may be hired to teach others; and as all or nearly all who had acquired these useful arts are susceptible of such employment, an estimate of national wealth ought to include the value of these attainments, however various in degree, and widely extended.

2dly. All the knowledge acquired by a superior education and superior talents, on account of a similar susceptibility, would have a greater claim to be included in the estimate. The possessors of religious and moral knowledge, though obtained without any view to the instruction of others for a pecuniary remuneration, would be ready to sell such instruction under a reverse of fortune. The same may be said of a knowledge of classical literature, mathematics, history, natural philosophy, chemistry, geology, mineralogy, botany, &c. &c. On the same principle, those who had learnt to dance, to sing, or to fence for their amusement might more or less imperfectly teach dancing, singing, or fencing, for money.

In short, if we include under the denomination of wealth all the qualities of the mind and body which are susceptible of being hired, we shall find that by the restriction of the term wealth, to that which has exchangeable value, we have advanced but little towards removing the confusion and uncertainty attendant upon the former definition; and all idea of estimating the increase of wealth in any country, or making any moderate approaches towards it, must be absolutely hopeless.

On the other hand, if we confine the definition of wealth to those objects which either have been exchanged, or are specifically intended to be exchanged, we shall attempt to draw a broad line of demarcation between things which in regard to their qualities are precisely similar; and further exclude from the category of wealth a great mass of articles, which have been included, and most correctly so, by Adam Smith, and by almost every person who makes use of the term, either in writing or conversation.

The various information acquired by private study, and destined for private use and enjoyment, may be exactly of the same kind as that which is intended to be let out if any body will hire it; yet the first, in this classification, is not to be called wealth, and the other is. The person who buys instruction, buys an amount of wealth, which it must be presumed is equal in value to what he has paid for it, while the self-taught person, who is in possession of much superior knowledge, has acquired no wealth. According to this definition wealth cannot be given; it can only be bought. The instructions of the schoolmaster are wealth; the same instructions given by a friend or father are not wealth. This is sufficiently inconsistent; but this is not all. By this definition of wealth, a very large and most important portion of material commodities is excluded from the denomination. In the business of agriculture, a considerable share of the produce is always destined to be consumed on the spot without being exchanged. The common farmer calculates how much of what he produces must go the support of his own family and working cattle, before he can determine how much he will have to sell. The gentleman farmer supports perhaps a large private establishment upon his farm, lives hospitably, receives numerous guests, and sells comparatively very little. Our feudal ancestors pursued this course in a much greater degree. In fact it was the only way in which they could spend the principal part of the products of their large possessions. The great Earl of Warwick is said to have supported thirty thousand people daily on his different manors; and at an earlier period, the elder Spencer in his petition to Parliament complains of the ravages made by the barons on his estates, and enumerates 20,000 sheep, 1,000 oxen and heifers, 12,000 cows with their breed for two years, 560 cart horses, 2,000 hogs, 10 tons of cyder, together with 600 bacons, 80 carcasses of beef, and 600 muttons in the larder. From this enumeration, Hume observes, "the plain inference is, that the greater part of Spencer's vast estates, as well as the estates of the other nobility was farmed by the landlord himself, managed by his stewards or bailiffs, and cultivated by his villains."

Little or none of it was let on lease to husbandmen. Its produce was consumed in rustic hospitality by the baron, or his officers.

Now this large mass of material commodities, increased as it would be by the flax and wool raised, spun, and wove for home consumption, few, it is conceived, would venture to exclude from the denomination of wealth; and yet this produce has neither actually been exchanged for money or other goods, nor has it been raised with the intention of being so exchanged, and therefore, according to the last definition, it ought not to be considered as wealth.

It must be allowed nevertheless, that it has exchangeable value; and here one of the great characteristic differences between material objects and objects which are not material appears in a striking point of view. Of the quantity and quality of the material commodities here noticed it would not be difficult to make an inventory. Many household books indeed furnish one; and knowing pretty nearly the quantity and quality of such articles, a fair approximation to their value might be attained by estimating them according to the market prices of the district at the time. But in regard to immaterial objects, the difficulty seems to be insurmountable. Where is an inventory to be found, or how is one to be made of the quantity and quality of that large mass of knowledge and talents reserved for the use and consumption of the individual possessors and their friends. Or supposing it were possible to form such an inventory, how could we make any moderate approaches towards a valuation of the articles it contained.

Consequently, if by objects which have value in exchange we mean objects which are susceptible of being exchanged, we shall include such a mass of the mental and physical qualities of mankind as to make the term wealth convey no tolerably distinct and useful meaning.

And if by objects which have value in exchange we mean only those objects which have actually been, or are specifically intended to be exchanged, we shall exclude from the denomination of wealth a large mass of material commodities which have always, and most justly, been classed under that head?

To get rid of these obvious embarrassments, it has sometimes been the practice to consider the labour which is hired, as the wealth which is purchased without reference to its results. But it seems very strange and incorrect to consider mere labour as wealth. No one would give anything for it if he were sure that it would yield no gratifying result. It is in the expectation of this result alone that labour is employed. The sick man employs a physician, not because he is pleased with the trouble which he gives him, but because he expects that his health may be benefited by the advice which he receives. The lawyer is consulted and feed, only because his client expects to derive some advantage from the opinion to be given, or the cause to be pleaded. And even the menial servant is not hired on account of the desire to see a man work, but on account of the trouble which he will save his master in performing certain offices for him, or the gratification afforded to his vanity by the shew of having a person at his command.

The natural consequences of these difficulties is, that the ablest writers who have deserted *matter*, in their definition of wealth, have fallen almost inevitably into contradictions and inconsistencies.

M. Say, for instance, in his chapter on immaterial products, which he defines to be, "des valeurs qui sont consommées au moment de leur production," and of such a nature "qu'on ne saurait les accumuler,"* can only refer to the personal services which are hired, or to some particular kinds of immaterial products. He cannot refer to immaterial products in general, because it is quite impossible to deny that knowledge, talents, and personal qualities are capable of being accumulated. Yet he says, "Une nation où il se trouverait une foule de musiciens, de prêtres, d'employés pourrait être une nation fort divertie, bien endoctrinée, et admirablement bien administrée; mais voilà tout; son capital ne recevrait de tous les travaux de ces hommes industrieux aucun accroissement direct, parce que leurs travaux seraient consommés à mesure qu'ils seraient créés."† A few pages further on, he observes that most immaterial products

* Traité d'Econ. Polit. Liv. I. c. xiii. 5th edit.

† Id. Ib. p. 148.

"sont le résultat d'un talent; tout talent suppose une étude préalable; et aucune étude ne peut avoir lieu sans des avances." He applies this to the advice of the physician, the consultation of the lawyer, and the song of the musician, and then expressly states that, "le talent d'un fonctionnaire public lui-même est un capital accumulé."* Now if it be true that the talents which produce music and good administrations are accumulated capitals, on what possible ground can it be asserted that musicians and employés, who can alone be the teachers of their arts to others, do not increase the national capital, particularly as the rapid consumption of the products of such capitals, so far from impeding accumulation, tends greatly to facilitate it, and to increase the number and skill of the capitalists.

M. Say, in a note to the second part of M. Storch's Cours d'Economie Politique, adverting to those objects which he thinks should be considered as riches, observes, "que, ce n'est que la possibilité de les déterminer, de connaître par conséquent quand, et comment les biens augmentent, quand et comment ils diminuent, et dans quelles proportions ils se distribuent qui a fait de l'économie politique une science positive qui a ses expériences, et fait connaître des resultats."†

Nothing can be more just than this. It is the main criterion to which, with a view to useful and practical conclusions, I should wish to refer. But M. Say, both in the last edition of his Traité d'Economie Politique, and still later in his Cours Complet‡ includes under the name of riches, all talents, natural and acquired; and I would ask in reference to such qualities, how it is possible to ascertain, "quand et comment ils augmentent, quand et comment ils diminuent, et dans quelles proportions ils se distribuent." In every improved country there must always be a vast mass of natural and acquired talents, which are never made the subject of regular exchange or valuation; and of this

* Traité d'Econ. Polit. pp. 150, 151.

† Livre I. c. ii. p. 229.

‡ Tome I. p. 7.

vast mass which would be included in M. Say's definition of riches, it may safely be affirmed that it is not composed of objects, "dont la quantité soit rigoureusement assignable, et dont l'accroissement ou le déclin soit soumis à des lois déterminées."*

One motive which seems to have induced M. Say to force into his definition of riches, "les plus nobles vertus, et les plus rare talens,"† is to enlarge and exalt the domain of political economy, which he says has been reproached with occupying itself upon worldly goods, and encouraging a spirit of avarice. But even if such a classification would give the subject more importance, this additional importance would be dearly purchased at the expense of the precision of its conclusions. The question, however, is not whether the results of useful labours may not very properly find a place in a Treatise on Political Economy, as they have done in the Inquiry of Adam Smith; but whether the specific term wealth should be so defined, as to make not only its own meaning quite indistinct, but to introduce still greater indistinctness into the terms of the science of morals.

Every moral writer, from the most ancient to the most modern, has instructed us to prefer virtue to wealth; and though it has been generally allowed that they may be united in the same person; yet it has always been supposed that they were essentially different in themselves, and that it was often necessary to place them in direct contradistinction one to the other.

If, however, virtue be wealth, how are we to interpret all those moral admonitions which instruct us to underrate the latter in comparison with the former? What is the meaning of not setting our hearts upon riches, if virtue be riches? What do we intend to express when we say of a person of our acquaintance, that he is a very virtuous and excellent man, but poor. The commonest terms used in moral discussions will become quite uncertain without constant circumlocutions, and the meanings of virtue, morals, rich and

* Cours d'Econ. Pol. Tome I. p. 99. † Id. Ib. p. 100.

poor, in our dictionaries, if applied in the ordinary way, and according to the best authorities, will lead us into perpetual error.

It will be recollected that it has never been a question, whether a preacher of the gospel, or a lecturer in moral philosophy who is remunerated for his instructions obtains wealth in exchange for them. The only question is, whether it would be a convenient and useful classification to consider all that was obtained by his hearers, as wealth under the absolute impossibility of appreciating it. That such knowledge has not in the ordinary language of society been called wealth, except metaphysically, must be allowed, and it is equally certain that there is no way of arriving at its amount. In estimating the usual cost of a material object, we are pretty sure of coming near to its usual price. Generally speaking, those commodities, the conditions of the supply of which have been the same, are found to have nearly the same exchangeable value, or if not, the estimate is very soon rectified by an appeal to the next market. But in regard to moral and intellectual qualities, the same expenses of production terminate in results as different as can well be imagined. Even in the learned professions of law and physic, in which the students acquire their knowledge for the express purpose of exchanging it, an attempt to estimate the skill and attainments of each person by the expenses of his education would lead to the most fallacious conclusions. And in the more general education obtained by the great mass of the higher classes of society, such an attempt would be perfectly ridiculous. Those who have paid the most for their instruction, are often those who have the least profited by it. If the products were material, and sold with a view to gain, their production would very soon come to an end ; but education still goes on, and most properly so, although the inequality of possessions arising from the same outlay is known to be prodigious, while in reference to the great mass of them, there are no means of rectifying the estimate founded on cost, by an appeal to their market values. How then is it possible to say with any truth, that morals, talents, and personal attainments may be placed with propriety in the category of wealth, because they are capable of being rigorously appreciated.

On the other hand, there seems to be no kind of incongruity in allowing that wealth, according to the most common acceptation of the term, may be employed in obtaining gratifications which it would be most inconvenient and embarrassing to call by the same name as the material products which were given for them. A man of fortune has the means of purchasing the gratification of leisure; he has often the means of collecting at his table persons from whom he is likely to hear the most agreeable and instructive conversation; he has the means of travelling into different countries, seeing the beauties of nature in her grandest forms, contemplating the finest models of art, ancient and modern, studying the character and polity of different nations, and laying in a stock of taste and information calculated to refine, improve, and enlarge his mind.

It will not be denied, that these are some of the modes of employing wealth, which are always, and most justly, considered as much superior in respectability, to the purchase of fine clothes, splendid furniture, or costly jewels. It is equally certain that the power of wealth to purchase these sources of intellectual gratification forms a most natural encouragement to the acquisition of it, and may therefore, with perfect propriety, be said to be indirectly productive of it. But it is a wide step in advance of these concessions, at once to place in the category of wealth, leisure, agreeable conversation, cultivated tastes, and general information. And yet if the gratification and information derived from a lecture on chemistry or the belles lettres, are to be considered as wealth, in consequence of a specific sum being paid for attendance, why should the taste and information acquired by a larger outlay in foreign travels be refused the same title.

The fact really is, that if we once desert matter in the definition of wealth, there is no subsequent line of demarcation which has any tolerable degree of distinctness, or can be maintained with any tolerable consistency, till we have included such a mass of immaterial objects as utterly to confuse the meaning of the term, and render it impossible to speak with any approach towards precision, either of the wealth of different individuals, or different nations.

If then we wish, with M. Say, to make political economy a positive science, founded on experience, and capable of making known its results, we must be particularly careful in defining its principal term, to embrace only those objects, the increase or decrease of which is capable of being estimated; and the line which it seems most natural and useful to draw, is that which separates material from immaterial objects.

Adam Smith has nowhere given a very regular and formal definition of wealth; but that the meaning which he attaches to the term is confined to material objects is, throughout his work, sufficiently manifest. His prevailing description of wealth may be said to be, "the annual produce of the land and labour." The objections to it as a definition are, that it refers to the sources of wealth before we are told what wealth is, and that it is not sufficiently discriminate, as it would include all the useless and unappropriated products of the earth, as well as those which are appropriated and enjoyed by man.

To avoid these objections, and to keep at an equal distance from a too confined, or a too indiscriminate sense of the term, I should define wealth to be the material objects, necessary, useful, or agreeable to man, which are voluntarily appropriated by individuals* or nations. The definition thus limited includes

* In my little work on the "Definitions in Political Economy," published in 1827, I defined wealth to be "The material objects necessary, useful, or agreeable to man, which have required some portion of human industry to appropriate or produce. The latter

nearly all the objects which usually enter into our conceptions when we speak of wealth or riches—an advantage of considerable importance, as long as we retain these terms both in common use, and in the vocabulary of political economy.

A *country* will therefore be rich or poor, according to the abundance or scarcity with which these material objects are supplied, compared with the extent of territory; and the people will be rich or poor, according to the abundance or scarcity with which they are supplied, compared with the population.

SECTION II.—*On Productive Labour.*

THE question of productive labour is closely connected with the definition of wealth. Both *the Economists* and Adam Smith have uniformly applied the term productive to that species of labour, which directly produces what they call wealth, according to their several views of its nature and origin. *The Economists* therefore, who confine wealth to the products of the soil, mean by productive labour, that labour alone which is employed upon the land. Adam Smith, who considers all the material objects which are useful to man as wealth, means by productive labour, that labour which realizes itself either in the production or increased value of such material objects.

This mode of applying the term productive labour to that labour which is directly productive of wealth,

part was added, in order to exclude air, light, rain, &c.; but there is some objection to the introduction of the term industry or labour into the definition, because an object might be considered as wealth which has had no labour employed upon it. A diamond accidentally found on the sea shore might have a high value; and the fruit at the top of a tree must be considered by the savage as necessary or agreeable to him, before he will make the exertions required to obtain it.

however wealth may be defined, is obviously of the greatest use in explaining the causes of the increase of wealth. The only essential objection to it is, that it seems to underrate the importance of all other kinds of labour—at least the term *unproductive labour*, used by Adam Smith to express all other kinds of labour, has been frequently so interpreted, and has formed in consequence the great objection to his classification. To remove this objection to a classification in other respects sufficiently correct for practical purposes, and beyond comparison more useful in explaining the causes of the wealth of nations, than any other which has hitherto been suggested, it might be desirable to substitute the term *personal services* for unproductive labour.

Labour may then be distinguished into two kinds, productive labour, and personal services, meaning by productive labour that labour which is so directly productive of material wealth as to be capable of estimation in the quantity or value of the object produced, which object is capable of being transferred without the presence of the producer; and meaning by personal services that kind of labour or industry, which however highly useful and important some of it may be, and however much it may conduce *indirectly* to the production and security of material wealth, does not realize itself on any object which can be valued and transferred without the presence of the person performing such service, and cannot therefore be made to enter into an estimate of national wealth.

This, though differing in name, is essentially the doctrine of Adam Smith. It has been controverted by two opposite parties, one of which has imputed to him an incorrect and unphilosophical extension of the term productive to objects which it ought not to include, and the other has accused him of a similar want of precision, for attempting to establish a distinction between two different sorts of labour where no distinction is to be found.

In proceeding to give my reasons for adopting the opinion of Adam Smith with the modification above suggested, I shall first endeavour to show that some such classification of the different sorts of labour is really called for in an inquiry into the causes of the wealth of nations, and that a considerable degree of confusion would be introduced into the science of political economy by an attempt to proceed without it. We shall be less disposed to be disturbed by plausible cavils, or even by a few just exceptions to the complete accuracy of a definition, if we are convinced that the want of precision which is imputed to it, is beyond comparison less in amount and importance than the want of precision which would result from the rejection of it.

In the first place, then, it will readily be granted, that as material capital is the specific source of that great department of the national revenue, peculiarly called profits, and is further absolutely necessary to that division of labour, and extended use of machinery, which so wonderfully increases the productive powers of human industry, its vast influence on the progress of national wealth must be considered as incontrovertibly established. But in tracing the cause of the different effects of the produce which is employed as capital, and the produce which is consumed as revenue, we shall find that it arises principally from the different kinds of labour directly maintained by each. It is obvious, for instance, that it is only the productive labour of Adam Smith, which can keep up, restore, or increase, the material capital of a country. It is also this kind of labour alone, that is, the labour which is realized in the production, or increased value of material objects, which requires a considerable amount of capital for its continued employment; but that, for which there is an effectual demand, will generally be supplied, and the practical consequence is such as might naturally be expected. In those countries which abound in the number, and especially in the skill of their productive labourers, capital and wealth abound. In those where personal services predominate, capital and wealth are comparatively deficient.

It is true, that what is called capital, is sometimes employed in the maintenance of labour, which is not called productive; as by the managers of theatrical exhibitions, and in the payment of the expenses of education. In regard to the first kind of expenditure, however, it would be excluded from coming under the head of capital, if capital were defined, as I have defined it, namely, that portion of the stock or material possessions of a country which is kept or employed with a view to profit in the production or distribution of wealth. But at all events, the amount of it is too inconsiderable to be allowed to interfere with a classification in other respects correct, and in the highest degree useful.

In regard to the expense of education, it should be recollected that no small portion of it is employed in acquiring the skill necessary to the production and distribution of material objects, as in the case of most apprenticeships; and as the persons who have the means of teaching this skill, are themselves employed in this sort of production and distribution; and that the skill so acquired will finally be realized, according to its value on material objects, the capital so employed must clearly be considered as maintaining productive labour, in the most natural sense of the term. The same may be said of all that is expended in the maintenance of those kinds of labour which, though they appear to have the same general character as personal services, are yet so necessary to the production and distribution of material objects, as to be estimated in the value of those objects when they reach the consumer.

In regard to the remaining expenditure in education, it will be excluded from coming under the denomination of capital, by the definition of capital above adverted to: and it may fairly be questioned whether the expenses of general education, and even, for the most part, the education for the learned professions, ought not properly to be considered as being paid from revenue rather than from capital. Practically they seem to be so considered. But in whatever light we view the expenditure upon these services, which are not realized upon any material products, it must be allowed that the great source of what is peculiarly called profits, and the great mass of what is usually called wealth, is directly derived from the employment of material capital in the maintenance of what Adam Smith has called productive labour. In speaking therefore, and treating of capital, it seems highly useful to have some term for the kind of labour which it generally employs, in contradistinction to the kind of labour which in general is employed directly by revenue, in order to explain the nature of productive labour, and its peculiar efficiency in causing the increase of wealth.

Secondly, it is stated by Adam Smith, that the produce which is annually saved is as regularly consumed, as that which is annually spent, but that it is consumed by a different set of people. If this be the case, and if saving be allowed to be the immediate cause of the increase of capital, it must be desirable in all questions relating to the progress of wealth, to distinguish by some particular title a set of people who appear to act so important a part in accelerating this progress. Almost all the lower classes of people of every society are employed in some way or other, and if there were no grounds of distinction in their employments with reference to their effects on the national wealth, it is difficult to conceive what would be the use of saving from revenue to add to capital, as it would be merely employing one set of people in preference to another. How in such a case are we to explain the nature of saving, and the different effects of parsimony and extravagance upon the national capital? No political economist of the present day can by saving mean mere hoarding; and beyond this contracted and inefficient proceeding, no use of the term in reference to the national wealth can well be imagined, but that which must arise from a different application of what is saved, founded upon a real distinction between the different kinds of labour maintained by it.

If the labour of menial servants be as productive of wealth as the labour of manufacturers, why should not savings be employed in their maintenance, not only without being dissipated, but with a constant increase of their amount? But menial servants, lawyers, or physicians, who save from their salaries are fully aware that *their* savings would be immediately dissipated again if they were advanced to persons like themselves, instead of being employed in the maintenance of persons of a different description. To consider the expenditure of the unproductive labourers of Adam Smith as advances made to themselves, and of the same nature as the advances of the master manufacturer to his workmen, would be at once to confound the very useful and just distinction between those who live upon wages, and those who live upon profits, and would render it quite impossible to explain the frequent and important operations of saving from revenue to add to capital, so absolutely necessary to the continued increase of wealth.

Some writers who refuse to adopt the classification of Adam Smith, endeavour to explain the nature of saving by substituting the term productive, or reproductive consumption for productive labour; but it does not seem to be agreed who are to be called the productive or reproductive consumers.

If, as some affirm, every person is a reproductive consumer who obtains for himself a value equal to that which he consumes, it is obvious that all menial servants kept for pomp or pleasure will be productive consumers; but it is quite impossible that a saving, or an increase of wealth and capital can result to any individual from the employment of a great number of such reproductive consumers.

If, on the other hand, a more correct meaning be

given to the expression productive consumption, if it be considered as a present sacrifice with a view to a future advantage, still every species of education would be included in the definition; and certainly it would be impossible to explain the nature of saving by stating that a country gentleman would equally increase his own and the national wealth and capital, whether he employed a considerable part of his revenue in improving his farms and increasing their saleable value, or in paying masters to teach his sons and daughters the most fashionable accomplishments. The latter sort of expenditure, to a certain extent, might be quite as proper and creditable as the former, or even more so; but that is not the question. The question is, what is saving? Now every body would readily pronounce that the first kind of expenditure judiciously applied, was a saving from revenue to add to capital; but few, I apprehend, could expect to be understood, if they pronounced that the second expenditure, in proportion to its extent, was an equal saving from revenue, and an equal addition to individual and national capital.

It appears then upon examination, that the use of the term productive consumption will not enable us to explain what is most usually and most correctly meant by individual and national saving, unless when it is so defined as to mean the very same thing that Adam Smith means by the employment of productive labour.

It has been said, that many of the unproductive labourers of Adam Smith save, and add to the national capital in the usual sense of the term. This is no doubt true; and it is equally true that any person who received a portion of wealth as a gift might save some of it, and add to the national capital. The power of saving, which is equally possessed by both, is not necessarily connected with the means by which their wealth was obtained. But on this point there is another circumstance not sufficiently noticed, which draws a marked line of distinction between productive labour and personal services. Workmen and mechanics who receive the common wages, and various higher salaries, which are realized upon material objects, have the means of saving just in the same manner as menial servants, and others engaged in personal services. In this respect the two classes are precisely on a level. But the productive labourers at the same time that they obtain wealth, and the means of accumulation for themselves, furnish a large surplus to that other most important class of society which lives upon the profits of capital. This distinction alone is quite sufficient to place in a different point of view the productive labourers of Adam Smith, and those engaged in personal services.

Thirdly, it has been stated by Adam Smith, and it is allowed to have been stated truly, that there is a balance very different from the balance of trade, which according as it is favourable or unfavourable, occasions the prosperity or decay of every nation. This is the balance of the annual production and consumption. If in given periods the produce of a country exceeds in a certain degree the consumption of those employed in its production, the means of increasing its capital will be provided; its population will increase, or the actual numbers will be better accommodated, and probably both. If the consumption in such periods fully equals the produce, no means of increasing the capital will be afforded, and the society will be nearly at a stand. If the consumption continually exceeds the produce, every succeeding period will see the society worse supplied, and its prosperity and population will be evidently on the decline.

But if a balance of this kind be so important; if upon it depends the progressive, stationary, or declining state of a society, surely it must be of importance to distinguish those who mainly contribute to render this balance favourable, from those who chiefly contribute to make the opposite scale preponderate. Without some such distinction we shall not be able to trace the causes why one nation is thriving, and another is declining ; nor will the superior riches of those countries where merchants and manufacturers abound, compared with those in which the retainers of a court and of a feudal aristocracy predominate, admit of an intelligible explanation. To such an explanation it is absolutely necessary, that by the balance of production and consumption, we should mean the production and consumption of material objects : for, if all the gratifications derived from personal services were to be included in the term produce, it would be quite impossible either to estimate such a balance, or even to say what was to be understood by it.

If a taste for idle retainers, and a profusion of menial servants, had continued among the great landholders of Europe from the feudal times to the present, the wealth of its different kingdoms would have been very different from what it is now. Adam Smith has justly stated that the growing taste of our ancestors for material conveniences and luxuries, instead of personal services, was the main cause of the change. While the latter continue to be the predominant taste, few comparatively will be living on the profits of capital. The great mass of society will be divided chiefly into two classes, the rich and the poor, one of which will be in a state of abject dependance upon the other. But a taste for material objects, however frivolous, almost always requires for its gratification the accumulation of capital, and the existence of a much greater number of manufacturers, merchants, wholesale dealers, and retail dealers.* The face of society is thus wholly changed. A middle class of persons, living upon the profits of stock, rises into wealth and consequence ; and an increasing accumulation of capital, almost exclusively derived from the industry of the

* There can hardly be a more important inquiry in political economy than that which traces the effects of different proportions of productive labour, and personal services in society ; but this inquiry cannot be conducted without the application of different terms to these two different kinds of labour ; and the distinction made by Adam Smith appears to me to be the simplest and the most convenient.

mercantile and manufacturing classes, effects to a considerable extent the division and alienation of those immense landed properties, which, if the fashion of personal services had continued, might have remained to this time nearly in their former state, and have prevented the increase of wealth on the land, as well as elsewhere.

Surely then some distinction between the different kinds of labour, with reference to their different effects on national wealth, must be admitted to be not only useful, but necessary; and if so, the question is what this distinction should be, and where the line between the different kinds of labour should be drawn.

The opinion that the term productive labour should be exclusively confined to the labour employed upon the land, has been maintained by a particular class of French Economists, and their followers. Without entering upon the general merits of their system, it will only be necessary to observe here, that whatever advantages their definition may claim in point of precision and consistency, yet for the practical and useful purpose of comparing different countries together, with regard to all these objects, which usually enter into our conception of wealth, it is much too confined. Two countries of the same territory and population might possess the same number of agricultural labourers, and even direct the same quantity of skill and capital to the cultivation of the soil, and yet if a considerable proportion of the remaining population in one of them consisted of manufacturers and merchants, and in the other of menial servants and soldiers, the former might have all the indications of wealth, and the latter all the symptoms of poverty. The number and skill of the agricultural labourers, therefore, cannot alone determine the national wealth. We evidently want some definition of productiveness, which refers to the effects of manufacturing and mercantile capital and skill; and unless we consider the labour which produces these most important results as productive of riches, we shall find it quite impossible to trace the causes of those different appearances in different nations, which all persons, whatever may be their theories on the subject, universally agree in calling different degrees of wealth.

The opinion which goes to the opposite extreme of the one here noticed, and calls all labour equally productive, has already been sufficiently considered, in the endeavour to shew that a distinction between the different kinds of labour is really wanted, in an inquiry into the nature and causes of the wealth of nations.

This distinction must be considered as so clearly the corner stone of Adam Smith's work, and the foundation on which the main body of his reasonings rests, that, if it be denied, the superstructure which he has raised upon it, must fall to the ground. Of course it is not meant to be said that his reasonings should not fall, if they are erroneous; but it appears inconsistent in those who allow of no distinction in the different kinds of labour, to entertain a very high opinion of an '*Inquiry into the nature and causes of the Wealth of Nations*,' in which, the increase of the quantity and skill of what is called productive labour is the main hinge on which the progress of national opulence and prosperity is made to turn.*

If in calling personal services productive of wealth, we do not look to the character of what is produced, but merely to its effect in stimulating other producers, this is introducing a new and separate consideration, which has no relation to the direct production of wealth. In this view, it will be seen that I consider personal services to a certain extent as very efficient; but this is evidently not as being productive themselves, but as encouraging the production of material objects to be exchanged for them, and as making a

* The annual produce of the land and labour of any country, can be increased in its value by no other means than by increasing either the number of its productive labourers, or the productive powers of those labourers who had before been employed. (Wealth of Nations, B. II. c. iii.) This is the general doctrine of the work.

demand in proportion to the payments received. It is no doubt true, that the desire to enjoy the convenience or parade of personal attendance, and the advantages of legal and medical advice, has a strong tendency to stimulate industry. But though the tendency of personal services to act as a stimulus to the production of wealth be fully allowed, they can never be said directly to create it, so long as the definition is confined to material objects. Under the circumstances most favourable to their influence, their operation can only be indirect; and if we were to include under the head of productive labour, all the exertions which may contribute, however indirectly, to the production of wealth, the term would cease to have any definite and useful signification, so as to admit of being applied with advantage to an explanation of the causes of the wealth of nations. It would at once confound the effects even of production and consumption, as there is certainly no indirect cause of production so powerful as consumption.

When we consider then the difficulties which present themselves on every supposition we can make, it may fairly be doubted whether it is probable that we shall be able to find a distinction more useful for practical purposes, and on the whole less objectionable in point of precision than that of Adam Smith; which draws the line that distinguishes riches from other kinds of value, between what is matter and what is not matter, between what is susceptible of accumulation and definite valuation, and what is without either one or both of these essential properties.

Some degree of duration and a consequent susceptibility of accumulation seems to be essential to our usual conceptions of wealth, not only because produce of this kind seems to be alone capable of forming those accumulations which tend so much to facilitate future production, but because they so essentially contribute to increase that store reserved for consumption, the possession of which is certainly one of the most distinguishing marks of riches compared with poverty. The characteristic of poverty seems to be, to live from hand to mouth: the characteristic of riches is, to have a store to apply to for the commodities wanted for immediate consumption; but in every case of productive labour as explained by Adam Smith, there is always a period, though in some cases it may be very short, when either the stock destined to replace a capital, or the stock reserved for immediate consumption is distinctly augmented by it; and to this quality of adding to the national stock, the term enriching, or productive of riches seems to be peculiarly appropriate.

But it is not enough that it should be susceptible of accumulation, and of adding to the national stock, to entitle it to be called productive according to the meaning of Adam Smith. In order to make the term useful for practical purposes, the results of the kind of labour to which it refers should be susceptible of some sort of definite valuation. The laws of the legislator, the precepts of the moralist, and the conclusions of the natural philosopher may certainly be said to be susceptible of accumulation and of receiving assistance from past labour; but how is it possible to estimate them, or to say to what amount the country has been enriched by them? On the other hand, the labour, which is the necessary condition of the supply of material objects is estimated in the price at which they are sold, and may fairly be presumed to add to the wealth of the country an amount at least equal to the value paid for such labour; and probably with few or no exceptions, the labour which is realized upon material products is the only kind that is at once susceptible of accumulation and definite valuation.

It has been observed by M. Garnier, in his valuable edition of the *Wealth of Nations*, that it seems very strange and inconsistent to denominate musical instruments riches, and the labour which produces them productive, while the music which they yield, and which is the sole object for which they are made, is not to be considered in the same light; and the performers who can alone put them to their proper use, are called unproductive labourers.* But the difference between material products and those which are not matter, sufficiently warrants the distinction, in point of precision and consistency; and the utility of it is immediately obvious from the facility of giving a definite valuation to the instruments, and the absolute impossibility of giving such a valuation to all the tunes which may be played upon them.

It has also been observed by the same authority, that it is still more inconsistent to denominate the clerk of a merchant a productive labourer, and a clerk employed by government, who may in some cases have precisely the same kind of business to do, an unproductive labourer.* To this, however, it may be replied, that in all business conducted with a view to the profit of individuals, it may be fairly presumed that there are no more clerks, or labourers of any kind employed, nor with higher salaries than necessary; but the same presumption cannot be justly entertained in regard to the business of government: and as the results of the labours of its servants are not brought to market, nor their salaries distributed with the same rigid attention to the exchangeable value of their services, no just criterion is afforded for determining this value.†

At the same time it may be remarked, that if a servant of government perform precisely the same kind of labour in the preparation or superintendence of material products as the servant of a merchant, he ought to be considered as a productive labourer. He is one among the numerous instances which are always occurring, of productive labourers, or labourers

* Vol. v. note xx.

† The application of Adam Smith's distinction, is in this, as in most other cases, preeminently clear. The merchant's clerk increases his master's wealth. He adds a value to the subject on which his labour is bestowed, for if he did not, he would not be employed. The same thing cannot be said of the Government clerk; however useful or necessary his services may be, he contributes nothing to the fund from whence be derives his remuneration. He lives at the expense of his employers, the nation at large, and is paid out of a tax or duty, not out of a profit or reproduction. *Ed.*

occasionally productive, to be found among those classes of society, which, in reference to the great mass of their exertions, may with propriety be characterized as unproductive. This kind of exception must of course frequently happen, not only among the servants of government, but throughout the whole range of menial service, and in every other situation in society. Almost every person, indeed, must occasionally do some productive labour; and the line of separation which Adam Smith has drawn between productive and unproductive labour may be perfectly distinct, although the denomination which he has given to the different classes of society, founded on their general character, must unavoidably be inaccurate with regard to the exertions of some individuals.

It should also be constantly borne in mind, that Adam Smith fully allows the vast importance of many sorts of labour, which he calls unproductive. From the enumeration, indeed, which he has made of these different sorts, he must have been aware, that some of them produce advantages to society, with which the results of the labour employed in making ribands and laces, or indeed of any other labour than that which directly supplies our most pressing physical wants, cannot for a moment be compared. Indirectly indeed, and remotely, there cannot be a doubt that even the supply of these physical wants, is most powerfully promoted by the labours of the moralist, the legislator, and those who have exerted themselves to obtain a good government; but a great part of the value of their labours, evidently depends upon the encouragement they give to the full development of industry, and their consequent invariable tendency to increase the quantity of material wealth. So far as they contribute to promote this supply, their general effect, though not the precise amount, will be estimated in the quantity of these material objects, which the country can command; and so far as they contribute to other sources of happiness, besides those which are derived from matter, it may be more correct, and more useful to consider them as belonging to a class of objects, most of which, cannot without the greatest confusion, enter into the gross calculations which relate to national wealth. To estimate the value of Newton's discoveries, or the delight communicated by Shakespeare and Milton, by the price at which their works have sold, would be but a poor measure of the degree in which they have elevated and enchanted their country; nor would it be less groveling and incongruous to estimate the benefit which the country has derived from the Revolution of 1688, by the pay of the soldiers, and all other payments concerned in effecting it.

On the whole, therefore, allowing that the labours of the moralist and the manufacturer, the legislator and the lacemaker, the agriculturist and the vocal performer, have all for their object the gratification of some want or wish of mankind, it may still be the most natural, the most correct, and pre-eminently the most useful classification which the subject will admit, first to separate under the name of wealth or riches, every thing which gratifies the wants of man by means of material objects, and then to denominate productive every kind of labour which is directly productive of wealth, that is, so directly, as to be estimated in the quantity or value of the objects produced.

The reader will see that this discussion is not introduced with a view to the establishment of any nice and subtle distinctions, without a practical object. Its purpose is to shew, that there is really some difficulty in the definitions of wealth and of productive labour; but that this difficulty should not deter us from adopting any classifications which are obviously useful in conducting inquiry; that in treating of the nature and causes of the wealth of nations, a distinction between the different sources of gratification, and the different kinds of labour, seems to be not only useful, but almost absolutely necessary; and consequently that we should be satisfied with the best classification which we can get on these subjects, although it may not in all its parts be unobjectionable.

CHAPTER II.

ON THE NATURE, CAUSES, AND MEASURES OF VALUE.

SECTION I.—*On the different sorts of Value.*

MOST writers in treating of value, have considered it as having two different meanings; one, value in use, and the other, value in exchange. We are not, however, much in the habit of applying the term in the first of these two senses. We do not often hear of the value of air and water, although they are bodies in the highest degree useful, and indeed essentially necessary to the life and happiness of human beings. Yet it may be admitted that the term, taken perhaps in a metaphorical, rather than in a literal sense, may imply, and is sometimes used to imply, whatever is in any way beneficial to us, and in this sense may apply without impropriety to an abundant spring of water, or to a fine air, although no question could arise respecting their value in exchange.

As this meaning therefore of the word value has already been admitted by many writers into the vocabulary of political economy, it may not be worth while to reject it; and it need only be observed, that as the application of the word value in this way, is very much less frequent than in the other, it should never appear alone, but should always be marked by the addition *in use*.

Value in exchange is the relation of one object to some other or others in exchange. To determine this relation accurately in any particular case, an actual exchange must take place; and every exchange must imply not only the power and will to give some object in exchange for one more wanted, but a reciprocal desire in the party possessing the commodity wanted, for the commodity or the labour proposed to be exchanged for it.

When this reciprocal desire exists, the rate at which the exchange is made, or the portion of one object which is given for an assigned portion of the other, will depend upon the estimation in which each is held by the parties concerned, founded on the desire to possess, and the difficulty of procuring possession of it.

Owing to the necessary difference of the desires of individuals, and their powers of producing, or purchasing, it is probable that the contracts thus made were, in the first instances, very different from each other. Among some individuals it might be agreed to give six pounds of bread for a pound of venison, and among others only two. But the man who was ready and willing to give six pounds of bread for a pound of venison, if he heard of a person at a little distance who would take two pounds for the same quantity, would of course not continue to give six; and the man who would consent to give a pound of venison for only two pounds of bread, if he could any where else obtain six, would not continue to make an exchange by which he could obtain only two.

After a certain time it might be expected that a sort of average would be formed, founded on all the offers of bread, compared with all the offers of venison; and thus, as is very happily described by Turgot, a current relative value of all commodities in frequent use would be established.

It would be known not only that a pound of venison was worth four pounds of bread, but that it was also worth perhaps a pound of cheese, a quarter of a peck of wheat, a quart of wine, a certain portion of leather, &c. &c. each of an average quality, the estimation in which each of these several objects was ordinarily held by the society, being determined by the ordinary desires of individuals to possess it, and the ordinary difficulty of procuring possession of it.

Each commodity would in this way measure the *relative* values of all others, and would in its turn be measured by any one of them. Each commodity would also be a representative of value. The possessor of a quart of wine might consider himself in possession of a value equal to four pounds of bread, a pound of cheese, a certain portion of leather, &c. &c. and thus each commodity would, with more or less accuracy and convenience, possess two essential properties of money, that of being both a representative and a measure of value.

But long before it is conceivable that this general valuation of commodities, with regard to each other should have taken place to any considerable extent, or with any tolerable degree of accuracy, a great difficulty in making exchanges, and in the determination of relative value would be constantly recurring from the want of a reciprocal demand. The possessor of venison might want bread, but the possessor of bread to whom he applied might not want venison, or not that quantity of it which the owner would wish to part with. This want of reciprocal demand would occasion in many instances, and in places not very remote from each other, the most unequal exchanges, and except in large fairs or markets where a great quantity and variety of commodities were brought together, would seem almost to preclude the possibility of any thing like such a general average valuation as has been just described.

Every man, therefore, in order to secure this reciprocal demand, would endeavour, as is justly stated by Adam Smith, so to carry on his business, as to have by him, besides the produce of his own particular trade, some commodity for which there was so general and constant a demand, that it would scarcely ever be refused in exchange for what he wanted. In order that each individual in a society should be furnished with that share of the whole produce, to which he is entitled, by his wants and powers, it is not only necessary that there should be some measure of this share, but some medium by which he can obtain it in the quantity and at the time best suited to him.

The constantly recurring want of some such medium

occasioned the use of various commodities for this purpose in the early periods of society.

Of these, cattle seem to have been the most general. Among pastoral nations, they are not only kept without difficulty or loss by those who obtain them, but as they form the principal possessions and wealth of society in this stage of its progress, they must naturally have been the subject of frequent exchanges, and their exchangeable value in consequence compared with other commodities would be pretty generally known.

It seems to be quite necessary indeed that the commodity chosen for a medium of exchange should, in addition to the other qualities which may fit it for that purpose, be in such frequent use that the estimation in which it was held, founded on the desire to possess it, and the difficulty of obtaining it, should be tolerably well established.

A curious and striking proof of this is, that notwithstanding the peculiar aptitude of the precious metals to perform the functions of a medium of exchange, they had not been used for that purpose in Mexico at the period of its conquest by the Spaniards, although these metals were in some degree of plenty as ornaments, and although the want of some medium of exchange was clearly evinced by the use of the nuts of cacao for that purpose.*

It is probable, that as the practice of smelting and refining the ores of the precious metals had not yet been resorted to, the supply of them was not sufficiently steady, nor was the use of them sufficiently general, or the degree of difficulty with which they were obtained sufficiently known, to fit them for the purpose required.

In Peru, where the precious metals were found by the Spaniards in much greater abundance, the practice of smelting and refining the richest ores had begun to prevail, although no shafts had been sunk to any depth in the earth.† But in Peru the state of

* Robertson's America, Vol. iii. Book vii. page 215.

† Ibid. page 252.

property was so peculiar, and there was so little commerce of any kind, that a medium of exchange seems not to have been called for; at least there is no account of the use of either of the precious metals, or of any other commodity in the capacity of money.

In the old world the art of smelting and refining the ores of gold, silver, and copper, seems to have been known to some of the most improved nations of which we have accounts, from the earliest ages; and as soon as the means used to obtain these metals, and a certain accumulation of them had rendered their supply in the market steady, and they had been introduced into common use in the shape of ornaments and utensils, their other peculiar and appropriate qualities, such as their durability, divisibility, uniformity of substance, and great value in a small compass would naturally point them out as the best commodity that could be selected to answer the purpose of a medium of exchange, and measure of value.

But when they were adopted as the general measure of value, it would follow, of course, that all other commodities would be most frequently compared with this measure. The nominal value of a commodity is strictly speaking its value in any one commodity named; but as the precious metals are on almost all occasions the commodity named, or intended to be named, the nominal value of a commodity, when no object is specifically referred to, is always understood to mean its value in exchange for the precious metals.

This sort of value has been usefully designated by the name of *price*. It is, properly speaking, another term for nominal value; and as such we may apply it to any particular commodity named, and say price in corn, price in cloth, or price in any other article, with which we wish to compare any given object; but whenever it occurs without the above additions, it is always understood to mean the value of a commodity estimated in the precious metals, or in the currencies of different countries which profess to represent them.

The introduction of a measure which determined the nominal and relative values of commodities with a medium which would be readily accepted by all persons, was a most important step in the progress of society, and tended to facilitate exchanges and stimulate production to an extent which, without such an instrument, would have been perfectly impossible.

It is very justly observed by Adam Smith, that it is the nominal value of goods, or their prices only, which enter into the consideration of the merchant.* It matters very little to him whether a hundred pounds, or the goods which he purchases with this sum, will command more or less of the labour, or of the necessaries and conveniences of life in Bengal than in London. What he wants is an instrument by which he can obtain the commodities in which he deals, and estimate the relative values of his sales and purchases. His returns come to him wherever he lives; and whether it be in London or Calcutta, or whether they come to him in goods, bills, or bullion, his gain will be in proportion to the excess of their money value above the amount which he has expended to obtain them. The variations which may take place in the value of money during the short period of a mercantile transaction will, in general, be so inconsiderable, that they may safely be neglected.

But though the precious metals are an accurate and unexceptionable measure of value at the same place, and nearly at the same time; and in those parts of the world where they are in general use answer the important purpose of determining the rate at which the products of the most distant countries shall exchange with each other, when brought to the same spot, and thus give the greatest encouragement to the production and distribution of wealth throughout the commercial world; yet we know from experience, that at different periods and in different countries, they are liable to great changes of value owing to the greater or less fertility of the mines, or the greater or

* Book I, ch. v. p. 55; 6th edit.

less facility of purchasing them; and that consequently given portions of them will, in many cases, express most imperfectly the difficulty of obtaining possession of the numerous objects for which they may be exchanged.

If we are told that a certain quantity of cloth in a particular country will exchange for ten ounces of silver, or that the revenue of a particular sovereign, seven or eight hundred years ago, was £400,000 a year, these statements of nominal value do not tell us whether the cloth is obtained with facility or difficulty, or whether the resources of the sovereign are abundant or scanty. Without further information on the subject, we should be quite at a loss to say, whether it would be necessary to sacrifice the worth of ten days labour to obtain the cloth, or a hundred days; whether the king in question might be considered as having a very inadequate revenue; or whether the sum mentioned was so great as to be incredible.*

It is quite obvious that in cases of this kind, and they are of constant recurrence, the values of commodities or incomes estimated in the precious metals, or in other commodities which are subject to considerable variations in the difficulty of obtaining them, may imply an increase or decrease of value merely in name, and would be of little use to us alone.

What we want further to know, is the estimation in which the cloth and money were held in the country, and at the time in question, founded on the desire to possess, and the difficulty of obtaining possession of them.

It is truly stated by Mr. Senior, that in comparing two commodities together, the power of one to purchase the other must depend upon two sets of causes, that is, upon the causes which affect the desire to possess, and the difficulty of obtaining possession of one of them, and the causes which affect the

* Hume very reasonably doubts the *possibility* of William the Conqueror's revenue being £400,000 a year, as represented by an ancient historian, and adopted by subsequent writers.

desire to possess, and the difficulty of obtaining possession of the other. The causes which affect the desire to possess, and the difficulty of obtaining possession of any one commodity, may with propriety be denominated the *intrinsic* causes of its power of purchasing; because the more these causes increase, the greater power will the commodity possess of purchasing all those objects which continue to be obtained with the same facility. The causes which affect the desire to possess, and the difficulty of obtaining possession of all the different commodities with which the first commodity might be exchanged, may with propriety be denominated the *extrinsic* causes of its power of purchasing; because while the desire to possess, and the difficulty of obtaining possession of the first commodity remains precisely the same, its power of purchasing other commodities may vary in any degree, owing to the variations in the desire to possess, and the difficulty of obtaining possession of all the other commodities with which it might be exchanged, that is, owing to causes *extrinsic* to those which operate on the first commodity.

Now it is obvious that these extrinsic causes must, from their nature, and the variety of commodities to which they would apply, be almost innumerable; and though it would certainly be desireable to have some measure of the power of purchasing the mass of commodities, or at least the principal necessaries and conveniences of life, as it would enable us to form an estimate of the wealth of those persons who were in possession of particular commodities, or of certain revenues in money, yet when we consider what such a measure implies, we must feel assured that no one object exists, or can be supposed to exist with such qualities as would fit it to become a standard measure of this kind. It would imply steadiness in the desire to possess, and the difficulty of obtaining possession, not merely of one object, but of a great variety of objects, which is contrary to all theory and experience.

But even if such a measure were attainable, though

it might be very desireable as a measure of wealth, it would not be a measure of value according to the most general use of the term.

When it is said that the exchangeable value of a commodity is proportioned to its general power of purchasing,* if the expression has any definite meaning, it must imply that while a commodity continues to purchase the same quantity of the mass of commodities, it continues of the same exchangeable value. If it will purchase more, it rises proportionally in value, if it will purchase less, it falls proportionally in value.

Now let us suppose, what is continually occurring, that from improvements in machinery, the fall of profits, and the increase of skill both in manufactures and agriculture, a large mass of manufactured articles can be obtained with much greater facility than before, while the increase of skill in agriculture prevents any increase in the difficulty of obtaining raw produce, can it be asserted with any semblance of correctness, that an object which under these changes would command the same quantity of agricultural and manufactured products of the same kind, and each in the same proportion as before, would be practically considered by the society as of the same exchangeable value. On the supposition here made, no person would hesitate for a moment to say, that cottons had fallen in value, that linen had fallen in value, that silks had fallen in value, that cloth had fallen in value, &c. and it would be a direct contradiction in terms, to add that an object which would purchase only the same *quantity* of all these articles, which had confessedly fallen in value, had not itself fallen in value.

The general power of purchasing, therefore, possessed by a particular commodity, cannot with any sort of propriety be considered as representing the variations in its exchangeable value, according to the most usual meaning attached to the term. The ex-

* Adam Smith defines the value of an object in exchange to be, "the power of purchasing other goods, which the possession of that object conveys." Book I. ch. iv. p. 42; 6th edit.

changeable value of a commodity can only be proportioned to its general power of purchasing so long as the commodities with which it is exchanged continue to be obtained with the same facility. But as it is known by experience that no considerable mass of commodities ever continues to be obtained with the same facility, it is observable that when we speak of the variations in the exchangeable value of a particular commodity, we refer almost invariably to its power of purchasing arising from intrinsic causes.

That this is so, is incontrovertibly proved by the manner in which we practically estimate the variations of value by money. In the same places, and for short periods, money is universally considered as a correct measure of value in the ordinary sense in which the term is used. If from any cause whatever the members of the society are willing and able to make a greater sacrifice in money, in order to obtain a particular commodity, we say that it has risen in value, without stopping to inquire into the state of other commodities. If corn be dear, on account of a deficient supply, we say that corn has risen in value; but if we still pay the same money for our coats, shirts, and shoes, we never think of saying that they have fallen in value, although on account of the rise in a great mass of raw produce, they will have diminished most essentially in their general power of purchasing. The corn is said to have risen in exchangeable value, because its power of purchasing has been affected by a cause *intrinsic* to the article itself, namely, a deficiency of its supply. The coats, shirts, and shoes, are said to have remained of the same value, because their supply, compared with the demand, appears to have remained the same, and nothing has operated to increase or diminish their power of purchasing arising from intrinsic causes. In neither case do we trouble ourselves about the *extrinsic* causes of their power of purchasing. During the short periods in which we consider the value of money as nearly constant, we invariably refer to the power of particular commodities to command, at different times, different quantities of money, as expressing distinctly the variations in their exchangeable values. But as a rise or fall of a commodity in money during the periods in which money is considered as constant, cannot indicate any other variations than those which arise from *intrinsic* causes, it follows necessarily, that when we refer to the variations in the values of commodities, in the ordinary sense in which the term is used, we refer exclusively to their purchasing power arising from intrinsic causes, or to that kind of value which may be denominated their intrinsic value in exchange.

If then we continue to apply the term value in the first sense mentioned, we shall have three sorts of value:

1. Value in use, which may be defined to be the intrinsic utility of an object.

2. Nominal value in exchange, or price, which, unless something else is specifically referred to, may be defined to be the value of commodities estimated in the precious metals.

3. Intrinsic value in exchange, which may be defined to be the power of purchasing arising from intrinsic causes, in which sense, the value of an object is understood when nothing further is added.* This definition is precisely equivalent to—The estimation in which a commodity is held, founded on the desire to possess, and the difficulty of obtaining possession of it; and accords entirely with the definition of the exchangeable value of a commodity, given in my work *On definitions in Political Economy*, namely,—The estimation in which a commodity is held at any place and time, determined in all cases by the state of the supply compared with the demand, and ordinarily by the elementary cost of production.

* There has been no more fruitful source of error in the very elements of political economy, than the not distinguishing between the power of purchasing generally, and the power of purchasing arising from intrinsic causes; and it is of the highest importance to be fully aware that, practically, when the rise or fall in the value of a commodity is referred to, its power of purchasing arising from extrinsic causes is always excluded.

SECTION II.—*Of Demand and Supply as they affect Exchangeable Value.*

The terms demand and supply are so familiar to the ear of every reader, and their application in single instances so fully understood, that in the slight use which has hitherto been made of them, it has not been thought necessary to interrupt the course of the reasoning by definitions and explanations. These terms, however, though in constant use, are by no means applied with precision. And before we proceed further, it may be advisable to clear this part of the ground as much as possible, that we may be certain of the footing on which we stand. This will appear to be the more necessary, as it must be allowed that of all the principles of political economy, there is none which bears so large a share in the phenomena which come under its consideration as the principle of supply and demand.

It has been already stated, that exchangeable value is the relation of one object to some other or others in exchange. And when, by the introduction of a medium of exchange and measure of value, a distinction has been made between buyers and sellers, the demand for any sort of commodities may be defined to be, the will of persons to purchase them, combined with their general means of purchasing; and supply, the quantity of the commodities for sale, combined with the desire to sell them.*

It is further evident, that when the use of the precious metals, as a medium of exchange and measure of value, has become general, and during those periods

* There may be sometimes a comparatively small quantity of certain commodities ready for sale, but if a large supply is soon expected, the desire to sell will be great, and the prices low. On the other hand, there may be a comparatively large quantity of the commodities ready for sale, yet if a future scanty supply is looked forward to, the dealers will not be anxious for an immediate sale, and the prices may be high.

when their value is considered as remaining the same, the demand will be represented and measured by the sacrifice in money which the demanders are willing and able to make in order to satisfy their wants.

In this state of things, the value of commodities in money or their prices are determined by the demand for them, compared with the supply of them. And this law appears to be so general, that probably not a single instance of a change of price can be found, which may not be satisfactorily traced to some previous change in the state of the demand or supply.

In examining the truth of this position, we must constantly bear in mind the terms in which it is expressed; and recollect, that when prices are said to be determined by demand and supply, it is not meant that they are determined either by the demand alone, or by the supply alone, but by their relation to each other.

But how is this relation to be determined? It has sometimes been said, that demand is always equal to supply; because no supply of any commodity can take place for which there is not a demand, which will take off all that is offered. In one sense of the terms in which demand and supply have been used, this position may be granted. The actual *extent* of the demand, compared with the actual *extent* of the supply are always nearly equal to each other. If the supply be ever so small, the *extent* of the demand cannot be greater; and if the supply be ever so great, the *extent* of the demand will in most cases increase in proportion to the fall of price occasioned by the desire to sell, and the consumption will finally equal the production. It cannot, therefore, be in this sense that a change in the proportion of demand to supply takes place; because in this sense demand and supply always bear nearly the same relation to each other. And this uncertainty in the use of these terms, renders it an absolutely necessary preliminary in the present inquiry, clearly to ascertain what is the nature of that change in the relation of demand and supply on which the prices of commodities so entirely depend.

Demand has been defined to be the will to purchase, combined with the means of purchasing.

The greater is the degree of this will, and of these means of purchasing when directed to any particular commodity wanted, the greater or the more intense may be said to be the demand for it. But, however great this will and these means may be among the demanders of a commodity, none of them will be disposed to give a high price for it, if they can obtain it at a low one; and as long as the means and competition of the sellers continue to bring the quantity wanted to market at a low price, the whole intensity of the demand will not show itself.

If a given number of commodities attainable by labour alone, were to become more difficult of acquisition, as they would evidently not be obtained unless by means of increased exertion, we might merely consider such increased exertion, if applied, as an evidence of a greater intensity of demand, or of a will and power to make a greater sacrifice in order to obtain them.

In the same manner, if while money is considered as of the same value, certain commodities, either from scarcity, or the greater cost of production become more difficult of acquisition, as they will certainly not be acquired except by those who are willing and able to sacrifice a greater amount of money in order to obtain them, such sacrifice, if made, must be considered as an evidence of greater intensity of demand.

In fact, it may be said, that the giving a greater price for a commodity, while the difficulty of obtaining money remains the same, necessarily implies a greater intensity of demand; and that the real question is, what are the causes which determine the increase or diminution of this intensity of demand, which shows itself in a rise or fall of prices.

It has been justly stated that the causes which tend to raise the price of any article estimated in some commodity named, and supposed, for short periods, not essentially to vary in the difficulty of its production, or the state of its supply compared with the demand, are, an increase in the number, wants, and means of the demanders, or a deficiency in the supply; and the causes which lower the price are a diminution in the number, wants, and means of the demanders, or an increased abundance in its supply.

Now the first class of these causes is obviously calculated to call forth the expression of a greater intensity of demand, and the other of a less.

If, for instance, a commodity which had been habitually demanded and consumed by a thousand purchasers, were suddenly to be wanted by two thousand, it is clear that before this increased extent of demand can be supplied, some must go without what they want; and it is scarcely possible to suppose that the intensity of individual demand should not exist in such a degree among a sufficient number of these two thousand demanders, as to take off the whole of the commodity produced at an increased price. At the same time, if we could suppose it possible, that the wills and means of the demanders, or the intensity of their demand would not admit of increase, it is quite certain that however the matter might be settled among the contending competitors, no rise of price could take place.*

In the same manner, if a commodity were to be diminished one half in quantity, it is scarcely possible to suppose that a sufficient number of the former demanders would not be both willing and able to take off the diminished quantity, at a higher price; but if they really would not or could not do this, the price could not rise.

* Sir Edward West seems to think, that a demand *in posse* cannot be called demand; but it does not appear to me that there is any impropriety in so applying the term; and it is quite certain that if there were not a greater intensity of demand *in posse* than *in esse*, no failure of supply could raise prices. In reality prices are determined by the demand *in posse* compared with the supply *in esse*.

On the other hand, if the permanent cost of producing the commodity were doubled, it is evident that such a quantity only could be permanently brought to market, as would supply the wants of those who were both able and willing to make a sacrifice for the attainment of their wishes, equal to double of what they did before. The quantity of the commodity which would be brought to market under these circumstances might be extremely different. It might be reduced to the supply of a single individual, or might remain precisely the same as before. If it were reduced to the supply of a single individual, it would be a proof that only one of all the former purchasers was both able and willing to make an effectual demand for it at the advanced price. If the supply remained the same, it would be a proof that all the purchasers were in this state, but that the expression of this intensity of demand had not before been rendered necessary on account of the facility with which the article had been previously produced, and the competition of the sellers. In the latter case there would be exactly the same quantity of the commodity supplied, and exactly the same effectual demand for it in regard to extent. But there would be a much greater intensity of demand called forth, the value brought to market to exchange for the commodity in question would have greatly increased; and this may be fairly said to be a most important change in the relation between the demand and the supply of the commodity. Without the increased intensity of demand, which in this case takes place, the commodity would cease to be produced, that is, the failure of the supply would be contingent upon the failure of the will or power to make a greater sacrifice for the object sought.*

* Adam Smith says, that "when the quantity of any commodity which is brought to market falls short of the effectual demand, all those who are willing to pay the whole value of the rent, wages, and profits, which must be paid in order to bring it thither, cannot be supplied with the quantity which they want. Rather than want it altogether some of them will be willing to give more." Now this willingness, on the part of some of the demanders, to

Upon the same principles, if, owing to an unusual supply, a commodity were to become much more abundant compared with the former number of purchasers, this increased supply could not be all sold, unless the price were lowered. Each seller wishing to dispose of that part of the commodity which he possessed under the fear of its remaining upon his hands, would go on lowering it till he had effected his object; and though the wills and means of the old purchasers might remain undiminished, yet as the commodity could be obtained without the expression of the same intensity of demand as before, this demand would of course not then show itself.

A similar effect would obviously take place from the consumers of a commodity requiring a less quantity of it.

If instead of a temporary abundance of supply compared with the demand, the cost of producing any particular commodity were greatly diminished, the fall of price would in the same manner be occasioned by an increased abundance of supply, either actual or contingent. In almost all practical cases it would be an actual and permanent increase; because the competition of the sellers would lower the price, and it

make a greater sacrifice than before, in order to satisfy their wants, is what I have called a greater intensity of demand. As no increase of price can possibly take place, unless the commodity be of such a nature as to excite in a certain number of purchasers this species of demand, and as this species of demand must always be implied whenever we speak of demand and supply as determining prices, I have thought that it ought to have a name. It is essentially different from effectual demand, which, as defined by Adam Smith, is the quantity wanted by those who are willing and able to pay the natural price; and this demand will of course generally be the greatest when the natural price is the least. But the increased intensity of demand, when actually called forth, uniformly implies an increased *value* offered, compared with the *quantity* of the commodity supplied, and is equally applicable to an article which is accidentally scarce, and one which has increased in its natural price. It is invariably and exclusively the intensity of demand, and not the effectual demand, which is referred to, when it is said, and correctly, that the prices of commodities vary as the demand directly, and the supply inversely.

very rarely happens that a fall of price does not occasion an increased consumption. On the supposition however, of the very rare case that a definite quantity of the commodity only was required, whatever might be its price, it is obvious that from the competition of the producers, a greater quantity would be brought to market than could be consumed, till the price was reduced in proportion to the increased facility of production; and this temporary excess of supply would be always contingent upon the circumstance of the price being at any time higher than that which would return average profits. In this case of a fall of prices, as in the other of a rise of prices, the actual quantity of the commodity supplied and consumed may possibly, after a short struggle, be the same as before; yet it cannot be said that no change has taken place in the demand. It may indeed exist latently in the same degree, and the actual consumers of the commodity might be perfectly ready to give what they gave before rather than go without it; but such has been the alteration in the means of supply, compared with the former demand, that the competition of the producers renders the making of the same sacrifice no longer necessary to effect the supply required; and not being necessary, it is of course not made, and the price falls.

It is evidently, therefore, not merely the extent of actual demand, nor even the extent of actual demand compared with the extent of the actual supply, which raises prices, but such a change in the relation between demand and supply, as renders necessary the expression of a greater intensity of demand, or the offer of a greater *value* compared with the *quantity* supplied, in order either peaceably to divide an actual produce, or to prevent the future produce of the same kind from failing.

And in the same manner, it is not merely the extent of actual supply, nor the extent of the actual supply compared with the extent of the actual demand, (which are generally nearly equal) that lowers prices;

but such a change in the relation of the supply compared with the demand as renders a fall of price necessary, in order to take off a temporary abundance, or to prevent a constant excess of supply contingent upon a diminution in the costs of production, without a proportionate diminution in the price of produce.

If the terms demand and supply be understood, and used in the way here described, there is no case of price, whether temporary or permanent, which they will not determine; and in every instance of bargain and sale, it will be perfectly correct to say, that the prices of commodities will depend upon the relation of the demand to the supply; or will vary as the demand (that is, the money ready to be offered) directly, and the supply inversely.

I wish it to be particularly observed, that in this discussion, I have not given a meaning to the terms demand and supply different from that in which they have been most frequently applied before. In the use which I have made of the words intense and intensity as applied to demand, my purpose has been to explain the meaning which has hitherto always been attached to the terms demand, when it is said to raise prices. Mr. Ricardo, in his chapter "*On the influence of demand and supply on prices*," observes, that "the demand for a commodity cannot be said to increase, if no additional quantity of it be purchased or consumed." But it is obvious, as I have before remarked, that it is not in the sense of mere extent of consumption that demand raises prices, because it is almost always when prices are the lowest, that the extent of demand and consumption is the greatest. This, therefore, cannot be the meaning hitherto attached to the term demand, when it is said to raise prices. Mr. Ricardo, however, subsequently quotes Lord Lauderdale's statements respecting value, and allows them to be true, as applied to monopolized commodities, and to the market prices of all other commodities, for a limited period. He would allow, therefore, that a deficiency in the usual quantity of an article in a market would occasion a greater demand for it compared with the supply, and raise its price, although in this case less than usual of the article must be purchased by the consumers. Demand in this sense is obviously quite different from the sense in which Mr. Ricardo had before used the term. The one is a demand in regard to extent, the increase of which implies a greater quantity of the commodity purchased; the other is demand in regard to intensity, the increase of which implies the will and power to make a greater sacrifice in order to obtain the object wanted. It is in this latter sense, I think, that the term is most frequently applied; at any rate, it is in this latter sense alone that demand raises prices.* It is in the nature of things absolutely impossible that any demand, in regard to extent, should raise prices, unaccompanied by a will and power on the part of the demanders to make a greater sacrifice, in order to satisfy their wants. And my object is to shew that, whenever we talk of demand and supply as determining prices, whether market, or natural, the terms must always be understood in the sense in which Mr. Ricardo, and every other person, has hitherto understood them, when speaking of commodities bought and sold in a market.

Section III.—*Of the Cost of Production as affected by the Demand and Supply, and on the mode of representing Demand.*

It may be said, perhaps, that even according to the view given of demand and supply in the preceding section, the permanent prices of the great mass of commodities will be determined by the ordinary cost of their production. This is unquestionably true, if we include all the component parts of price stated by

* Of course it must often happen that an increased intensity of demand, and an increased extent of demand go together. In fact, an increased intensity of demand, when not occasioned by an increased difficulty of production, is the greatest encouragement to an increase of produce and consumption.

Adam Smith. Yet, still it is true, that in all transactions of bargain and sale, there is a principle in constant operation, which can determine, and does actually determine, the prices of commodities, independently of any considerations of cost, or of the ordinary wages, profits, and rent expended in their production. And this is found to operate, not only permanently upon that class of commodities which may be considered as monopolies, but temporarily and immediately upon all commodities, and strikingly and pre-eminently so upon all sorts of raw produce.

It has never been a matter of doubt, that the principle of demand and supply determines exclusively, and very regularly and accurately, the prices of monopolized commodities, without reference to the ordinary cost of their production; and our daily and uniform experience shows us that the prices of raw products, particularly those which are most affected by the seasons, are at the moment of their sale determined always by the higgling of the market, and differ widely in different years, and at different times, while the outgoings required to produce them, may have been very nearly the same, and the general rate of profits has not varied.

With regard, therefore, to a class of commodities of the greatest extent, it is acknowledged that the existing market prices are, at the moment they are fixed, determined upon a principle distinct from the cost of production, and that these prices are in reality almost always different from what they would have been, if this cost had exclusively regulated them.

There is indeed another class of commodities, such as manufactures, particularly those in which the raw material is cheap, where the existing market prices much more frequently coincide with the costs of production, and may appear therefore to be exclusively determined by them. Even here, however, our familiar experience shews us, that any alteration in the proportion of the demand to the supply quite overcomes for a time the influence of these costs; and further, when we come to examine the subject more closely, we find that the cost of production itself only influences the prices of these commodities, as the payment of this cost is the necessary condition of their continued supply in proportion to the extent of the effectual demand for them.

But if this be true, it follows that the great law of demand and supply is called into action to determine what Adam Smith calls natural prices, as well as what he calls market prices.

It has been shown that no change can take place in the market prices of commodities, without some previous change in the relation of the demand to the supply; and the question is, whether the same position is true in reference to natural prices? This question must of course be determined by attending carefully to the nature of the change which an alteration in the cost of production occasions in the state of the demand and supply, and particularly to the specific and immediate cause by which the change of price which takes place is effected.

We all allow that when the cost of production diminishes, a fall of price is almost universally the consequence; but what is it, specifically, which forces down the price of the commodity. It has been shown in the preceding section, that it is an actual or contingent excess of supply.

We all allow that when the cost of production increases, the prices of commodities rise. But what is it specifically which forces up the price? It has been shown that it is an actual or contingent failure of supply. Remove these actual or contingent variations of the supply; that is, let the extent of the supply remain exactly the same, without excess or failure, whether the cost of production rises or falls; and there is not the slightest ground for supposing that any variation of price would take place.

If, for instance, all the commodities which are produced in this country, whether agricultural or manufactured, could be produced during the next ten years without labour, but could only be supplied exactly in the same quantities as they would be in the actual state of things; then, supposing the wills and means of the purchasers to remain the same, there cannot be a doubt that all prices would also remain the same. But if this be allowed, it follows that the relation of the supply to the demand is the dominant principle in the determination of prices whether market or natural, and that the cost of production can do nothing but in subordination to it, that is, merely as it affects the ordinary relation which the supply bears to the demand.

It is not, however, necessary to resort to imaginary cases in order to fortify this conclusion. Actual experience shows the principle in the clearest light.

In the well known instance noticed by Adam Smith of the insufficient pay of curates, notwithstanding all the efforts of the legislature to raise it, a striking proof is afforded that the permanent price of an article is determined by the demand and supply, and not by the cost of production. The real cost of the education would in this case be more likely to be increased than diminished by the subscriptions of benefactors; but a large part of it being paid by these benefactors, and not by the individuals themselves, it does not regulate and limit the supply; and this supply, on account of such encouragement, becoming and continuing abundant, the price is naturally low, whatever may be the real cost of the education given.

The effects of the poor-rates, in lowering the wages of independent labour, present another practical instance of the same kind. It is not probable that public money should be more economically managed than the income of individuals. Consequently the cost of rearing a family cannot be supposed to be diminished by parish assistance; but a part of the expense being borne by the public, and applied more largely to labourers with families, than to single men, a fair and independent price of labour, adequate to the maintenance of a certain family, is no longer a necessary condition of a sufficient supply. As by means of parish rates so applied, this supply can be obtained without such wages, the real costs of supplying labour no longer regulate the ordinary wages of independent labour.

In fact, in every kind of bounty upon production, the same effects must necessarily take place; and just in proportion that such bounties tend to lower prices, they show that prices depend upon the supply compared with the demand, and not upon the costs of production.

But the most striking instance which can well be conceived to show that the cost of production only influences the prices of commodities, as it influences their supply compared with the demand, is continually before our eyes in the artificial value which is given to bank-notes by limiting their amount. Mr. Ricardo's admirable and efficient plan for this purpose proceeded upon the just principle, that if you can limit the supply of notes, so that they shall not exceed the quantity of gold which would have circulated if the currency had been metallic, you will keep the notes always of the same value as gold. And I am confident he would have allowed, that if this limitation could be completely effected without the paper being exchangeable for gold, the value of the notes would not be altered, while the same demand for a circulating medium continued. But if an article which costs comparatively nothing, though it performs the most important function of gold, can be kept to the value of gold, by being supplied in the same quantity; it is the clearest of all possible proofs that the value of gold itself no further depends upon the cost of its production, than as this cost influences the supply compared with the demand: and that if the cost were to cease, provided the supply were not increased compared with the demand, the value of gold in this country would still remain the same.

It does not, however, in any degree follow from what has been said, that the costs of production have not a most powerful effect upon prices. But the true way of considering these costs is as the necessary condition of the supply of the objects wanted.

Although at the time of the actual purchase of a commodity, no circumstance affects it but the relation of the supply to the demand; yet as almost all the objects of human desire are obtained by the instrumentality of human exertion, it is clear that the supply of these objects must be regulated—First, by the quantity, skill, and direction of this exertion; Secondly, by the assistance which it may receive from previous accumulations; and Thirdly, by the abundance or scarcity of the materials on which it has to work, and of the food of the labourer. It is of importance therefore to consider the different conditions which must be fulfilled, in order that any commodity should continue to be brought to market in the quantity wanted to supply the effectual demand.

The first condition is, that the labour expended upon it should be so remunerated in the quantity of desirable objects given in exchange for it, as to encourage the exertion of a sufficient quantity of industry in the direction required, as without such adequate remuneration, the supply of the commodity must necessarily fail. If this labour should be of a very severe kind, few comparatively would be willing or able to engage in it; and upon the common principles of exchangeable value before explained it would rise in price. If the work were of a nature to require an uncommon degree of dexterity and ingenuity, a rise of price would take place in a greater degree; but not merely on account of the esteem which men have for such talents, as stated by Adam Smith, but on account of their rarity, and the consequent rarity of the effects produced by them. In all these cases the remuneration will be regulated, not by the intrinsic qualities, or utility of the commodities produced, but by the state of the demand for them, compared with the supply; and of course by the demand and supply of the sort of labour which produced them. If the commodities have been produced by manual labour exclusively, aided at least only by the unappropriated bounties of nature, and brought to market immediately, the whole remuneration will of course belong to the labourer, and the usual money price of this remuneration in the existing state of the society would be the usual price of the commodity.

The second condition to be fulfilled is, that the assistance which may have been given to the labourer, by the previous accumulation of objects which facilitate future production, should be so remunerated as to continue the application of this assistance to the production of the commodities required. If by means of certain advances to the labourer of machinery, food and materials previously collected, he can execute eight or ten times as much work as he could without such assistance, the person furnishing them might appear at first to be entitled to the difference between the powers of unassisted labour, and the powers of labour so assisted. But the prices of commodities do not depend upon their intrinsic utility, but upon the supply and demand. The increased powers of labour would naturally produce an increased supply of commodities; their prices would consequently fall, and the remuneration for the capital advanced would soon be reduced to what was necessary in the existing state of the society, to encourage the application of such capital to the production in question, in the quantity required by the effectual demand. With regard to the labourers employed, as neither their exertions, nor their skill would necessarily be greater than if they had worked unassisted, their remuneration in money would be nearly the same as before, and would depend entirely upon the kind of labour employed, estimated in the usual way, by the money demand compared with the supply. But the price of labour so determined would, under the influence of good machinery, give the labourer a greater *quantity* than before of the produce obtained, though not necessarily a greater proportion of it. It is not, therefore, correct to represent, as Adam Smith does, the profits of capital as a deduction from the produce of labour. They are only a fair remuneration for that part of the production contributed by the capitalist, estimated exactly in the same way as the contribution of the labourer.

The third condition to be fulfilled is, that the prices of commodities should be such as to effect the continued supply of the food and raw materials used by the labourers and capitalists; and we know that this price cannot be paid without yielding a rent to the landlord on almost all the land actually in use. In speaking of the landlords, Adam Smith's language is again exceptionable. He represents them, rather invidiously, as loving to reap where they have not sown, and as obliging the labourer to pay for a license to obtain those natural products which, when land was in common, cost only the trouble of collecting.* But he would himself be the first to acknowledge, that if land were not appropriated, its produce would be very much less abundant compared with the demand, and that consequently the producers and consumers would be much worse off; and if it *be* appropriated, some persons or other must necessarily be the proprietors. It matters not to the society, whether these persons are the same or different from the actual cultivators of the land. The price of the produce will be determined by the general supply compared with the general money demand, and will be the same, or very nearly so, whether the cultivator pays a rent, or uses the land without rent. The only difference would be, that, in the latter case, what remains of this price after paying the necessary labour and profits, will go to the same person that advanced the capital, which is equivalent to saying that the farmer would be better off if he were also the possessor of land, a fact not to be disputed; but it cannot imply, that the labourer or farmer, who in the lottery of human life has not drawn a prize of land, suffers any hardship or injustice

* Wealth of Nations, B. I. ch. vii. p. 74, 6th edit.

in being obliged to give something in exchange for the use of what belongs to another. The possessors of land, whoever they may be, conduct themselves, with regard to their possessions, exactly in the same way as the possessors of labour and of capital, and let out or exchange what they have for as much money as the demanders are willing to give them for it.

The three conditions, therefore, above specified, must necessarily be fulfilled in every society, in order to obtain the continued supply of by far the greater part of the commodities which it wants; and the compensation which fulfils these conditions, or the ordinary price of any exchangeable commodity, may be considered as consisting of three parts; that which pays the wages of the labourers employed in its production; that which pays the profits of the capital, including the advances to the labourers, by which such production has been facilitated; and that which pays the rent of land,* or the compensation for the use of those powers attached to the soil which are in the possession of the landlord; the price of each of these component parts being determined exactly by the same causes as those which determine the price of the whole.

The price which fulfills these conditions is precisely what Adam Smith calls the natural price; and when a commodity is sold at this price, he says it is sold for precisely what it is worth. But here I think he has used the term worth in an unusual and improper sense. Commodities are continually said to be worth more than they have cost, ordinary profits included; and according to the customary and proper use of the term worth, we could never say that a given quantity

* Though it is quite true, as will appear in the next chapter, that rent has little effect in determining the prices of raw produce, yet, in almost all commodities, a part of the price is resolvable into rent. The reason is, that the same kinds of products which sell for exactly the same prices, have a very different quantity and value of rent in them; but the greater is the value of the rent, the less is the value of the labour and profits; and therefore the varying value of rent in commodities has but little effect on their prices.

of claret, of corn, or of any other article, was not worth more when it was scarce, although the cost of its production, on the supposition of ordinary profits, had remained the same. The worth of a commodity, in the place where it is estimated, is its market price, not its natural price. It is its intrinsic value in exchange, determined by the state of the supply compared with the demand at the time, and not its ordinary cost. It need hardly be observed, that the payment of taxes of any kind, where required, is an incidental condition of the supply of commodities which contributes to increase their cost of production and limit their quantity.

But if it appear generally that the ordinary cost of production only determines the usual prices of commodities, as the payment of this cost is the necessary condition of their supply; and that the component parts of this cost are themselves determined by the same causes which determine the whole, it is obvious that we cannot get rid of the principle of demand and supply, by referring to the cost of production.* Natural and necessary prices appear to be regulated by this principle, as well as market prices; and the only difference is, that the former are regulated by the ordinary and average relation of the supply to the demand; and the latter, when they differ from the former, are determined by the extraordinary and accidental relations of the supply to the demand.

It has sometimes been said that there is no such thing as natural price; but explained as Adam Smith has explained it, it is not only a very intelligible, but a very useful term. If the natural price of a commodity be considered as made up of all the money wages which have been paid in the various parts of

* One of the two main elements of the cost of production, namely, the rate of profits, is peculiarly variable and pre-eminently dependent on supply and demand. Under the greatest variations in the rates of wages, we may suppose many commodities still to require in their production the same *quantities* of labour of the same kind; but under great variations in the rate of profits, we cannot suppose that any commodities should still require for their production the same amount of profits.

the process of its production for the specific kinds of labour required, of all the ordinary money profits of the other capitals employed during the periods of various lengths for which they have been advanced, and of all the money rent concerned in the necessary materials and food obtained by the assistance of those powers of nature which are attached to the soil, then supposing things to be in their ordinary and average state and untaxed, it is quite certain that this price, and the ordinary and average prices of commodities, will be found to agree. To this price, which may fairly and usefully be called the natural, necessary, or ordinary price, the market prices are always tending. And this price determines the rate at which commodities usually exchange for each other. So understood, nothing can be more simple, or more generally applicable. The natural price of an acre of copse wood, or of a hundred sheep from the highlands of Scotland, which in a country generally well cultivated must be composed chiefly of rent, is as easily explicable as the natural price of corn on the last land taken into cultivation, where rent is quite inconsiderable. And the natural price of those sorts of goods where a large proportion of fixed capital is employed, and the returns of the circulating capital are unusually slow, and where consequently the price must consist chiefly of profits, may be as satisfactorily accounted for as the price of a straw bonnet, or piece of Brussels lace. Where the materials are of scarcely any value, the capital required is quite inconsiderable, and the expense of production must consist almost entirely of labour.

It is obvious that when, from any cause whatever, the money cost of producing a commodity increases, without some increased facility of obtaining money, the estimation in which such a commodity is ordinarily held, or its exchangeable value arising from intrinsic causes, proportionally increases.

In explaining the effects of demand and supply on the values of commodities, whether arising from temporary causes, or from the ordinary costs of production, I have thought that the subject would be best illustrated by referring first to those periods in which the value of money is practically considered as constant; and it is allowed that during such periods, it is the uniform practice of society to represent demand by money. But it is evident that we cannot extend these periods to any considerable length. We well know, that although the precious metals, from their durability, and the consequent steadiness of their supply, are subject to slow changes of value; yet that at distant periods, and in different countries, their value has been, and is, essentially different.

It is absolutely necessary, therefore, to consider how a demand may be represented and measured under any changes which may take place in the value of money.

An effectual demand for a commodity, is such a demand as will fulfill the natural and necessary conditions of the supply; or, as it has been defined, it is the sacrifice which the demanders must make in order to effectuate the continued supply of the commodity in the quantity required under the actual circumstances.

Now it is obvious, that if money varies essentially, as compared with the natural and necessary conditions of the supply of commodities, a given amount of money cannot possibly represent a given demand, or a given sacrifice.

In every country there are a few commodities obtained by labour alone; and, if the advance of a certain quantity of labour be the necessary condition of the supply of a particular commodity, then the money which will command such labour will represent the effectual demand for the commodity; that is, a demander able and willing to make such a sacrifice as will effectuate the supply. But if, subsequently, money falls in value in relation to the required labour, the same quantity of money obviously ceases to represent the same demand. No one, I apprehend, would venture to affirm that an ounce of pure silver, applied as a demand, would at the present time effectuate the supply of the same quantity of a commodity produced by labour alone, as an equal weight of silver would have effectuated under similar circumstances in the reign of Edward III.; since which period the value of silver, as compared with labour, has fallen five or six times.

Under any changes, however, which may take place in money, if the conditions of the supply of any commodity, or the elementary costs of its production, require a certain quantity of labour of a given description, the power of setting to work that quantity of labour, whether paid for by a larger or smaller quantity of produce or money, will be an effectual demand for it. Now it is obvious that this cannot be said of any *product* of labour whatever.

In the first place, there is no product of labour which is the *sole* condition of the supply of any one commodity. Consequently, while the necessary conditions of the supply of any commodity are a given quantity of labour of a certain description, no given quantity of any *product* of labour can continue, like a given quantity of labour itself, always to represent the same effectual demand for such commodity.

Secondly, there is no product of labour, which, applied directly, enters, as labour itself does, into the composition of all commodities that have value, and constitutes the *chief* element in the conditions of their supply. Consequently there is no *product* of labour which can represent the most important condition of the supply of all commodities, namely the quantity of labour absolutely necessary to their production; and we cannot say that a definite quantity of money, a definite quantity of corn, a definite quantity of cloth, or a definite quantity of any product of labour, subject, as they all are, to variations in their relation to labour, can continue to afford an effectual demand for that definite quantity of labour, without which the mass of commodities cannot by possibility be produced.

But if, when commodities are selling at their natural prices, the quantity of labour directly applied to the production of a particular article were to absorb exactly one half, three fourths, or any definite proportion of the whole value, as the demand for this proportion, whatever it might be, the *half* we will suppose, might be represented and measured by an amount of labour equal in quantity and quality to that which had been actually employed upon the commodity, it is obvious that an equivalent to *double* the quantity of such labour would be an effectual demand for the whole article produced, involving profits, rent, taxes, or any other accession to the difficulty of bringing the commodity to market, besides that which is occasioned by the necessary quantity of labour to be advanced.

Having this πȣ στω, this foundation to go upon, in all commodities, namely, the quantity of immediate labour actually worked up in them, the above conclusion seems to follow necessarily; that is, if a certain quantity of labour will represent and measure the demand for an aliquot part of the value of a commodity, the proper multiple of that quantity of labour must represent and measure the demand for the whole; and as there is no object but labour which can represent and measure the demand for that aliquot of the value of a commodity which consists of immediate labour, it follows necessarily that there is no object but labour which can represent and measure the demand for the whole of a commodity, the value of which is made up of various ingredients besides labour.

When, therefore, owing to changes in the value of money, relatively to labour, we can no longer represent a given demand by a given quantity of money, it appears that we may with accuracy represent such demand by a given quantity of labour.

It follows, therefore, that the power of commanding a given quantity of labour of a given character, together with the will to advance it, represents a given demand. It should be particularly observed, however, that this power is never possessed by the labourers themselves, but by those employers of labour who are both able and willing to pay the quantity of money or of commodities, whether great or small, which is necessary in the actual circumstances of the society to command the required quantity of labour.

Section IV.—*Of the Labour which has been employed on a Commodity considered as a Measure of its Exchangeable Value.*

In the two last sections, the causes which affect and determine the exchangeable values of commodities have been investigated; and these appear to consist of every circumstance which contributes in any degree to enhance the difficulty of obtaining them: such as, the necessity of paying the wages of a certain quantity of labour, without which the commodity cannot be produced, the necessity of certain advances of other capital, which no one will continue to make without the ordinary remuneration in the shape of profits, and the frequent necessity of further payments owing to rents, tithes, taxes, natural and artificial monopolies, and temporary deficiencies of supply, arising from accident, or the state of the seasons. These are all sources of difficulty, which, in proportion to the degree in which they prevail, must raise the exchangeable value of commodities arising from intrinsic causes; and it has further appeared, that the result of all these causes of value is expressed in the state of the supply compared with the intensity of the demand.

We come now to inquire more particularly into the *measures* of value—an inquiry obviously not identical with an inquiry into the *causes* of value, as it is only in a very few cases that they can properly be represented by the same object.*

* The labour worked up in a commodity is the principal *cause* of its value, but it will appear in this chapter that it is not a measure of it. The labour which a commodity will command is *not* the *cause* of its value, but it will appear in the next chapter to be the measure of it.

A measure of value is wanted for two most important purposes.

First, to measure easily and conveniently the relative values of all commodities, compared one with another, and to enable all dealers to estimate the profits which they make upon their sales. This purpose is completely answered by money.

Secondly, to measure the difficulty with which a commodity is obtained, including all the conditions of its supply; and when two or more commodities have in the course of time altered in their exchangeable relations to each other, to enable us to ascertain in which, and to what extent in each, the change has taken place.* This is most important information, particularly in reference to commodities of the same country, at different times; but it is evident, that as money, in periods of some length, is liable to alter greatly in its exchangeable value, arising from intrinsic causes, it is impossible that, applied as a measure, it can give the information required.

It remains, therefore, to be considered whether any other object can perform the functions of a general measure of value, and answer the purposes above described.

Adam Smith, in his chapter† on the real and nominal price of commodities, in which he considers labour as a universal and accurate measure of value, has introduced some confusion into his inquiry, by not adhering strictly to the same mode of applying the labour which he proposes for a measure.

Sometimes he speaks of the value of a commodity as being measured by the quantity of labour which its production has cost, and sometimes by the quantity of labour which it will command in exchange.

It is in the latter sense, however, in which he ap-

* Nothing appears to me more essential, in an "Inquiry into the nature and causes of the Wealth of Nations," than to have the means of distinguishing between the rise of one commodity and the fall of another.

† Book I. ch. v.

plies it much the most frequently, and on which he evidently lays the chief stress. "The value of any commodity," he says, "to the person who possesses it, and who means not to use or consume it himself, but to exchange it for other commodities, *is equal to the quantity of labour which it enables him to purchase or command. Labour, therefore, is the real measure of the exchangeable value of all commodities.*"* Other expressions in the same chapter apply labour as a measure of value in the same way;† and on another occasion, in his digression on the value of silver during the four last centuries, he takes an opportunity to say, "*Labour*, be it remembered, and not any commodity, or mass of commodities, is the *sole measure* of the value of silver, and of all other commodities."‡

These passages may be said to determine the prevailing sense in which he considers labour as a general measure of exchangeable value. It would not then be worth while to inquire how far labour may be considered as a measure of value, when applied in the way which Adam Smith has practically rejected in reference to the more advanced stages of society, if this mode of applying it had not been adopted by some distinguished modern writers as the foundation of a new theory of value. But as this is the case, the inquiry seems to be called for; and it should be particularly noticed, that the question embraces not merely the propriety of a definition, but the truth of a proposition. It is not merely what should be the definition and the measure of value in exchange, but a question of fact, whether the labour worked up in commodities either determines or measures the rate at which they exchange with each other; and in no stage of society with which we are acquainted does it do this. At a very early period profits will be found to enter largely into the question of exchangeable value as a necessary condition of the supply. To make

* Book I. ch. v. p. 44, 6th edit. † P. 54.
‡ Book I. ch. xi. p. 303.

even a bow and arrow, it is obviously necessary that the wood and reed should be properly dried and seasoned, and *the time* which these materials require to be kept by the workman before his work is completed, introduces at once a new element into the computation of value. The varying quickness of the returns is likewise an entirely new element, which has nothing to do with the quantity of labour employed upon the capital; and yet in every period of society, the earliest as well as the latest, it is of the utmost importance in the determination of exchangeable value.

The fixed capital necessary to hollow out a canoe may consist of little more than a few stone hatchets and shell chisels, and the labour necessary to make them might not add much to the labour subsequently employed in the work to which they were applied; but it is likewise necessary that the workman should previously cut down the timber, and employ a great quantity of labour in various parts of the process long before there is a possibility of receiving the returns for his exertions, either in the use of the canoe, or in the commodities which he might obtain in exchange for it; and during this time, he must of course advance to himself the whole of his subsistence. But the providence, foresight, and postponement of present gratification for the sake of future benefit and profit, which are necessary for this purpose, have always been considered as rare qualities in the savage; and it can scarcely admit of a doubt that the articles which were of a nature to require this long preparation would be comparatively very scarce, and would have a great exchangeable value in proportion to the quantity of labour which had been actually employed upon them, and on the capital necessary to their production. On this account it is not improbable that a canoe might in such a state of society possess double the exchangeable value of a number of deer, to produce which successively in the market might have cost precisely the same number of days' labour, including the necessary fixed capital, consisting of the bows and arrows,

&c. used for killing them; and the great difference of value in this case would arise from the circumstance, that the returns for the labour of killing each successive deer always came in within a few days after it had been advanced, while the returns for the labour expended upon the canoe were delayed probably beyond the year. Whatever might be the rate of profits, the comparative slowness of these returns must tell proportionally on the price of the article; and, as there is reason to think that among savages, the advances necessary for a work of slow returns would be comparatively seldom made, the profits of capital would be extremely high, and the difference of exchangeable value in different commodities, which had cost in their production and in the production of the necessary capital the same quantity of labour, would be very great.

Mr. Ricardo, speaking of the different implements which might be necessary, in an early stage of society, to kill the beaver and the deer, says,* that those who furnished these capitals might, under different circumstances, "have a half, a fourth, or an eighth of the produce obtained, the remainder being paid as wages to those who furnished the labour; yet this division could not affect the relative value of these commodities, since, whether the profits of capital were greater or less, whether they were 50, 20, or 10 per cent. or whether the wages of labour were high or low, they would operate equally on both employments." But it is quite obvious from what has been said, that if for the employment of killing a deer, we substitute the employment of making a canoe, which would not be completed in less than a year, or perhaps two, and suppose what is here supposed with great probability, that profits might be 50 per cent., the difference between the value of such a product, and the value of a deer, which, on account of its being sold almost the next day, could hardly be affected by profits, would, in reference to the same quantity of labour employed

* P. 17, 3rd edit.

upon each, be as much as 50 per cent. Consequently, in the early stages of society, the relative values of commodities is not determined or measured by the relative quantities of labour employed upon them.

In countries advanced in civilization, it is obvious that the same cause of variation in the exchangeable value of commodities, independent of the labour which has been employed upon them, must prevail as in the early periods of society; and, as might be expected, some others. The profits of capital, indeed, are not so high, and consequently the slowness or quickness of the returns will not, as far as the rate of profits is concerned, produce the same proportionate difference of prices; but to make up for this, the difference in the quantity of fixed capital employed is prodigious, and scarcely the same in any two commodities, and the difference in the returns of capital varies from two or three days, to two or three years, and in some cases many more.

The proposition of Mr. Ricardo, which states that a rise in the price of labour lowers the price of a large class of commodities, has undoubtedly a very paradoxical air; but it is, nevertheless, true, and the appearance of paradox would vanish, if it were stated more naturally and correctly.

Mr. Ricardo has allowed, that the effect he contemplated and attributed to a rise in the wages of labour is produced by a fall of profits, which he considers as the same thing;* and undoubtedly no one could have thought the proposition paradoxical, or even in the slightest degree improbable, if he had stated that a fall of profits would occasion a fall of price in those commodities, where, from the quantity of fixed capital employed, the profits of that capital had before formed the principal ingredient in the cost of production. But this is what he has in substance said. In a par-

* "Every rise of wages, therefore, or, which is the same thing, every fall of profits, would lower the relative value of those commodities which were produced with a capital of a durable nature." P. 37, 3rd edit.

ticular case which he has taken to illustrate his proposition, he supposes the application of a very durable machine worth £20,000, which requires very little labour either to work it, or keep it in constant repair; and, consequently, the price of the yearly produce of this machine would be composed almost entirely of the ordinary profits of the £20,000 which it had cost.* Now it is quite certain, that if, from any cause whatever, the ordinary profits of stock should fall, the price of the commodity so produced would fall nearly in proportion. A fall of profits from 20 to 10 per cent. would reduce its price nearly one half.† This is sufficiently obvious. But the effects arising from an opposite supposition were not at first considered, and the general result was overlooked.

The state of the case, in a general view of it, seems to be this. There is a very large class of commodities, in the production of which a great quantity of fixed capital is used, and a long time elapses before the returns of the capital, whether fixed or circulating, come in. In such commodities, the proportion which the capital bears to the quantity of labour which it yearly employs, is in various degrees very considerable: and, in all these cases, it is natural to suppose that the fall of price, arising from the fall of profits, should in various degrees more than counterbalance the rise of price, which would naturally be occasioned by a rise in the price of labour. Consequently, on the supposition of a rise in the price of labour, and a fall in the rate of profits, all these commodities will, in various degrees, naturally fall in price.

On the other hand, there is a large class of commodities, where, from the absence of fixed capital, and the rapidity of the returns of the circulating capital,

* P. 37, 3rd edit.

† In a case of this kind brought forward in the first edition, Mr. Ricardo distinctly allows that a change in the relative values of two commodities might take place to the extent of 68 per cent. from the fall of profits, without any change having taken place in the relative quantities of labour employed on each.

the proportion which the capital bears to the quantity of labour it employs is very small. A capital of a hundred pounds, which was returned every week, could employ as much labour annually as £2,600, the returns of which came in only at the end of the year; and if the capital were returned nearly every day, as it is practically in some few cases, the advance of little more than the wages of a man for a single day might pay above three hundred days' labour in the course of a year. Now it is quite evident, that out of the profits of these trifling capitals, it would not only be absolutely impossible to take a rise in the price of labour of 7 per cent., but it would be impossible to take a rise of ½ per cent. On the first supposition, a rise of only ½ per cent. would, if the price of the produce continued the same, absorb more than all the profits of the £100; and, in the other case, much more than all the capital advanced. If, therefore, the prices of commodities, where the proportion of labour is very great compared with the capital which employs it, do not rise upon an advance in the price of labour, the production of such commodities must at once be given up. But they certainly would not be given up. Consequently, upon a rise in the money price of labour and fall of profits, there will be a large class of commodities which will rise in price.

There will undoubtedly, however, be a class of commodities which, from the effects of these two opposite causes, will remain stationary in price; but, from the very nature of the case, this class must theoretically form little more than a line. Wherever this line may be placed, it can embrace but a small class of objects; and upon a rise in the price of labour and fall of profits, all the rest will either fall or rise in price, although exactly the same quantity of labour continues to be employed upon them.*

* In this discussion, I have assumed money to be obtained in the way suggested by Mr. Ricardo; in which case the results will be as I have described, and as he has allowed in his third edition (p. 45); but his money, as we shall see, is not so constituted as

What then becomes of the doctrine that the exchangeable value of commodities is proportioned to the labour which has been employed upon them? Instead of their remaining of the same value while the same quantity of labour is employed upon them, it appears that from well-known causes of constant and universal operation, the prices of all commodities, with very few exceptions, vary with the variations in the rate and quantity of profits.

There are other causes practically in operation which prevent the exchangeable value of commodities from being proportioned to the quantity of labour which has been employed upon them. But as those which have been already more particularly adverted to, are so very powerful, and so completely decisive of the question, it is not necessary to refer specifically to others. It is scarcely possible, indeed, to take up two commodities of different kinds, which will be found to exchange with each other in proportion to the quantity of labour worked up in each. Nothing, indeed, could make such a rate of exchange, in reference to commodities generally, approach towards the truth, but the assumption that profits are the wages of accumulated labour, and that, therefore, profits may be called labour. But profits are altogether different from wages, and are regulated by quite different principles, as most justly stated by Adam Smith.* Such an assumption is so completely unphilosophical, so calculated to defeat all the useful purposes of a just nomenclature, and to create confusion in the ordinary language of political economy, that it cannot for a moment be admitted.† We might just as correctly call rent labour.

to be a proper measure of value. In reality, *all* commodities obtained by the same quantity of labour fall with a fall of profits.

* Book I. ch. 6.

† We may measure the value which the element of profits gives to a commodity by labour, as I have said in another place; but how we can say that more labour has been employed upon a commodity, merely because it must be kept longer before it is brought to market, is what I cannot understand.

It may be safely affirmed, then, that however curious and desirable it may be to know the exact quantity of labour, accumulated and immediate, which has been employed in the production of commodities, it is certainly not this labour alone which either determines or measures their relative values in exchange at the same place, and at the same time.

But if, at the same place and at the same time, the relative values of commodities are not measured by the labour which they have cost in production, including the labour employed on the capitals concerned, it is quite clear that such labour cannot measure their relative values at different places and at different times.

In regard to intrinsic value in exchange, it is still more clear that the value of the labour actually employed in the production of a commodity, never represents or is proportioned to the value of the completed commodity, except in the rare case when labour alone is employed, and the produce is brought to market immediately. In the vast majority of cases, there are other intrinsic causes of value, acting sometimes with great power, which increase the difficulty of obtaining the object desired, in addition to the labour actually employed. The slightest attention to what is passing around us, at any one period, and in any one place, must convince us of this truth; and, at different periods, and in different places, the labour actually employed upon a commodity, considered as a measure of its value, must partake of all the inaccuracies which necessarily belong to it at the same time and place.

It appears, then, that the quantity of labour actually employed in the production of commodities, answers neither of the two great objects of a measure of value. It neither measures the rate at which commodities exchange with each other at the same place and time, like money, nor does it measure the whole of the difficulty to be overcome, or the sacrifice to be made, in obtaining commodities at the same or different times, and in different countries, and enable us to say when two or more commodities have varied in relation to each other, in which, and to what extent in each, the variations have taken place.*

SECTION V.—*Of the Labour which a Commodity will command, considered as a Measure of Value in Exchange.*

WHEN we consider labour as a measure of value in the sense in which it is most frequently applied by Adam Smith, that is, when the value of an object is estimated by the quantity of labour of a given description which it can command, it will appear to be a measure essentially distinct from all others, and to approach as near to a standard measure, both of re-

* Mr. Ricardo, at the conclusion of the sixth section of his first chapter, has the following passage: "It is necessary for me to remark that I have not said, because one commodity has so much labour employed upon it as will cost £1000, and another so much as will cost £2000, that therefore one would be of the value of £1000, and the other of £2000; but I have said that their value will be to each other as 2 to 1, and that in these proportions they will be exchanged. It is of no importance to the truth of this doctrine, whether one of these commodities sells for £1100, and the other for £2200, or one for £1500, and the other for £3000; into that question I do not at present inquire: I affirm only that their relative values will be governed by the relative quantities of labour bestowed on their production." It is on this view of *relative* value, that all Mr. Ricardo's calculations in the rest of his book depend, without any modifications, although in two previous sections he had acknowledged that considerable modifications were necessary. My object in the present section has been to show that the *relative* values of commodities are not only not governed, but are very far from being governed, by the relative quantities of labour bestowed on their production, as stated in the passage quoted: and, in the passage itself, it is positively denied, that because a commodity has so much labour bestowed upon it as will cost £1000, that *therefore* it is of the value of £1000. Mr. Ricardo did not fall into the unaccountable error of *calling* labour profits, and of confounding the accumulated labour actually worked up in fixed capitals and materials with the *profits* upon such capitals and materials, things totally distinct.

lative and of intrinsic value in exchange, as the nature of the subject will admit.

It is universally allowed that in the same place, and within moderately short periods of time, the precious metals are an unexceptionable measure of the relative values of commodities; but whatever is true of the precious metals with respect to the relative and nominal values of commodities is true of labour applied in the way proposed.

It is obvious, for instance, that in the same place, and at the same time, the different quantities of day labour which different commodities can command, will be exactly in proportion to their relative values in exchange; and if any two of them will purchase the same quantity of labour of the same description, they will invariably exchange with each other.

The merchant might safely regulate his dealings, and estimate his commercial profits by the excess of the quantity of labour which his imports would command, compared with his exports. Whether the value of the commodity had arisen principally from the limitation of its supply, occasioned by a strict or partial monopoly; whether it had arisen principally from the scarcity of the raw material, the peculiar sort of labour required in its construction, or from unusually high profits; whether its value had been increased by an increased cost of production, or diminished by the application of improved machinery; whether its value at the moment depended chiefly upon permanent or temporary causes—in all cases and under all circumstances, the quantity of labour which it will command, or what comes to the same thing, the quantity of labour's worth which people will give to obtain it, will be a very exact measure of its relative value in exchange. In short, this measure will, in the same place and at the same time, exactly accord with the money prices of commodities.

It will probably be objected, that in the same place, and at the same time, every commodity may be considered as an accurate measure of the relative values of others, and that what has just been said of labour may be said of cloth, cotton, iron, hops, or any other article. Any two commodities, which at the same time and in the same place will purchase or command the same quantity of cloth, cotton, iron, or hops of a given quality, will have the same value, or will exchange even with each other. This is no doubt true, if we take the same time precisely, and if we wish merely to know the relation of one commodity to some other or others in exchange; but the comparison utterly fails if we take different periods, and more especially if we refer to the main characteristic of the value of a commodity, namely, the difficulty of obtaining it, or the limitation of its supply compared with the demand.

One of the most important reasons why practically money makes a much better measure of value than any other *commodity* is, that its relation to common labour not only changes more slowly than cloth, cotton, iron, hops, &c. but that having been adopted as the almost universal medium of exchange, its relation to labour in any particular place must always be known to the inhabitants of that place; and while such relation is known and remains constant, the money prices of commodities will not only express their relations to each other, but also the difficulty of obtaining them, the conditions of their continued supply, if they are in an ordinary state, and the supply compared with the demand in whatever state they may be, which will include of course their power of purchasing arising from all the intrinsic causes of value which may have operated upon them.

Consequently money, under these circumstances, that is, while its relation to labour is known and remains constant, is a measure both of relative and intrinsic value in exchange.

But if the only cause which prevents money from being such a measure is, that its relation to labour is not constant, it would appear, that as the labour which a commodity will command is necessarily a measure of relative value like money, the substitution of labour so applied instead of money will give the measure we want.

It remains, therefore, to be considered more particularly how far the labour which a commodity will command appears to be an adequate measure of value in exchange at different periods and in different countries, according to the most usual and correct sense in which the term is practically applied; and it will be recollected that I have endeavoured to show, and I trust with success, that this sense is not the general power of purchasing possessed by a particular commodity, but its power of purchasing arising from intrinsic causes, which includes all the causes, of whatever kind they may be, which have contributed to the limitation of its supply compared with the demand.

Keeping in mind, therefore, the meaning attached to the term *value of a commodity* at a particular time and place, let us compare the values of two commodities, one of which was produced in the time of Edward III. and the other in the time of William IV.

And first let us suppose, for the sake of clearness, that the common agricultural labour of each period, which may be taken as the standard, is exactly of the same degree of strength, and is employed for the same number of hours, and further, that there are some commodities which, both at these periods and during the whole of the interval between them, are produced by this kind of labour alone, and brought to market immediately.

Perhaps these suppositions have not been very far from the truth in this country since the time of Edward III. I should suppose that the physical strength of the men of that period was nearly the same as at present, and that an ordinary day's work of agricultural labour was nearly of the same length; and it is generally allowed that at all times there are a few commodities produced by labour alone.

It is obvious that commodities so produced would, at any particular period, exchange with one another, on an average according to the quantity of labour employed to obtain them; and in comparing the values of commodities so produced at one period with the commodities so produced at the other period, it seems scarcely possible not to allow that those commodities which had been produced at each period with exactly the same quantity of labour of the same description, and brought to market immediately, would be supplied ordinarily in the same proportion to the demand at each period, and be considered as of the same value.

Now in regard to commodities produced by labour alone, and brought to market immediately, it is evident that the labour employed upon them must on an average be precisely the same as the labour which they will command. But it is allowed that the relations of all commodities to one another, however variously composed, are at the same time and place, exactly in proportion to the quantity of labour which they will severally command. Consequently if the values of the commodities produced by labour alone in the time of Edward III. be to the values of commodities produced by labour alone in the time of William IV. as the quantities of labour which at each period they will command, it follows necessarily, that the values of all and each of the commodities in the time of Edward III. however variously composed, must be to the values of all and each of the commodities in the time of William IV. however composed, in the proportion of the quantity of labour which all and each will severally command.

The value, therefore, of any commodity at either period, whether arising from the intrinsic cause of labour alone, or from labour combined in various proportions with profits, rent, and taxes, or affected by temporary scarcity or abundance, will be measured by the quantity of the labour of each period which it will command.

And that the correctness of so measuring the values of commodities, will not be in any degree disturbed by the varying quantity of produce, or the varying wages which the labourer may receive, will be obvious from the following considerations.

Let us suppose, what is probably not far from the truth, that a man who employs himself in shrimping, earns about the same remuneration as the common agricultural labourer, and let us further suppose, that the shrimper in the time of Edward III. could on an average bring home 800 shrimps a day. Now if at a subsequent period of some extent, shrimps were to frequent the shores in greater abundance, so that 1600 might ordinarily be obtained by a day's labour, and the supply of shrimps were doubled, it is quite certain that we should say, and correctly say, that shrimps had proportionably fallen in value, not that labour had proportionably risen. In the same manner, if from a diminished afflux of shrimps to our shores, only 400 could be obtained by a day's labour, it is equally certain that we should say, and correctly say, that shrimps had risen in value, not that labour had fallen.

The value of the shrimps would be determined by the supply compared with the demand. The demand, in this case, for the produce of a day's shrimping would be accurately represented by the power of commanding a day's labour, whether the means of supporting the labourer were abundant or scanty; and the demand being given, the value of a given number of shrimps would be inversely as the supply.

If it would take the same man the same quantity of labour to obtain 100 prawns, as it would to obtain 400 shrimps, and yet he found it advantageous to continue getting prawns, it would be a great absurdity to say that labour was altered in value on account of the difference in the returns; and it would be little less absurd in the case previously supposed, if when the labour advanced was exactly of the same character, and employed for the same time, to say that the difference in the produce obtained, arising from the plenty or scarcity of the article compared with the given demand of a day's labour, would make any kind of difference in the value of the labour advanced.

If the changes were in the quantity of labour employed, not in the quantity of fish obtained, the effects would not be different. Though the whole demand might be increased in the case of an increased population, or diminished in the case of a diminished population, yet the power of commanding a day's labour would still represent a given and unchanged demand in regard to intensity; and if on account of a greater number of competitors in the one case, and a smaller number in the other, each man could obtain in a day a smaller or greater number of fish, the fish would become scanty or abundant as compared with a given demand; and their value would still vary inversely as their supply, and be measured in both cases by the quantity of labour which a certain quantity of them would command.

It appears then that the varying quantity of produce obtained by the same quantity of labour of a given character, where labour alone is concerned, while it implies great alterations in the value of a given portion of the produce, does not alter the value of a given quantity of labour.

And it is equally true that the varying wages, whether in corn or money, paid to the labourer at different periods for labour of the same character, when this labour enters into the composition of commodities combined with profits, rent, taxes, or any other intrinsic causes of value, does not alter the value of the labour itself, or disqualify it from being used as a measure.

In our own country there was a period subsequent to the reign of Edward III. namely from 1444, to the end of the reign of Henry VII. when, as far as the documents on the subject can be trusted, the labourer earned nearly two pecks of wheat a day, while he earned less than a peck in the time of Edward III. and much less than a peck towards the end of the reign of Elizabeth. Now it is quite certain that the labourer could not for so long a time have had his corn wages nearly doubled, if from some cause or other, or probably from a union of different causes, the supply of corn had not become more abundant in relation to the consumers; and whether this was occasioned by the destruction of the population during the civil wars, or by the increased growth of corn on the breaking up of the feudal system, or by a union of both, the effect would be just the same on the supply as compared with the demand. Man, with his wants and powers, it must be always recollected, is the primary source of all demand; and in this respect the increase or decrease of population is distinct from the increase or decrease of any commodity. If the quantity of cotton goods were to be greatly diminished, this would probably create a greater, rather than a less demand for woollen goods, whereas if population be diminished, all the articles before consumed by it will for a time become comparatively redundant, and some perhaps may long continue to be produced with greater facility.

The labourer, therefore, during the period alluded to, was able to command a greater quantity of corn, which was unquestionably an increase of wealth to him; but he obtained this increase of wealth because corn had fallen in value, not because labour had risen in value.

Any object which continues of the same value must necessarily purchase more of an object which has fallen in value.

The same reasoning applies to the labourer's varying money wages. In the time of Edward III. the wages of common labour were about three half-pence a day, which allowing for the difference in the quantity of metal contained in the same nominal sum would be equal to about four-pence of our money. Consequently, supposing, the present money wages of common labour to be twenty-pence or two shillings, the money price of labour since the time of Edward III. will appear to have risen five or six times. But no person, I conceive, imagines that the *value* of labour has so risen. We all know very well that the value of money has fallen, and if the labour has remained unchanged in its character, the conditions of the supply of a given quantity of silver, the elementary costs of its production, the average state of its supply as compared with the demand, or its power of purchasing at these different periods arising from intrinsic causes, will be exactly represented by the quantity of labour which the given quantity of silver will command at each period.

If we now consider the values of commodities in different countries at the same period, and suppose the character of the agricultural labour to be of the same kind, the same conclusion will necessarily follow. Yet here an actual exchange is practicable; and it is quite certain that the products of the same quantities of labour of the same character, will, under different circumstances exchange for very different quantities of money, while we well know that money prices regulate the rate at which all actual exchanges are made.

But in cases of this kind, and they are constantly occuring, it is obvious, that the difference in the money price of the products of the same quantity of labour in different countries, arises from the difference in the value of money, and not from the difference in the value of the labour. Metallic money in all countries which have no mines of the precious metals, is only to be obtained by exportable commodities; and the soil, situation, and habits of some countries may occasion a comparatively scanty production of exports, although their labourers work with as much energy, and sometimes in regard to domestic commodities with as much skill, as the great mass of the labourers of those countries, where exportable commodities abound.

If two nations quite unconnected were to employ the same quantity of labour of the same character in working two silver mines, one of which had double the fertility of the other, there can be no doubt that the supply of silver compared with the demand, or its value in exchange arising from intrinsic causes, would be very much lower in the one country than in the other; and we should not hesitate in saying, that the difference in prices so occasioned, was owing to the difference in the value of money, not in the value of the labour.

Nor ought the conclusion, in my opinion, to be different, if the application of excellent machinery in the one case, and very indifferent machinery in the other mines of the same natural fertility, were to produce the same difference in the state of the supply of silver compared with the demand, and the same purchasing power arising from intrinsic causes as in the former case. In the country of machinery, not only the labour of the miner, but all labour would be high in money price; and in comparing the two countries together, the natural and useful language would be, that while the value of the labour was the same in both countries, the value of silver was most essentially different. The same sacrifice of physical force, supposing the profits and other circumstances in both countries to have been the same, had probably produced in one country double the quantity of silver which it had produced in the other.

From all the accounts we have of the Chinese settlers in different parts of the East, it appears that the labouring classes in China, are remarkable for their industry and energy, and even for their skill in making those domestic articles where superior machinery is not required. We cannot therefore justly say that Chinese labour, independent of machinery, or other particular advantages, is not as effective as our own. Yet we well know that the money price of labour is extremely low in China, and this is obviously owing to the small amount of exports compared with the population, and the prodigious extent of territory, including a large part of Tartary, over which the precious metals which are imported into China will be necessarily spread, so as to throw the greatest imaginable obstacles in the way of a fall in their value; the consequence of which naturally is, that they have fallen comparatively but little in value since the discovery of the American mines; and the elementary cost of producing a pound of silver, the quantity of Chinese labour, profits, rent, &c. which must be worked up in the commodities exported to purchase it, are very much greater than in Europe. Under these circumstances it would surely be most preposterous to measure the value of Chinese labour in China by money, instead of measuring the money by the labour.

Yet, still it is perfectly true, that a Chinese commodity carried to Hamburgh would be sold at its China money price, with the addition of the freight, insurance, profits, &c. of the last voyage; and an English merchant purchasing Hamburgh and Chinese goods, would unquestionably estimate their relative values by their cost in money, without the least reference to the very different quantities of labour which had been employed in obtaining them; or if he chanced to hear something about the greater quantity of Chinese labour employed on the articles from China, for which he had paid the same price as for the Hamburgh goods, he would be inclined, and not very unnaturally, to estimate the value of Chinese labour very low. It is most justly observed by Adam Smith, that the merchant, in all his transactions, has only to consider money prices.

To a merchant, therefore, living in London and purchasing goods at Hamburgh, Chinese labour, if estimated at all, would necessarily be estimated at a low value. But he would fall into a gross error if he were to infer that it was therefore low in China. When the value of money, or of any other article *in China* is spoken of, it would imply a gross perversion of language to suppose that the person speaking meant the value of Chinese money, Chinese goods, or Chinese labour in Hamburgh or London. The expression *in China*, cannot mean in Hamburgh, or in London. What alone can be correctly meant by the value of money, or of any other commodity *in China* is, the estimation in which such money is held in China, determined at all times by the state of the supply compared with the demand, and ordinarily by the elementary costs of its production in China, or what comes to the same thing, the value of money in China, is its power of purchasing in China, arising from intrinsic causes. And as it is obvious, that the quantity of Chinese labour which a pound of silver will command, must measure its power of purchasing in China, arising from intrinsic causes; it follows, that the value of money or of any other commodity in China, is measured by the quantity of Chinese labour which a given portion of it will command.

It is thought by some persons, that the cheap food and small quantity of it which is supposed to be earned by the Chinese labourer, must imply a low value of labour; but if things are in their natural state, what it really implies, is, that this food, however low in value it may appear to us, is of high value in China. The great demanders of the commonest sort of food in all countries are the labouring classes; and if a labourer in ordinary employment, and working with ordinary energy and skill, can, on an average, only obtain a comparatively small quantity of such food, it is a proof that its permanent supply compared with the demand is very scanty, and on the common principle of supply and demand, it must be of high value there.

To come to an instance nearer home. There is reason to believe that the common labourer of the Netherlands is as strong, and works for as many hours in the day as the English labourer. In the great business of agriculture, in which so large a part of the population of every country is employed, he is supposed to be peculiarly skilful, and in many manufactures he has been generally considered as excelling the workmen of most of the countries of Europe. Yet his wages measured in money are decidedly lower than in England. Is this owing to the lower value of *labour* in the Netherlands, or the higher value of *money*? To the latter most assuredly; and the cause of it unquestionably is, that though the great mass of the labourers in the Netherlands may work with as much energy and skill as the great mass of English labourers; yet a certain proportion of the latter, assisted by superior machinery, more abundant capitals and cheaper fuel, are able to produce a large quantity of exportable manufactures at a lower money price than they can be produced in the Netherlands; which, together with some superiority in colonial products, enables England to maintain her exchanges, although she pays a higher money price for her labour, the difference in profits being inconsiderable.

It will be said, perhaps, that the higher money price of corn and labour in England is entirely owing to the corn laws, which prevent the money price of English corn from falling to the price of corn in the Netherlands. It is indeed nearly certain, that if the corn laws were repealed, English labour and the general scale of English prices would be lower. But it is still more certain, that no possible corn laws could prevent the prices of our corn and labour from falling to the level of the rest of Europe, if we possessed no natural or artificial advantages in regard to our exportable commodities. Supposing the price of English common labour to be twenty-pence or two shillings, and of continental labour fourteen or sixteen-pence, each bearing the same relation in each country to manufacturing labour, with no more difference of profits than at present prevails, it is quite obvious, that without some peculiar advantages to balance the price of our labour, we could not *possibly* maintain our exchanges, and could not, in fact, export a single yard of cloth or calico, till the exchanges had continued against us a sufficient time to raise the value of money and lower the money prices of labour and corn to the level of the principal countries with which we were connected in commerce.

An instance of somewhat a different kind will tend further to illustrate this subject.

It is generally considered that labour is very scarce, and of very high value in the United States of America, and that in consequence the agricultural labourer is paid much higher both in wheat and money than in England. In wheat it is supposed that he earns 18 or 20 quarters in the year, while the English labourer only earns 9 or 10. But is it properly the American labour which is of so much higher value than the English labour; or the American wheat which is of so much lower value in America, than the English wheat in England? It is in the nature of things quite impossible, as we have said before, that the labourers of any country can continue to be paid an amount of products of so high a value as the value of what they are themselves able to produce for their employers; because if they were so paid, their employers would always be losing by so employing them. Consequently the American labourers, paid as above stated, must be able to produce considerably more than 18 or 20 quarters; because, we know that profits are high in the United States; while it may fairly be presumed that on lands in England which yield the least rent, the English labourer produces a less excess above the 9 or 10 quarters than the American labourer above the 18 or 20 quarters. Can any thing show more clearly that the difference is in the lower value of the corn, and not in the higher value of the labour. And this difference is obviously occasioned by the great abundance of fertile land in America, and the consequent facility with which corn is obtained.

But the American labourer is also paid higher in bullion, in the currency of the commercial world; and how comes it that bullion should be obtained with more facility in the United States than in England, when it is well known that the English labourer works for as many hours in the day, with as much strength, and with at least as much skill as the American labourer?

The lower value of money in England compared with the value of money in most of the states of Europe, has appeared to arise principally from the cheapness of our exportable manufactures, derived from our superior machinery, skill, and capital. The still lower value of money in the United States is occasioned by the cheapness and abundance of her raw products derived from the advantages of her soil, climate, and situation. Notwithstanding the scarcity of labour in the

United States, it would be obviously impossible for the country to maintain the money price which she actually pays for her labour, if, in spite of such price, she were not able from her situation, and the state of her soil, to produce raw cotton, tobacco, corn, timber, &c. in large quantities at a lower money price than most of her competitors in the European markets. The state of the demand in these markets for corn, tends to raise the price of the American corn, which is exported towards the level of the money prices in Europe. The price of the American corn which is exported naturally raises the money price of American corn in general; and the very great demand for labour in America compared with corn, by awarding to the labourer a large quantity of it, necessarily makes the money wages of labour high; while the abundant exports of other raw products obtained with great facility, afford the means of maintaining the exchanges under so high a bullion price of labour.

As a matter of unquestionable fact, the elementary cost of obtaining a pound of silver in the United States is less than in any country of Europe. A much smaller quantity of labour, of a character and quality hardly equal to that of England, is employed, with other outgoings estimated in the same kind of labour, to produce the articles which purchase it; and neither the difference in profits, nor the difference in the price of labour, is such as to counterbalance this facility of production, and prevent the abundance of exports.

Unquestionably the American labourer is richer, and much better off than the English labourer. He obtains the command of a quantity of food more than sufficient to maintain the largest family; and from the high bullion price of his labour, he can afford in general to purchase a fair quantity both of home and foreign manufactured goods. But he evidently does not purchase what he obtains by a greater sacrifice than the English labourer. He does not give more for what he receives, but receives more for what he gives; and unless we mean to make *quantity* of products the measure of value, which would lead us into the most absurd and inextricable difficulties, we must measure the value of what the labourer receives in the United States by the labour which he gives for it. We must make the proper distinction between value and riches, and say that he is rich, not because he possesses a greater value to give in exchange for what he wants, but because what he wants, or the main articles which constitute his riches, are obtained with much more facility, and are really more abundant and cheaper than they are in Europe.

In those numerous cases, therefore, where the great mass of the day labour of different countries is of the same character in regard to physical strength and duration, such labour must be a measure of value exactly of the same kind as the labour of the same country at different periods. And while we avoid the gross error of confounding the value of money, or of any other commodity in one country with the value of the same quantity of money, or of any other commodity in another country, or in the general market of Europe, it will appear that the labour of each country for which any commodity will exchange, must measure its exchangeable value in that country, or its power of purchasing in that country arising from intrinsic causes.

Hitherto we have assumed that the labour of the same description in different periods and countries, is of the same character as to strength, skill, and duration. It remains to be considered, whether in different countries at the same period, where it is known that the character of the labour is essentially different, and in the same country at different periods, when it may be supposed that the character of the labour has changed, the proposed measure may still be considered as correct.

And here it is probable that the measure will not be considered so satisfactory as in those cases where the labour is exactly of the same character. Yet, while it is obvious that the relative values of all commodities in every country may be accurately measured by the labour which they will command in that country, it must be allowed that there is no other way of approximating towards the other great object of a measure of the values of commodities, namely, a knowledge of the desire to possess, and the difficulty of obtaining possession of them, or the limitation of their supply compared with the demand, than by comparing them with the labour of the country in which they are produced or exchanged, whatever may be its character. And it appears, that if we adhere to that definition of the value of a commodity, which on other grounds has been shown to be the most useful and correct, such labour will measure it: and as no other object or objects will approach to such a measure, it may with propriety be considered as the standard.

The definition of the value of a commodity at a particular place and time, is stated to be " the estimation in which it is held at that place and time, determined in all cases by the state of the supply compared with the demand, and, ordinarily, by the elementary costs of its production, which regulate that state ;" or what comes to the same thing, its power of purchasing at that place and time, arising from intrinsic causes.

Now supposing that in India the labourers do not work either with so much strength, or for so many hours in the day, as the English labourers, what will be the result? Will not every article produced by labour be more scantily supplied compared with the numbers and wants of the population? And to obtain such an article must not a greater number of days labour, with the necessary wages to support the labourer for the greater number of days, be unavoidably sacrificed? That is, every such article will be of higher value, as determined by the state of the supply compared with the demand, and ordinarily by the elementary costs of production. But it has been shown that in every place at any one time, the value of a commodity produced by labour alone is to the value of a commodity however complicated in its mode of production, as the quantity of labour which the simple commodity will command to the quantity of labour that the complicated commodity will command. Consequently, if a certain piece of muslin in England commands five days English labour, and a piece of muslin in India, the same in quantity and quality, will command thirty days Indian labour, the natural inference is that the piece of muslin in India is held there in six times greater estimation than in England, founded on the limitation of its supply compared with the demand, and the greater elementary costs of its production; or, in other words, that its purchasing power in India, arising from intrinsic causes, is six times greater, which, according to the definition, is the same as saying, that the values of two similar pieces of muslin in the two different places, is measured by the quantity of labour in each place which they will respectively command.

But the value of money at any particular place and time can only be determined and measured exactly in the same way as the value of any other commodity. Consequently, the value of money at any particular place and time in India will be there and then determined by the state of its supply compared with the demand, and ordinarily by the elementary costs of its production, and will be measured by the quantity of the standard labour of the country which it will command.

It follows, as a necessary consequence, that the money prices of all commodities produced in different countries, at the same elementary costs, and existing in the same state of the supply compared with the demand, will, when brought to a common market in Europe, be proportioned inversely to the value of money in the country where they are produced. And this, I believe, is the rate at which all foreign commodities practically sell for in any common mart of Europe, after the money expenses and profits of the last voyage are allowed for.

Recollecting then always, that I have not been inquiring for some object which approximates to a standard measure of value in exchange, on the supposition that the proper definition of the value of a commodity is its power of purchasing *generally*, but upon the supposition that the most usual, the most useful, and therefore the most correct* interpretation of the term, is its power of purchasing *arising from intrinsic causes*, we may safely consider labour as the object which will answer the purpose required; and say, that the value of a commodity at any time, and at any place, may be measured by the quantity of the standard labour of that time and place, which it will exchange for or command.

SECTION VI.—*On the Practical Application of the Measure of Value, and its general Use and Advantages.*

THE practical application of the measure of value proposed, will not in general be difficult. In this respect it has a prodigious superiority over the general power of purchasing, a measure which it is impossible practically to apply with any approach towards precision. But when we confine our view to the power of purchasing arising from intrinsic causes, we are able to measure the variations in this power, by the varying quantity of a specific object for which it will exchange; and the practical application of this object is rendered easy, by referring to the money prices of commodities and labour.

Thus, if the relations of two or three commodities in exchange, such as cloth, silver, and corn, for instance, have altered in this country, since the time of

* I cannot help thinking, that if a certain interpretation of a particular term is at once the most usual, and the most useful, it may justly be considered as the most correct, and the one which ought to be adopted in a proper nomenclature.

In all the successful instances of entirely new nomenclatures in any science, it is their obvious and pre-eminent *utility*, which makes up for the disadvantage of their novelty.

Henry VII., and we wish to know, in which, and to what extent in each, a change of value has taken place, we must begin by inquiring what were the money prices of cloth, wheat, and of common labour in the time of Henry VII. compared with what they are now.

It appears from a statute passed in the fourth of Henry VII. that the ordinary price of a broad yard of the finest scarlet grained, or other grained cloth of the finest make, was 16 shillings, and 16 shillings at that time contained the same quantity of silver as 24 of our shillings, before the late new coinage. At present there is reason to believe that cloth of the same, or probably of superior quality, could be obtained for 20 shillings. But the proportion between 24 and 20 would express merely the relation between cloth and silver at these different periods, and would give us no sort of information as to the relative difficulty with which each of these objects was obtained, or the degree in which one or both had altered in value. For this purpose we must refer to the money prices of standard labour. The money price of common agricultural labour in the time of Henry VII. was 4 pence a day, containing as much silver as 6 pence of our present money. If we take the present money wages of common labour at 10 shillings a week, or 20 pence a day, and compare the price of cloth with this price of labour, it will appear that a yard of fine cloth in the time of Henry VII. would command 48 days labour, and a yard of fine cloth at the present time 12 days labour; from which we may safely infer, that supposing these prices to have been what Adam Smith calls natural prices, the difficulty of obtaining cloth of the same quality, or the ordinary supply of cloth compared with the demand, had increased four times.

Comparing in the same manner silver with labour, it appears that as in the time of Henry VII. 6 pence would command the same quantity of labour of the same character, as 20 pence at the present time, silver will appear to have fallen in value $3\frac{1}{3}$ times. And further, if we compare corn and labour at these two periods, it will appear that wheat instead of falling in value like cloth and money, had risen very considerably. In the time of Henry VII. the price of labour as before stated was 4 pence a day, and the average price of the quarter of wheat was 6*s*. 3¼*d*. from which it appears that a quarter of wheat would only purchase 18 ⅘ days labour, whereas taking labour at 20 pence a day, and the present price of wheat at 60 shillings a quarter, the quarter will command 36 days labour. The labourer in the time of Henry VII. could purchase a peck and $\frac{7}{10}$ of a peck by a day's labour; at present he can only purchase $\frac{8}{9}$ of a peck; and altogether the value of wheat has risen in the proportion of 10 to above 19, or has nearly doubled.*

We must of course proceed in the same manner in estimating the values, and the changes in the values of commodities in different countries.

It is proper, however, to mention, that in taking the average money price of labour in different countries, and at different times, a caution is necessary similar to that which is given by Adam Smith, in speaking of the general equality of wages. He very justly observes, that they must be in their natural and ordinary state, and the sole or principal support of the labourer; and particularly remarks, that the labour of cotters will often be cheaper in appearance than it is in reality. In the cotter system, the labourers receive a certain portion of land from a landlord or farmer, which is paid for in labour, at a very low additional remuneration when that labour is called for. During the greater part of the year, however, their labour is not wanted, and the cultivation of their own little portion of land not being sufficient to occupy the time which is left at their own disposal, they are generally

* The reader should be aware that this refers only to a particular period, from about 1444 to 1509, when wheat seems to have been unusually plentiful, and low in value. Taking a century earlier, wheat was of about the same value as at present, and a century later it was of much higher value, and the labourer was much worse off than at present.

willing to offer their labour for a very small recompense to any body who will employ them. But it is evident that the daily or weekly recompense which such labourers receive in money, either from their proper masters or others, is not the whole price of their labour, though, as Adam Smith observes, it has been considered as the whole of it by many writers; and in consequence the wages of labour have been in these cases represented as much below the truth. This was the state of things not long since in Scotland; and it still prevails very generally in Ireland.

A similar observation applies in those cases where the wages of labour are paid in part out of the Parish rates. The money which the labourer receives from his employer is not the whole of what goes to the maintenance of himself and his family. It would not fulfil the necessary conditions of the supply of such labour, and cannot therefore be considered as its natural remuneration in the district in which it is employed.

A further caution to be noticed is, that in estimating the price of agricultural labour in any district, it must be the labour which is actually and with average constancy employed and paid, and not that the price of labour which in a temporary deficiency or excess in the demand for labour, may fall so low, or rise so high, that it cannot be maintained. It must not in short be the average yearly wages of those who are only half employed, or the daily wages of a time of harvest.

When these circumstances, however, have been properly attended to, and the wages we take as the ordinary wages of any particular country or district are the whole of the natural and necessary conditions of the supply of labour, we may fairly presume, that whether the quantity of money, or of necessaries paid to the labourer be great or small, the value of this quantity will be the same.

In general where the facility of production is great, the labourer will obtain a large quantity of them, as in new colonies favourably circumstanced, and in the United States of America. On the other hand, where from the demand of a greatly increased population, cultivation is pushed upon poor land, and production is difficult, the labourer, though he may obtain a larger proportion of what he produces, will receive a smaller quantity of produce. But it is obvious that the smaller quantity in the latter case is obtained with just as much difficulty as the greater quantity in the former case.

There are, however, instances where it may at first sight appear that what the labourer receives as wages is produced with facility, and yet the quantity he receives is very small; but it must always be recollected, that the labour actually employed in the production of wages, is never the sole element of their value. Profits are universally another element, and in some cases, taxes and unnatural rents may raise the value of produce in an unusual proportion beyond the labour employed in its production. In those countries where the sovereign is the proprietor of the soil, if he requires an exorbitant proportion of the produce from all the land that is cultivated, he may leave the poor cultivator only what is just sufficient to support him, although the last land taken into cultivation may be fertile. In this case many of the effects of natural exhaustion and barrenness are produced artificially. Much good land is left uncultivated, and the population presses hard against the limits of that quantity of necessaries which can alone be obtained by the labourer. To earn a very scanty support, he must make a great sacrifice; and a small quantity of produce thus becomes of great value, owing to the limitation of the supply compared with the demand, notwithstanding the real facility of production. Some parts of India have unquestionably at times exemplified this state of things;* and such instances form no exception to the general rule, that the value of the wages given to the labourer in any

* It is said that under Hyder Ally and Tippoo Sultan, $\frac{2}{3}$ of the produce were often taken as rent. If this were general, much fertile land might be kept out of cultivation, and the labourer might be paid miserably, although the productiveness of labour on the poorest land cultivated was great.

country can only be measured by the quantity of the ordinary labour of that country which he gives in exchange for them.

But the Indian labourer receives a smaller quantity of money as well as of necessaries for his day's work; and this is because money also is very difficult of attainment in India, the manufactures sent abroad to purchase it, having cost a great mass of labour, profits, and rent.

It follows that in measuring the value of money at any time and place, and the rise or fall of this value at different times and in different places, we have only to refer, with the cautions above mentioned, to the money price of common agricultural labour. In every country, this sort of labour, as I have said, may be considered as the standard into which every other kind of labour is resolvable, and no difficulty will arise from the acknowledged fact that a great part of the labour of every country is of a higher value than the standard. If the labour of a common journeyman watchmaker be paid at the rate of ten shillings a day, and that of a common agricultural labourer at twenty-pence, the only effect will be that each day's labour employed on the watch, will communicate to that watch a value in exchange arising from intrinsic causes equivalent to that of six days of the standard labour; and the power of the standard labour to measure the difficulty of obtaining the watch will in no degree be impaired. This observation applies to all commodities by whatever kind of labour they are produced. In short, if we are entitled to assume, as I think we are, from what has been said in the preceding sections, that in the natural and ordinary state of things, a given quantity of standard labour applied to the production of any commodity, communicates to it a *given* value in exchange arising from intrinsic causes; and if by value in exchange, when nothing else is added to the term, we mean value in exchange arising from intrinsic causes, it follows, that, contrary to the usual impressions on the subject, there must be a measure of the values, of commodities however composed, and that measure can only be labour.

The specific reason, as it appears to me, why it has been generally supposed that there cannot be anything like a standard measure of value, is, that the principal founder of the *science* of political economy, Adam Smith, has given a definition of value in exchange,* not only different from that meaning in which it is practically, and most frequently, applied, but quite inconsistent with the specific measure of value which he has himself proposed. If by the value of an object in exchange, be meant, as Adam Smith has stated, the power of purchasing other goods which the possession of that object conveys, then, as it is quite certain that such power may increase from the facility of producing other goods as well as from the difficulty of producing the object in question, it is equally certain that there can be no measure of the value of such object; and that when in the same page he speaks of the real measure of this exchangeable value, and afterwards distinctly proposes the labour which a commodity will command at that measure, and enters upon an elaborate inquiry into the value of silver during the four last centuries, he proceeds upon a principle in the application of which he contradicts at every step his first definition. These contradictions were no doubt calculated to produce impressions unfavourable to the existence of a standard measure of value. Such at least were the impressions produced on myself. If, however, he had limited his definition of the exchangeable value of a commodity to its power of purchasing arising from intrinsic causes, or the estimation in which it is held determined by the state of the supply compared with the demand, and, ordinarily, by the elementary costs of its production, which is unquestion-

* "The word value, it is to be observed, has two different meanings, and sometimes expresses the utility of some particular object, and sometimes *the power of purchasing other goods*, which the possession of that object conveys. The one may be called value in use, *the other value in exchange*." Book I. ch. iv. p. 42, 6th edition.

ably the sense in which he applies it himself, and in which it is most frequently applied by others, the measure he has proposed would have been consistent with his definition, and both would have been just.

The question, therefore, of the existence of a measure of value depends upon the sense in which we understand the term value in exchange; and I have fully given my reasons for thinking, not only that the limited sense just adverted to is the sense in which the term is most frequently applied, but that it is the sense in which it is most useful and important to know the exchangeable value of an object, and the only sense in which we can arrive at any practical conclusions approaching towards distinctness and precision, when we speak of a rise or fall in the values of commodities.

It is not a little discreditable to a branch of knowledge which claims to be called a science, that the meaning of a term which is constantly met with in every work on political economy, and constantly heard in every conversation on the subject, should not yet be settled. But while it is most frequently used in a sense different from that in which it has been most frequently defined, it must be allowed that the question relating to the most correct and useful definition of it, is still open for discussion; and though it is well known from experience that those who have once publicly supported particular opinions are not likely to change them; yet looking to the future when it is scarcely possible to suppose that the point should not be settled, every effort to contribute to what is conceived to be a just and useful decision on the *very elements* of the science must be fully warranted.

The language of political economy has been much facilitated, and much indistinctness and unnecessary circumlocution has been prevented by the definite meaning which has been given to the term *price*, or nominal value. Though it is allowable to say price in corn, price in cloth, or price in any other article *named;* yet, when the term price occurs, as it generally does, without any such adjunct, it is universally understood to mean money price.

A similar advantage would be gained, if, when the term value of a commodity, or its value in exchange, were made use of, as it generally is, without any adjunct, it were universally understood to mean value in exchange arising from intrinsic causes, which value it has been shown may be measured by labour.

It cannot be too often repeated, that for short periods when the value of money is considered as nearly constant, we uniformly measure the variations of value, as well as the variations of price by money; and it is quite certain that money, under these circumstances, can only measure the variations in the value of a commodity arising from intrinsic causes, and has nothing to do with causes which are extrinsic.

It may indeed sometimes be desirable to know how far a particular commodity, or a certain quantity of money may go in the purchase of other goods; but even in this case, if it were possible to conceive an article which would represent the mass of all others, it may be doubted whether the power of commanding such an article would give the information wanted. When such inquiries are made, it is generally with a view to the power of the incomes of particular classes to enable them to live in the way they wish.*

The most interesting and useful inquiry of this kind is to ascertain the amount of necessaries, and of ordinary conveniences and luxuries which can be obtained in different countries by the money wages of labour. But if the value of the money wages received by the labourer could be measured by some article which would represent the mass of all purchasable commodities, as such a measure would be affected by a large quantity of commodities unconnected with the wants of the poorer classes of purchasers, it would not give us the information required respecting the condition of the labourer.

On the other hand, if the inquiry related to the power

* When it is said that the exchangeable value of a commodity is determined by its power of purchasing *other goods*, it may most reasonably be asked, *what goods?* It would be absolutely impossible to apply all goods as a measure.

of an income of three thousand a year in different countries, the prices of many of those commodities which only tended to render the measure incorrect in the former case, would probably be the most important in the latter.

It is obvious, therefore, that a measure representing the mass of commodities, or the general power of purchasing, even if attainable, which, however, is impossible, would not only, as formerly stated, fail entirely in reference to the main characteristic * of value, but would be very unsatisfactory in the inquiries above mentioned. And in such cases we ought never to use the term value, or value in exchange by itself, but add specifically the kind of articles, in the purchase of which the incomes would be chiefly spent.

When, therefore, the value of a commodity at any place and time is spoken of, without expressing some object or objects with which it is intended to compare it, we may safely understand by it that value which arises from intrinsic causes; and if labour, applied in the mode proposed, be considered as the measure of such value, it follows necessarily that neither money, nor any other commodity, can ever correctly perform the functions of such a measure, except while it continues to bear the same relation to labour.

It has been justly stated by Adam Smith, that corn is a better measure of value from century to century, than money, and the specific reason which he gives for it is, that its relation to labour is more constant than that of any other commodity.† But if this be the reason why corn at distant periods may be considered as a better measure of value than any other product of labour, it implies distinctly that it cannot be so good a measure of value as labour itself.

It is not a little surprising that the Marquis de Garnier, M. Say, and some other writers, seeing the impossibility of applying the mass of commodities as a

* The quantity of goods which a commodity will command, does not ascertain the difficulty of getting possession of it.

† Book I. ch. v. p. 54, 6th edit.

measure of value, and wishing, therefore, to refer to some one object which might make the nearest approach to it, should have preferred referring to corn instead of labour, when it is well known that corn not only varies greatly in the difficulty of obtaining it, from temporary abundance, or scarcity, but that very great alterations may take place for fifty or sixty years together in the same country, and in different countries, at different periods in the progress of cultivation, for a much longer period.

Adam Smith himself, in his "Digression concerning the value of silver during the four last centuries," by referring most unaccountably to the prices of corn, instead of to the measure which he had himself proposed, has fallen into the very gross error of making the value of silver *rise* in the proportion of from two to three in the interval between the middle of the fourteenth, and the end of the fifteenth century, instead of *falling* in the proportion of from three to two, which would have been the just conclusion, if he had applied labour as his measure instead of corn; and surely he was bound to do this, after saying "Labour, it must always be remembered, and not any commodity, or set of commodities, is the measure not only of silver, but of all other commodities."* In the instance of error to which I have referred, corn had so essentially altered in its relation to labour for fifty or sixty years together, and had fallen so much in value, that a day's labour would purchase nearly two pecks of wheat instead of one. The same quantity of wheat, therefore, instead of representing nearly the same quantity of labour from century to century, as intimated by Adam Smith, represented very little more than the half of that quantity, and his inference respecting the rise in the value of silver was quite reversed.

Of the doctrine that the term value of a commodity ought never to be used without at the same time specifying distinctly the article with which it is intended to be compared, and that any one article measures this

* Book I. ch. xi. p. 291, 6th edit.

value as well as any other; it need only be observed that in this case the term value becomes perfectly superfluous and useless. It has exactly the same meaning as price, or nominal value, that is, the value of one commodity in any other commodity named; and if value admits of no other meaning than this, it would certainly be much better to discard it at once from the vocabulary of political economy, as only tending to create confusion. We ought in this case, however, to invent some other term to express what is so much wanted, namely, the relation which commodities bear to the difficulty of obtaining them, or the estimation in which they are held at different times, and in different countries. But as this is the most usual sense in which the term value is now practically applied, we cannot surely do better than retain it in this sense.

SECTION VII.—*On the Variations in the Value of Money in the same, and different Countries.*

MONEY is beyond all question the most convenient practical measure of value; and while its relation to labour is known and constant, it fully answers the purpose required: It is, however, subject to variation like all other products; but this variation is for the most part so slow, that for short periods, as we have stated, its value has been considered as nearly constant.

We cannot be surprised therefore, that writers in tracing the causes of the rise or fall of the values of particular commodities in the progress of society, should be inclined, with a view to illustration, to suppose this constancy permanent, in order that they might have a standard to refer to. It was specifically with this view that Mr. Ricardo proposed that gold should be considered as produced always in a particular and uniform manner so as to prevent it from deviating, except in a very trifling degree, from a uniform value.

"If then, (he observes) I may suppose myself to

be possessed of a standard so nearly approaching to an invariable one, the advantage is, that I shall be enabled to speak of the variations of other things without embarrassing myself on every occasion with the consideration of the possible alteration in the value of the medium in which price and value are estimated."

"To facilitate then the object of this enquiry, although I fully allow that money made of gold is subject to most of the variations of other things, I shall suppose it to be invariable, and therefore all alterations in price to be occasioned by some alterations in the value of the commodity of which I may be speaking."*

But if, as suggested by Mr. Ricardo, we adopt money obtained under such circumstances as to render profits an element of its value, it is obvious that such a measure must vary with the commodities to be measured when profits either rise or fall.

We may reasonably enough suppose, by way of illustration, that a given quantity of bullion is always obtained by the same quantity of labour, while other commodities may require different quantities, because the circumstance of certain commodities in the progress of society requiring more or less labour in their production, does not necessarily prevent a particular commodity from requiring only the same quantity. But this is not true in regard to the rate of profits, which applies to all commodities, and is allowed to

* Mr. Ricardo, in the first edition of his work (page 11) has given the following description of an invariable measure of value. "If any one commodity could be found, which now, and at all times required precisely the same quantity of labour to produce it, that commodity would be of unvarying value, and would be eminently useful as a standard by which the variations of other things might be measured. Of such a commodity we have no knowledge, and consequently are unable to fix on any standard of value. It is, however, of considerable use towards attaining a correct theory, to ascertain what the essential qualities of a standard are, that we may know the causes of the variations in the relative values of commodities; and that we may be enabled to calculate the degree in which they are likely to operate."

Nothing can be more just and satisfactory than this passage; but unfortunately it was given up.

be nearly the same in all the different employments of capital. We cannot then make the supposition, that the capitals employed in obtaining the precious metals always yield 10 per cent., while the capitals engaged in other employments of the same country vary from 20 per cent. to 5 per cent. It is quite certain therefore, that an article chosen for a standard measure of value must not consist of profits as one of its elements. Gold obtained by labour alone, without profits would far more completely than on any other supposition, measure the variations in the values of all other commodities.

It may perhaps be dangerous to dwell much upon any supposition respecting a mode of obtaining the precious metals, which is essentially different from the truth, because high and low prices under such a supposition will be different from the high and low prices of common language, yet the same terms being used, it will be extremely difficult to avoid confusion. But as Mr. Ricardo was disposed to overlook this objection, and thought that it would on the whole facilitate inquiry, if he were allowed to consider gold as invariable in value, he was surely bound to adopt such a supposition in regard to the mode of obtaining it, as would make it approach the nearest to the invariability required; and it cannot be doubted that this would be best accomplished by supposing the same quantity of gold always to be obtained by the same quantity of labour, without the aid of any advances but the food of a single day; instead of which he has supposed gold to be "produced with such proportions of the two kinds of capital as approach the nearest to the average quantity employed in the production of most commodities."* He is of course compelled to acknowledge in the outset, that a measure so constituted, "would be a perfect measure of value for all things produced under the same circumstances precisely as itself, but for no others." But what a prodigious concession this is! What a full and entire

* Principles of Political Economy, ch. I. sec. vi. p. 44, 3rd. edition.

acknowledgment is it at once that the measure can be of no use. It is really almost like proposing a measure of length which will measure no other commodities than those formed of the same materials with itself.*

What we want is, something to measure the values of commodities under all the variations to which they may be subject; whether their value consists almost wholly in the profits of fixed capitals, or in the labour employed by circulating capitals, whether the commodity is completed for sale in two or three days, or two or three years: whether it is composed in part of other ingredients, such as rents, tythes and taxes, or is made up exclusively of labour and profits; and whether its value is determined by the accidental, or by the ordinary state of the demand and the supply. Now gold obtained by an uniform quantity of labour alone, without capital, would measure all these variations. This then is the measure which Mr. Ricardo, when looking for as near an approximation to a standard measure of value as could be theoretically conceived, should have adopted. And of course, if it seems successful with a view to illustration, to assume that the precious metals are invariable in their value in a particular country; they must be considered as obtained by labour without capital, and as always therefore bearing the same constant relation to labour.

It may be proper however to observe, that this constancy in the money price of labour, can only be a supposition adopted for the sake of illustration; because money is practically obtained by *accumulated* labour and profits, as well as immediate labour and profits, which render profits a necessary condition of its supply; and consequently if the same quantity of labour continue to be applied, while profits rise or

* The obvious defect of such a measure is, that, whether applied to commodities produced under the same circumstances as itself, or to any others, it can never measure the variations to which *they* are subject occasioned by the general rise or fall of profits, because it must *itself* necessarily vary in *that* respect precisely as they do.—*Ed.*

fall, money must rise or fall like all other commodities in the same predicament.

With a view to distinguish the necessary tendency to a fall in the value of money occasioned by the accumulation of capital, the progress of cultivation, and the fall of profits, from the incidental fall occasioned by the varying fertility of the mines, and the possession of an abundance of exportable commodities, it might be useful to distinguish the differences in the value of money into two kinds: first, that which is occasioned by the high or low rate of profit, arising from the progress of capital and cultivation, and which may be denominated the necessary cause of the high or low value of money; and secondly, that which is occasioned by the varying fertility of the mines, the skill with which they are worked, the difficulty or facility of communication with them, and the deficiency or abundance of exportable commodities, which may be denominated the incidental causes of the high or low value of money. These two different kinds of causes will sometimes act in conjunction, and sometimes in opposition, and it may not always be easy to distinguish their separate effects; but as these effects have really a different origin, it is important to keep them as separate as we can.

The marks which distinguish a fall in the value of the precious metals, arising from what has been called the necessary cause, are, a rise in the money prices of corn, raw produce, and labour, without a general rise in the prices of wrought commodities. All of them, indeed, so far as they are composed of raw products, will have a tendency to rise; but in a large class of commodities, this tendency to rise will be much more than counterbalanced by the effect of the fall of profits. Some, therefore, will rise and some will fall according to the nature of the capitals employed upon them, compared with those which produce money; and while the money prices of corn and labour very decidedly increase, the prices of wrought commodities taken on an average, might possibly remain not far from the same.

On the other hand, when the value of money falls from the incidental causes above noticed, without a fall of profits, there will be a tendency to a proportionate rise of all commodities, as well as corn and labour, though in some cases it may take a considerable time before the proportionate rise of all objects are completed. This was remarked, at the time of the influx of the precious metals, from the discovery of the American mines, and also on the issue of an abundant paper currency, during the war which terminated in 1815.

As a necessary consequence of the distinction above made, it may be of use to recollect, that whenever a fall in the value of money takes place, without a fall in the rate of profits, an event which is generally open to observation, it is to be attributed to the incidental causes affecting the relations of money and labour, and not to that which is connected with the accumulation of capital, and the necessity of taking poorer land into cultivation, without improvements in agriculture.

It is certain, however, that those causes operating upon the value of money in different countries and periods, which I have called incidental, are much more powerful and prominent than those which take place necessarily in the progress of society, from the fall of profits. Even in such a country as the United States, where capital is scarce and profits are comparatively high, the fall of profits, which will certainly occur, in the progress of wealth and population, will probably be more than counterbalanced by the effect of a diminution in the facility of producing exportable commodities. And in reference to the fuller peopled countries of Europe, there is no room for such a fall of profits as can approach to the effects which have arisen, and may yet arise from the increased fertility of the mines; or the diminished quantity of labour, which in a particular country, owing to superior skill and machinery, is required to purchase the precious metals, while the cost of obtaining them at the mines of America, and the quantity imported into the whole of Europe remain nearly the same.

The effects of this last cause have never been sufficiently appreciated. It is a just and most important observation of Mr. Ricardo, that, "Gold and silver having been chosen for the general medium of circulation, are by the competitions of commerce distributed in such proportions amongst the different countries of the world, as to accommodate themselves to the natural traffic which would take place if no such metals existed, and the trade between countries was purely a trade of barter."* This distribution is effected by the varying state of the exchanges. If one country possesses peculiar advantages in regard to its exportable commodities, its exchanges will for a time be steadily in its favour, and an influx of the precious metals will take place till the rise in the money price of labour balances the peculiar advantages, and a trade of barter is restored.† On the other hand, if a country loses its advantages in regard to exportable commodities, it will lose a portion of its precious metals by an adverse exchange, and the fall of prices will continue till the reduced money price of labour balances the disadvantages, and the trade of barter returns.

It is on this principle that the different value of money in different countries is accounted for. As Mr. Ricardo most justly observes, "it will explain to us why the prices of home commodities, and those of great bulk, though of comparatively small value, are, independently of other causes, higher in those countries where

* Principles of Political Economy, ch. vii. p. 143, 3rd edit.

† Practically in countries where a large part of the currency consists of paper, the actual influx of bullion is continually checked by an increased issue of bank notes and bills of exchange; but as long as there is no difference between paper and gold, the effect in lowering the value of money is precisely the same. Repeated experience appears to have shewn us that in the case of a brisk demand, no difficulty is ever found in furnishing the means of a considerable rise of prices in some classes of commodities, without any tendency to a fall in others. Currency is always at hand. The important question is, whether the exchanges can be maintained under such prices; and we know too well that they have often risen higher than the exchanges would allow so as to keep paper and gold together.

manufactures flourish. Of two countries having precisely the same population, and the same quantity of land, of equal fertility in cultivation, with the same knowledge too of agriculture, the prices of raw produce will be the highest in that where the greater skill and the better machinery is used in the manufacture of exportable commodities. The rate of profits will probably differ but little; for wages, or the real reward of the labourer, may be the same in both; but those wages, as well as raw produce, will be rated higher in money in that country into which, from the advantages attending their skill and machinery, an abundance of money is imported in exchange for their goods."

The following passage, which occurs in the same chapter of Mr. Ricardo's work, is so just, and so well calculated to dispel some unfortunate prejudices which at present prevail, that I cannot resist the temptation of bringing it afresh before the public.*

"An improvement in the facility of working the mines, by which the precious metals may be produced with a less quantity of labour, will sink the value of money generally. It will then exchange for fewer commodities in all countries; but when any particular country excels in manufactures, so as to occasion an influx of money towards it, the value of money will be lower, and the prices of corn and labour will be relatively higher in that country than in any other.

"This lower value of money will not be indicated by the exchange; bills may be negotiated at par, although the prices of corn and labour should be ten, twenty, or thirty per cent. higher in one country than another.†

* I have always considered the first part of Mr. Ricardo's chapter (vii) on foreign trade as essentially erroneous; but the greater part of the chapter is not only new, but unquestionably true, and of the highest importance.

† Mercantile men are too apt to measure the value of money in different countries by the difference in the exchanges, which merely measures the rate at which the money of one country exchanges for the money of another, and has little to do with the elementary cost of money, or the difficulty of obtaining it in each country, or even with the power of purchasing the mass of those commodities which

Under the circumstances supposed, such a difference of prices is the natural order of things; and the exchange can only be at par when a sufficient quantity of money is introduced into the country excelling in manufactures, so as to raise the price of its corn and labour."*

If this doctrine be true, and I most firmly believe it is, it appears that a rise in the money price of corn and labour is a necessary consequence of commercial prosperity; and though I would distinctly allow, that in reference to our own country at present the corn laws keep the prices of corn and labour higher than they would be, if things were left to take their natural course: yet still it is unquestionable, that the actual prices of corn and labour indicate a low value of money, and not a high value of corn, and that they operate in a totally different way from taxes on the labouring classes.

It is certainly true that the money wages of independent labour, notwithstanding their fall of late years, are higher in this country than in any other country in

are least liable to change in their cost of production. Of all commodities, those which are exported are the most liable to changes in the cost of their production, and are therefore the last which should be referred to with any view to a measure of the value of money.

In my first publication on rent in the shape of a pamphlet, which appeared in 1815, two years before the first edition of Mr. Ricardo's work came out, the following passage occurs in a note:

" The precious metals are always tending to a state of rest, or such a state of things as to make their movement unnecessary. But when this state of rest has been nearly attained, and the exchanges of all countries are nearly at par, the value of the precious metals in different countries estimated in corn and labour, or in the mass of commodities, is far indeed from being the same. To be convinced of this, it is only necessary to look at England, France, Poland, Russia, and India, when the exchanges are at par."

In reality, the quantity of money in each country is determined by the quantity wanted to maintain its general exchanges at par; and the greater are the advantages of any country in regard to its exportable commodities, the more money will it retain, and the higher will be the price of its corn and labour, when its exchanges are at par. If England should lose her advantages in this respect, her corn and labour would fall to the level of the rest of Europe, in spite of any corn laws that could be imagined.

* Ch. vii. p. 156, 3rd edit.

Europe, and there is every reason to believe that the English labourer with his money earnings can purchase as great a quantity of wheat as any European labourer of the same description. If this be so, it is a distinct proof that the higher price of corn in this country, as compared with the continent, is not at present owing to a greater difficulty of obtaining it, but to a higher scale of money prices, or lower value of money, which operates upon *all* commodities, though it is more than counterbalanced in that class of commodities where skill and superior machinery have most prevailed, and it is of these that our principal exports will naturally consist.

In all cases it is of the greatest use and importance to distinguish between a rise or fall in the value of money, and a rise or fall in the values of other commodities. As long as the varying prices of other commodities do not affect the money price of the standard labour in any country, we may consider the value of money as remaining the same, and attribute the relative variations between money and commodities to causes exclusively affecting the commodities, such as the cheapness of products arising from the improvements in machinery, or their dearness from an increased elementary cost of production. But if the money price of the standard labour rises generally, it is a sign that the elementary cost of obtaining money has fallen, and that a smaller sum of labour, profits, rent, and taxes, is given to obtain a certain quantity of it. If, on the other hand, the money price of labour falls, it is a sign that the elementary cost of obtaining money has risen, and that a greater sum of labour, profits, rent, and taxes, must be given to obtain the same quantity of it. And we should be aware that these effects may be, and frequently are produced by causes operating in the first instance on commodities.

This has been practically exemplified in this country of late years. The raised price of corn, commencing with the year 1795, and continuing, with but few exceptions, till 1813, occasioned necessarily a rise in the money price of labour. Without such a rise, the conditions of the supply of the quantity of labour demanded would not have been fulfilled; and the great relative superiority of our manufacturing industry at that time over the rest of Europe enabled us to maintain our exchanges under such a high money price of labour. While this high price continued in the standard labour of the country, with a price of manufacturing labour generally proportioned to it, it is hardly possible to deny that the elementary cost of obtaining bullion in this country was diminished, whatever might be the case in other countries, or whatever might be the costs of producing bullion at the mouths of the mines from which it was obtained. The fact that the quantity of manufactures which would purchase an ounce of gold would, under the circumstances supposed, purchase a smaller quantity of standard labour than usual, proves at once the fact, that the elements in the cost of obtaining gold in England, consisting of labour, profits, rents, and taxes, were, taken altogether, less in value than before, or, in other words, that the elementary cost of obtaining gold in England had diminished.

On the same principle it follows, that the cost of obtaining gold in England has since decidedly increased. Owing to the great fall in the prices of manufactured goods, a greater quantity of them is required to purchase a given quantity of gold—greater than in proportion to the cheapness arising from increased skill, and improvements in machinery. Consequently, such goods so exchanged for gold contain a greater value of English labour, profits, rents, and taxes; and the cost of obtaining gold in England has unquestionably increased.

How far this increased cost of obtaining bullion may have been aggravated by circumstances, which are known to have diminished considerably the supplies from the American mines since 1810, it is not easy to calculate. It has been said that, reckoning the defalcation at the highest, it would bear so small a proportion to the whole quantity of bullion in the world, that it could hardly be expected to have a perceptible effect. But the annual supplies of bullion, though they would operate slowly, even in those countries which were most in the way of receiving them, would still operate much more powerfully than in the proportion which they might bear to the whole mass of bullion in the world. We have good reason to believe that it was a very long time before even the great discovery of the mines of America began to operate sensibly on India, China, Tartary, and other parts of Asia, where no inconsiderable part of the bullion of the world is either slowly circulating, or is buried in the earth. It cannot be doubted that the active part of the commercial world might be powerfully influenced by the varying supply of the American mines, while central Asia was scarcely sensible of any change.

No very satisfactory conclusion, therefore, can be drawn respecting the cause of the late rise in the value of money in the greater part of Europe, and the United States of America, from the smallness of the defalcation in the mines, as compared with the whole mass of bullion in the world.

On the other hand, it must be owned that the circumstance of gold having increased in the cost of its production about as much as silver, without our being able to trace an equal defalcation in its supply, seems to indicate that other causes have been more powerful than the state of the mines of gold and silver; and the object of this digression is to shew that such causes are frequently more efficient in altering the value of the precious metals, especially in particular countries, than moderate changes in the state of their annual supply from the mines.

Adam Smith has justly observed, that the natural effect of the increase of wealth is to raise the value of the precious metals; and it is quite certain that a great increase of produce and population, supposing the supplies of the precious metals, and all other circumstances affecting currency, to remain the same, would render bullion scarcer compared with the demand, and occasion the necessity of its being bought at a greater elementary cost.

Now it is well known that since the war which terminated in 1815, there has been a very great increase of produce and population in most of the countries of the commercial world, and from the necessity that has occurred of withdrawing a great part of the paper which was in circulation in these countries during the war, and the frequent failure of credit from overspeculation subsequently, there is reason to think that the great increase of produce and population has not been balanced by a proportionate increase of currency and credit; and under these circumstances a fall in the prices of produce and labour was inevitable.

As long as the price of labour was not affected by these low prices of commodities, the elementary cost of obtaining the precious metals would not be increased. Although more cottons would be given for an ounce of gold, this would be merely giving a larger quantity of an article which had fallen in the cost of obtaining it, and the elementary cost of obtaining gold might remain the same; but as soon as the price of the standard labour began generally to fall, more labour must be given for the same quantity of silver, and the elementary cost of producing the precious metals would necessarily rise; and in the actual state of things it seems almost impossible to deny that such an increase of their value has really taken place.

In all conclusions, however, relating to variations of value, it would be unreasonable to expect that they can be ascertained with the same precision as the variations of length and weight. Neither the object to be measured, nor the instrument of measurement comes within the pale of that certainty which belongs to the stricter sciences. A given length is the same all over the world; but the *estimation* in which a commodity is held, its elementary cost of production, and the state of its supply compared with the demand is liable to vary at every different place, and in every different period. The standard labour also in different countries is neither the same in different districts, nor does it at all times bear the same relation to other kinds of labour; and it is not always easy to ascertain its money price, particularly when it is in the act of rising or falling, and the change is not completed. Yet notwithstanding these drawbacks, as great confusion would be occasioned by not distinguishing value from price, as all political economists are constantly in the habit of using the term value; and as we cannot speak of a rise or fall of value with any consistency, without some kind of measure of it, it is surely of the greatest use at once to adopt that measure which beyond all comparison approaches the nearest to accuracy, and which in fact may be said to be *exclusively* capable of measuring value in the sense in which the term is in practice most frequently applied.

Labour is in this respect entirely distinct from all the *products* of labour, and the selection of it as a measure of the difficulty of obtaining possession of a commodity in the place where such commodity is estimated, seems to be pointed out by the nature of things, and cannot be called arbitrary.

A measure, to whatever it may be applied, must itself increase or decrease according to quantity. The standard labour of a country which is actually employed, and in the district where the demand is made for it, is *the only object the value of which is proportioned to its quantity*, under the greatest differences both in place and time, both in different countries and in different periods of the same country.

CHAPTER III.

OF THE RENT OF LAND.

SECTION I.—*Of the Nature and Causes of Rent.*

THE rent of land may be defined to be that portion of the value of the whole produce which remains to the owner of the land, after all the outgoings belonging to its cultivation, of whatever kind, have been paid, including the profits of the capital employed, estimated according to the usual and ordinary rate of the profits of agricultural capital at the time being.

It sometimes happens that, from accidental and temporary circumstances, the farmer pays more, or less, than this; but this is the point towards which the actual rents paid are constantly gravitating, and which is therefore always referred to when the term is used in a general sense.

Rent then being the excess of the value of the whole produce, or if estimated in money, the excess of the price of the whole produce, above what is necessary to pay the wages of the labour and the profits of the capital employed in cultivation, the first object which presents itself for inquiry, is, the cause or causes of this excess of price.

After very careful and repeated revisions of the subject, I do not find myself able to agree entirely in the view taken of it, either by Adam Smith, or the *Economists* of the school of M. Quesnay; and still less, by some more modern writers.

Almost all these writers appear to me to consider rent as too nearly resembling, in its nature, and the laws by which it is governed, that excess of price above the cost of production, which is the characteristic of a common monopoly.

Adam Smith, though in some parts of the eleventh chapter of his first book he contemplates rent quite in its true light,* and has interspersed through his work more just observations on the subject than any other writer, has not explained the most essential cause of the ordinary excess of the price of raw produce above its cost of production with sufficient distinctness, though he often touches on it; and by applying occasionally the term monopoly to the rent of land, without stopping to mark its more radical peculiarities, he leaves the reader without a definite impression of the real difference between the cause of this excess in the price of the necessaries of life, and in common monopolized commodities.

Some of the views which the *Economists* of the school of Quesnay have taken of the nature of rent appear to me also, to be quite just; but they have mixed them with so much error, and have drawn such unwarranted inferences from them, that what is true in their doctrines has produced little effect. Their great practical conclusion, namely, the propriety of taxing exclusively the neat rents of the landlords, evidently depends upon their considering these rents not only as completely disposeable, like that excess of price above the cost of production, which distinguishes a common monopoly, but also that every indirect tax operates as a deduction from neat rents in proportion to its amount.

M. Say, in his valuable Treatise on Political Economy, in which he has explained with great clearness many points not sufficiently developed by Adam Smith,

* I cannot, however, agree with him in thinking that all land which yields food must *necessarily* yield rent. The land covered with wood which is successively taken into cultivation in new colonies for the production of food, may only pay profits and labour. A fair profit on the capital employed, including, of course, the payment of labour, will always be a sufficient inducement to cultivate. But, practically, the cases are very rare, where land is to be had by any body who chooses to take it, and it is true perhaps universally, that all appropriated land which yields food *in its natural state*, yields a rent, whether cultivated or uncultivated.

has not treated the subject of rent in a manner entirely satisfactory. In speaking of the different natural agents which, as well as the land, co-operate with the labours of man, he observes: "Heureusement personne n'a pu dire, le vent et le soleil m'appartiennent, et le service qu'ils rendent doit m'être payé."* And, though he acknowledges that, for obvious reasons, property in land is necessary, yet he evidently considers rent as almost exclusively owing to such appropriation, and to external demand.

In the excellent work of M. de Sismondi, *De la Richesse Commerciale*, he says, in a note on the subject of rent: "Cette partie de la rente foncière est celle que les Economistes ont décorée du nom du *produit net*, comme étant le seul fruit du travail qui ajoutât quelque chose à la richesse nationale. On pourroit, au contraire, soutenir contre eux, que c'est la seule partie du produit du travail, dont la valeur soit purement nominale, et n'ait rien de réelle: c'est en effet le résultat de l'augmentation de prix qu'obtient un vendeur en vertu de son privilège, sans que la chose vendue en vaille réellement davantage."†

The prevailing opinions among the modern writers in our own country have appeared to me to incline towards a similar view of the subject; and, not to multiply citations, I shall only add, that in a very respectable edition of the *Wealth of Nations*, published by Mr. Buchanan, of Edinburgh, the idea of monopoly is pushed still farther. And, while former writers, though they considered rent as governed entirely by the laws of monopoly, were still of opinion that this monopoly in the case of land was necessary and useful, Mr. Buchanan sometimes speaks of it even as preju-

* Vol. ii. p. 124, 2nd edit. In his 5th edition, vol. ii. p. 346, he describes the subject anew, but he does not seize the right view of it. He still considers the price of the produce of land which occasions rent too much as the result of a common monopoly.

† Vol. i. p. 49. M. de Sismondi, in his later work, *Nouveaux Principes d'Economie Politique*, has given a different and more correct view of rent.

dicial, and as depriving the consumer of what it gives to the landlord.

In treating of productive and unproductive labour in the last volume, he observes, that,* "The neat surplus by which the *Economistes* estimate the utility of agriculture, plainly arises from the high price of its produce, which, however advantageous to the landlord who receives it, is surely no advantage to the consumer who pays it. Were the produce of agriculture to be sold for a lower price, the same neat surplus would not remain, after defraying the expenses of cultivation; but agriculture would be still equally productive to the general stock; and the only difference would be, that, as the landlord was formerly enriched by the high price, at the expense of the community, the community will now profit by the low price, at the expense of the landlord. The high price in which the rent or neat surplus originates, while it enriches the landlord who has the produce of agriculture to sell, diminishes, in the same proportion, the wealth of those who are its purchasers; and on this account it is quite inaccurate to consider the landlord's rent as a clear addition to the national wealth."

In other parts of this work he uses the same, or even stronger language, and in a note on the subject of taxes, he speaks of the high price of the produce of land as advantageous to those who receive it, but proportionably *injurious* to those who pay it. "In this view," he adds, "it can form no general addition to the stock of the community, as the neat surplus in question is nothing more than a revenue transferred from one class to another, and, from the mere circumstance of its thus changing hands, it is clear that no fund can arise out of which to pay taxes. The revenue which pays for the produce of land exists already in the hands of those who purchase that produce; and, if the price of subsistence were lower, it would still remain in their hands, where it would be just as available for taxation, as

* Vol. iv. p. 134.

when by a higher price it is transferred to the landed proprietor."*

That there are some circumstances connected with rent, which have a strong affinity to a natural monopoly, will be readily allowed. The extent of the earth itself is limited, and cannot be enlarged by human demand. The inequality of soil occasions, even at an early period of society, a comparative scarcity of the best lands; and this scarcity is undoubtedly one of the causes of rent properly so called. On this account, perhaps the term *partial monopoly* may be fairly applicable to it. But the scarcity of land, thus implied, is by no means alone sufficient to produce the effects observed. And a more accurate investigation of the subject will show us how different the ordinary excess of the price of raw produce above its cost of production is, both in its nature and origin, and the laws by which it is governed, from the high price of a common monopoly.

The causes of the ordinary excess of the price of raw produce above the costs of production, may be stated to be three.

First, and mainly, That quality of the soil, by which it can be made to yield a greater quantity of the necessaries of life than is required for the maintenance of the persons employed on the land.

Secondly, That quality peculiar to the necessaries of life, when properly distributed, of creating their own demand, or of raising up a number of demanders in proportion to the quantity of necessaries produced.

And, thirdly, The comparative scarcity of fertile land, either natural or artificial.

The quality of the soil here noticed as the primary cause of the excess in the price of raw produce above the costs of its production, is the gift of nature to man. It is quite unconnected with monopoly, and yet is so absolutely essential to the existence of rent, that without it no degree of scarcity or monopoly could have occasioned an excess of the price of raw produce above

* Vol. iii. p. 212.

what was necessary for the payment of wages and profits.

If, for instance, the soil of the earth had been such, that, however well directed might have been the industry of man, he could not have produced from it more than was barely sufficient to maintain those whose labour and attention were necessary to obtain its products; though, in this case, food and raw materials would have been evidently scarcer than at present, and the land might have been in the same manner monopolized by particular owners; yet it is quite clear, that neither rent nor any essential surplus produce of the land in the form of high profits and high wages could have existed.

On the other hand, it will be allowed, that in whatever way the produce of a given portion of land may be actually divided, whether the whole is distributed to the labourers and capitalists, or a part is awarded to a landlord, the *power* of such land to yield rent is exactly proportioned to its natural or acquired fertility, or to the general surplus which it can be made to produce beyond what is strictly necessary to support the labour and keep up the capital employed upon it. If this surplus be as 1, 2, 3, 4, or 5, then its *power* of yielding a rent will be as 1, 2, 3, 4, or 5: and no degree of monopoly—no possible increase of external demand can essentially alter these different *powers*.

But if no rent can exist without this surplus, and if the *power* of particular soils to pay rent be proportioned to this surplus, it follows that this surplus from the land, arising from its fertility, must evidently be considered as the foundation or main cause of all rent.

Still however, this surplus, necessary and important as it is, would not be sure of possessing a value which would enable it to command a proportionate quantity of labour and other commodities, if it had not a power of raising up a population to consume it, and, by the articles produced in return, of creating an effective demand for it.

It has been sometimes argued, that it is mistaking

the principle of population to imagine, that the increase of food or of raw produce alone can occasion a proportionate increase of population. This is no doubt true; but it must be allowed, as has been justly observed by Adam Smith, that "when food is provided, it is comparatively easy to find the necessary clothing and lodging."* And it should always be recollected, that land does not produce one commodity alone, but in addition to that most indispensable of all articles —food, it produces the materials for clothing, lodging, and firing.†

It is therefore strictly true, that land produces the necessaries of life—produces the means by which, and by which alone, an increase of people may be brought into being and supported. In this respect it is fundamentally different from every other kind of machine known to man; and it is natural to suppose that the use of it should be attended with some peculiar effects.

If an active and industrious family were possessed of a certain portion of land, which they could cultivate so as to make it yield food, and the materials of clothing, lodging, and firing not only for themselves but for five other families, it follows, from the principles of population, that, if they properly distributed their surplus produce, they would soon be able to command the labour of five other families, and the value of their landed produce would soon be worth five times as much as the value of the labour which had been employed in raising it. But if, instead of a portion of land which would yield all the necessaries of life, they possessed only, in addition to the means of their

* Book I. c. xi. p. 255, 6th edit.

† It is however certain that, if either these materials be wanting, or the skill and capital necessary to work them up be prevented from forming, owing to the insecurity of property or any other cause, the cultivators will soon slacken in their exertions, and the motives to accumulate and to increase their produce will greatly diminish. But in this case there will be a very slack demand for labour: and, whatever may be the nominal cheapness of provisions, the whole body of labourers will not really be able to command such a portion of the necessaries of life, including, of course, clothing, lodging, &c. as will occasion an increase of population.

own support, a machine which would produce hats or coats for fifty people besides themselves, no efforts which they could make would enable them to ensure a demand for these hats or coats, and give them in return a command over a quantity of labour considerably greater than their fabrication had cost. For a long time, and by possibility for ever, the machine might be of no more value than that which would result from its making hats or coats for the family. Its further powers might be absolutely thrown away from the want of demand; and even when, from external causes totally independent of any efforts of their own, a population had risen to demand the fifty hats, other similar machines might be made, and the value of the hats in the command of labour and other commodities might permanently exceed but very little the value of the labour employed in making them.

After the new cotton machinery had been introduced into this country, a hundred yards of muslin of a certain quality would not probably command so much labour as twenty-five yards would before; because the supply had increased in a greater degree than the demand, and there was no longer a demand for the whole quantity produced at the same price. But after great improvements in agriculture have been adopted upon a limited tract of land, a quarter of wheat will in a short time command just as much labour as before; because the increased produce, occasioned by the improvements in cultivation, if properly distributed, is found to create a demand proportioned to the supply, which must still be limited; and the value of corn is thus prevented from falling like the value of muslins.

Thus the fertility of the land gives the power of yielding a rent, by yielding a surplus quantity of necessaries beyond the wants of the cultivators; and the peculiar quality belonging to the necessaries of life, when properly distributed, tends strongly and constantly to give a value to this surplus by raising up a population to demand it.

These qualities of the soil and of its products have been, as might be expected, strongly insisted upon by the *Economists* in different parts of their works; and they are evidently admitted as truths by Adam Smith, in those passages of the *Wealth of Nations*, in which he approaches the nearest to their doctrines. But modern writers have in general been disposed to overlook them, and to consider rent as regulated upon the principles of a common monopoly, although the distinction is of great importance, and appears obvious and striking in almost any instance that we can take.

If the fertility of the mines of the precious metals all over the world were diminished one half, it will be allowed that, as population and wealth do not necessarily depend upon gold and silver, such an event might not only be consistent with an undiminished amount of population and wealth, but with a considerable increase of both. In this case however it is quite certain that the rents, profits, and wages paid at the different mines in the world might not only not be diminished, but might be considerably increased. But if the fertility of all the lands in the world were to be diminished one half;* inasmuch as population and wealth strictly depend upon the quantity of the necessaries of life which the soil affords, it is quite obvious that a great part of the population and wealth of the world would be destroyed, and with it a great part of the effective demand for necessaries. The largest portion of the lands in most improved countries would be thrown completely out of cultivation, and wages, profits, and rents, particularly the latter, would be greatly diminished on all the rest. There is hardly any land in this country employed in producing corn, which yields a rent equal in value to the

* Mr. Ricardo has supposed a case (p. 490, third edit.) of a diminution of fertility of one-tenth, and he thinks that it would increase rents by pushing capital upon less fertile land. I think, on the contrary, that in any well cultivated country it could not fail to lower rents, by occasioning the withdrawing of capital from the poorest soils. If the last land before in use would do but little more than pay the necessary labour, and a profit of 10 per cent. upon the capital employed, a diminution of a tenth part of the gross produce would certainly render many poor soils no longer worth cultivating, and would therefore reduce rents.

wages of the labour and the profits of the stock necessary to its cultivation. If this be so, then, in the case supposed, the quantity of produce being only the half of what was before obtained by the same labour and profits, it may be doubted whether any land in England could be kept in tillage.

The produce of certain vineyards in France, which, from the peculiarity of their soil and situation, exclusively yield wine of a certain flavour, is sold, of course, at a price very far exceeding the cost of production, including ordinary profits. And this is owing to the greatness of the competition for such wine, compared with the scantiness of its supply, which confines the use of it to so small a number of persons that they are able, and, rather than go without it, willing to give an excessively high price. But, if the fertility of these lands were increased so as very considerably to increase the produce, this produce might so fall in value as to diminish most essentially the excess of its price above the cost of production. While, on the other hand, if the vineyards were to become less productive, this excess might increase to almost any extent.*

The obvious cause of these effects is, that, in all common monopolies, the demand is exterior to, and independent of, the production itself. The number of persons, who might have a taste for scarce wines, and would be desirous of entering into a competition for

* Mr. Ricardo observes, (p. 492, third edit.) in answer to this passage, that, "*given the high price*, rent must be high in proportion to abundance and not scarcity," whether in peculiar vineyards or on common corn lands. But this is begging the whole of the question. The price cannot be given. By the force of external demand and diminished supply the produce of an acre of Champaigne grapes might permanently command fifty times the labour that had been employed in cultivating it; but, supposing the labourers employed in cultivation to live upon the corn they produce, no possible increase of external demand or diminution of supply could ever enable the produce of an acre of corn to command permanently so many labourers as it would support: because in that case the labourer would be absolutely without the means of supporting a family, and keeping up the population.

the purchase of them, might increase almost indefinitely, while the produce itself was decreasing; and its price, therefore, would have no other limit than the numbers, powers, and caprices of the competitors for it.

In the production of the necessaries of life, on the contrary, the demand is dependent on the produce itself, and the effects are therefore widely different. In this case it is physically impossible that, beyond a certain narrow limit, the number of demanders should increase, while the quantity of produce diminishes, since the demanders can only exist by means of the produce.

In all common monopolies, an excess of the value of the produce above the value of the labour and ordinary profits required to obtain it, may be created solely by external demand, and a scanty supply. In the partial monopoly of the land which produces necessaries, such an excess can only be permanently created by the fertility of the soil.

In common monopolies, and all productions except necessaries, the laws of nature do very little towards proportioning their value in exchange to their value in use. The same quantity of grapes or cottons might, under different circumstances, be worth permanently three or three hundred days labour. In the production of the necessaries of life alone, the laws of nature are constantly at work to regulate their exchangeable value according to their value in use; and though from the great difference of external circumstances, and particularly the greater plenty or scarcity of land, this is seldom or never fully effected; yet the exchangeable value of a given quantity of necessaries always tends to approximate towards the value of the quantity of labour which it can maintain in such a manner as to support at least a stationary population, or in other words, to its value in use.

In all common monopolies, the price of the produce, and consequently the excess of price above the cost of production, may increase without any definite bounds. In the partial monopoly of the land which produces necessaries, the excess of their price above the cost of production is subjected to an impassable limit. This limit is the surplus of necessaries which the land can be made to yield beyond the lowest wants of the cultivators, and is strictly dependent upon the natural or acquired fertility of the soil. Increase this fertility, the limit will be enlarged, and the land may be made to yield a high rent; diminish it, the limit will be contracted, and a high rent will become impossible; diminish it still further, the limit will coincide with the cost of production, and all rent will disappear.

In short, in the one case, the *power* of the produce to exceed in price the cost of the production depends upon the degree of the monopoly, and of the external demand, in the other, this power depends entirely upon the degree of fertility, natural or acquired. This is surely a broad and striking distinction.*

Is it, then, possible to consider the ordinary excess of the price of the necessaries of life above their costs of production as regulated upon the principle of a common monopoly? Is it possible, with M. de Sismondi, to regard rent as the sole produce of labour, which has a value purely nominal, and the mere result of that augmentation of price which a seller obtains in consequence of a peculiar privilege: or, with Mr. Buchanan, to consider it as no addition to the national wealth, but merely as a transfer of value, advantageous only to the landlords, and proportionably *injurious* to the consumers?†

Must we not, on the contrary, allow that rent is the

* Yet this distinction does not appear to Mr. Ricardo to be well founded! c. xxxi. p. 492, 3rd edit.

† It is extraordinary that Mr. Ricardo (p. 486) should have sanctioned these statements of M. Sismondi and Mr. Buchanan. Strictly, according to his own theory, the price of corn is always a natural or necessary price, and, independent of agricultural improvements, the natural and necessary condition of an increased supply of produce. In what sense then can he agree with these writers in saying, that it is like that of a common monopoly, or advantageous only to the landlords, and proportionably *injurious* to the consumers?

natural result of a most inestimable quality in the soil, which God has bestowed on man—the quality of being able to maintain more persons than are necessary to work it? Is it not a part, and we shall see farther on that it is an absolutely necessary part, of that general surplus produce from the land, which has been justly stated to be the source of all power and enjoyment; and without which, in fact, there would be no cities, no military or naval force, no arts, no learning, none of the finer manufactures, none of the conveniences and luxuries of foreign countries, and none of that cultivated and polished society, which not only elevates and dignifies individuals, but which extends its beneficial influence through the whole mass of the people?*

SECTION II.—*On the necessary Separation of the Rent of Land from the Profits of the Cultivator and the Wages of the Labourer.*

So much of violence, and unjust monopoly has attended the appropriation of land in the early times of all long settled states, that in order to see the natural foundation and natural progress of rents, it is necessary to di-

* After what had been said and written on the subject of rent, I confess I was a good deal surprised that Colonel Perronet Thompson should come forward with a pamphlet, entitled "The True Theory of Rent, in opposition to Mr. Ricardo and others," and should state that the simple cause of rent is every where the same as that which gives rise to the rent of the vineyard which produces Tokay. The statement is the more remarkable in Colonel Thompson, as in the course of his pamphlet he acknowledges the truth of the main results of the new theory; which are,

First, That in a progressive country with gradations of soil, which is the state of almost every known country, the actual average price of corn is a necessary price, or the price necessary to obtain the actual amount of the home supply under the existing state of agricultural skill, and existing value of money.

Secondly, That no degree of monopoly could make land which produces the food on which the people live yield a rent, if it did not yield a greater produce than was sufficient to support the cultivators.

Thirdly, That the ordinary price of corn is so strictly limited that

rect our attention to the establishment and progressive cultivation of new colonies. In the settlement of a new colony, where the knowledge and capital of an old society are employed upon fresh and fertile land, the surplus produce of the soil shews itself chiefly in high profits, and high wages, and appears but little in the shape of rent. While fertile land is in abundance, and may be had by whoever asks for it, nobody of course will pay a rent to a landlord. But it is not consistent with the laws of nature, and the limits and quality of the earth, that this state of things should continue. Diversities of soil and situation must necessarily exist in all countries. All land cannot be the most fertile: all situations cannot be the nearest to navigable rivers and markets. But the accumulation of capital beyond the means of employing it with the same returns on land of the greatest natural fertility, and the most advantageously situated, must necessarily lower profits; while the rapid increase of population will tend to lower† the wages of labour.

it cannot by possibility continue so high as to prevent the ordinary money wages of the labouring classes from purchasing more corn than is required to support the individuals actually employed.

Now, it is unquestionably true, First, that the price of Tokay is not a necessary price. The same quantity would be produced, although the price were considerably lower. Secondly, That neither the purchasers of Tokay, nor the cultivators of it, live upon the produce. And Thirdly, That there is no limit to the price of Tokay, but the tastes and fortunes of a few opulent individuals.

How then can it possibly be said with truth, that the simple cause of rent is every where the same as that which gives rise to the rent of the vineyard which produces Tokay; and how entirely inapplicable is a reference to Tokay as an illustration of the true theory of rent.

With regard to the grand fallacy on which Colonel Thompson dwells so much, it is obvious that the incautious language in which the new doctrine of rent has been sometimes announced, does not affect its substance. The errors arising from this cause had been pointed out in the first edition of this work long before Colonel Thompson entered upon the question.

† After what has been stated respecting the constancy of the *value* of labour in the last chapter, it will be understood that whenever I speak of *high* or *low* wages, or of the *rise* or *fall* of wages, I always mean to refer to their greater or less amount, or to the in-

The costs of production in corn wages and profits will thus be diminished; but the value of the produce, that is, the quantity of labour which it can command, instead of diminishing, will have a tendency to increase. There will be an increasing number of people demanding subsistence, and ready to offer their services in any way in which they can be useful. The value of food will be in excess above the value of the labour and profits which are the condition of its supply; and this excess is that portion of the general surplus derived from land which has been peculiarly denominated rent.

The quality of the earth first mentioned, or its power to yield a greater quantity of the necessaries of life than is required for the maintenance of the persons employed in cultivation, is obviously the foundation of this rent, and the limit to its possible increase. The second quality noticed, or the tendency of an abundance of food to increase population, is necessary both to give a value to the surplus of necessaries which the cultivators can obtain on the first land cultivated; and also to create a demand for more food than can be procured from the richest lands.* And the third cause, or the comparative scarcity of fertile land, which is clearly the natural consequence of the second, is finally necessary to separate a portion of the general surplus from the land, into the specific form of rent to a landlord.†

crease or diminution of the *quantity* of necessaries, &c. awarded the labourer, or of the money wherewith he purchases those necessaries, and which is variable in its value.

It would, perhaps, have been better, in order to avoid ambiguity, always to have applied these latter terms to wages, instead of the former ones, but the expressions high and low wages, and the rise and fall of wages, being so constantly used in common conversation, and being always understood in the sense in which I explain them, the retaining them is not likely to create confusion in the mind of the reader.

* If, commencing with a new colony the increase of population did not create a demand for more food than could be produced with the same profits from the richest lands, no rent could arise, and no inferior land could be taken into cultivation.

† Mr. Ricardo quite misunderstood me, when he represents me as saying that rent immediately and necessarily rises or falls with

Nor is it possible that in a country increasing in wealth and population, the whole produce could continue to be divided only between the capitalists and labourers, as the profits of capital and the wages of labour. If profits and corn wages were not to fall, then, without particular improvements in cultivation, none but the very richest lands could be brought into use. The fall of profits and wages which practically takes place, undoubtedly transfers a portion of produce to the landlord, and forms a part, though, as we shall see farther on, only a *part* of his rent. But if this transfer can be considered as injurious to the consumers, then every increase of capital and population not resulting specifically from improvements in agriculture, must be considered as injurious; and a country which might maintain well ten millions of inhabitants ought to be kept down to a million. The transfer from profits and wages, and such a value of the produce as yields rent, which have been objected to as injurious, and as depriving the consumer of what it gives to the landlord, are absolutely necessary in order to obtain any considerable addition to the wealth and numbers of the first settlers in a new country; and are the natural and unavoidable consequences of that increase of capital and population for which nature has provided in the propensities of the human race.

the increased or diminished fertility of the land. (p. 489, 3d edit.) How far my former words would bear this interpretation the reader must judge: but I certainly could not be aware that they would be so construed. Having stated three causes as necessary to the production of rent, I could not possibly have meant to say that rent would vary always and exactly in proportion to one of them. I distinctly stated, indeed, that in new colonies, the surplus produce from the land, or its fertility, appears but little in the shape of rent. Surely he expressed himself more inadvertently while correcting me, by referring to the comparative scarcity of the most fertile land as the only cause of rent, (p. 490, 3d edit.) although he has himself acknowledged, that without positive fertility, no rent can exist. (p. 491.) If the *most* fertile land of any country were still very poor, such country would yield but very little rent, however scarce such land might be; and if there were no excess of necessaries above what are required for the maintenance of the cultivators, there would be no excess of price.

When such an accumulation of capital has taken place, as to render the returns of an additional quantity employed on the lands first chosen less than could be obtained from inferior land,* it must evidently answer to cultivate such inferior land. But the cultivators of the richer land, after profits and wages had fallen, if they paid no rent, would cease to be mere farmers, or persons living upon the profits of agricultural stock; they would evidently unite the characters of landlords and farmers—a union by no means uncommon, but one which does not alter in any degree the nature of rent, or its essential separation from profits and wages.

If the profits of capital on the inferior land taken into cultivation were thirty per cent., and portions of the old land would yield forty per cent., ten per cent. of the forty would obviously be rent by whomsoever received: and when capital had further accumulated and corn wages fallen † on the more eligible lands of a country, other lands, less favourably circumstanced with respect to fertility or situation, might be occupied with advantage. The quantity of produce required to replace wages and profits, having fallen, poorer land, or land more distant from rivers and markets, though yielding at first no rents, might fully repay these expenses, and fully answer to the cultivator. And again, when either the profits of stock, or the corn wages of labour, or both, have still further fallen, land still poorer or still less favourably situated,

* The immediate motive for the cultivation of fresh land can only be the prospect of employing an increasing capital to greater advantage than on the old land.

† When a given value of capital yields smaller returns, whether on new land or old, the loss is generally divided between the labourers and capitalists, and wages and profits fall at the same time. This is quite contrary to Mr. Ricardo's language. But the wages we refer to are totally different. He speaks of the mere labour cost of producing the necessaries of the labourer; I speak of the necessaries themselves. The reader will be aware that when corn wages have fallen, the value of corn has risen, owing to a greater intensity of demand for it, or the power and will to purchase it by the sacrifice of a greater quantity of labour.

might be taken into cultivation. And at every step of this kind it is clear, that the rent of land must rise.

It may be laid down, therefore, as an incontrovertible truth, that as a nation reaches any considerable degree of wealth, and any considerable fullness of population, the separation of rents, as a kind of fixture upon lands of a certain quality, is a law as invariable as the action of the principle of gravity; and that rents are neither a mere nominal value, nor a value unnecessarily and injuriously transferred from one set of people to another; but a most important part of the whole value of the annual produce, necessarily resulting from its continued increase, and placed by the laws of nature on the land, by whomsoever possessed, whether by few or many, whether by the landlord, the crown, or the actual cultivator.

This then is the mode in which rent would separate itself from profits and wages, in a natural state of things, the least interrupted by bad government, or any kind of unnecessary monopoly; but in the different states in which mankind have lived, it is but too well known that bad governments and unnecessary monopolies have been frequent; and it is certain that they will essentially modify this natural progress, and often occasion a premature formation of rent.

In most of the great eastern monarchies, the sovereign has been considered in the light of the owner of the soil. This premature monopoly of the land joined with the two properties of the soil, and of its products first noticed, has enabled the government to claim, at a very early period, a certain portion of the produce of all cultivated land; and under whatever name this may be taken, it is essentially rent. It is an excess both of the quantity, and of the value of what is produced above the costs of cultivation.*

* This view of the subject includes all the different kinds of rent referred to by Mr. Jones, in his late valuable account of the state of rents, and the various modes of paying labour in different parts of the world. Whether the labourer is paid in money, in produce, or by a portion of land which he is to work himself with

But in most of these monarchies there was a great extent of fertile territory; the natural surplus of the soil was very considerable; and while the claims upon it were moderate, the remainder was sufficient to afford such profits and wages as would allow of a great increase of population.

It is obvious, however, that it is in the power of a sovereign who is owner of the soil in a very rich territory to obtain, at an early stage of improvement, an excessive rent. He might, almost from the first, demand all that was not necessary to allow of a moderate increase of the cultivators, which, if their skill were not deficient, would afford him a larger *proportion* of the whole produce in the shape of a tax or rent, than could probably be obtained at any more advanced period of society; but then of course only the most fertile lands of the country could be cultivated; and profits, wages and population would come to a premature stop.

It is not to be expected that sovereigns should push their rights over the soil to such an extreme extent, as it would be equally contrary to their own interest, and to that of their subjects; but there is reason to believe that in parts of India, and in many other southern and eastern countries, and probably even in China, the progress of taxation on the land, founded upon the sovereign's right to the soil, together with other customary payments out of the raw produce, have forcibly and prematurely lowered the profits of capital, and the wages of labour on the land, and have thrown great obstacles in the way of progressive cultivation and population in latter times, while much good land has remained waste. This will always be the case,

a part of his labour, while he gives the other part to his lord, the foundation of rent is exactly the same, depending always upon the value of the excess of what the whole of the lord's land produces, above that which under the actual circumstances is received by the cultivators, and the amount of rent which can be received from a given extent of land will rise according to all the different degrees of fertility above that which will only support the actual cultivators.

when, owing to an unnecessary monopoly, a greater portion of the surplus produce is taken in the shape of rent or taxes, than would have been separated by the natural fall of profits and wages occasioned by the increase of capital and population. But whatever may be the nature of the monopoly of land, whether necessary or artificial, it will be observed that the power of paying a rent or taxes on the land, is completely limited by its fertility; and those who are disposed to underrate the importance of the two first causes of rent which I have stated, should look at the various distributions of the produce in kind which take place in many parts of India, where, when once the monopoly has enabled the sovereign to claim all the produce which remains above what is required for the cultivation of the soil, his resources obviously depend upon the surplus of necessaries which the land yields, and the power of these necessaries to command labour.

It may be thought, perhaps, that rent could not be forcibly and prematurely separated from profits and wages so as unnaturally to reduce the two latter, because capital and labour would quit the land if more could be made of them elsewhere; but it should be recollected, that the actual cultivators of the soil in these countries are generally in a very low and degraded condition; that very little capital is employed by them, and scarcely any which they can remove and employ in another business; that the surplus produce possessed by the government soon raises up a population to be employed by it, so as to keep down the price of labour in other departments to the level of the price in agriculture; and that the small demand for the products of manufacturing and commercial industry, owing to the poverty of the great mass of society, affords no room for the employment of a large capital, with high profits in manufactures and commerce.

On account of these causes which tend to lower profits, and the difficulty of collecting money, together with the risk of lending it which tends to raise interest, I have long been of opinion, that though the rate of interest in different countries is almost the only criterion from which a judgment can be formed of the rate of profits; yet that in such countries as India and China, and indeed in most of the eastern and southern regions of the globe, it is a criterion subject to the greatest uncertainty. In China, the legal interest of money is said to be three per cent. per month.* But it is impossible to suppose, when we consider the state of China, so far as it is known to us, that capital employed on the land can yield profits to this amount; or, indeed, that it can be employed in any steady and well-known trade with such a return.

In the same way extraordinary accounts have been given of the high rate of interest in India; but the state of the actual cultivators completely contradicts the supposition, that, independently of their labour, the profits upon their stock is so considerable; and the late reduction of the government paper to six per cent. fully proves that, in common and peaceable times, the returns of capital, which can be depended upon in other sorts of business, are by no means so great as to warrant the borrowing at a very high rate of interest.

It is probable that, with the exception of occasional speculations, the money which is borrowed at the high rates of interest noticed in China and India, is borrowed in both countries, rather with a view to expenditure, the payment of debts, or some pressing necessity, than with a view to regular profits.

Some of the causes, which have been noticed as tending prematurely and irregularly to raise rents and lower profits in the countries of the east, operated without doubt to a certain extent in the early stages of society in Europe. At one period most of the land was cultivated by slaves; and on the *metayer* system which succeeded, the division of the crop was so ar-

* Penal Code, Staunton, p. 158. The market-rate of interest at Canton is said, however, to be only from twelve to eighteen per cent. Id. note XVII.

ranged as to allow the cultivator but little more than a scanty subsistence. In this state of things the rate of profits on the land could have but little to do with the general rate of profits. The peasant could not, without the greatest difficulty, realize money and change his profession; and it is quite certain that no one who had accumulated a capital in manufactures and commerce, would employ it in cultivating the lands of others as a *metayer*. There would thus be little or no interchange of capital between trade and agriculture, and the profits in each might in consequence be very unequal.

It is probable however, as in the case of China and India above mentioned, that profits would not be excessively high. This would depend indeed mainly upon the supply of capital in manufactures and commerce; if capital were scarce, compared with the demand for the products of these kinds of industry, profits would certainly be high; and all that can be said safely is, that we cannot infer that they were very high, from the very high rates of interest occasionally mentioned.

Rent then has been traced to the same common nature with that general surplus from the land, which is the result of certain qualities of the soil and its produce; and it has been found to commence its separation from profits and wages, as soon as they begin to fall from the scarcity of fertile land whether occasioned by the natural progress of a country towards wealth and population, or by any premature and unnecessary monopoly of the soil.

SECTION III.—*Of the Causes which tend to raise Rents in the ordinary Progress of civilized and improved Societies.*

IN tracing more particularly the laws which govern the rise and fall of rents, the main causes which practically tend to increase the difference between the price of the produce, and the expenses of cultivation including ordinary profits, require to be more specifically enumerated. The principal of these seem to be four:—1st, Such an accumulation of capital compared with the means of employing it, as will lower the profits of stock; 2dly, such an increase of population as will lower the corn wages of labour; 3dly, such agricultural improvements, or such increase of exertions as will diminish the number of labourers necessary to produce a given effect; and 4thly, such an increase in the *price* of agricultural produce, from increased demand, as, while it probably raises the money price of labour, or occasions a fall in the value of money, is nevertheless, accompanied by a diminution either temporary or permanent, of the money outgoings of the farmer, compared with his money returns.

If capital increases in some departments, and the additional quantity cannot be employed with the same profits as before, it will not remain idle, but will seek employment either in the same or in other departments of industry, although with inferior returns, and this will tend to push it upon less fertile soils.

In the same manner, if population increases faster than the funds for the maintenance of labour, the labourers must content themselves with a smaller quantity of necessaries. The *value* of produce will consequently rise; the same quantity of corn will set more labour in motion, and land may be cultivated which could not have been cultivated before.

These two first causes sometimes act so as to counterbalance one another. An increase of capital tends to raise the wages of labour, and a fall of wages tends to raise the profits of stock; but these are only temporary effects. In the natural and regular progress of a country towards its full complement of capital and population, the rate of profits and the corn wages of labour permanently fall together. Practically this is often effected by a rise in the money price of corn, accompanied by a rise, but not a proportionate rise, in the money wages of labour. The greater rise in the money price of corn as compared with labour, is more than counterbalanced to the cultivator by the diminished quantity of produce obtained by the same agricultural capital; and the profits of all other capitalists are diminished, by having to pay out of the same money returns higher money wages; while the command of the labourer over the necessaries of life is of course contracted by the inadequate rise of the price of labour as compared with that of corn.

But this exact and regular rise in the money price of corn and labour is not necessary to the fall of profits. Profits and corn wages may fall, and rent be separated, under any variations of the value of money. All that is necessary to the most regular and permanent fall of profits, is, that an increased proportion of the produce obtained by a given quantity of labour should be absorbed in paying that labour. In the continued progress of cultivation, this is generally effected by a diminution of the produce, obtained by the same labour without a proportionate diminution of the quantity absorbed by labour, which leaves less for profits, at the same time that the corn wages of the labourer are diminished. But it is obvious that if a smaller quantity of produce be sufficient to remunerate both the capitalist and the labourer,* the outgoings neces sary to cultivation will be diminished, rents will tend to rise on all the old lands, and poorer lands may be cultivated with advantage.

The third cause enumerated as tending to raise rents by lowering the expenses of cultivation compared with the price of the produce is, such agricultural improve-

* Mr. Ricardo has observed (p. 499, 3rd edit.) in reference to the second cause which I have here stated, as tending to raise rents, "that no fall of wages can raise rents; for it will neither diminish the portion, nor the value of the portion of the produce which will be allotted to the farmer and labourer together." And yet in reality there is no other rise in the *value* of corn, but that which is accompanied by a fall in the corn wages of labour. The fact is, that the *value* allotted to the farmer and labourer together, measured in labour, or money of a fixed value, is very far from remaining the same. All his calculations are built upon the fundamental error of omitting the consideration of profits in estimating the value of wages, and thus making the value of labour

ments, or such increase of exertions, as will diminish the number of labourers necessary to produce a given effect.

In improving and industrious countries, not deficient in stimulants, this is a cause of great efficacy. If the improvements introduced were of such a nature as considerably to diminish the costs of production, without increasing in any degree the quantity of produce, then, as it is quite certain that no alteration would take place in the price of corn, the extravagant profits of the farmers would soon be reduced by the competition of capitals from manufactures and commerce; and as the whole *arena* for the employment of capital would rather have been diminished than increased, profits on the land as well as elsewhere would soon be at their former level, and the increased surplus from the diminished expenses of cultivation would go to increase the rents of the landlords.

But if these improvements, as must always be the case, would facilitate the cultivation of new land, and the better cultivation of the old with the same capital, more corn would certainly be brought to market. This would lower its price; but the fall would be of short duration. The operation of that important cause noticed in the early part of this chapter, which distinguishes the surplus produce of the land from all others, namely, the power of the necessaries of life, when properly distributed, to create their own demand, or in other words the tendency of population to press against the means of subsistence, would soon restore the prices

rise, instead of making it constant. The value obtained by a given quantity of labour, or the value allotted to the farmer and labourer together, must always fall with the fall of profits. If it does not in Mr. Ricardo's money, it is precisely because his money is so constructed as to vary with the article it measures. The high corn wages of America will finally go to rent, not to profits. If labourers were permanently to receive the value of half a bushel of wheat a day, none but the richest lands could pay the expense of working them. An increase of population, and a fall of very high corn wages are absolutely necessary to the cultivation of poor land. How then can it be said that a fall of wages is not one of the causes of a rise of rents?

of corn and labour, and reduce the profits of stock to their former level, while in the mean time every step in the cultivation of poorer lands facilitated by these improvements, and their application to all the lands of a better quality before cultivated, would universally have raised rents: and thus, under an improving system of cultivation, rents might continue rising without any rise in the value of corn, or any fall in the corn wages of labour, or in the general rate of profits.

The very great improvements in agriculture which have taken place in this country are clearly demonstrated by the profits of stock having been as high in 1813 as they were nearly a hundred years before, when the land supported but little more than half the population. And the power of the necessaries of life, when properly distributed, to create their own demand is fully proved by the palpable fact, that the exchangeable value of corn in the command of labour and other commodities was for many years before that period, undiminished, notwithstanding the many and great improvements which had been successively introduced into cultivation, both by the use of better implements, and by a more skilful system of managing the land. In fact, the increase of produce had gone almost wholly to the increase of rents and the payment of taxes, tithes, and poor's rates.

It may be added that, when in particular districts, improvements are introduced which tend to diminish the costs of production, the advantages derived from them go immediately, upon the renewal of leases, to the landlords, as the profits of stock must necessarily be regulated by competition, according to the general average of the whole country. Thus the very great agricultural improvements which have taken place in some parts of Scotland, the north of England, and Norfolk, have raised, in a very extraordinary manner, the rents of those districts, and left profits where they were.

It must be allowed then, that facility of production

in necessaries,* unlike facility of production in all other commodities, is rarely or never attended with a permanent fall of their value. They are the only commodities of which it can be said that their permanent command of labour has a constant tendency to keep pace with the increase of their quantity. And consequently, in the actual state of things, all savings in the cost of producing them will permanently increase the surplus which goes to rent.

The fourth cause which tends to raise rents, is such an increase in the money price of agricultural produce from increased demand, as while it raises the money price of labour, or lowers the value of money, is accompanied by a *comparative* diminution, either temporary or permanent, in the money outgoings of the farmer.†

I have already adverted to a rise in the money price of raw produce, which may take place in consequence of a regular increase of capital and population, and a regular fall of profits and corn wages. But this sort of rise is confined within narrow limits, and has little share in those great variations in the price of corn, which are most frequently the subject of observation. The kind of increased price, the effects of which I wish now more particularly to consider, is a rise of price from increased demand, terminating in a diminished value of the precious metals.

If a great and continued demand should arise among surrounding nations for the raw produce of a particular country, the price of this produce would of course rise considerably; and the expenses of culti-

* Properly speaking, facility of production in necessaries can only be temporary where there are gradations of land as far as barrenness, except when capital is prevented from increasing by the want of power or will to save, arising from bad government. It may then be permanent. But though corn will, in that case, cost but little labour, the labour which it will command, or its value, will be comparatively high.

† This cause is partly included in the preceding ones; but as it frequently occurs, and has a different origin, it is worth while to consider it separately, and trace its practical operation.

vation rising only slowly and gradually to the same proportion, the price of produce might for a long time keep so much a head as to give a prodigious stimulus to improvement, and encourage the employment of much capital in bringing fresh land under cultivation, and rendering the old much more productive. If however the demand continued, the price of labour would ultimately rise to its former level, compared with corn; a decided fall in the value of money supported by the abundant exportation of raw produce might generally take place, in which case labour would become extremely productive in the purchase of all foreign commodities, and rents might rise without a fall of profits or wages.

The state of money prices, and the rapid progress of cultivation in the United States of America, tend strongly to illustrate the case here supposed. The price of wheat in the eastern states has been often nearly as high as in France and Flanders; and owing to the continued demand for hands, the money price of day-labour has been at times nearly double what it is in England.* But this high price of corn and labour has given great facilities to their farmers and labourers in the purchase of clothing and all sorts of foreign necessaries and conveniences. And it is cer-

* According to Pitkin's Statistical View of the United States, (p. 112, 2nd ed.) the average price of the bushel of wheat for eleven years, from 1806 to 1816 inclusive, at the principal places of exportation, was rather above 1½ dollars, or 54 shillings per quarter; and, according to Fearon's Sketches, common labour was above a dollar a day.

The state of things in 1821 was essentially different, and shews how much the value of money in any country depends upon the demand and supply of produce. Corn and labour, it is said, had fallen at that time one half. The former high prices were no doubt in part owing to paper, but before the war with England, for seven years out of the eleven referred to, silver and paper were at par, and during this period wheat at the ports of the Eastern States was above 50 shillings a quarter. A rise in the price of corn, and other sorts of raw produce in an exporting country with plenty of good land, enables it to purchase money with a smaller quantity of labour, which is likely to render it cheap, or to make the money price of labour high.

tain that if the money prices of corn and labour had been both lower, yet had maintained the same proportion to each other, land of the same quality could not have been cultivated with the same advantage, nor could equal rents have been obtained with the same rate of profits and the same corn wages of labour.

Effects of a similar kind took place in our own country from a similar demand for corn during the twenty years from 1793 to the end of 1813, though the demand was not occasioned in the same way. For some time before the war, which commenced in 1793, we had been in the habit of importing a certain quantity of foreign grain to supply our habitual consumption. The war naturally increased the expense of this supply by increasing the expense of freight, insurance, &c.; and, joined to some bad seasons and the subsequent decrees of the French government, raised the price, at which wheat could be imported, in the quantity wanted to supply the demand, in a very extraordinary manner.*

This great rise in the price of imported corn, although the import bore but a small proportion to what was grown at home, necessarily raised in the same proportion the whole mass, and gave the same sort of stimulus to domestic agriculture as would have taken place from a great demand for our corn in foreign countries. In the mean time, the scarcity of hands, occasioned by an extending war, an increasing commerce, and the necessity of raising more food, joined to the ever ready invention of an ingenious people when strongly stimulated, introduced so much saving of manual labour into every department of industry, that the new and inferior land taken into culti-

* During the period alluded to, corn rose far beyond what was necessary to defray the increased expense of freight, insurance, &c., occasioned by the war. The *cause* of the rise was therefore, *independent* of the increased cost of importation. It doubtless originated in the profuse expenditure of the state, and the increased activity of commercial and manufacturing industry at the time.—*Ed.*

vation, to supply the pressing wants of the society, was worked at a less expense of labour than richer soils had been some years before. Yet still the price of grain necessarily kept up as long as the most trifling quantity of foreign grain, which could only be obtained at a very high price, was wanted in order to supply the existing demand. With this high price, which at one time rose to nearly treble in paper and above double in bullion, compared with the prices before the war, it was quite impossible that the money price of labour should not rise nearly in proportion, and with it, of course, as profits had not fallen, all the commodities into which labour had entered.

We had thus a general rise in the prices of labour and commodities, or a fall in the value of the precious metals, compared with other countries, which our increasing foreign commerce and abundance of exportable commodities enabled us to sustain, and this is one of the signal instances in which the value of money arising from incidental causes entirely overwhelmed and obscured the effects arising from the necessary cause. Profits instead of falling rose; and the value of money ought therefore to have risen, and the money price of labour to have fallen; but the secondary causes arising from the demand for corn and labour, and the increasing money value of our exported commodities quite overcame the natural effects of the rise of profits, and occasioned a very decided fall, not only in the value of our currency but in the value of our bullion compared with labour. That the last land taken into cultivation in 1813 did not require more labour to work it than the last land improved in the year 1790, is proved by the acknowledged fact, that the rate of interest and profits was higher in the later period than the earlier, while the corn wages of labour were nearly the same. But still the profits were not so much higher as not to have rendered the interval extremely favourable to the rise of rents. This rise, during the interval in question, was the theme of universal remark; and though a severe check, from a combination of circumstances, has since occurred; yet the great drainings and permanent improvements, which were the effects of so powerful an encouragement to agriculture, have acted like the creation of fresh land, and have increased the real wealth and population of the country, without increasing the labour and difficulty of raising a given quantity of grain.

It is obvious then that a fall in the value of the precious metals, commencing with a rise in the price of corn, has a strong tendency, while it is going on, to encourage the cultivation of fresh land and the formation of increased rents.

A similar effect would be produced in a country which continued to feed its own people, by a great and increasing demand for its manufactures. These manufactures, if from such a demand the money value of their amount in foreign countries was greatly to increase, would bring back a great increase of money value in return, which increase could not fail to increase the money price of labour and raw produce. The demand for agricultural as well as manufactured produce would thus be augmented; and a considerable stimulus, though not perhaps to the same extent as in the last case, would be given to every kind of improvement on the land.

This result generally takes place from the introduction of improved machinery, and a more judicious division of labour in manufactures. It almost always happens in this case, not only that the quantity of manufactures is very greatly increased, but that the value of the whole mass is augmented, from the great extension of the demand for them both abroad and at home, occasioned by their cheapness. We see, in consequence, that in all rich manufacturing and commercial countries, the value of manufactured and commercial products bears a very high proportion to the increased raw products;* whereas, in compara-

* According to the calculations of Mr. Colquhoun, the value of our trade, foreign and domestic, and of our manufactures, ex-

tively poor countries, with few manufactures and little foreign commerce, the value of their raw produce, though small compared with their extent of territory, constitutes almost the whole of their wealth.

In those cases where the stimulus to agriculture *originates* in a prosperous state of commerce and manufactures, it sometimes happens that the first step towards a rise of prices is an advance in the money wages of commercial and manufacturing labour. This will naturally have an immediate effect upon the price of corn, and an advance in the price of agricultural labour will follow. It is not, however, necessary, even in those cases, that labour should rise first. If, for instance, the population were increasing as fast as the mercantile and manufacturing capital, the only effect might be an increasing number of workmen employed at the same money wages, which would occasion a rise in the price of corn before any rise had taken place in the wages of labour.

We are supposing, however, now, that the price of labour does ultimately rise nearly to its former level compared with corn, that both are considerably higher, and that money has suffered a decided change of value. Yet in the progress of this change, the other outgoings, besides labour, in which capital is expended, can never all rise at the same time, or even finally in the same proportion. A period of some continuance can scarcely fail to occur when the difference between the price of produce and the cost of production is so increased as to give a great stimulus to agriculture; and as the increased capital, which is employed in consequence of the opportunity of making great temporary profits, can seldom be entirely removed from the land, a part of the advantage so derived is permanent; together with the whole of that which may be occasioned by a greater perma-

clusive of raw materials, is nearly equal to the gross value derived from the land. In no other large country probably is this the case.—Treatise on the Wealth, Power, and Resources of the British Empire, p. 96.

nent rise in the price of corn than in some of the materials of the farmer's capital.

It is acknowledged that, when a fall takes place in the value of money, taxed commodities will not rise in the same proportion with others; and, on the supposition of such fall being peculiar to a particular country, the same must unquestionably be said of all the various commodities which are either wholly or in part imported from abroad, many of which enter into the capital of the farmer. He would, therefore, derive an increased power from the increased money price of corn compared with those articles. A fall in the value of money cannot indeed be peculiar to one country without the possession of peculiar advantages in exportation; but with these advantages, which we know are very frequently possessed, and are often increased by stimulants, such a fall, whether arising generally from an increased supply from the mines, or partially from a demand for corn and labour in a particular country, can scarcely fail to encourage the outlay of more capital in agriculture, to increase the power of cultivating poorer lands, and to advance rents.

In speaking, however, of the advantages sometimes derived from a fall in the value of money, it should always be recollected, that if it goes to a greater extent than can be permanently maintained—an event very likely to take place, it will surely be followed by a retrograde movement, which, though it may not undo all the effects of the previous encouragement given to production, in reference to the general wealth of the country, will be felt by all the parties concerned, landlords, capitalists, and labourers, as so painful a reverse that they may well wish that they had not been subjected to the stimulus. Still, however, it is proper to consider the effects of such a stimulus during the time it lasts.

Whenever then, by the operation of the four causes above mentioned, the difference between the price of produce and the cost of the instruments of production increases, the rents of land will rise.

It is, however, not necessary that all these four causes should operate at the same time; it is only necessary that the difference here mentioned should increase. If, for instance, the price of produce were to rise, while the money wages of labour and the price of the other branches of capital did not rise in proportion,* and at the same time improved modes of agriculture were coming into general use, it is evident that this difference might be increased, although the profits of agricultural stock were not only undiminished, but were to rise decidedly higher.

Of the great additional quantity of capital employed upon the land in this country during the twenty years, from 1793 to 1813, by far the greater part is supposed to have been generated on the soil, and not to have been brought from commerce or manufactures. And it was unquestionably the high profits of agricultural stock, occasioned by improvements in the modes of agriculture, and by the constant rise of prices, followed only slowly by a proportionate rise in the materials of the farmer's capital, that afforded the means of so rapid and so advantageous an accumulation.

In this case, cultivation was extended, and rents rose, although one of the instruments of production, capital, was dearer.

In the same manner a fall of profits, and improvements in agriculture, or even the latter separately, might raise rents, notwithstanding a rise of corn wages.

It is further evident, that no fresh land can be taken into cultivation till rents have risen, or would allow of a rise upon what is already cultivated.

Land of an inferior quality requires a greater advance of labour and capital to make it yield a given produce; and if the actual price of this produce be not such as fully to compensate the cost of produc-

* This would in fact be a fall in the corn wages of labour, though it might be made up to the labourer by the comparative cheapness of some other articles, and more constant employment for all the members of his family.

tion, including profits, the land must remain uncultivated. It matters not, whether this compensation is effected by an increase in the money price of raw produce, without a proportionate increase in the money price of the instruments of production; or by a decrease in the price of the instruments of production, without a proportionate decrease in the price of produce. What is absolutely necessary is, a greater *relative* cheapness of the instruments of production, to make up for the quantity of them required to obtain a given produce from poor land.

But whenever, by the operation of one or more of the causes before mentioned, the instruments of production become relatively cheaper, and the difference between the price of produce and the expenses of cultivation increases, rents naturally rise. It follows therefore as a direct and necessary consequence, that it can never answer to take fresh land of a poorer quality into cultivation till rents have risen, or would allow of a rise, on what is already cultivated.

It is equally true, that without the same tendency to a rise of rents,* it cannot answer to lay out fresh capital in the improvement of old land; at least upon the supposition, that each farm is already furnished with as much capital as can be laid out to advantage, according to the actual rate of profits.

It is only necessary to state this proposition to make its truth appear. It certainly may happen, (and I fear it happens very frequently) that farmers are not provided with all the capital which could be employed upon their farms at the actual rate of agricultural profits. But supposing they are so provided, it implies distinctly, that more could not be applied without loss, till, by the operation of one or more of the causes above enumerated, rents had tended to rise.

It appears then, that the power of extending culti-

* Rents may be said to have a tendency to rise, when more capital is ready to be laid out upon the old land, but cannot be laid out without diminished returns. When profits fall in manufactures and commerce from the diminished price of goods, capitalists will be ready to give higher rents for old farms.

vation and increasing produce, both by the cultivation of fresh land and the improvement of the old, depends entirely upon the existence of such prices, compared with the expense of production, as would raise rents in the actual state of cultivation.

But though cultivation cannot be extended and the produce of a country increased, except in such a state of things as would allow of a rise of rents ;* yet it is of importance to remark, that this rise of rents will not necessarily be *in proportion* to the extension of cultivation or to the increase of produce.

A slight rise in the value of corn may allow of the employment of a considerable quantity of additional capital ; and when either new land is taken into cultivation, or the old improved, the increase of produce is often greater than the increase of rents. We frequently see in consequence, that, in the progress of a country towards a high state of cultivation, the quantity of capital employed upon the land, and the quantity of produce yielded by it, bears an increasing proportion to the amount of rents, unless counterbalanced by extraordinary improvements in the modes of cultivation.†

In the early state of cultivation upon the Metayer system, with small capitals, the proportion of the produce which went to the landlord was generally one half. Even in the United States, where profits and

* This, it must be recollected, is upon the supposition above adverted to, that the farmer has had the means and the will to employ all the capital, both fixed and circulating, which can be applied at the actual rate of profits.

† To the honour of Scotch cultivators it should be observed, that they have applied their capitals so very skilfully and economically, that at the same time that they have prodigiously increased the produce, they have increased the landlord's proportion of it. The difference between the landlord's share of the produce in Scotland and in England is quite extraordinary—greater than can be accounted for by the absence of tithes and poor's-rates. It must be referred therefore to superior skill and economy, and improvements in cultivation.—See Sir John Sinclair's valuable Account of the Husbandry of Scotland ; and the General Report, published in 1813 and 14—works replete with the most useful and interesting information on agricultural subjects.

corn wages have been such as would allow of a large transfer to the landlords, produce seems to have increased faster than rents. And according to the returns made to the board of agriculture in 1813, the average proportion which rent bears to the value of the whole produce seems to be little more than one-fifth;* whereas formerly, when there was more land in pasture, less capital employed, and less produce obtained, the proportion amounted to one-fourth, one-third, or even two-fifths.† Still, however, the numerical difference between the price of produce and the expenses of cultivation increases with the progress of improvement; and though the landlord may have a less *share* of the whole produce, yet this less share from the great increase of the produce, owing to the conversion of natural pastures into arable land, will command more labour, and consequently be of greater value to him. If the produce of land be represented by the number six, and the landlord has one-fourth of it, his share will be represented by one and a half. If the produce of land be as ten, and the landlord has

* See Evidence before the House of Lords, given by Arthur Young, in the Report respecting the corn laws, 1814, p. 66.

† In that state of things where land is in great abundance, and rents very low, the capital, and particularly the fixed capital employed, is generally very inconsiderable. Mr. Ricardo, in illustrating his doctrine of rent, has supposed a capital of £3000 employed with low corn wages to obtain a produce worth £720, before the commencement of rent. But this is so directly contrary to the real state of things before rent has commenced, as to destroy all just illustration. In the present advanced state of cultivation under a large mass of rents, a capital of £1000 is considered as adequate to obtain the above value of produce. It was the very disproportionate amount of capital, with the low corn wages assumed, which enabled Mr. Ricardo to contemplate an extraordinary rise of rents, occasioned exclusively by a transfer from profits. This apparent result was further assisted by the adoption of a money as his measure of value, which, (as I have already shown, p. 124-125) must necessarily vary with the commodity which it was to measure. When all labour, all raw products, and many manufactured products had risen in his money, he still supposed his money to remain of the same value, whereas it had in fact fallen in value from the fall of profits, without which fall the appearances he contemplates could not possibly take place.

one-fifth of it, his share will be represented by two. In the latter case, therefore, though the proportion of the landlord's share to the whole produce is greatly diminished, the value of his rent, independent of nominal price, will be increased in the proportion of from three to four.

We see then that a progressive rise of rents seems to be necessarily connected with the progressive cultivation of new land, and the progressive improvement of the old: and that this rise is the natural and necessary consequence of the operation of four causes, which are the most certain indications of increasing prosperity and wealth—namely, the accumulation of capital, the increase of population, improvements in agriculture, and a rising market price of raw produce, occasioned either by a great demand for it in foreign countries, or by the extension of commerce and manufactures.

SECTION IV.—*Of the Causes which tend to lower Rents.*

THE causes which lead to a fall of rents are, as may be expected, exactly of an opposite description to those which lead to a rise: namely, diminished capital, diminished population, an operose system of cultivation, and a falling price of raw produce from deficiency of demand. They are almost always* indications of poverty and decline, and are necessarily connected with the throwing of inferior land out of cultivation, and the continued deterioration of the land of a superior quality.

The necessary effects of a diminished capital and diminished population in lowering rents, are too obvious to require explanation; nor is it less clear that an operose and bad system of cultivation might prevent the formation of rents, even on fertile land, by checking the progress of population and demand beyond what could be supplied from the very richest

* The only practical exception is in the case of importing foreign corn, the effects of which will be considered more particularly in the next section, and a subsequent part of this chapter.

qualities of soil. I will only therefore advert to the fourth cause here noticed.

We have seen that a rise in the price of corn, terminating in a diminished value of the precious metals, would give a considerable stimulus to cultivation for a certain time, and some facilities permanently, and might occasion a considerable and permanent rise of rents. And this case was exemplified by what happened in this country during the period from 1794 to 1814.

It may be stated in like manner, that a fall in the price of corn terminating in a rise in the value of money, must, upon the same principles, tend to throw land out of cultivation and lower rents. And this may be exemplified by what happened in this country at the conclusion of the war. The fall in the price of corn at that period necessarily disabled the cultivators from employing the same quantity of labour on their land. Many labourers, therefore, were unavoidably thrown out of employment; and, as the land could not be cultivated in the same way, without the same number of hands, some of the worst soils were no longer worked, much agricultural capital was destroyed, and rents universally fell; while this great failure in the power of purchasing, among all those who either rented or possessed land, naturally occasioned a general stagnation in all other trades. But the fall in the money price of labour* from the competition of the labourers, and the poverty of the cultivators; together with the fall of rents, from the want of power to pay the former rents, would tend to restore the former relations of produce, wages, and rents to each other, though

* This is an instance of the incidental causes of the high or low value of money prevailing over the necessary cause just in an opposite direction to that noticed in the last section. Profits unquestionably fell after the war, and the value of money ought to have fallen, and the money price of labour to have risen; but the rise in the value of money, owing to the slackness of the circulation, the withdrawing of much paper, and the comparative want of demand for corn and labour, combined with the diminished money value of our exported commodities, quite overcame the natural effects of the fall of profits, and occasioned a decided rise in the value of money.

they would all be lower in price than they were before. The land which had been thrown out of tillage might then again be cultivated with advantage ; but in the progress from the lower to the higher value of money, a period would have elapsed of diminished produce, diminished capital, and diminished rents. The country would recommence a progressive movement from an impoverished state; and, owing to a fall in the value of corn greater than in taxed commodities, in foreign commodities, and in others which form a part of the capital of the farmer and of the necessaries and conveniences of the labourer, the permanent difficulties of cultivation would be great compared with the natural fertility of the worst soil actually in tillage.

It has appeared that, in the progress of cultivation and of increasing rents, it is not necessary that all the causes which tend to advance rents should operate at the same time; and that the difference between the price of produce and the expense of cultivation might increase, although either the profits of stock or the wages of labour might be higher, instead of lower.

In the same manner, when the produce of a country is declining from a diminution of demand, and rents in consequence falling, it is not necessary that all the causes which tend to lower rents should be in action. In the natural progress of such a decline, the profits of stock must be low ; because it is specifically the want of adequate returns which occasions this decline. After some capital has been destroyed, money wages will fall ; but the low price of raw produce may more than counterbalance the low money wages of labour, and prevent the profitable cultivation of land where much capital is required.

It has appeared also, that in the progress of cultivation, and of increasing rents, if not accompanied by very decided agricultural improvements, rent, though greater in positive amount, often bears a less proportion to the quantity of capital employed upon the land, and the quantity of produce derived from it. According to the same principle, when produce diminishes and rents fall, though the amount of rent will be less, the proportion which it bears to capital and produce may be greater. And as, in the former case, the diminished proportion of rent was owing to the necessity of yearly taking fresh land, consisting of rough pasture and wood, into cultivation, and proceeding in the improvement of old land, when it would return only the common profits of stock, with little or no rent; so, in the latter case, the higher proportion of rent is owing to the discouragement of a great expenditure in agriculture, and the necessity of employing the reduced capital of the country in the exclusive cultivation of the richest lands, and leaving the remainder to yield what rent can be got for them in natural pasture, which, though small, will bear a large *proportion* to the labour and other capital employed. In proportion, therefore, as the relative state of prices is such as to occasion a progressive fall of rents, more and more land will be gradually thrown out of cultivation, the remainder will be worse cultivated, and the diminution of produce will generally proceed still faster than the diminution of rents.*

If the doctrine here laid down respecting the laws which govern the rise and fall of rents be near the truth, the doctrine which maintains that, if the produce of agriculture were sold at such a price as to yield less neat surplus, agriculture would be equally productive to the general stock, must be very far from the truth. And if, under the impression that the ordinary excess of the price of raw produce above the costs of production which occasions rent on the great mass of land is as injurious to the consumer as it is advantageous to the landlord, a rich and improved nation were determined by law to lower the price of its produce, till no surplus in the shape of rent any where remained, it would inevitably throw not only all the poor land, but all except the very best land, out of cultivation, and probably reduce its produce and population to less than one-tenth of their former amount.

* It should be recollected, however, that both the results here contemplated will be essentially affected by taxes which fall on the land.

SECTION V.—*On the Dependance of the actual Quantity of Produce obtained from the Land, upon the existing Prices of Produce, and existing Rents, under the same Agricultural Skill and the same Value of Money.*

FROM the preceding account of the progress of rent, it follows that the actual amount of the natural rent of land in the actual state of agricultural skill, is, with very little drawback, necessary to the actual produce; and that the price of corn in every progressive country, must be just about equal to the cost of production on land of the poorest quality actually in use, with the addition of the rent it would yield in its natural state; or to the cost of raising additional produce on old land, which additional produce yields only the usual returns of agricultural capital with no rent.

It is quite obvious that under the existing value of money, the price cannot be less;* or such land would not be cultivated, nor such capital employed. Nor can it ever much exceed this price, because it will always answer to the landlord to continue letting poorer and poorer lands, as long as he can get any thing more than they will pay in their natural state;

* The reader will be aware from what was said in the last chapter, that, though in speaking of the relation between the price of the produce and its money cost at any given time, money is always a correct measure; yet that in speaking of the price of the produce without such reference, it is necessary that the existing value of money should be expressed, or understood; and I trust that the reader will allow of the latter, when the meaning is clear from the context. As I measure the value of money by labour, the price of the produce under the existing value of money is exactly equivalent to the expression *value* of the produce. In reality it may be said, that in the natural and ordinary state of things, it is the actual *value of the produce*, or its actual power of commanding labour, which is necessary to the supply of the actual produce. In these cases it might be better at once to use the term value instead of price; but I fear it would not yet be so readily understood.

and because it will always answer to any farmer who can command capital, to lay it out on his land, if the additional produce resulting from it will fully repay the profits of his capital, although it yields nothing to his landlord.

It follows then, that corn, in a cultivated and improving country, is sold nearly at its necessary price, that is, at the price necessary to obtain the actual amount of produce if no rents were paid; although by far the largest part is sold at a price much above that which is neccessary to its production without rent, owing to this part being produced at less expense, while its price remains undiminished.

The difference between the price of corn and the price of manufactures, with regard to natural or necessary price, is this; that if the price of any manufacture were essentially depressed, the whole manufacture would be entirely destroyed; whereas, if the price of corn were equally depressed, the *quantity* of it only would be diminished. There would be some machinery in the country still capable of sending the commodity to market at the reduced price.

The earth has been sometimes compared to a vast machine, presented by nature to man for the production of food and raw materials; but, to make the resemblance more just, as far as they admit of comparison, we should consider the soil as a present to man of a great number of machines, all susceptible of continued improvement by the application of capital to them, but yet of very different original qualities and powers.

This great inequality in the powers of the machinery employed in obtaining raw produce, forms the most remakable feature which distinguishes the machinery of the land from the machinery employed in manufactures.

When a machine in manufactures is invented, which will produce more finished work with less expenditure than before, if there be no patent, or as soon as the patent has expired, a sufficient number of such machines may be made to supply the whole demand, and to supersede entirely the use of all the old machinery. The natural consequence is, that the price is reduced to the price of production from the best machinery, and if the price were to be depressed lower, the whole of the commodity would be withdrawn from the market.

The machines which produce corn and raw materials, on the contrary, are the gifts of nature, not the works of man; and we find, by experience, that these gifts have very different qualities and powers. The most fertile and best situated lands of a country, those which, like the best machinery in manufactures, yield the greatest products with the least expenditure, are never found sufficient, owing to the second main cause of rent before stated, to supply the effectual demand of an increasing population. The price of raw produce, therefore, naturally increases till it answers to pay the cost of raising it with inferior machines, and by a more expensive process; and, as there cannot be two prices for corn of the same quality, all the other machines, the working of which requires less expenditure compared with the produce, must yield rents in proportion to their goodness.

Every extensive country may thus be considered as possessing a gradation of machines for the production of corn and raw materials, including in this gradation not only all the various qualities of poor land, of which every large territory has generally an abundance, but the inferior machinery which may be said to be employed when good land is further and further forced for additional produce. As the price of raw produce continues to rise, these inferior machines are successively called into action; and as the price of raw produce continues to fall, they are successively thrown out of action. The illustration here used serves to show at once the necessity of the existing price of corn to the existing produce, in the actual state of most of the countries with which we are acquainted, and the different effect which would attend a great reduction in the price of any particular manufacture, and a great reduction in the price of raw produce.

We must not, however, draw too large inferences from this gradation of machinery on the land. It is what actually exists in almost all countries, and accounts very clearly for the origin and progress of rent, while land still remains in considerable plenty. But such a gradation is not strictly necessary, either to the original formation, or the subsequent regular rise of rents. All that is necessary to produce these effects, is, the existence of the two first causes of rent formerly mentioned, with the addition of limited territory, or a scarcity of fertile land.

Whatever may be the qualities of any commodity, it is well known that it can have no exchangeable value, if it exists in a great excess above the wants of those who are to use it. But such are the qualities of the necessaries of life that, in a limited territory, and under ordinary circumstances, they cannot if properly distributed be permanently in excess; and if all the land of this country were precisely equal in quality, and all as rich, as the best, there cannot be the slightest doubt, that after the whole of the land had been taken into cultivation, both the profits of stock, and the real wages of labour, would go on diminishing till profits had been reduced to what was necessary to keep up the actual capital, and the wages to what was necessary to keep up the actual population, while the rents would be high, just in proportion to the fertility of the soil natural or acquired, and the mass of rents very much greater than at present.

Nor would the effect be essentially different, if the capital which could be employed with advantage upon such fertile soil were extremely limited, so that no further outlay were required for it than what was wanted for ploughing and sowing. Still there can be no doubt that capital and population might go on increasing in other employments, till both the profits of capital and the wages of labour had so fallen as to come nearly to a stand, and rents had reached the limits prescribed by the powers of the soil, and the habits of the people.

In these cases it is obvious that the rents are not regulated by the gradations of the soil, or the different products of capital on the same land; and that it is an incorrect inference from the theory of rent to conclude with Mr. Ricardo, that "It is only because land is of different qualities with respect to its productive powers, and because in the progress of population, land of an inferior quality, or less advantageously situated, is called into cultivation, that rent is ever paid for the use of it." *

There is another inference which has been drawn from the theory of rent, which involves an error of much greater importance, and should therefore be very carefully guarded against.

In the progress of cultivation, as poorer and poorer land is taken into tillage, without improvements in agriculture, the rate of *profits* must be limited in amount by the powers of the soil last cultivated, as will be shewn more fully in a subsequent chapter. It has been inferred from this, that when land is successively thrown out of cultivation, the rate of profits will be high in proportion to the superior natural fertility of the land which will then be the least fertile in cultivation.

If land yielded no rent whatever in its natural state, whether it were poor or fertile, then the whole produce being divided between profits and wages, and the corn wages of labour being supposed to

* Principles of Political Economy, ch. ii. p. 54. This passage was taken from the first edition. It is altered in the second and third; but not sufficiently to make it true. In the third, (p. 56) the passage is as follows: "It is only then because land is not unlimited in quantity and uniform in quality, and because in the progress of population land of an inferior quality, or less advantageously situated, is called into cultivation, that rent is ever paid for the use of it." Now it is quite obvious, as stated above, that if land as fertile as the best were merely limited in quantity, without being different in quality, it would, in the progress of population, yield altogether a much higher rent than the same quantity of land would with gradations of soil.

remain nearly the same, the inference would be just. But the premises are not such as are here supposed. In a civilized and appropriated country uncultivated land always yields a rent in proportion to its natural power of feeding cattle or growing wood; and of course, when land has been thrown out of tillage, particularly if this has been occasioned by the importation of cheaper corn from other countries, and consequently without a diminution of population, the last land so thrown out may yield a moderate rent in pasture, though considerably less than before. As was said in the preceding section, rent will diminish, but probably not so much in proportion either as the capital employed on the land, or the produce derived from it. No landlord will allow his land to be cultivated by a tillage farmer paying little or no rent, when by laying it down to pasture, and saving much yearly expenditure of capital upon it, he can obtain a greater rent. Consequently, as the produce of the worst lands actually cultivated can never be wholly divided between profits and wages, the state of such land or its degree of fertility cannot regulate the rate of profits upon it.

If to the effect of the cause here noticed we add its natural consequence, viz. a rise in the value of money, and a greater fall of corn than of foreign commodities, taxed commodities and probably of labour and working cattle, it is obvious that permanent difficulties may be thrown in the way of cultivation, and that richer land may not yield superior profits. The higher rent paid for the last land employed in tillage, together with the greater expense of the materials of capital compared with the price of produce, may fully counterbalance, or even more than counterbalance, the difference of natural fertility.

With regard to the capital which the tenant may lay out on his farm in obtaining more produce without paying additional rent for it, the rate of its returns must obviously conform itself to the general rate of profits determined by other causes. It must always follow, but can never lead or regulate. It is true that when the price of corn had settled itself, there would be some corn produced on the old cultivated land, the cost of producing which without rent would be just about equal to such price. But it is quite certain that if instead of laying out so much additional capital on the lands in tillage, the capitalists could have obtained the untilled land without rents, the price of corn would not have risen so high, or have required so much labour and other capital to produce the actual quantity; and consequently the rents of such lands clearly add to the price of corn, and form a part of the costs of production.

It should be added, that in the regular progress of a country towards general cultivation and improvement, and in a natural state of things, it may fairly be presumed, that if the last land taken into cultivation be rich, capital is scarce, and profits will then certainly be high; but if land be thrown out of cultivation on account of means being found of obtaining corn cheaper elsewhere, no such inference is justifiable. On the contrary, capital may be abundant, compared with the demand for corn and commodities, in which case and during the time that such abundance lasts, whatever may be the state of the land, profits must be low. These are all points of great practical consequence which have been much overlooked. The doctrine of the gradations of soils is a most important one, but in drawing practical conclusions from it, great care should be taken to apply it correctly.

It will be observed, that the rents paid for what the land will produce in its natural state, though they make a difference in the questions relating to profits and the component parts of price, do not invalidate the important doctrine that, in countries in their usual state with gradations of soil, corn is sold nearly at its natural or necessary price, that is, at the price necessary to bring the actual quantity to market. This price must on an average be at the least equal to the costs of its production on the worst land actually cultivated, together with the rent of such land in its natural state: because, if it falls in any degree below this, the cultivator of such land will not be able to pay the landlord so high a rent as he could obtain from the land without cultivation, and consequently the land will be left uncultivated, and the produce will be diminished. In progressive countries, however, this rent is trifling, and the price of corn is little more than is necessary to pay the wages of the labour and the profits of the capital required to obtain it. But in the case of land being thrown out of cultivation under an abundance of capital and labour, the rent of the worst land cultivated for corn might by no means be trifling. Still however the actual price of the corn under the same value of money would be necessary to obtain the actual home supply, because if the farmers paid no rents, it would not answer to them to produce corn which would not yield so profitable a return as the products of rough pasture, or land in copse wood, or plantations.

I hope to be excused for presenting to the reader in various forms the doctrine, that corn, in reference to the quantity actually produced is sold at nearly its necessary price, like manufactures; because I consider it as a truth of high importance, which has been entirely overlooked by the Economists, by Adam Smith, and by all those writers who have represented raw produce as selling always at a monopoly price.

Section VI.—*Of the Connexion between great comparative Wealth, and a high comparative Price of raw Produce.*

Adam Smith has very clearly explained in what manner the progress of wealth and improvement tends to raise the price of cattle, poultry, the materials of clothing and lodging, the most useful minerals, &c. compared with corn; but he has not entered into the explanation of the natural causes which tend to determine the price of corn. He has left the reader indeed to conclude, that he considers the price of corn as determined only by the state of the mines, which at the time supply the circulating medium of the commercial world.* But this is a cause, which, though it may account for the high or low price of corn in reference to the whole of the commercial world, cannot account for the differences in its price, in different countries, or as compared with certain classes of commodities in the same country.

I entirely agree with Adam Smith, that it is of great use to inquire into the causes of high price, as from the result of such inquiries it may turn out, that the very circumstance of which we complain, may be the necessary consequence and the most certain sign of increasing wealth and prosperity. But of all inquiries of this kind, none surely can be so important, or so generally interesting, as an inquiry into the causes which affect the price of corn, and occasion the differences in this price so observable in different countries.

The two principal causes of these effects are—

1. A difference in the value of the precious metals in different countries, in whatever way such difference may have arisen.

2. A difference in the elementary cost of producing a given quantity of corn.

The principal causes of the differences in the value of money in different countries have been already stated, in the last section of the preceding chapter; and it is certain that they occasion the greatest portion of that inequality in the price of corn which is the most striking and prominent. More than three-fourths of the prodigious difference between the price of corn in Bengal and England is occasioned by the difference in the value of money in the two countries; and far the greater part of the high price of

* B. I. ch. v. p. 53, 6th ed.

corn in this country, compared with its price in most of the states of Europe, is occasioned in the same way. If the profits of stock in Flanders be nearly the same as in England (which I believe is the case), and the corn wages of labour rather lower than higher, it follows necessarily that the elementary cost of producing corn is nearly the same in both countries, and that the higher money price of corn in England is occasioned by the lower value of money, and not by the increased quantity of labour and other conditions of supply required to produce corn.

The second cause of the high comparative price of corn is the greater elementary cost of its production. If we could suppose the value of money, or the money wages of standard labour, to be the same in all countries, then the cause of the higher money price of corn in one country compared with another, would be the greater quantity of labour, and other conditions of the supply required to produce it; and the reason why the price of corn would be high and tend to rise in countries already rich, and still advancing in prosperity and population, would be to be found in the necessity of resorting to poorer land, without proportional improvements in agriculture, that is, to machines which would require a greater expenditure to work them; and which consequently occasion each fresh addition to the raw produce of the country to be purchased at a greater cost—in short it would be found in the important truth that corn in a progressive country is sold at the price necessary to yield the actual supply, and that as this supply becomes more difficult the price must rise in proportion. On the supposition which we have made of the value of money being the same in different countries, the price of corn would rise without being followed by a rise in the money price of labour.

The prices of corn in different countries, as determined by the two causes above mentioned, must of course be affected by every circumstance in each country that affects either the value of money, or the elementary cost of producing corn, such as the prosperity of foreign commerce, improvements in the modes of cultivation; the saving of labour on the land, direct and indirect taxation; and particularly the importations of foreign corn. The latter cause, indeed, may do away, in a considerable degree, the usual effects of great wealth on the price of corn; and this wealth will then shew itself in a different form.

Let us suppose seven or eight large countries not very distant from each other, and not very differently situated with regard to the mines; and further, that neither their soils nor their skill in agriculture are essentially unlike; that there are no taxes; and that every trade is free, except the trade in corn. Let us now suppose one of them very greatly to increase in capital and manufacturing skill above the rest, and to become much more rich and populous without increased skill in agriculture. I should say, that this comparative increase of riches could not take place, without a comparative increase in the prices of corn and labour; and that such increase of prices would, under the circumstances supposed, be the natural sign and necessary consequence, of the increased wealth and population of the country in question.

Let us now suppose the same countries to have the most perfect freedom of intercourse in corn, and the expenses of freight, &c. to be quite inconsiderable: And let us still suppose one of them to increase very greatly above the rest, in manufacturing capital and skill, in wealth and population: I should then say, that as the importation of corn would prevent any great difference in the prices of corn and labour, it would prevent any great difference in the amount of capital laid out upon the land, and the quantity of corn obtained from it; that consequently, the great increase of wealth could not take place without a great importation of corn from other nations; and that this importation, under the circumstances supposed, would be the natural sign and necessary consequence of the increased wealth and population of the country in question.

These I consider as the two alternatives necessarily belonging to a great comparative increase of wealth; and the supposition here made will, with proper allowances, apply to the general state of Europe.

In most countries the expenses attending the carriage of corn are considerable. They form a natural barrier to importation; and even the country, which habitually depends upon foreign corn, must have the price of its food higher than the general level. Practically, also, the prices of raw produce in the different countries of Europe are variously modified by different soils, different degrees of taxation, and different degrees of improvement in the science of agriculture. But the principles laid down are the general principles on the subject; and in applying them to any particular case, the particular circumstances of such case must always be taken into the consideration.

With regard to improvements in agriculture, which in similar soils is the great cause which retards the advance of price under an increase of produce; although they are sometimes most powerful, and of very considerable duration, we know from experience that they have not been sufficient to balance the effects of applying to poorer land, or inferior machines. Corn is obtained with less labour in the United States of America than in any European country. In this respect, raw produce is essentially different from manufactures.

The elementary cost of manufactures, or the quantity of labour and other conditions of the supply necessary to produce a given quantity of them, has a constant tendency to diminish; while the quantity of labour and other conditions of the supply necessary to procure the last addition which has been made to the raw produce of a rich and advancing country, has a constant tendency to increase.

We see in consequence, from the combined operation of the two causes, which have been stated in this section, that in spite of continued improvements in agriculture, the price of corn is generally the highest in the richest countries; while notwithstanding the high prices of corn and labour, the prices of many manufactures still continue lower than in poorer countries.

I cannot then agree with Adam Smith, in thinking that the low value of gold and silver is no proof of the wealth and flourishing state of the country where it takes place. Nothing of course can be inferred from it, taken absolutely, as such high price may depend merely upon the abundance of the mines; but taken relatively to other commodities and in comparison with the state of other countries at no great distance, and connected with each other, much may be inferred from it. If we are to estimate the value of the precious metals in different countries by the measure which he has himself proposed, it appears to me that whether we consider the first or second cause which has been referred to in this section, there are few more certain signs of wealth than the high average price of raw produce. If the value of money were the same in all countries, then, independently of importation and improvements in agriculture, the wealth and population of similar countries, though not the condition of the labouring classes, would be proportioned to the high price of their corn. And in the actual state of things, with great differences in the value of money, arising from the incidental causes above noticed, as those countries not possessed of mines where the money prices of corn and labour are high must have had very flourishing manufactures, or an abundance of raw products fitted for exportation, such countries will generally be found either rich, or in the way rapidly to become rich.

It is of importance to ascertain this point; that we may not complain of one of the most certain proofs of the prosperous condition of a country.

Section VII.—*On the causes which may mislead the Landlord in letting his Lands, to the Injury both of himself and the Country.*

In the progress of a country towards a high state of improvement, the positive wealth of the landlord ought, upon the principles which have been laid down, gradually to increase; although his relative condition and influence in society will probably rather diminish, owing to the increasing number and wealth of those who live upon the profits of capital.

The progressive fall, with few exceptions,* in the value of the precious metals throughout Europe; the still greater fall, which has occurred in the richest countries, together with the increase of produce which has been obtained from the soil, must all conduce to make the landlord expect an increase of rents on the renewal of his leases. But, in re-letting his farms, he is liable to fall into two errors, which are almost equally prejudicial to his own interests, and to those of his country.

In the first place, he may be induced, by the immediate prospect of an exorbitant rent, offered by farmers bidding against each other, to let his land to a tenant without sufficient capital to cultivate it in the best way, and make the necessary improvements upon it. This is undoubtedly a most short-sighted policy, the bad effects of which have been strongly noticed by the most intelligent land-surveyors in the evidence brought before Parliament; and have been particularly remarkable in Ireland, where the imprudence of the landlords in this respect, combined perhaps with some real difficulty in finding substantial tenants, has aggravated the discontents of the country, and thrown the most serious obstacles in the way of an improved system of cultivation. The conse-

* Among these exceptions, the period since the war of the French revolution forms an important one.

quence of this error is the certain loss of all that future source of rent to the landlord, and wealth to the country, which arises from the good farming of substantial tenants.

The second error to which the landlord is liable, is that of mistaking a mere temporary rise of prices, for a rise of sufficient duration to warrant an increase of rents. It frequently happens that a scarcity of one or two years, or an unusual demand arising from any other cause, may raise the price of raw produce to a height at which it cannot be maintained. And the farmers, who take land under the influence of such prices, will, on the return of a more natural state of things, probably fail, and leave their farms in a ruined and exhausted state. These short periods of high price are of great importance in generating capital upon the land, if the farmers are allowed to have the advantage of them; but if they are grasped at prematurely by the landlord, capital is destroyed instead of being accumulated; and both the landlord and the country incur a loss, instead of gaining a benefit.

Some delay also is desirable in raising rents, even when the rise of prices seems as if it would be permanent. In the progress of prices and rents, rent ought always to be a little behind; not only to afford the means of ascertaining whether the rise be temporary or permanent, but even in the latter case, to give a little time for the accumulation of capital on the land, of which the landholder is sure to feel the full benefit in the end.

There is no just reason to believe, that if, in the present state of this country, the landlords were to give the whole of their rents to their tenants, corn would be in any marked degree cheaper. If the view of the subject, taken in the preceding inquiry, be correct, the last additions made to our home produce are sold at nearly the cost of production, and independent of agricultural improvements the same quantity could not be produced from our own soil at an essentially less price, even without rent, supposing the value of money to remain the same. The effect of transferring all rents to tenants, would be merely the turning them into landlords, and tempting them to cultivate their farms under the superintendence of careless and uninterested bailiffs, instead of the vigilant eye of a master, who is deterred from carelessness by the fear of ruin, and stimulated to exertion by the hope of a competence. The most numerous instances of successful industry, and well-directed knowledge, have been found among those who have paid a fair rent for their lands; who have embarked the whole of their capital in their undertaking; and who feel it their duty to watch over it with unceasing care, and add to it whenever it is possible.

But when this laudable spirit prevails among a tenantry, it is of the very utmost importance to the progress of riches, and the permanent increase of rents, that there should be the power as well as the will to accumulate; and an interval of advancing prices, not immediately followed by a proportionate rise of rents, furnishes the most effective power of this kind. These intervals of advancing prices, when not succeeded by retrograde movements, most effectually contribute to the progress of national wealth. And practically I should say, that when once a character of industry and economy has been established, temporary high profits are a more frequent and powerful source of accumulation than any other cause that can be named.* It is the only cause which seems capable of accounting for the prodigious accumulation among individuals, which must have taken place in this country during the last war, and which left us with a greatly increased capital, notwithstanding the vast annual destruction of stock for so long a period.

* Adam Smith notices the bad effects of high profits on the habits of the capitalist. They may perhaps sometimes occasion extravagance; but generally, I should say, that extravagant habits were a more frequent cause of a scarcity of capital and high profits, than high profits of extravagant habits.

Among the temporary causes of high price, which may sometimes mislead the landlord, it is necessary to notice changes in the value of the currency from the issue of paper. When they are likely to be of short duration, they must be treated by the landlord in the same manner as years of unusual demand. But when they continue so long as they did at one time in this country, it is impossible for the landlord to do otherwise than regulate his rent accordingly, and take the chance of being obliged to lessen it again, on the return of the currency to its natural state.

With the cautions here noticed in letting farms, the landlord may fairly look forward to a gradual and permanent increase of rents; and in general, not only to an increase proportioned to the rise in the *price* of produce, but to the increase of its quantity occasioned by the extension of cultivation, and agricultural improvements.

If in taking rents, which are equally fair for the landlord and tenant, it is found that in successive lettings notwithstanding the increase of cultivation, they do not rise more than in proportion to the price of produce, it will generally be owing to heavy taxation.

Though it is by no means true, as stated by the Economists, that all taxes fall on the neat rents of the landlords, yet it is certainly true that they have little power of relieving themselves. It is also true that they possess a fund more disposeable, and better adapted for taxation than any other. They are in consequence more frequently taxed, both directly and indirectly. And if they pay, as they certainly do, many of the taxes which fall on the capital of the farmer and the wages of the labourer, as well as those directly imposed on themselves, they must necessarily feel it in the diminution of that portion of the whole produce, which under other circumstances would have fallen to their share.

SECTION VIII.—*On the strict and necessary Connection of the Interests of the Landlord and of the State.*

IT has been stated by Adam Smith, that the interest of the landholder is "strictly and inseparably connected with the general interest of the society:" and that whatever either promotes or obstructs the one, necessarily promotes or obstructs the other.* The theory of rent, as laid down in the present chapter, seems strongly to confirm this statement. If under any given natural resources in land, the main causes which conduce to the interest of the landholder are increase of capital, increase of population, improvements in agriculture, and an increasing demand for raw produce occasioned by the prosperity of commerce, it seems scarcely possible to consider the interests of the landlord as separated from the general interests of the society.

Yet it has been said by Mr. Ricardo that, "the interest of the landlord is always opposed to that of the consumer and the manufacturer,"† that is, to all the other orders in the state. To this opinion he has been led, very consistently, by the peculiar view he has taken of rent, which makes him state, that it is for the interest of the landlord that the cost attending the production of corn should be increased,‡ and that improvements in agriculture tend rather to lower than to raise rents.

If this view of the theory of rent were just, and it were really true, that the income of the landlord is increased by increasing the difficulty, and diminished

* Wealth of Nations, Book I. c. xi. p. 394. 6th edit.

† Mr. Ricardo in his 3rd edit. (c. xxiv. p. 399.) allows that the landlord has a *remote* interest in improvements; but still dwells without sufficient reason on the interval of injury which he sustains.

‡ Ibid.

by increasing the facility of production, the opinion would unquestionably be well founded. But if, on the contrary, the landlord's income is practically found to depend chiefly upon natural fertility of soil, improvements in agriculture, and inventions to save labour, we may still think, with Adam Smith, that the landlord's interest is not opposed to that of the country.

It is so obviously true, as to be hardly worth stating, that if the land of the greatest fertility were in such excessive plenty compared with the population, that every man might help himself to as much as he wanted, there would be no rents or landlords properly so called. It will also be readily allowed, that if in this or any other country you could suppose the soil suddenly to be made so fertile, that a tenth part of the surface, and a tenth part of the labour now employed upon it, could more than support the present population, you would for some time considerably lower rents.

But it is of no sort of use to *dwell upon*, and draw general inferences from suppositions which never can take place.

What we want to know is, whether, living as we do in a limited world, and in countries and districts still more limited, and under such physical laws relating to the produce of the soil and the increase of population as are found by experience to prevail, the interests of the landlord are generally opposed to those of the society. And in this view of the subject, the question may be settled by an appeal to the most incontrovertible principles confirmed by the most glaring facts.

Whatever fanciful suppositions we may make about sudden improvements in fertility, nothing of this kind which we have ever seen or heard of in practice, approaches to what we know of the power of population to increase up to the additional means of subsistence.

Improvements in agriculture, however considerable they may finally prove, are always found to be partial and gradual. And as, where they prevail to any extent, there is generally an effectual demand for labour, the increase of population occasioned by the increased facility of procuring food, soon overtakes the additional produce. Instead of land being thrown out of cultivation, more land is cultivated, owing to the cheapness of the instruments of cultivation, and under these circumstances rents rise instead of fall. These results appear to me to be so completely confirmed by experience, that I doubt, if a single instance in the history of Europe, or any other part of the world, can be produced, where improvements in agriculture have been *practically* found to lower rents.

I should further say, that not only have improvements in agriculture never lowered rents, but that they have been hitherto, and may be expected to be in future, the *main* source of the increase of rents, in almost all the countries with which we are acquainted.*

It is a fundamental part of the theory which has been explained in this chapter, that, as most countries consist of a gradation of soils, rents rise as cultivation is pushed on poorer lands; but still the connexion between rent and fertility subsists in undiminished force. The rich lands are those which yield the mass of rents, not the poor ones. The poor lands are cultivated, because the increasing capital and population are calling for more produce, and if there were no poor soils, there would still be rents; a limited territory, however fertile, would soon be peopled; and as the demand for

* In an article of the Edinburgh Review, on Mr. Jones' Theory of Rent, the reviewer alludes to the error of Mr. Ricardo in regard to the effects of agricultural improvements on the rents of the landlords; and says, "Had Mr. Jones been the first to point out this mistake of Mr. Ricardo, and to rectify it, he would have done some little service to the science." For the *first* rectification of the mistake, a reference is made to what had been published twelve months previously to the appearance of Mr. Jones' work, in the second edition of Mr. M'Culloch's Political Economy.

Now as the reviewer was so ready to accuse Mr. Jones of not knowing what had been done by others, he should not himself have been ignorant that the mistake had been rectified in this work, not merely twelve months, but nearly twelve years before, that is, in 1820, before Mr. Ricardo's 3rd edit. came out.

corn increased compared with the supply, rents would rise.

It is evident then, that difficulty of production has no connection with increase of rent, except as, in the actual state of most countries, it is the natural consequence of an increase of capital and population, and a fall of profits and corn wages; or, in other words, of an increase of wealth.

But after all, the increase of rents which results from an increase of price occasioned solely by the greater quantity of labour and other conditions of supply, necessary to produce a given quantity of corn on fresh land, is very much more limited than has been supposed; and by a reference to most of the countries with which we are acquainted, it will be seen that, practically, improvements in agriculture and the saving of labour on the land, both have been, and may be expected in future to be, a very much more powerful source of increasing rents.

It has already been shown, that for the very great increase of rents which has taken place in this country during nearly the last hundred years, we are mainly indebted to improvements in agriculture, as profits have rather risen than fallen, and little or nothing has been taken from the wages of families, if we include parish allowances, and the earnings of women and children. Consequently these rents must have been a creation from the skill and capital employed upon the land, and not a transfer from profits and wages, as they existed nearly a hundred years ago.

The peculiar increase of rents, which has taken place in Scotland during the last half century, is well known to have been occasioned by improvements in agriculture, a greater expenditure in manure, a better rotation of crops, and the saving of labour on the land.

In Ireland, neither the wages of the individual labourer, nor the profits of agricultural capital, seem as if they could admit of any considerable reduction; but there can be no doubt that a great augmentation of rents might be effected by an improved system of cultivation, and a prosperous commerce, which, at the same time that it would sweep into flourishing cities the idlers which are now only half employed upon the land, would occasion an increasing demand for the products of agriculture, while the rates of profits and wages might remain as high as before.

Similar observations may be made with regard to Poland, and indeed almost all the countries of Europe. There is not one in which the real wages of labour are high, and scarcely one in which the profits of agricultural capital are known to be considerable. If no improvements whatever in agriculture were to take place in these countries, and the future increase of their rents were to depend upon an increase of price occasioned solely by the increased quantity of labour necessary to produce food, I am inclined to think that the progress of their rents would be very soon stopped. The present rates of profits and wages are not such as would admit of much diminution; and without increased skill in cultivation, and especially the saving of labour on the land, it is probable that no soils *much* poorer than those which are at present in use, would pay the expense of cultivation.

Even the rich countries of India and South America are not very differently circumstanced. From all the accounts we have received of these countries, it does not appear that *agricultural* profits are high, and it is certain that wages in reference to the condition of the labourer are in general small in amount. And although rents might receive some augmentation from such profits and wages, yet I conceive that their possible increase in this way would be quite trifling, compared with what it might be under an improved system of cultivation, a prosperous commerce, and an effectual demand for a greater quantity of raw produce, even without any transfer from the labourer or cultivator.

The United States of America seem to be almost the only country with which we are acquainted where the present wages of labour and the profits of agricultural stock are sufficiently high to admit of a considerable transfer to rents without improvements in agriculture. And probably it is only when the skill and capital of an old and industrious country are employed upon a new, rich, and extensive territory, under a free government, and in a favourable situation for the export of raw produce, that this state of things can take place.

In old states, experience tells us that the wages of the individual labourer may be inconsiderable,* and the profits of the cultivator not high, while vast tracts of good land remain uncultivated. It is obvious, indeed, that an operose and ignorant system of cultivation, combined with such a faulty distribution of property as to check the progress of demand, might keep the profits of cultivation low, even in countries of the richest soil. And there is little doubt, from the very large proportion of people employed in agriculture in most unimproved territories, that this is a case which not unfrequently occurs. But in all instances of this kind, it must be allowed, that the great source of the future increase of rents will be improvements in agriculture, and the demand occasioned by a prosperous external and internal commerce, and not the increase of price occasioned by the additional quantity of labour required to produce a given quantity of corn.

If, however, in a country which continues to grow nearly its own consumption of corn, or the same proportion of that consumption, it appears that every sort of improvement which has ever been known to take place in agriculture, manufactures, or commerce, by which a country has been enriched, tends to increase rents, and every thing by which it is impoverished, tends to lower them, it must be allowed that the inte-

* If, partly from indolence, and partly from the want of demand for labour, which is the great parent of indolence in these countries, the labourer works only two or three days in the week, wages, though they may be low in reference to the condition of the labourer, may be high in reference to the outgoings of the capitalist.

rests of the landlord, and those of the state are, under the circumstances supposed, inseparable.

Mr. Ricardo, as I have before intimated, appears to take only one simple and confined view of the progress of rent. He considers it as occasioned solely by the increase of price, arising from the increased difficulty of production.* But if rents in many countries may be doubled or trebled by improvements in agriculture, while in few countries they could be raised a fourth or a fifth, and in some not a tenth, by the increase of price arising from the increased difficulty of production, must it not be acknowledged, that such a view of rent embraces only a very small part of the subject, and consequently that any general inferences from it must be utterly inapplicable to practice?

It should be further observed, in reference to improvements in agriculture, that the mode in which Mr. Ricardo estimates the increase or decrease of rents is quite peculiar; and this peculiarity in the use of his terms tends to separate his conclusions still farther from truth as enunciated in the accustomed language of political economy.

In speaking of the division of the whole produce of the land and labour of the country between the three classes of landlords, labourers, and capitalists, he has the following passage.

"It is not by the absolute quantity of produce obtained by either class, that we can correctly judge of the rate of profit, rent, and wages, but by the quantity of labour required to obtain that produce. By improvements in machinery and agriculture the whole produce may be doubled; but if wages, rent and profits be also doubled, they will bear the same proportions to one another as before. But if wages partook not of the whole of this increase; if they, instead of

* Mr. Ricardo always seems to assume, that increased difficulties thrown in the way of production will be overcome by increased price, and that the same quantity will be produced as would have been produced if no increased difficulty had occurred. But this is quite an unwarranted assumption.

being doubled, were only increased one half; if rent, instead of being doubled, were only increased three-fourths, and the remaining increase went to profit, it would, I apprehend, be correct for me to say, that rent and wages had fallen while profits had risen. For if we had an invariable standard by which to measure the value of this produce, we should find that a less value had fallen to the class of labourers and landlords, and a greater to the class of capitalists than had been given before."*

A little farther on, having stated some specific proportions, he observes, "In that case I should say, that wages and rent had fallen and profits risen, though, in consequence of the abundance of commodities, the *quantity* paid to the labourer and landlord would have increased in the proportion of 25 to 44."†

But, to estimate rent and wages by the *proportion* which they bear to the whole produce, must, in an inquiry into the nature and causes of the wealth of nations, lead to perpetual confusion and error. For what does it require us to say? We must say that the rents of the landlord have fallen and his interests have suffered, when he obtains as rent above three-fourths more of raw produce than before, and with that produce will shortly be able, according to Mr. Ricardo's own doctrines, to command three-fourths more labour. In applying this language to our own country, we must say that rents have fallen considerably during the last forty years, because, though rents have greatly increased in exchangeable value,—in the command of money, corn, labour and manufactures, it appears, by the returns to the Board of Agriculture, that they are now only a fifth of the gross produce,‡ whereas they were formerly a fourth or a third.

In reference to the price of labour, we must say that it is low in America, although we have been hitherto in the habit of considering it as very high. And

* Principles of Political Economy, ch. i. p. 49, 3rd edit.

† Id. p. 50.

‡ Reports from the Lords on the Corn Laws, p. 66.

we must call it high in Sweden; because, although the labourer only earns low money wages, and with them can obtain but few of the necessaries and conveniences of life; yet, in the division of the whole produce of a laborious cultivation on a poor soil, a larger proportion may go to labour.*

Into this unusual language Mr. Ricardo has been betrayed by the fundamental error of adopting a measure of value, which varied with the thing to be measured.

If, however, we were to use a really invariable measure, the result would be totally different from that which he has stated. Let us suppose, for instance, that a produce of 110 quarters of corn were divided into 60 quarters for the advances of labour and other capital, 40 for rent, and 10 for the farmer's profits, and that subsequently labour became doubly productive, so that the same quantity of labour and other capital produced 220 quarters instead of 110, and were divided as supposed by Mr. Ricardo, that is one half more produce awarded to the labourer, three fourths to rent, and the remainder to profits. The result would be as follows:

While the produce was 110 quarters,

The labourers had . .	60
The landlords . . .	40
The capitalists . . .	10

After the increase to 220 quarters,

The labourers would have .	90
The landlords . . .	70
The capitalists . . .	60

Now, if we measure these incomes in money of an invariable value, and with a view to simplify the cal-

* It is specifically this unusual application of common terms which has rendered Mr. Ricardo's work so difficult to be understood by many people. It requires indeed a constant and laborious effort of the mind to recollect at all times what is meant by high and low rents, and high or low wages. In other respects, it has always appeared to me that the style in which the work is written, is perfectly clear. It is never obscure, but when either the view itself is erroneous, or terms are used in an unusual sense.

culation, suppose that in the first case each quarter is worth £1, that four men are employed for the year in immediate labour, and advances equivalent in value to the wages of two men are made in accumulated labour and profits, that the capital employed is therefore £60, and that the wages of labour are 10 quarters, or £10 a year, the following will be the results on the increase of produce.

1. The price of the quarter will fall from £1 to 13*s*. 4*d*.,* £60 being the price of 90 quarters.

2. The price of the whole produce will rise from £110 to £146. 13*s*. 4*d*., this sum being the price of 220 quarters, at 13*s*. 4*d*. a quarter.

3. The money will rise from £40 to £46. 13*s*. 4*d*., this sum being the price of 70 quarters, at 13*s*. 4*d*. a quarter.

4. The rate of profits will rise from 16⅔ per cent. to 66⅔ per cent. the difference being the advance of 60 quarters with the return of 70, and of 90 with the return of 150.

5. The corn wages of labour will increase from 10 quarters to 15 quarters, 90 quarters instead of 60 being divided among the six labourers; but the price of the 90 quarters being the same as that of the 60 quarters, the value of the wages paid will remain exactly the same.

It will indeed be perfectly true that the 15 quarters of corn now paid to each labourer can be raised at a less expense of mere labour than the 10 quarters were before, and it is on this account specifically that Mr. Ricardo would say that labour had fallen; but he throws quite out of consideration the prodigious difference of profits under which the wages of the labourer are produced in the two cases considered. Now though it may be said that when the value of

* Mr. Ricardo thought that it would fall to 10*s*., because he supposes the same amount of labour and capital to yield double the amount of corn. But as according to his own supposition, 90 quarters, instead of 120, will pay the six labourers, it is obvious that the price of the quarter will only fall to 13*s*. 4*d*.: and the values of the whole produce, and of the rent vary accordingly.

commodities is made up of labour and profits, if profits be the same, their relative value will depend exclusively on the labour employed, yet it is obviously quite impossible that this should be the case, when profits are most essentially different, as in the case stated.

In the present instance the difference is between a profit of 16⅔ per cent., and 66⅔ per cent. Supposing the 60 quarters which in the first case pay the wages of 6 men to be produced with a profit of 16⅔ per cent., the quantity of labour employed to produce them would be 5.14. Supposing the 90 quarters which in the second case pay the wages of the 6 men to be produced with a profit of 66⅔ per cent., the quantity of labour employed would be 3.6. This is no doubt a very great difference; but the very great difference in the rate of profits exactly counterbalances it, and renders the *value* of the labour of 6 men for the year in both cases just the same.

The foregoing cases shew further how fundamentally erroneous it is to consider the rise of rent, when measured by an invariable standard, as depending entirely upon a rise in the price of corn, which must proportionally injure the consumer. We have here an instance of the fall of the money price of corn from £1 a quarter to 13*s*. 4*d*., while the money rent rises on the first division proposed, from £40 to £46. 13*s*. 4*d*.* But it is not consistent with the natural tendency to accumulation, and the principle of population, that such profits as 66⅔ per cent., and such wages as 15 quarters a year, should continue for any length of time; and if owing to the rapid increase of capital and population which, if the pro-

* Mr. Ricardo by his proposed division of the produce has assumed that the demand is such as to occasion the produce to be so divided; and then the results stated will follow. But in reality if the labour on the land were to become at once doubly productive, there would certainly be a glut of corn, and the division of the produce would be very different from that which he has supposed.

duce were properly distributed, would unquestionably take place, we were to suppose them gradually to return to their former rates, and the money price of corn to its former price, we should find that after an interval of great prosperity to all classes, and without any subsequent pressure upon the capitalist, the labourer, or consumer, greater than before the extraordinary improvement supposed, corn rent on the same land would have risen from 40 quarters to 160 quarters, and money rent from £40 to £160.

Now if we compare this prodigious increase of rent, occasioned by facility of production, with any increase which could have taken place owing to difficulty of production, we shall see the great superiority of the former source of rent over the latter.

The labouring classes could not probably admit of a greater reduction in their corn wages than from 10 quarters a year to 8 quarters a year, in which case if corn were estimated in money of a fixed value, the price could not rise higher than from £1 to £1. 5*s*. Nor is it probable that profits would admit of a greater reduction than from $16\frac{2}{3}$ to $6\frac{2}{3}$ before accumulation would be nearly at a stand. On these suppositions the division of the produce of 110 quarters would be as follows:—

6 labourers at 8 quarters a year .	48 qrs.
Profits upon advances of 48 quarters at $6\frac{2}{3}$ per cent.	$3\frac{1}{5}$
	$51\frac{1}{5}$

The remainder of the 110 quarters, equal to $58\frac{4}{5}$ quarters, will be corn rent; and $58\frac{4}{5}$ quarters, at £1. 5*s*., equal to £73. 10*s*., will be money rent.

It is obvious that if we had set out with a lower and more usual rate of profits and corn wages, such as profits of 10 or 9 per cent, and wages of 9 or $8\frac{1}{2}$ quarters, the increase of rent would have been comparatively trifling, and that in those countries where the wages of labour are at what Mr. Ricardo has called the natural price, that is, at such a price as is only sufficient to maintain a stationary population, no permanent rise in the price of corn or increase of rent arising solely from the reduction of profits and wages is possible.

The only doubt which can exist respecting the strictest union between the interest of the landlord, and that of the state, is in the question of importation. And here it is evident that at all events the landlord cannot be considered as placed in a more invidious situation than other producers. No person has ever doubted that if some foreign nations were to excel us in machinery, the individual interests of the actual manufacturers of woollen, silk, linen, or cotton goods, in this country might be injured by foreign competition; and few would deny that the importation of a large body of labourers would tend to reduce wages. Under the most unfavourable view therefore that we can take of the subject, the case of the landlord is not separated from that of other producers.*

And if to this we add that in a state of perfectly free intercourse, it is eminently the interest of those who live upon the rents of land that capital and population should increase, while to those who live upon the profits of stock and the wages of labour, an increase of capital and population is, to say the least of it, a much more doubtful benefit, it may be most safely asserted that the interest of no other class in the state is so nearly and necessarily connected with its wealth, prosperity, and power, as the interest of the landowner.

* Colonel Torrens concludes the second edition of his Treatise on a Free Corn Trade with the following passage: "The class of land proprietors have not any more than the capitalists and labourers an interest in imposing restrictions on the importation of foreign corn." If this be so, the identity of the interests of landlords and of the state is even more complete than I had ventured to express it.

SECTION IX.—*General Remarks on the Surplus Produce of the Land.*

IT seems rather extraordinary that the very great benefit which society derives from that surplus produce of the land which, in the progress of society, falls mainly to the landlord in the shape of rent, should not yet be fully understood and acknowledged. I have called this surplus a bountiful gift of Providence, and am most decidedly of opinion, that it fully deserves the appellation. But Mr. Ricardo has the following passage:—

"Nothing is more common than to hear of the advantages which the land possesses over every other source of useful produce, on account of the surplus which it yields in the form of rent. Yet when land is most abundant, when most productive and most fertile, it yields no rent; and it is only, when its powers decay, and less is yielded in return for labour, that a share of the original produce of the more fertile portions is set apart for rent. It is singular that this quality in the land, which should have been noticed as an imperfection, compared with the natural agents by which manufactures are assisted, should have been pointed out as constituting its peculiar pre-eminence. If air, water, the elasticity of steam, and the pressure of the atmosphere were of various qualities, if they could be appropriated, and each quality existed only in moderate abundance, they, as well as the land, would afford a rent, as the successive qualities were brought into use. With every worse quality employed, the value of the commodities in the manufacture of which they were used would rise, because equal quantities of labour would be less productive. Man would do more by the sweat of his brow, and nature perform less, and the land would be no longer pre-eminent for its limited powers."

"If the surplus produce which the land affords in

the form of rent be an advantage, it is desirable that every year the machinery newly constructed should be less efficient than the old, as that would undoubtedly give a greater exchangeable value to the goods manufactured, not only by that machinery, but by all the other machinery in the kingdom; and a rent would be paid to all those who possessed the most productive machinery."*

What has been stated in the last section, distinctly shows how very erroneous this view of the subject is; but additional considerations press upon us here. In referring to a gift of Providence, we should surely speak of its value in relation to the laws and constitution of our nature, and of the world in which we live. But, if any person will take the trouble to make the calculation, he will see that if the necessaries of life could be obtained and distributed without limit, and the number of people could be doubled every twenty-five years, the population which might have been produced from a single pair since the Christian æra, would have been sufficient, not only to fill the earth quite full of people, so that four should stand in every square yard, but to fill all the planets of our solar system in the same way, and not only them, but all the planets revolving round the stars which are visible to the naked eye, supposing each of them to be a sun, and to have as many planets belonging to it as our sun has. Under this law of population, which, excessive as it may appear when stated in this way is, I firmly believe, best suited to the nature and situation of man, it is quite obvious that some limit to the production of food, or some other of the necessaries of life, must exist. Without a total change in the constitution of human nature, and the situation of man on earth, the whole of the necessaries of life could not be furnished in the same plenty as air, water, the elasticity of steam, and the pressure of the atmosphere. It is not easy to conceive a more disastrous present—

* Princ. of Polit. Econ. ch. ii. p. 63, 3rd edit.

one more likely to plunge the human race in irrecoverable misery, than an unlimited facility of producing food in a limited space. A benevolent Creator then, knowing the wants and necessities of his creatures, under the laws to which he had subjected them, could not, in mercy, have furnished the whole of the necessaries of life in the same plenty as air and water. This shows at once the reason why the former are limited in quantity, and the latter poured out in profusion. But if it be granted, as it must be, that a limitation in the power of producing food is obviously necessary to man confined to a limited space, then the value of the actual quantity of land which he has received, depends upon the small quantity of labour necessary to work it, compared with the number of persons which it will support; or, in other words, upon that specific surplus so much under-rated by Mr. Ricardo, which by the laws of nature terminates in rent.

If manufactured commodities, by the gradations of machinery supposed by Mr. Ricardo, were to yield a rent, man, as he observes, would do more by the sweat of his brow;* and supposing him still to obtain the same quantity of commodities, (which, however, he would not,) the increase of his labour would be in proportion to the greatness of the rent so created. But the surplus, which a given quantity of land yields in the shape of rent, is totally different. Instead of being a measure of the increase of labour, which is necessary altogether to produce the quantity of corn which

* That is, supposing the gradations were towards worse machinery, some of which it was necessary to use, as in the case of land, but not otherwise. The reason why manufactures and necessaries will not admit of comparison in regard to rents is, that necessaries, in a limited territory, are always tending to the same exchangeable value, whether they have cost little or much labour; but manufactures, if not subjected to an artificial monopoly, must fall in value with the facility of producing them. We cannot therefore suppose the price to be given; but if we could, facility of production would, in both cases, be equally a measure of relief from labour.

the land can yield, it is finally an exact measure of the *relief* from labour in the production of food granted to him by a kind Providence. If this final surplus be small, the labour of a large portion of the society must be constantly employed in procuring, by the sweat of their brows, the mere necessaries of life, and society must be most scantily provided with conveniences, luxuries, and leisure; while, if this surplus be large, manufactures, foreign luxuries, arts, letters, and leisure may abound.

It is a little singular, that Mr. Ricardo, who has, in general, kept his attention so steadily fixed on permanent and final results, as even to define the *natural* price of labour to be that price which would maintain a stationary population, although such a price cannot generally occur under moderately good governments, and in an ordinary state of things, for hundreds of years, has always, in treating of rent, adopted an opposite course, and referred almost entirely to temporary effects.

It is obviously with this sort of reference, that he has objected to Adam Smith for saying that, in rice countries a greater share of the produce would belong to the landlord than in corn countries, and that rents in this country would rise, if potatoes were to become the favourite vegetable food of the common people, instead of corn.* Mr. Ricardo could not but allow, indeed he has allowed,† that rents would be finally higher in both cases. But he immediately supposes that this change is put in execution at once, and refers to the temporary result of land being thrown out of cultivation. Even on this supposition however, all the lands which had been thrown up, would be cultivated again in a very much less time, than it would take to reduce the price of labour, in a natural state of things, to the maintenance only of a stationary population. And therefore, with a view to permanent and final results, which are the results which Mr. Ri-

* Wealth of Nations, Vol. I. book i. p. xi. pp. 248—250. 6th ed.

† Princ. of Polit. Econ. ch. xxiv. p. 398. 3rd edit.

cardo has principally considered throughout his work, he ought to have allowed the truth of Adam Smith's statements.

But, in point of fact, there is every probability that not even a temporary fall of rent would take place. No nation ever has changed or ever will change the nature of its food all at once. The process, both in reference to the new system of cultivation to be adopted, and the new tastes to be generated, must necessarily be very slow. In the greater portion of Europe, it is probable, that a change from corn to rice could never take place; and where it could, it would require such great preparations for irrigation, as to give ample time for an increase of population fully equal to the increased quantity of food produced. In those countries where rice is actually grown, the rents are known to be very high. Dr. Buchanan, in his valuable travels through the Mysore, says, that in the watered lands below the Ghâts, the government was in the habit of taking two-thirds of the crop.* This is an amount of rent which probably no lands cultivated in corn can ever yield; and in those parts of India and other countries, where an actual change has taken place from the cultivation of corn to the cultivation of rice, I have little doubt that rents have not only finally risen very considerably, but have risen even during the progress of the change.

With regard to potatoes, we have very near to us on opportunity of studying the effects of their becoming the vegetable food of the great mass of a people. The population of Ireland has increased faster during the last hundred years, than that of any other country in Europe; and under its actual government, this fact cannot be rationally accounted for, but from the introduction and gradual extension of the use of the potatoe. I am persuaded, that had it not been for the potatoe, the population of Ireland would not have much more than doubled, instead of much more than

* Vol. ii. p. 212.

quadrupled, during the last century. This increase of population has prevented lands from being thrown out of cultivation, or given greater value to natural pasture, at the same time that it has occasioned a great fall in the comparative money wages of labour. This fall, experience tells us, has not been accompanied by a proportionate rise of profits, and the consequence is a considerable rise of rents. The wheat, oats, and cattle of Ireland are sold to England, and bear English money prices, while they are cultivated and tended by labour paid at half the money price; a state of things which must greatly increase either the revenue derived from profits, or the revenue derived from rents; and practical information assures us, that it is the latter which has derived the greatest benefit from it.

Although, therefore, it must lead to great errors, not to distinguish very decidedly the temporary rates of wages from their final rates, it would lead to no such error to consider the temporary effects of the changes of food which have been referred to, as of the same kind with their final effects, that is, as tending always to raise rents. And if we make our comparisons with any tolerable fairness, that is, if we compare countries under similar circumstances, with respect to extent, and the quantity of capital employed upon the soil, which is obviously the only fair mode of comparing them, we shall find that rent will be in proportion to the natural and acquired fertility of the land.

If the natural fertility of this island had been double what it is, and the people had been equally industrious and enterprising, the country would, according to all just theory, have been at this time doubly rich and populous, and the rents of land much more than double what they are now. On the other hand, if the soil of the island had possessed only half its present fertility, a small portion of it only, as I stated on a former occasion, would have admitted of corn cultivation, the wealth and population of the country would have been quite inconsiderable, and rents not nearly one half of what they are now. But if, under similar circumstances, rent and fertility go together, it is no just argument against their natural connexion to say that rent is higher in England, where a great mass of capital has been employed upon the land, than in the more fertile country of South America, where, on the same extent of territory, not a twentieth part has been employed, and the population is extremely scanty.

The fertility of the land, either natural or acquired, may be said to be the only source of permanently high national returns for capital. If a country were exclusively manufacturing and commercial, and were to purchase all its corn at the market prices of Europe, it is absolutely impossible that the national returns for its capital should for any great length of time be high. In the earlier periods of history, indeed, when large masses of capital were extremely rare, and were confined to very few towns, the sort of monopoly which they gave to particular kinds of commerce and manufactures tended to keep up profits for a much longer time; and great and brilliant effects were undoubtedly produced by some states which were almost exclusively commercial. But in modern Europe, the general abundance of capital, the easy intercourse between different nations, and the laws of domestic and foreign competition prevent the possibility of large permanent returns being received for any other capitals than those employed on the land. No great commercial and manufacturing state in modern times, whatever may have been its skill, has yet been known permanently to make much higher profits than the average of the rest of Europe. But the capitals successfully employed on moderately good land, may permanently and without fear of interruption or check, sometimes yield twenty per cent., sometimes thirty or forty, and sometimes even fifty or sixty per cent.

A striking illustration of the effects of capitals employed on land compared with others, appeared in the returns of the property-tax in this country. The taxable income of the nation derived from the capitals employed on land, was such as to yield to the property-tax nearly 6½ millions; while the income derived from the nearly equal capitals employed in commerce and manufactures was only such as to yield two millions.* It is probably true, that a larger proportion of the incomes derived from the capitals employed in trade and manufactures, escaped the tax, partly from their subdivision, and partly from other causes; but the deficiency so occasioned could in no respect make up for the extraordinary productiveness of the capitals employed in agriculture.† And indeed it is quite obvious that, in comparing two countries together with the *same* capitals and the *same* rate of profits, one of which has land on which to grow its corn, and the other is obliged to purchase it, that which has the land, particularly if it be fertile, must be much richer, more populous, and have a larger disposable income for taxation.

Another most desirable benefit belonging to a fertile soil is, that states so endowed are not obliged to pay so much attention to that most distressing and disheartening of all cries to every man of humanity—the cry of the master manufacturers and merchants for low wages, to enable them to find a market for their exports. If a country can only be rich by running a successful race for low wages, I should be disposed to say at once, perish such riches! But, though a nation which purchases the main part of its food from foreigners, is condemned to this hard alternative, it is not so with the possessors of fertile land. The peculiar products and manufactures of a country, though never probably sufficient to enable it to im-

* The Schedule D. included every species of professions. The whole amounted to three millions, of which the professions were considered to be above a million.

† It must always be recollected, that the *national* profits, or the increase of value to the nation obtained by the capitals employed on the land, must be considered as including rents as well as the common agricultural profits.

port a large proportion of its food as well as of its conveniences and luxuries, will generally be sufficient to give full spirit and energy to all its commercial dealings, both at home and abroad; while a small sacrifice of produce, that is, the not pushing cultivation too far without agricultural improvements, would, with prudential habits among the poor,* enable it to maintain the whole of a large population in wealth and plenty. Prudential habits with regard to marriage carried to a considerable extent, among the labouring classes of a country mainly depending upon manufactures and commerce, might injure it. In a country of fertile land, such habits would be the greatest of all conceivable blessings.

Among the inestimable advantages which belong to that quality in the land, which enables it to yield a considerable rent, it is not one of the least, that in the progress of society it affords the main security to man that nearly his whole time, or the time of nearly the whole society, shall not be employed in procuring mere necessaries. Mr. Ricardo seems to think that the whole amount of the revenue derived from profits might be diminished† in the progress of accumulation; and the probability I fear is, that the labourer will be

* Under similar circumstances, with respect to agricultural skill, &c., it is obvious that land of the same degree of barrenness could not be cultivated, if by the prevalence of prudential habits the labourers were very well paid; but to forego the small increase of produce and population arising from the cultivation of such land, would, in a large and fertile territory, be a slight and imperceptible sacrifice, while the happiness which would result from it to the great mass of the population, would be beyond all price.

† Princ. of Polit. Econ. chap. vi. p. 124, 3rd edit.

The truth of this opinion depends upon the question whether upon increasing the capital of a country in a certain proportion, profits will be diminished in a greater proportion. It is probable that this would be the case if accumulation were pushed to a very great extent, as in the ratio assumed in Mr. Ricardo's instance, which is of course taken at random. For the purpose merely of illustration, I am inclined to think, however, that as one very large class of society lives upon the profits of stock, accumulation would cease from the want of power or motive to save, before the general income derived from capital was actually diminished.

obliged to employ a greater quantity of labour to procure that portion of his wages which must be spent in necessaries. Both these great classes of society, therefore, may be expected to have less power of giving leisure to themselves, or of commanding the labour of those who administer to the enjoyments and intellectual improvement of society, as contradistinguished from those who administer to its necessary wants. But, fortunately for mankind, the neat rents of the land, under a system of private property, can never be diminished by the progress of cultivation. Whatever proportion they may bear to the whole produce, the actual amount must always go on increasing, and will always afford a fund for the enjoyments and leisure of the society, sufficient to leaven and animate the whole mass.

If the only condition on which we could obtain lands yielding rent were, that they should remain with the immediate descendants of the first possessors, though the benefits to be derived from the present would no doubt be very greatly diminished, yet from its general and unavoidable effects on society, it would be most unwise to refuse it as of little or no value. But, happily, the benefit is attached to the soil, not to any particular proprietors. Rents are the reward of present valour and wisdom, as well as of past strength and abilities. Every day lands are purchased with the fruits of industry and talents.* They afford the great prize, the "*otium cum dignitate*" to every species of laudable exertion; and, in the progress of society, there is every reason to believe, that, as they become more valuable from the increase of capital and population, and the improvements in agriculture,

* Mr. Ricardo himself was an instance of what I am stating. He became, by his talents and industry, a considerable landholder; and a more honourable and excellent man, a man who for the qualities of his head and heart more entirely deserved what he had earned, or employed it better, I could not point out in the whole circle of landholders.

It is somewhat singular that Mr. Ricardo, a considerable receiver of rents, should have so much underrated their national the benefits which they yield may be divided among a much greater number of persons.

In every point of view, then, in which the subject can be considered, that quality of land which, by the laws of our being, must terminate in rent, appears to be a boon most important to the happiness of mankind; and I am persuaded, that its value can only be underrated by those who still labour under some mistake, as to its nature, and its effects on society.

CHAPTER IV.

OF THE WAGES OF LABOUR.

SECTION I.—*On the Definition of the Wages of Labour, and their Dependance upon Supply and Demand.*

THE wages of labour are the remuneration to the labourer for his exertions.

They may be divided into nominal and real.

The nominal wages of labour consist of money; for it is in money that the labourer is generally paid in civilized countries.

The real wages of labour consist of the necessaries, conveniences, and luxuries of life, which the money wages of the labourer enable him to purchase.

It has been shown in the fifth section of the second chapter of this work, that the average wages of a given

importance; while I, who never received, nor expect to receive any, should probably be accused of overrating their importance. Our different opinions, under these circumstances, may serve at least to show our mutual sincerity, and afford a strong presumption, that to whatever bias our minds may have been subjected in the doctrines we have laid down, it has not been that, against which perhaps it is most difficult to guard, the insensible bias of situation and interest.

number of common agricultural labourers, or what has been called standard wages, are always of the same *value*, that is, they are always obtained in each country, and at all times, at the same elementary cost. But it is well known that the quantity of money, of corn, or of the necessaries and conveniences of life, which is awarded to the labourer, is subject to great variations, all dependant upon the demand and supply of these objects compared with the demand and supply of labour.

If the society can purchase a given quantity of money by commodities which require a smaller sacrifice of labour, profits, &c. to obtain them than is necessary to purchase or obtain the labour for which that money has before been usually exchanged, the money price of labour will rise. If either from the scarcity of money, or the plenty of labour,* a *greater* sacrifice must be made to obtain the given quantity of money, the money price of labour will fall. And whatever may be the state of the effectual demand for labour, it is obvious that the money price of labour must, on an average, be so proportioned to the price of the funds for its maintenance, as to effectuate the desired supply. It is as the condition of the supply, that the prices of the necessaries of life have so important an influence on the price of labour. A certain portion of these necessaries is required to enable the labourer to maintain a stationary population, a greater portion to maintain an increasing one; and consequently, whatever may be the prices of the necessaries of life, the money wages of the labourer must be such as to enable him to purchase these portions, or the supply cannot take place in the quantity required.

The corn wages of labour are still more strikingly determined by the state of the demand and supply than money wages, on account of the variations in the quantity of corn being much greater in short periods

* It must always be recollected, that a plenty of labour, if that labour be employed, always tends to increase the competition for money, and raise its value.

than in the quantity of money. The great variations in the prices of corn in different seasons, while the money price of labour remains the same, are universally observed and acknowledged; but the variations of a more permanent kind in corn wages are sometimes not much less considerable. When the last land taken into cultivation in any country is fertile, and yet worked with some skill, there will be a large produce to divide between profits and wages, and it will depend upon the abundance of this produce and the manner in which it is divided, but chiefly on the former, whether the average corn wages are high or low. In the United States of America, for instance, the plenty and fertility of the land are such as to enable the farmers to pay to their labourers as much as 18 or 20 quarters of wheat in the year, above double the quantity usually paid in the greatest part of Europe, and yet to retain good profits. But it is known that the labouring classes of a country can more than keep up their numbers when paid only 8 or 9 quarters in the year. The question therefore whether the labourer shall be paid, on an average, 8 or 18 quarters, or any intermediate quantity, must depend upon the demand and supply of corn compared with the demand and supply of labour; and it is obvious that the labourer could not, for many years together, receive the larger quantity in any country where corn was not essentially of low value, that is obtained with a small quantity of labour.

If instead of corn wages, or wages estimated in the prime necessary of life, we consider wages as consisting of the general necessaries and conveniences in which the money earnings of the labouring classes are usually spent, then if we suppose the agricultural labourer to be paid in the first instance in corn, his wages in necessaries and conveniences will depend partly upon the quantity of corn which he earns, and partly upon the value of that corn in exchange for the other necessaries of which he stands in need, such as clothing, housing, firing, soap, candles, leather,

&c.; the one depending on the varying supply of corn to labour, and the other on the varying supply of corn to the other commodities wanted. Usually wages estimated in general necessaries and conveniences are more steady than corn wages; because most of the articles besides corn, of which they are composed, are less affected by the seasons, and consequently more regular in their supply than corn; but if these articles are compared directly with labour instead of corn, the quantity of them which shall be given to the labourer will still depend not only upon the varying powers of labour in their production, but upon that ordinary state of the demand for them compared with the supply which, in any given condition of the productive powers of labour, determines the proportion of such necessaries which is awarded to the labourer.

Adam Smith is practically quite correct, when he says, that, "the money price of labour is necessarily regulated by two circumstances; the demand for labour; and the price of the necessaries and conveniences of life."* But it is of great importance to a thorough understanding of the subject, to keep constantly under our view the causes which determine the relative prices of labour and commodities, and to see clearly and distinctly the constant and predominant action of the principle of supply and demand on both.

In all those cases which Adam Smith has so happily explained and illustrated, where an apparent irregularity takes place in the wages of different kinds of labour, it will be found, universally, that the causes to which he justly attributes them, are causes of a nature to influence the supply of labour in the particular departments in question, and to determine such wages by the demand compared with the supply of the kind of labour required. The five principal circumstances, which, according to him, make up for a

* Wealth of Nations, Book i. ch. viii. p. 130, 6th edit.

small pecuniary gain in some employments, and counterbalance a great one in others, namely; 1. The agreeableness or disagreeableness of the employments themselves. 2. The easiness and cheapness, or the difficulty and expense of learning them. 3. The constancy or inconstancy of employment in them. 4. The small or great trust which must be reposed in those who exercise them; and 5. The probability or improbability of success in them,* are all obviously of this description; and in many of the cases stated, it would not be easy to account for their effects on the price of the different kinds of labour, upon any other principle. One hardly sees, for instance, why the cost of producing a poacher should be less than that of a common labourer, or the cost of producing a coal-heaver much greater; yet they are paid very differently. It is not easier to resolve the effects on wages of the small or great trust which must be reposed in a workman, or, the probability or improbability of success in his trade, into the quantity of labour, profits, &c. which has been employed to bring him into the market. Adam Smith satisfactorily shews, that the whole body of lawyers is not remunerated sufficiently to pay the expenses which the education of the whole body has cost;† and it is obvious that particular skill, both in trades and professions, is paid high, with but little reference to the labour employed in acquiring it, which, owing to superior talent, is often less than that which is frequently applied to the acquisition of inferior proficiency. But all these cases are accounted for in the easiest and most natural manner, upon the principle of supply and demand. Superior artists are paid high on account of the scanty supply of such skill, whether occasioned by unusual labour or uncommon genius, or both. Lawyers, as a body, are not well remunerated, because the prevalence of other motives,

* Wealth of Nations, B. i. ch. x. part i. p. 152, 6th edit.
† Id. p. 161.

besides mere gain, crowds the profession with candidates, and the supply is not regulated by the cost of the education; and in all those instances, where disadvantages or difficulties of any kind accompany particular employments, it is obvious that they must be paid comparatively high, because if the additional remuneration were not sufficient to balance such disadvantages, the supply of labour in these departments would be deficient, as, *cæteris paribus*, every person would choose to engage in the most agreeable, the least difficult, and the least uncertain occupations. The deficiency so occasioned, whenever it occurs, will naturally raise the price of labour; and the advance of price, after some little oscillation, will rest at the point where it is just sufficient to occasion a supply suited to the effectual demand.

Adam Smith has in general referred to the principle of supply and demand in cases of this kind, but he has occasionally forgotten it:—"If one species of labour," he says, "requires an uncommon degree of dexterity and ingenuity, the *esteem* which men have for such talents will give a value to their produce, superior to what would be due to the time employed about it."* And in another place, speaking of China, he remarks, "That if in such a country, (that is, a country with stationary resources,) wages had ever been more than sufficient to maintain the labourer, and enable him to bring up a family; the competition of the labourers and the interest of the masters, would soon reduce them to the lowest rate which is consistent with *common humanity*."† The reader will be aware, from what has been already said, that in the first case here noticed, it is not simply the esteem for the dexterity and ingenuity referred to, or a disinterested wish to reward such skill, which raises the price of the commodity, but their scarcity, and the consequent scarcity of the articles produced by them, compared with the demand. And in the latter case,

* Wealth of Nations, B. i. ch. vi. p. 71, 6th edit.

† Id. ch. vii. p. 108.

it is not common humanity which interferes to prevent the price of labour from falling still lower. If humanity could have successfully interfered, it ought to have interfered long before, and prevented any premature mortality from being occasioned by bad or insufficient food. But unfortunately, common humanity cannot alter the funds for the maintenance of labour. While these are stationary, and the habits of the lower classes prompt them to supply a stationary population cheaply, the wages of labour will be scanty; but still they cannot fall below what is necessary, under the actual habits of the people, to keep up a stationary population; because, by the supposition, the funds for the maintenance of labour are stationary, not increasing or declining; and consequently the principle of demand and supply would always interfere to prevent such wages as would either occasion an increase or diminution of people.

SECTION II.—*Of the Causes which principally affect the Habits of the Labouring Classes.*

THE natural price of labour has been defined by Mr. Ricardo to be "that price which is necessary to enable the labourers one with another to subsist, and to perpetuate their race, without either increase or diminution."* This price I should really be disposed to call a most unnatural price; because in a natural state of things, that is, without unnatural impediments to the progress of accumulation, such a price could not permanently occur in any country, till the cultivation of the soil, or the power of importation had been pushed as far as possible. But if this price be really rare, and, in an ordinary state of things, at a great distance in point of time, it must evidently lead to great errors to consider the market-prices of labour as only temporary deviations above and below that fixed price, to which they will very soon return.

* Polit. Econ. c. v. p. 86, 3rd edit.

The natural or necessary price of labour in any country I should define to be that price which, in the actual circumstances of the society, is necessary to occasion an average supply of labourers, sufficient to meet the effectual demand.* And the market price I should define to be, the actual price in the market, which from temporary causes is sometimes above, and sometimes below, what is necessary to supply this demand.

The condition of the labouring classes of society must evidently depend, partly upon the rate at which the funds for the maintenance of labour and the demand for labour are increasing; and partly, on the habits of the people in respect to their food, clothing, and lodging.

If the habits of the people were to remain fixed, the power of marrying early, and of supporting a large family, would depend upon the rate at which the funds for the maintenance of labour and the demand for labour were increasing. And if these funds were to remain fixed, the comforts of the lower classes of society would depend upon their habits, or the amount of those necessaries and conveniences, without which they would not consent to keep up their numbers to the required point.

It rarely happens, however, that either of them remains fixed for any great length of time together. The rate at which the funds for the maintenance of labour increase is, we well know, liable, under varying circumstances, to great variation; and the habits of a people though not so liable, or so necessarily subject to change, can scarcely ever be considered as permanent. In general, their tendency is to change together. When the funds for the maintenance of labour are rapidly increasing, and the labourer commands a large portion of necessaries, it is to be ex-

* We might with almost as much propriety define the natural rate of *profits* to be that rate which would just keep up the capital without increase or diminution. This is in fact the rate to which profits are constantly tending.

pected that if he has the opportunity of exchanging his superfluous food for conveniences and comforts, he will acquire a taste for these conveniences, and his habits will be formed accordingly. On the other hand, it generally happens that, when the funds for the maintenance of labour become nearly stationary, such habits, if they ever have existed, are found to give way; and, before the population comes to a stop, the standard of comfort is essentially lowered.

Still, however, partly from physical, and partly from moral causes, the standard of comfort differs essentially in different countries, under the same rate of increase in their funds for the maintenance of labour. Adam Smith, in speaking of the inferior food of the people of Scotland, compared with their neighbours of the same rank in England, observes, "This difference in the mode of their subsistence is not the cause, but the effect, of the difference in their wages, though, by a strange misapprehension, I have frequently heard it represented as the cause."* It must be allowed, however, that this correction of a common opinion is only partially just. The effect, in this case as in many others, certainly becomes in its turn a cause; and there is no doubt, that if the continuance of low wages for some time, should produce among the labourers of any country habits of marrying with the prospect only of a mere subsistence, such habits, by supplying the quantity of labour required at a low rate, would become a constantly operating cause of low wages.

It would be very desirable to ascertain what are the principal causes which determine the different modes of subsistence among the lower classes of people of different countries; but the question involves so many considerations, that a satisfactory solution of it is hardly to be expected. Much must certainly depend upon the physical causes of climate and soil; but still more perhaps on moral causes, the formation

* Wealth of Nat. Book I. chap. viii. p. 114. 6th edit.

and action of which are owing to a variety of circumstances.

From high real wages, or the power of commanding a large portion of the necessaries of life, two very different results may follow; one, that of a rapid increase of population, in which case the high wages are chiefly spent in the maintenance of large and frequent families; and the other, that of a decided improvement in the modes of subsistence, and the conveniences and comforts enjoyed, without a proportionate acceleration in the rate of increase.

In looking to these different results, the causes of them will evidently appear to be the different habits existing among the people of different countries, and at different times. In an inquiry into the causes of these different habits, we shall generally be able to trace those which, in old countries,* produce the first result, to all the circumstances which contribute to depress the lower classes of the people, which make them unable or unwilling to reason from the past to the future, and ready to acquiesce, for the sake of present gratification, in a very low standard of comfort and respectability; and those which produce the second result, to all the circumstances which tend to elevate the character of the lower classes of society, which make them act as beings who "look before and after," and who consequently cannot acquiesce patiently in the thought of depriving themselves and their children of the means of being respectable, virtuous, and happy.

Among the circumstances which contribute to the character first described, the most efficient will be found to be despotism, oppression, and ignorance: among those which contribute to the latter character, civil and political liberty, and education.

Of all the causes which tend to generate prudential

* In new countries, such as the United States, the funds for the maintenance of labour are so ample, and are increasing so rapidly, that for a considerable time the prudential check to early marriages may hardly be necessary.

habits among the lower classes of society, the most essential is unquestionably civil liberty. No people can be much accustomed to form plans for the future, who do not feel assured that their industrious exertions, while fair and honourable, will be allowed to have free scope; and that the property which they either possess, or may acquire, will be secured to them by a known code of just laws impartially administered. But it has been found by experience, that civil liberty cannot be permanently secured without political liberty. Consequently, political liberty becomes almost equally essential; and in addition to its being necessary in this point of view, its obvious tendency to teach the lower classes of society to respect themselves by obliging the higher classes to respect them, must contribute greatly to aid all the good effects of civil liberty.

With regard to education, it might certainly be made general under a bad form of government, and might be very deficient under one in other respects good; but it must be allowed, that the chances, both with regard to its quality and its prevalence, are greatly in favour of the latter. Education alone could do little against insecurity of property; but it would powerfully assist all the favourable consequences to be expected from civil and political liberty, which could not indeed be considered as complete without it.

According as the habits of the people had been determined by such unfavourable or favourable circumstances, high wages, or a rapid increase of the funds for the maintenance of labour, would be attended with the first or second of the results before described; or at least by such results as would approach to the one or the other, according to the different degrees in which all the causes which influence habits of improvidence or prudence had been efficient.

Ireland, during the course of the last century, may be produced perhaps as the most marked instance of the first result. On the introduction of the potatoe into that country, the lower classes of society were in such a state of oppression and ignorance, were so little respected by others, and had consequently so little respect for themselves, that as long as they could get food, and that of the cheapest kind, they were content to marry under the prospect of every other privation. The abundant funds for the support of labour occasioned by the cultivation of the potatoe in a favourable soil, which often gave the labourer the command of a quantity of subsistence quite unusual in the other parts of Europe, were spent almost exclusively in the maintenance of large and frequent families; and the result was, a most rapid increase of population, with little or no melioration in the general condition and modes of subsistence of the labouring poor.

An instance somewhat approaching to the second result may be found in England, in the first half of the last century. It is well known, that during this period the price of corn fell considerably, while the price of labour is stated to have risen. During the last forty years of the 17th century, and the first twenty of the 18th, the average price of corn was such as, compared with the wages of labour, would only enable the labourer to purchase, with a day's earnings, about two-thirds of a peck of wheat. From 1720 to 1750 the price of wheat had so fallen, while wages had risen, that instead of two thirds the labourer could purchase the whole of a peck of wheat with a day's labour.*

This great increase of command over the first necessary of life did not, however, produce a proportionate increase of population. It found the people of this country living under a good government, and enjoying all the advantages of civil and political liberty in an unusual degree. The lower classes of people had been in the habit of being respected, both by the laws and the higher orders of their fellow citizens, and had learned in consequence to respect themselves. The result was, that their increased corn wages, instead of occasioning an increase of population ex-

* See Section IV. of this chapter.

clusively, were so expended as to occasion a decided elevation in the standard of their comforts and conveniences.

During the same period, the funds for the maintenance of labour in Scotland do not appear to have increased so fast as those of England; but since the middle of the last century, the former country has perhaps made a more rapid progress than the latter; and the consequence has been, that from the same causes, these increased resources have not produced, exclusively, an increase of population, but a great alteration for the better in the food, dress, and houses of the lower classes of society, in that country.

The general change from bread of a very inferior quality to the best wheaten bread, seems to have been peculiar to the southern and midland counties of England, and may perhaps have been aided by adventitious circumstances.

The improving cultivation of the country after 1720, together with the state of the foreign markets, as opened by the bounty, appears to have diminished, in some districts, the usual difference in the prices of the different kinds of grain. Though barley was largely grown and largely exported, it did not fall in price so much as wheat. On an average of the twenty years ending with 1705, compared with an average of twenty years ending with 1745, the quarter of wheat fell from £1. 16*s*. 3*d*. to £1. 9*s*. 10*d*. but malt during the same period remained at the same price, or, if any thing, rather rose;* and as barley is supposed to be not a cheaper food than wheat, unless it can be purchased at $\frac{2}{3}$ of the price,† such a relative difference would have a strong tendency to promote the change.

From the small quantity of rye exported, compared with wheat and barley, it may be inferred that it did not find a ready vent in foreign markets; and this cir-

* Eden's State of the Poor. Table, vol. iii. p. 79. In this table, a deduction is made for $\frac{2}{9}$ for the quarter of middling wheat of eight bushels, which is too much.

† Tracts on the Corn Trade, Supp. p. 199.

cumstance, together with the improving state of the land, diminished its cultivation and use.

With regard to oats, the prohibitory laws and the bounty were not so favourable to them as to the other grains, and more were imported than exported. This would naturally tend to check their cultivation in the districts which were capable of growing the sort of grain most certain of a market; while the Act of Charles II. respecting the buying up of corn to sell again, threw greater obstacles in the way of the distribution of oats than of any other grain.

By this Act, wheat might be bought up and stored for future sale when the price did not exceed 48*s.*; barley, when the price did not exceed 28*s.*; and oats, when the price did not exceed 13*s.* 4*d.* The limited prices of wheat and barley were considerably above their ordinary and average rates at that period, and therefore did not often interfere with their proper distribution; but the ordinary price of oats was supposed to be about 12*s.* the quarter, and consequently the limit of 13*s.* 4*d.* would be very frequently exceeded,* and obstacles would be continually thrown in the way of their transport from the districts of their growth to the districts where they might be wanted. But if, from the causes here described, the labouring classes of the South of England were partly induced, and partly obliged, to adopt wheat as their main food, instead of the cheaper kinds of grain, the rise of wages would at once be accounted for, consistently with the fall in the price of wheat; an event which, under an apparently slack demand for labour at the time, has been considered as so improbable by some writers, that the accuracy of the accounts has been doubted. It is evidently, however, possible, either on the supposition of a voluntary determination on the part of the labouring classes to adopt a superior description of food, or a sort of obligation to do it, on account of the introduction of a new system of cultivation adapted

* Tracts on the Corn Trade, p. 50.

to a more improved soil: and, in either case, the effects observable from 1720 to 1750 would appear; namely, an increased power of commanding corn, without a proportionate increase of population. It is probable that both causes contributed their share to the change in question. When once the fashion of eating wheaten bread had become general in some countries, it would be likely to spread into others, even at the expense of comforts of a different description; and in all cases where particular modes of subsistence, from whatever causes arising, have been for any time established, though such modes always remain susceptible of change, the change must be a work of time and difficulty. A country, which for many years had principally supported its peasantry on one sort of grain, must alter its whole system of agriculture before it can produce another sort in sufficient abundance; and the obstinacy with which habits are adhered to by all classes of people, as in some countries it would prevent high wages from improving the quality of the food, so in others it would prevent low wages from suddenly deteriorating it; and such high or low wages would be felt almost exclusively in the great stimulus or the great check which they would give to population.

SECTION III.—*Of the Causes which principally influence the Demand for Labour, and the Increase of the Population.*

THERE is another cause, besides a change in the habits of the people, which prevents the population of a country from keeping pace with the *apparent* command of the labourer over the means of subsistence. It sometimes happens that corn wages are comparatively high without a proportionate demand for labour. This is the most likely to take place when the price of raw produce has fallen without a fall in the price of labour, so as to disable the cultivators from employing the same quantity of labour as before. If the fall be considerable, and not made up in value by increase of quantity, so many labourers will be thrown out of work that wages, after a period of great distress, will generally be lowered in proportion. But if the fall be gradual, and partly made up in exchangeable value by increase of quantity, the money wages of labour will not necessarily sink; and the result will be merely a slack demand for labour, not sufficient perhaps to throw the actual labourers out of work, but such as to prevent or diminish task-work, to check the employment of women and children, and to give but little encouragement to the rising generation of labourers. In this case the quantity of the necessaries of life actually earned by the labourer and his family, may be really less than when, owing to a rise of prices, the daily pay of the labourer will command a smaller quantity of corn. The command of the labouring classes over the necessaries of life, though apparently greater, is really less in the former than in the latter case, and, upon all general principles, ought to produce less effect on the increase of population.

This disagreement between apparent wages and the progress of population will be further aggravated in those countries where poor laws are established, and it has become customary to pay a portion of the labourers' wages out of the parish rates. If, when corn rises, the farmers and landholders of a parish keep the wages of labour down, and make a regular allowance for children, it is obvious that there is no longer any necessary connexion between the apparent corn wages of day labour and the real means which the labouring classes possess of maintaining a family. When once the people are reconciled to such a system, the progress of population might be rapid, at a time when the real wages of labour, independently of parish assistance, were only sufficient to support a wife and one child, or even a single man without either wife or child, because there might still be both encouragement to marriage, and the means of supporting children.*

When the population of a country increases faster than usual for any time together, the labouring classes must have the command of a greater quantity of food than they had before possessed, or at least than they had before applied to the maintenance of their families. This may be obtained in various ways—by higher corn wages, by saving in conveniences, by adopting a cheaper kind of food, by more task-work and the more general employment of the women and children, or by parish allowances. But the actual application of the greater quantity of food seems to be necessary to the increase of population; and wherever such increase has taken place, some of these causes, by which a greater quantity of food is procured, will always be in action, and may generally be traced.

The high wages, both in corn and money, of the United States, occasioned by the rapid accumulation of capital, and the power of selling produce, obtained by a comparatively small quantity of labour, at European prices, are unquestionably the cause of the very rapid progress of the American population. A very great demand for labour has, in this case, accompanied a low comparative value of produce, a union not necessary nor frequent, but, when it does occur, calculated to occasion the most rapid increase of population.

The peculiar increase of the population of Ireland, compared with other European countries, has obviously been owing to the adoption of a cheaper food, which might be produced in large quantities, and which, aided by the Cotter system of cultivation, has

* It is most fortunate for the country and the labouring classes of society, that the bill which passed the House of Commons, for taking from their parents the children of those who asked for relief, and supporting them on public funds, did not pass the House of Lords. Such a law would have been the commencement of a new system of poor laws beyond all comparison worse than the old.

allowed the increase of people greatly to exceed the demand for labour.

The great increase of population of late years in England and Scotland has been owing to the power of the labouring classes to obtain a greater quantity of food, partly by temporary high wages in manufactures, partly by the increased use of potatoes, partly by increased task-work and the increased employment of women and children, partly by increased parish allowances to families, and partly by the increased relative cheapness of manufactures and foreign commodities.

In general perhaps more of these causes will be called into action by a rise of prices which sometimes lowers the command of a day's labour over the necessaries of life, than by a fall of prices which raises it.

What is essentially necessary to a rapid increase of population is a great and continued demand for labour; and this is proportioned to the rate of increase in the quantity and value of those funds, whether arising from capital or revenue, which are actually employed in the maintenance of labour.

It has been generally considered, that the demand for labour is proportioned only to the circulating, not the fixed capital of a country. But in reality the demand for labour is not *proportioned* to the increase of capital in any shape; nor even, as I once thought, to the increase of the exchangeable value of the whole annual produce. It is proportioned only, as above stated, to the rate of increase in the quantity and value of those funds which are actually employed in the maintenance of labour.

These funds consist principally in the necessaries of life, or in the means of commanding the food, clothing, lodging, and firing of the labouring classes of society. Now it is quite evident that if the capital of a society were directed in the most judicious and skilful manner to the production of these necessaries, and that the neat surplus above what was required for the maintenance of the persons so employed, and of their employers, were spent in the maintenance of menial servants, soldiers, and sailors, all the demand for labour that the resources of such a country called out in the most effective manner would admit of, might exist, with little of that great mass of capital, which in most improved countries is employed in producing luxuries and superior conveniences.* But if this be so, it is obvious that capital, and even the exchangeable value of the whole produce may increase without any increase in the demand for labour. If the circulating capital applied to the production of luxuries and conveniences employed only those persons who would otherwise be maintained as unproductive labourers by the surplus of necessaries, not only no addition is thereby made to the demand for labour, but if the persons before engaged in personal services were dismissed faster than they could be employed in the production of luxuries and superior conveniences a diminished demand for labour might take place under an increasing circulating capital. And if a large portion of the exchangeable value of the whole produce of a country cannot be resolved into necessaries, it is clear that the whole produce may increase in exchangeable value without a greater value of the necessaries of life being actually employed in the maintenance of labour.

But though it is unquestionably true that without the capital employed in luxuries and superior conveniences the same demand for labour might exist; yet practically, if the neat revenue of a country could only be employed in the maintenance of menial servants and soldiers, there is every reason to think that the stimulus to production in modern states would be very greatly diminished, and that the cultivation of the soil would be carried on with the same kind of indolence and slackness as in the feudal times.

* This view of the subject was stated by me above thirty years ago in the quarto edition of the Essay on Population, p. 421, and by Mr. Ricardo in his 3rd edition, p. 475.

On the other hand, if the whole of the surplus produce beyond what was required for the support of those who were employed in the production of necessaries could be spent in no other way than in the production and purchase of *material* luxuries and conveniences, if no menial servants could be kept to take care of houses, furniture, carriages, horses, &c. it is quite clear that the demand for material luxuries and conveniences would very soon abate, and the owners of land and capital would have very slender motives to employ them in the most productive manner.

It is clearly then the operation of both stimulants, under the most favourable proportions, which is likely to give the most effective encouragement even to the production of necessaries. And though it is quite certain that an increase in the value of the funds for the maintenance of labour is not strictly proportioned to the increase in the exchangeable value of the whole produce estimated in labour; yet, in ordinary times, and when no great changes are taking place in the proportion of personal services to productive labour, an increase of such exchangeable value is generally followed by an increased demand for labour, since its ordinary and natural effect is to increase the value of the funds destined for the maintenance of labour.

Whenever the introduction of fixed capital has for a time the effect of diminishing the demand for labour, it will generally be found that the value of the whole annual produce is at the same time diminished: but in general the use of fixed capital is favourable to the abundance of circulating capital; and if the market for the products can be proportionally extended, the whole value of the capital and revenue of a state is greatly increased by it, as well as the value of the funds for the maintenance of labour, and a great demand for labour created.

The increase in the whole value of cotton products, since the introduction of the improved machinery, is known to be prodigious; and it cannot for a moment be doubted that both the circulating capital and the demand for labour in the cotton business have very greatly increased during the last fifty years. This is indeed sufficiently proved by the greatly increased population of Manchester, Glasgow, and the other towns where the cotton manufactures have most flourished.

A similar increase of value, though not to the same extent, has taken place in our hardware, woollen, and other manufactures, and has been accompanied by an increasing demand for labour, notwithstanding the increasing use of fixed capital.

Even in our agriculture, if the fixed capital of horses, which from the quantity of produce they consume, is the most disadvantageous description of fixed capital, were disused, it is probable, that a great part of the land which now bears corn would be thrown out of cultivation. Land of a poor quality would never yield sufficient to pay the labour of cultivating with the spade, of bringing manure to distant fields in barrows, and of carrying the products of the earth to distant markets by the same sort of conveyance. Under these circumstances, as there would be a diminution in the quantity of corn produced, there would be a diminution in the whole value of the produce; and the value of the funds for the maintenance of labour being impaired, the demand for labour would be diminished in proportion.*

On the other hand, if, by the gradual introduction of a greater quantity of fixed capital, we could cultivate and dress our soil and carry the produce to market at a much less expense, we might increase our produce very greatly by the cultivation of all our

* It has lately been stated, that spade cultivation will yield both a greater gross produce and a greater neat produce. I am always ready to bow to well established experience; but if such experience applies in the present case, one cannot sufficiently wonder at the continued use of ploughs and horses in agriculture. Even supposing however that the use of the spade might, on some soils, so improve the land, as to make the crop more than pay the additional expense of the labour, taken separately; yet, as horses must be kept to carry out dressing to a distance

waste lands and the improvement of all the land already in cultivation; and if the substitution of this fixed capital were to take place in the only way in which we can suppose it practically to take place, that is, gradually, there is no reason to doubt that the value of raw produce would keep up nearly to its former level; and its greatly increased quantity, combined with the greater proportion of the people which might be employed in manufactures and commerce, while it would occasion a very great increase in the exchangeable value of the general produce, would increase at the same time the value of the funds destined for the maintenance of labour, and thus cause a great demand for labour and a great addition to the population.

There is no occasion therefore to fear that the introduction of fixed capital, as it is likely to take place in practice, will diminish the effective demand for labour; indeed it is to this source that we are to look for the main cause of its future increase. At the same time, it is certainly true, as will be more fully stated in a subsequent part of this work, that if the substitution of fixed capital were to take place much faster than an adequate market could be found for the more abundant supplies derived from it and for the new products of the labour that had been thrown out of employment, a slack demand for labour and distress among the labouring classes of society would be universally felt. But in this case, the whole produce would fall in value, owing to a temporary excess of supply compared with the demand.

In the formation of the value of the whole funds

and to convey the produce of the soil to market, it could hardly answer to the cultivator to employ men in digging his fields, while his horses were standing idle in his stables. As far as experience has yet gone, I should certainly say, that it is commerce, price and skill, which will cultivate the wastes of large and poor territories—not the spade.

No inference whatever in regard to the cultivation of a large country can be drawn from what may be done on a few acres in the immediate neighbourhood of houses and manure.

specifically destined for the maintenance of labour, (the rate of the increase of which regulates the demand for labour,) a part depends upon the value of a given portion of such funds, and a part upon their amount in kind, or in other words, a part depends upon their price, and a part upon their quantity. That part which depends merely upon price is in its nature less durable and less effective than that which depends upon quantity. An increase of price with little or no increase of quantity, has obvious limits, and must be followed very soon in most cases by a nearly proportionate increase of money wages; while the command of these increased money wages over the necessaries of life going on diminishing, the population must come to a stop, and no further rise of prices can occasion an effective demand for labour.

On the other hand, if the quantity of produce be increased so fast that the value of the whole diminishes from excessive supply, it may not command so much labour this year as it did in the last, and for a time there will be a very slack demand for workmen.

These are the two extremes, the one arising from increased value without increased quantity; and the other from increased quantity without increased value.

It is obvious that the object which it is most desirable to attain is the union of the two. There is somewhere a happy mean, where, under the actual resources of a country, both the increase of wealth and the demand for labour may be a maximum. A taste for conveniences and comforts not only tends to create a more steady demand for labour, than a taste for personal services; but by cheapening manufactures and the products of foreign commerce, including many of the necessaries of the labouring classes, it actually enlarges the limits of the effectual demand for labour, and renders it for a longer time effective.

An increase in the quantity of the funds for the maintenance of labour, with steady prices, or even slightly falling, may occasion a considerable demand for labour; but in the actual state of things, and in the way in which the precious metals are actually distributed, some increase of prices generally accompanies the most effective demand for produce and population. It is this increase both of quantity and price which most surely increases the *value* of the funds for the maintenance of labour, creates the greatest demand for labourers, excites the greatest quantity of industry, and generally occasions the greatest increase of population.

SECTION IV.—*A Review of the Corn Wages of Labour from the Reign of Edward III.*

SOME writers of great ability have been of opinion that rising prices, occasioned by an influx of bullion, are very unfavourable to the labouring classes of society; and certainly there are some periods of our history which seem strongly to countenance this opinion: but I am inclined to think, that if these periods, and the circumstances connected with them, be examined with more attention, the conclusion which has been drawn from them will not appear so certain as has been generally imagined. It will be found that, in the instances in question, other causes were in operation to which the effect referred to might more justly be attributed.

The period of our history more particularly noticed is the 16th century, from the end of the reign of Henry VII. to the end of the reign of Elizabeth. During this period it is an unquestionable fact that the corn wages of labour fell in an extraordinary degree, and towards the latter end of the century they would not command much above one-third of the quantity of wheat which they did at the beginning of it.

Sir F. M. Eden has noticed the price of wheat in nineteen out of the twenty-four years of Henry VII.'s reign, and in some of the years two or three times.*

* State of the Poor, vol. iii. p. xli.

Reducing the several notices in the same year first to an average, and then taking the average of the nineteen prices, it comes to 6*s*. 3¼*d*. the quarter, rather less than 9½*d*. the bushel, and 2⅜*d*. the peck.

By a statute passed in 1495 to regulate wages, the price of common day labour seems to have been 4*d*. or 4½*d*. without diet. All labourers and artificers, not specifically mentioned, are put down at 4*d*.; but in another part of the statute, even a woman labourer (I suppose in hay time) is set down at 4½*d*. and a carter at 5*d*.*

At the price of wheat just stated, if the wages of the labourer were 4*d*. he would be able to purchase, by a day's labour, a peck and three quarters of wheat, within half a farthing; if his wages were 4½*d*. he would be able to purchase half a bushel, within a farthing.

The notices of the price of day labour in the subsequent years are extremely scanty. There are none in the reigns of Henry VIII., Edward, and Mary. The first that occurs is in 1575, and the price mentioned is 8*d*.† Taking an average of the five preceding years in which the prices of wheat are noticed, including 1575, having previously averaged the several prices in the same year, as before, it appears that the price of the quarter of wheat was 1*l*. 2*s*. 2*d*. which is 2*s*. 9½*d*. the bushel, and 8¼*d*. the peck. At this price, a day's labour would purchase a peck of corn, within a farthing, or $\frac{16}{17}$ of a peck.

This is a diminution of nearly a half in the corn wages of labour; but at the end of the century, the diminution was still greater.

The next notice of the price of labour, with the exception of the regulations of the justices in some of the more northern counties, which can hardly be taken as a fair criterion for the south, is in 1601, when it is mentioned as 10*d*. Taking an average from the Windsor table of five years, which includes, however, one

* State of the Poor, vol. iii. p. lxxxix.

† Ibid. vol. iii. p. lx.

excessively dear year, and subtracting $\frac{1}{9}$ to reduce it to Winchester measure, it appears that the price of the quarter was 2*l.* 2*s.* 0*d.* which is 5*s.* 3*d.* the bushel, and 1*s.* 3¾*d.*, the peck. A day's labour would at this price purchase less than $\frac{2}{3}$ of a peck.*

This is unquestionably a prodigious fall in the corn wages of labour. But it is of great importance to inquire whether the rate from which they fell was not as extraordinary as the rate to which they sunk; and here I think we shall find that the wages the most difficult to be accounted for are the high corn wages of the 15th, rather than the low corn wages of the 16th century.

If we revert to the middle of the 14th century, at the time when the first general statute was passed to regulate wages, the condition of the labourer will appear to be very inferior to what it was during the greatest part of the 15th century. This fact may be established on unexceptionable evidence. Statutes or regulations to fix the price of labour, though they do not always succeed in their immediate object, (which is generally the unjust one, of preventing it from rising,) may be considered as undeniable testimonies of what the prices of labour had been not long previous to the time of their passing. No legislature in the most ignorant age could ever be so rash as arbitrarily to fix the prices of labour without reference to some past experience. Consequently, though the prices in such statutes cannot be depended upon with regard to the future, they appear to be quite conclusive with regard to the past. In the present case, indeed, it is expressly observed, that servants should be contented with such liveries and wages as they re-

* The year 1597 seems to have been an extraordinary dear one, and ought not to be included in so short an average. If an average were taken of the five years beginning with 1598, the labourer would appear to earn about $\frac{5}{7}$ of a peck; and, on an average of ten years, from the same period, he would earn about $\frac{4}{5}$ of a peck. During the five years from 1594 to 1598 inclusive, the price of wheat seems to have been unusually high from unfavourable seasons.

ceived in the 20th year of the king's reign, and two or three years before.*

From this statute, which was enacted in 1350, the 25th of the King, for the most unjust and impolitic purpose of preventing the price of labour from rising after the great pestilence, we may infer that the price of day labour had been about 1½*d.* or 2*d.* Common agricultural labour, indeed, is not specifically mentioned; but the servants of artificers are appointed to take 1½*d.*, common carpenters 2*d.*, and a reaper, the first week in August, also 2*d.*, all without diet; from which we may conclude that the wages of common day labour must have been as often 1½*d.* as 2*d.*†

Sir F. M. Eden has collected notices of the prices of wheat in sixteen out of the twenty-five years of Edward III. previous to the time of the passing of the statute. Taking an average as before, the price of wheat appears to have been about 5*s.* 4*d.* the quarter, which is 8*d.* the bushel, and 2*d.* the peck.

At this price of wheat, if the labourer earned 1½*d.* a day, he could only purchase by a day's labour ¾ of a peck of wheat; if he earned 2*d.* he could purchase just a peck. In the former case, he would earn less than half of the corn earned by the labourer of Henry VII.; and in the latter case, very little more than half.

But in the subsequent period of Edward III.'s reign, the labourer appears to have been much worse off. The statute of labourers was renewed, and, it is said, enforced very rigidly, notwithstanding a considerable rise in the price of corn.‡ On an average of the thirteen years out of twenty-six, in which the prices of wheat are noticed, the quarter is about 11*s.* 9*d.* which is about 1*s.* 5½ the bushel, and 4¼*d.* the peck.

At this price, if the money wages of labour had not risen, the condition of the labourer would have been very miserable. He would not have been able to pur-

* Eden's State of the Poor, vol. i. p. 32. † Ibid. p. 33.
‡ Ibid, p. 36. 42.

chase so much as half-a-peck of wheat by a day's labour, about a fourth part of what he could subsequently command in the reign of Henry VII. It is scarcely possible, however, to conceive that the money wages of labour should not have risen in some degree, notwithstanding the statute and its renewal; but even if they rose one half, they would not have nearly kept pace with the price of corn, which more than doubled; and during the last twenty-five years of the reign of Edward III. the earnings of the labourer in corn were probably quite as low as during the last twenty-five years of Elizabeth.

In the reigns of Richard II. and Henry IV. the price of wheat seems to have fallen nearly to what it was in the first half of the reign of Edward III. From 1377 to 1398 inclusive, it was about 5*s*. 7*d*. the quarter; and from 1399 to 1411, about 6*s*. 1*d*.* It is difficult to ascertain how much the money wages of labour had advanced; but if they had risen so as to enable the labourer to support himself, through the last twenty-six years of the reign of Edward III. and had not sunk again, in consequence of the subsequent fall, which is probable, the labourer, during these reigns, must have been well paid.

During the reign of Henry V. and the first part of Henry VI. to the passing of the statutes in 1444, the price of the quarter of wheat was about 8*s*. 8*d*.† This would be 1*s*. 1*d*. the bushel, and 3¼*d*. the peck. For the greater part of these thirty-two years, the wages of day labour seem to have been about 3*d*. They did not probably rise to what they were appointed to be in 1444, that is 4*d*. or 4½*d*., till the ten dear years preceding the statute, during which, the average price of the quarter was 10*s*. 8*d*. On an average of the whole period of thirty-two years, the wages of day labour appear to have purchased about a peck of corn, rather less perhaps, than more, in reference to the greater portion of the period.

* Eden's State of the Poor, vol. iii. p. xxv. et seq.

† Eden's State of the Poor, Table of Prices, vol. iii.

From 1444 to the end of the century, the average money price of wheat was about 6*s.* while the wages of day labour continued at 4*d.* or 4½*d.** At the latter of these prices of labour, wages would purchase exactly two pecks of wheat, or half a bushel, and at the former price $\frac{8}{9}$ of half a bushel.

From the passing of the first statute of labourers in 1350 to the end of the 15th century, a period of 150 years, successive changes had been taking place in the quantity of metal contained in the same nominal sum; so that the pound of silver, which in the middle of the reign of Edward III. was coined into 1*l.* 2*s.* 6*d.* was, in the reign of Henry VII., coined into 1*l.* 17*s.* 6*d.*

One should naturally have expected, that this depreciation of the coin would have shown itself first, and most conspicuously, in some exportable commodity, such as corn, rather than labour; and so it probably would, as it did afterwards in the reign of Elizabeth, if wheat had not at the same time been cheap in the rest of Europe, particularly in France. In fact, however, this great fall in the intrinsic value of the coin was in no respect made up by the slight rise in the nominal price of wheat which occurred in the course of that period. This rise was only from about 5*s.* 4*d.* to 6*s.* or 6*s.* 3*d.* Consequently a very considerable fall had really taken place in the bullion price of wheat.

But the nominal price of labour, instead of rising in the same slight degree as wheat, rose from 1½*d.* or 2*d.* to 4*d.* or 4½*d.*, a rise much more than sufficient to cover the deterioration of the coin; so that the bullion price of labour rose considerably, during the time that the bullion price of wheat fell. It is singular, that Adam Smith, in his *Digression concerning the value of silver during the four last centuries*, should not

* Mr. Hallam, in his valuable Work on the Middle Ages, has overlooked the distinction between the reigns of Edward III. and Henry VI. with regard to the state of the labouring classes. The two periods appear to have been essentially different in this respect.

have noticed this circumstance. If he had been aware of this rise in the bullion price of labour, his principles, which led him to consider corn as a good measure of value, merely because it is the best measure of labour, should have led him to a very different conclusion from that which he has stated. Referring to labour which, it has been shown in this work, is the true standard measure of value, and in fact, is the standard which Adam Smith himself proposes, it appears that the value of silver from the middle of the 14th to the end of the 15th century, when the effect contemplated was the greatest, instead of rising to nearly double in value, fell in the proportion of from about 3 to 2.*

It was during the favourable part of this period that Sir John Fortesque wrote his work on *Absolute and Limited Monarchy*, and contrasted the prosperous and happy condition of the peasantry of England with the miserable state of the peasantry of France.†

But it is not sufficient to show that the condition of the lower classes of people in England during the last half of the 15th century, was much superior to what it was either in the preceding century, or subsequently during the depreciation of money occasioned by the discovery of the American mines. To prove that it was peculiar, we must compare it with the condition of the people after the depreciation had ceased.

According to Adam Smith, the effects of the dis-

* The nominal price of labour rose from about 1½*d.* or 2*d.* to 4*d.* or 4½*d.* If we combine these proportions of 3 to 8, and 4 to 9 together, and correct the result by the diminution of the quantity of metal contained in the same nominal sum in the latter period, which was in the proportions of 1*l.* 17*s.* 6*d.* to 1*l.* 2*s.* 6*d.*, or of 5 to 3, it will appear that the bullion price of labour rose nearly in the proportion of from 2 to 3, and consequently that the value of silver fell nearly in the proportions of from 3 to 2.

† The rise in the bullion price of labour, while the bullion price of corn was falling, proved not only, that the English labourer could command a greater quantity of corn than usual, but that at the same time there was a great demand for labour, and all who were willing to work might be employed, two events which do not always go together, but which when they do, are most favourable to the labouring classes.

covery of the American mines seemed to be at an end about 1638 or 40. In 1651 the wages of day-labour, as established by the justices in Essex at the Chelmsford quarter-sessions, were for the summer half year, harvest excepted, 1*s.* 2*d.* This is a considerable rise in the money price of labour from the time of Elizabeth; but we shall find that it is hardly proportionate to the rise of the price of wheat. If we take an average of the five years preceding 1651,* the period to which the regulation would probably for the most part refer; it appears that the price of the quarter of wheat in the Windsor market, deducting $\frac{1}{9}$ to reduce it to Winchester measure, was 3*l.* 4*s.* 7*d.*† the quarter, which would be about 8*s.* the bushel, and 2*s.* the peck. At this price of wheat, with wages at 14*d.* the labourer would only earn $\frac{7}{12}$ of a peck, half a peck, and $\frac{1}{12}$.

In 1661, soon after the accession of Charles II., wages were again regulated by the justices in Essex, at the Easter Sessions, and the price of common day-labour during the summer half year, with the exception of harvest time, was continued at 14*d.*

If we take an average of the price of wheat for the five years preceding 1661, as before, it appears that the quarter was 2*l.* 9*s.* 3*d.* This is 6*s.* 2*d.* the bushel, and 18½*d.* the peck. At this rate the labourer would earn about ¾ of a peck. It is true that the averages of the prices of corn here taken refer to dear times; but the wages were appointed just at these times: and in the regulations of 1651 it is expressly stated, that they are appointed, "having a special regard and consideration to the prices at this time of all kinds of victuals and apparel, both linen and woollen, and all other necessary charges wherewith artificers, labourers and servants have been more grievously charged with than in times past."‡

* As the regulation passed in April, the year 1651 is not included in the average.

† Encyclopædia Brit. Supp. Artic. Corn Laws, where a table is given with the $\frac{1}{9}$ deducted.

‡ Eden's State of the Poor, vol. iii. p. 98.

If we take an average of the twenty years from 1646 to 1665 inclusive, we shall find that the price of wheat was rather above than below that of the five years preceding 1661. The average price of the quarter of wheat during these twenty years was £2. 10*s*. 0$\frac{3}{4}$*d*.* which is 6*s*. 3*d*. the bushel, and nearly 19*d*. the peck. At this price, with wages at 14*d*. the labourer for these twenty years would hardly be able to earn so much as $\frac{3}{4}$ of a peck.

After 1665 the price of corn fell, but money wages seem to have fallen at the same time.

In 1682 wages at Bury in Suffolk were appointed to be 6*d*. in summer, and 5*d*. in winter with diet, and double without. This makes the summer wages 1*s*.; and according to the price of wheat in the preceding five years, the labourer who earned a shilling a day, could hardly command so much as $\frac{3}{4}$ of a peck of wheat.

The average price of the quarter of wheat from 1665 to 1700 was about £2. 2*s*. 6*d*. If we suppose the wages of labour during this period to have been about 1*s*. the earnings of the labourer would be about $\frac{3}{4}$ of a peck of wheat. But there is reason to think that the average money wages were not so high as 1*s*.

In the regulations of the justices at Warwick in 1685,† common labourers were allowed to take only 8*d*. a day for the summer half year. Sir George Shuckburgh puts down only 7$\frac{1}{2}$*d*. for the period from 1675 to 1720;‡ and Arthur Young estimates the average price of labour during the whole of the 17th century at 10$\frac{1}{4}$*d*.§ If on these grounds we were to estimate the wages of labour from 1665 to the end of the century at 10$\frac{1}{2}$*d*. it would appear that the earnings of the labourer, in the 17th century, after the depreciation of money had ceased, were only sufficient to purchase $\frac{}{3}$ of a peck of wheat. Taking however

* Windsor Table, deducting $\frac{1}{9}$.

† Eden's State of the Poor, vol. iii. p. 104.

‡ Philosoph. Trans. for 1798. Part i. p. 176.

§ Annals of Agriculture, No. 270, p. 88.

the more favourable supposition of 1*s.* a day as the earnings of the labourer, they would purchase, as before stated, about ¾ of a peck.

During the first twenty years of the 18th century, the price of corn fell, but not much; and it may be doubted whether the price of labour rose.

In 1725, a few years later than the period alluded to, the wages of labour were settled by the justices at Manchester. The best husbandry labourer, from the middle of March till the middle of September, was not to take more than 1*s.* a day without meat and drink; but common labourers, and hedgers, ditchers, palers, thrashers, or other task-work, only 10*d.* Mr. Howlett, as quoted by Sir F. Eden,* states the price of day-labour, so late as 1737, at only 10*d.* a day; and Sir F. Eden, writing in 1796, observes, that from various information he had collected in different parts of England, he had reason to think that the wages of labour had doubled* during the last sixty years, which could hardly be true, unless wages in the early part of the century had been lower than 1*s.*

The average price of wheat for the first twenty years of the century was rather less than £2.; and if the wages of labour were only 10*d.* or 10½*d.*, the labourer would earn considerably less than ¾ of a peck. If the wages were 1*s.* he would earn ⅘ of a peck.

From 1720 to 1755 corn fell and continued low, while the wages of labour seem to have been about 1*s.* During these thirty-five years the price of wheat was about 33*s.* the quarter, or a little above 1*s.* the peck, and the labourer therefore, on an average of thirty-five years together, would be able to earn about a peck of wheat.

From this time corn began gradually to rise, while wages do not appear to have risen in the same proportion. The first authentic accounts that we have of the price of labour, after corn had begun to rise,

* Vol. i. p. 385.

is in the extensive Agricultural Tours of Arthur Young, which took place in 1767, 1768 and 1770. The general result of the price of labour from these tours, on the mean rate of the whole year, was 7*s*. 4¼*d*. a week.* Taking an average of the five years, from 1766 to 1770 inclusive, the price of the quarter of wheat was £2. 7*s*. 8*d*. or nearly 48*s*.† which would be 6*s*. the bushel, and 1*s*. 6*d*. the peck. At these prices of labour and wheat, the labourer would earn very nearly $\frac{5}{6}$ of a peck.

In 1810 and 1811, accounts from thirty-seven counties, which, according to Arthur Young, were quite satisfactory, make the wages of day-labour for the mean rate of the year 14*s*. 6*d*.‡ a week, or nearly 2*s*. 6*d*. a day. The price of wheat for five years ending with 1810 was 92*s*.—ending with 1811, 96*s*.§ The prices both of labour and wheat appear to have doubled; and the labourer, in 1810 and 1811, could earn just about the same quantity of wheat as he could about forty years before, that is $\frac{5}{6}$ of a peck. The intermediate periods must necessarily have been subject to slight variations, owing to the uncertainty of the seasons, and an occasional advance in the price of corn, not immediately followed by an increased price of labour; but, in general, the average must have been nearly the same, and seldom probably for many years together differed much from $\frac{5}{6}$ of a peck.

Since the accounts given by Arthur Young, there has been no general calculation, that I am acquainted with, of the average money wages of agricultural labour, over districts sufficiently extensive to represent

* Annals of Agriculture, No. 271, p. 215.

† Deducting $\frac{1}{9}$ from the prices in the Windsor Table. Arthur Young deducts another 9th for the quality; but this is certainly too much, in reference to the general average of the kingdom to which the latest tables apply. I have therefore preferred adhering all along to the Windsor prices; and the reader will make what allowances he thinks fit for the quality, which, according to Mr. Rose, is not much above the average.

‡ Annals of Agriculture, No. 271, p. 215 and 216.

§ Windsor Table, Supp. to Encyclopædia Brit. Art. Corn Laws.

the whole. There are great differences in the prices of labour in different counties, and even in different parishes not very distant from each other. But from the numerous statements in the Agricultural Report, and what I have heard from other quarters, I should think that, making allowance for the difference between gold and paper during the high prices, the fall in the money price of standard labour has not been less than between 20 and 25 per cent.* As however the fall in the price of wheat has been much greater, it follows, that the labourer who is fully employed can now earn more wheat than he could at any period of the high prices. According to the calculations just referred to, when wheat on an average of 5 years ending with 1811 was 12*s*. a bushel, and 3*s*. a peck, the labourer with his half crown a day could only earn $\frac{5}{6}$ of a peck; whereas now if he earns only 20*d*. a day, and wheat is 52*s*. a quarter, or 6*s*. 6*d*. a bushel, he can purchase a whole peck, and have a halfpenny remaining. If his wages were 2*s*. a day he could purchase nearly a peck and a quarter. If the price of the quarter of wheat, instead of 52*s*. were 48*s*. the quarter, which is higher than it has been for some time latterly, the labourer earning 12*s*. a week or 2*s*. a day could purchase a peck and $\frac{1}{3}$, and earning only 20*d*. a day could purchase a peck and $\frac{1}{9}$, which is a

* In many cases the apparent fall has been in the proportion of 15 to 10, and even greater. In the North Riding of Yorkshire wages of the same description are said to have fallen from 3*s*. 6*d*. to 2*s*. and 2*s*. 3*d*. (Agricultural Report, Merry, p. 112.) In Shropshire from 2*s*. 4*d*. to 1*s*. 6*d*. (White, p. 24.) In Northamptonshire, Leicestershire, and Nottinghamshire, from 15*s*. and 18*s*. to 10*s*. since 1824. (Buckly, p. 398.) In Scotland, harvest wages from 2*s*. 6*d*. and 2*s*. to 1*s*. 6*d*. and 1*s*., and from 15*s*. and 12*s*. to 10*s*. and 8*s*. 6*d*. (Oliver, pp. 128 and 126.) Generally in the Lowlands the principal portion of the wages of labour is paid in kind, and the money value of that portion must therefore fall with the fall in the price of corn. The part paid in money has fallen, but not in proportion. In a private account which I received some years ago from the stewartry of Kircudbright, where the wages were all paid in money, it appears that from 1811 to 1822 the fall of summer wages was from 22*d*. to 15*d*., and of winter wages from 18*d*. to 1*s*.

greater quantity than the labourer has been able to command since 1575, when the price of labour is first stated in the reign of Elizabeth.

It is certainly true therefore that for some time, nearly perhaps ever since the war, the fully employed labourers have been able, in spite of the corn laws, to purchase a more than usual quantity of wheat. The specific evil of the present times in regard to agricultural labourers is, that from the low price of corn as compared with the price of labour and the other outgoings of the farmer, he is unable to farm with spirit, and the consequence is that a considerable number of men are unemployed except by the parish. Nothing can shew more clearly that a brisk demand for labourers depends upon an increase of the funds for their maintenance, *without a proportionate fall in their value*.

Section V.—*On the Conclusions to be drawn from the preceding Review of the Prices of Corn and Labour during the five last Centuries.*

From this review of the prices of corn and labour, during nearly the five last centuries, we may draw some important inferences.

In the first place, I think it appears that the great fall in the corn wages of labour which took place in the 16th century, must have been occasioned mainly by the great and unusual elevation which they had previously attained, and not by the discovery of the American mines and the consequent fall in the value of money. When we compare the corn wages of labour during the last half of the 15th century, with what they were both before and subsequently, it appears that whatever may have been the cause of these high wages, they were evidently peculiar, and could not therefore be permanent. This indeed is evident, not only by comparing them with previous and subsequent periods, but by considering their positive amount. Earnings of the value of nearly two pecks or half a bushel of wheat a day would allow of the earliest marriages, and the maintenance of the largest families. They are nearly the same as the earnings of the labourer in the United States. In such a country as England was, even at that time, such wages could only be occasioned by temporary causes. Among these we must reckon, a general improvement in the system of cultivation after the abolition of villanage, which increased the plenty of corn; and the comparatively rapid progress of commerce and manufactures, which occasioned a great demand for labour; while, owing to the wars in France, the civil wars between the Houses of York and Lancaster, and above all perhaps the slow change of habits among a people lately emancipated, this increase of produce and demand had not yet been followed by a proportionate effect on the population.

Certain it is that corn was very cheap both in France * and England; and labour in this country could not possibly have risen and kept high for so long a period as between sixty and seventy years, unless some peculiar cause or causes had restrained the supply of population, compared with the supply of corn and the demand for labour.

It is with the fact however of the very high wages of labour in the 15th century rather than with the causes of it, that we are chiefly concerned at present,

* It is a very curious fact, that the bullion price of corn continued unusually low in France from 1444 to 1510. (*Garnier's Richesse des Nations*, vol. ii. p. 184.) just during the same period that it was low in England. Adam Smith is inclined to attribute this fall and low price to a deficiency in the supply of the mines, compared with the demand; (B. i. ch. xi.) but this solution in no respect accounts for the rise of the bullion price of labour in England, at the time that the bullion price of corn was falling. Nothing can account for this fact, but a relative plenty of corn compared with labour—a state of things which has little to do with the mines. The low prices in France were probably connected with the abolition of villanage, and an extended cultivation in the reign of Charles VII. and his immediate successors, after the ravages of the English were at an end.

and of the fact there can be no doubt; but if the fact be allowed, it follows, that such wages must have very greatly fallen during the course of the following century, if the mines of America had not been discovered.

What effect the depreciation of money might have had in aggravating that increasing poverty of the labouring classes of society, which, with or without such a depreciation, would inevitably have fallen upon them, it is not easy to say. But from the still lower wages which prevailed in the 17th century after the depreciation had ceased, and from what has happened of late years (which shall be more fully noticed presently) I should not be disposed to consider a general rise in the price of corn, occasioned by an alteration in the value of money, and not by bad seasons, as likely to affect the labouring classes prejudicially for more than a few years. Still, however, it is quite certain that the condition of the labouring classes was growing much worse during the time that the depreciation of money from the discovery of the American mines was taking place; and whatever may have been the cause, as the people would always be comparing their situation with what it had been, in their own recollection and that of their fathers, it would inevitably excite great complaints; and, after it had grown comparatively very bad, as in the latter end of the reign of Elizabeth, it was likely to lead to those measures relating to the poor, which marked that period of our history.

Another inference which we may draw from the review is, that during the course of nearly 500 years, the earnings of a day's labour in this country have probably been more frequently below than above a peck of wheat; that a peck of wheat may be considered as something like a middle point, or a point rather above the middle, about which the corn wages of labour, varying according to the demand and supply, have oscillated; and that the population of a country may increase with some rapidity, while the wages of labour are even under this point.

The wages of day labour in France during the two last centuries, are said to have been pretty uniformly about the 20th part of a *septier* of wheat,* which would be a little above $\frac{4}{5}$ of a peck; but just before the revolution, at the time of Arthur Young's tour in France, they were only about $\frac{3}{4}$ of a peck. For some time subsequently to the revolution, they appear to have risen so as to command more than a peck.

A third inference which we may draw from this review is, that the seasons have a very considerable influence on the price of corn, not only for two or three years occasionally, but for fifteen or twenty years together, and sometimes much longer. These periods of unfavourable seasons seem to supersede all the other causes which may be supposed to have the greatest influence upon prices. An instance of this occurs after the great pestilence in the time of Edward III. One should naturally have thought that the quantity of good land being abundant, compared with the population, corn would have been very cheap. It was, however, on the contrary, dear during the twenty-five subsequent years,—a fact which cannot be accounted for but from unfavourable seasons.

Another instance of the same kind had occurred in the reign of Edward II., during the whole of which, the average price of wheat was more than double what it had been during the greatest part of the reign of Edward I., and the first half of the reign of Edward III.—evidently owing to unfavourable seasons.

A third instance occurs during the civil wars of the 17th century. So far from thinking that civil wars have a necessary tendency to make corn dear, I am disposed to agree with Sir F. Eden, in attributing a part of the high price of labour and the cheapness of corn in the 15th century, to the circumstance of a greater destruction of men than of cultivation having been occasioned in the civil wars of the Houses of York and Lancaster. But in the civil wars of the 17th century, no such cheapness of corn took place. On

* Wealth of Nations, b. i. c. xi. p. 313.

the contrary, in the period from 1646 to 1665 the price of corn was higher both in France and England than it had ever been known for twenty years together, either before or since, exclusive of the prices in this country during the war of the French Revolution. For shorter periods, these unfavourable seasons are of frequent recurrence, and must essentially affect the condition of the labourer during ten or five years. It depends upon their continuance and other concomitant circumstances, whether they raise money wages, or leave them as they were.

The periods of the lowest corn wages have been, when a considerable rise in the price of corn has taken place under circumstances not favourable to a proportionate rise in the price of labour. This is the most likely to happen in unfavourable seasons, when it would be impossible for the price of labour to rise in proportion to the price of corn. It may also happen when a fall is taking place in the value of money, if any previous causes have given an extraordinary stimulus to the progress of population. In this case, though the funds for the maintenance of labour may be increasing fast, the population may be increasing faster, and the money wages of labour will not rise in proportion to the price of corn. To this cause I am strongly disposed to attribute the inadequate rise of the money wages of labour during the reigns of Henry VIII., Mary, Edward VI., and Elizabeth. The state of things in the early part of the 16th century must have given a powerful stimulus to population; and considering the extraordinary high corn wages at this period, and that they could only fall very gradually, the stimulus must have continued to operate with considerable force during the greatest part of the century. In fact, depopulation was loudly complained of at the end of the 15th and beginning of the 16th centuries, and a redundancy of population was acknowledged at the end of the 16th. And it was this change in the state of the population, and not the discovery of the American mines, which occasioned so marked a fall in the corn wages of labour.

If the discovery of the American mines had found the labouring classes of the people earning only the same wages which they appear to have earned in the latter half of the reign of Edward III., and if the same increase of capital and produce had taken place during the 16th century, as really did take place, there is every probability that the money wages of labour would have increased as much as the money price of corn. Indeed when an increase of currency is accompanied, as it frequently is, by a rapid increase of capital, there is one reason, why, in the natural state of things, the price of labour should feel it more than other commodities. The encouragement given to population by such increase of resources, could not appear with any considerable effect in the market under sixteen or eighteen years;* and before that time the demand compared with the supply of labour might be greater than the demand compared with the supply of most other commodities.

It is on this account, that in the fall in the value of money which took place from 1793 to 1814, and which was unquestionably accompanied by a great increase of capital, and a great demand for labour, there is strong reason to believe, that if the price of labour had not been kept down by artificial means, it would have risen higher in proportion than the average price of corn. According to the last authentic accounts which had been obtained of the price of labour, previous to 1814, it appears by the statements of Arthur Young, that on an average of the returns of thirty-seven counties in 1810 and 1811, the weekly wages of day labour were 14*s.* 6*d.*,—a price, which, compared with the wages of 1767, 1768 and 1770,† is equal to the rise in the price of wheat during the same period. Now it is known that in many counties and districts in the

* The increase of the funds for the maintenance of labour would however have some effect soon, by diminishing mortality, both among those rising to the age of puberty, and the full grown labourers.

† Annals of Agriculture, No. 271. pp. 215 and 216.

southern parts of England, wages in 1810 and 1811 were unnaturally kept down to 12*s*., 10*s*., 9*s*. and even 7*s*. 6*d*. by the baneful system of regularly maintaining the children of the poor out of the rates; it may therefore fairly be concluded that if this system had not prevailed over a large part of England, the money wages of labour would have risen higher than in proportion to the price of wheat.

This conclusion is still further confirmed by what happened in Scotland and some parts of the north of England. In these districts, all accounts agree that the rise of money wages was in fact greater than the rise of corn, and that the condition of the labourer till 1814 was decidedly improved, even in spite of the taxes, many of which certainly bore heavily on the conveniences and comforts of the labourer, though they affected but little his command over strict necessaries.

In considering the corn wages of labour in the course of this review, it has not been possible always to make a distinction between the effects of a fall in the price of corn, and a rise in the money price of labour. In merely comparing the two objects with each other, the result is precisely similar; but their effects on the demand for labour and the encouragement to population are sometimes dissimilar, as I have before intimated. A great demand for labour is perfectly consistent with a fall in the price of raw produce, because, notwithstanding this fall, the whole *value* of the funds for the maintenance of labour may still be increasing; but it sometimes happens that a fall in the price of raw produce is accompanied by a diminished power on the part of the farmer to employ labour; and in this case the demand for labour and the encouragement to population will not be in proportion to the corn wages of labour.

If the labourer commands a peck instead of $\frac{5}{6}$ of a peck of wheat a day, in consequence of a rise of money wages, all the labourers who are willing and able to work may be employed, and probably also their wives and children; but if he is able to command this additional quantity of wheat on account of a fall in the price of corn which diminishes the value of the farmers' returns, the advantage is more apparent than real, and though the price of labour may not nominally fall for some time, yet as the demand for labour may be stationary, if not retrograde, its current price will not be a criterion of what might be earned by the united labours of a large family, or the increased exertions of the head of it in task-work.*

It is certain, therefore, that the same current corn wages will, under different circumstances, have a different effect, both on the demand for labour, and the general condition of the labouring classes.†

It should be observed, that in estimating the corn wages of labour I have uniformly taken wheat, the dearest grain. I have taken one grain to the exclusion of other necessaries, in order to avoid complicating the subject; and have chosen wheat because it is the main food of the greatest part of the population in England. But it is evident that at those periods, or in those countries, in which the main food of the people does not consist of wheat, the wheat wages which can be earned by a family will not form a just criterion of the encouragement given to population. Although the wheat wages might be very unequal at two different periods, or in two different countries, yet if in one case an inferior grain were habitually consumed, the encouragement to the population might be the same. The Irish labourer cannot command the support of so large a family upon wheat as the English labourer, but he can command in general the support of a larger family upon the food on which he is accustomed to live; and consequently, population has increased much faster during the last century in Ireland than in England.

* Under all ordinary circumstances, more labour may be set in motion, before any increase of population has taken place.

† This is frequently noticed in the Agricultural Report.

It appears then, that in order to form a just estimate of the demand for labour, the encouragement to population, and the condition of the labourer, we must first consider the increase of the funds specifically destined for the maintenance of labour, instead either of the increase of wealth, the increase of capital, or the increase in the exchangeable value of the whole produce.

Secondly, in estimating these funds we must consider their whole value, not merely their whole quantity, and make a proper allowance for those other parts of the wages of labour which do not consist of corn.

And thirdly, in estimating the amount of food and necessaries earned by the labouring classes, which amount principally affects their condition, we must make a careful distinction between the earnings of a whole family, when employment is difficult to be found, and their earnings when there is a demand for more work to be done than there are hands to do it.

It is further of the utmost importance always to bear in mind that a great command over the necessaries and conveniences of life may be effected in two ways, either by a rapid increase in the quantity and value of the funds destined for the maintenance of labour, or by the prudential habits of the labouring classes; and that as the former mode of improving their condition is neither in the power of the poor to carry into effect themselves, nor can in the nature of things be permanent, the great resource of the labouring classes for their happiness must be in those prudential habits which, if properly exercised, are capable of securing to them a fair proportion of the necessaries and conveniences of life, from the earliest stage of society to the latest.

I have said nothing of the rise or fall of wages according to the language adopted by Mr. Ricardo. Such wages, namely proportionate wages, only determine, or rather are determined by, the rate of profits, and will be considered in the next chapter. They have often little to do with the condition of the labourer, as, in reference to the proportion of the produce which he obtains, his wages are low in the United States of America, and high in countries where he may be starving. If indeed wages as well as profits were estimated by proportions, it would be perfectly true, as stated by Mr. Ricardo, that they could not both rise or fall together. If wages rose, profits must fall, and if wages fell, profits must rise. This is the necessary consequence of the language adopted. But Mr. Ricardo, I believe, was the first who used the term wages in this sense. Profits, indeed, and interest, had always been, and must always be estimated by proportions; but wages had always been, and always should be estimated by quantity, either by the quantity of money which the labourer earns, or by the quantity of the necessaries and conveniences of life, which that money enables him to purchase; and in reference to a period of any considerable length, by the latter, and not by the former.

Let it be remembered then, that this is the usual sense affixed to the term, wages, except when the word *proportionate* is added for some particular purpose. And consequently, according to the ordinary and most correct language of society, we frequently see high profits and high wages, low profits and low wages going together; in using which expressions, *high* and *low*, as applied to profits, always refer to their *rate* or *proportion*, and as applied to wages, to their *quantity* or *amount*.

CHAPTER V.

OF THE PROFITS OF CAPITAL.

SECTION I.—*Of the Nature of Profits, and the Mode in which they are estimated.*

IT has been usual in speaking of that portion of the national revenue which goes to the capitalist in return for the employment of his capital, to call it by the name of the profits of stock. But stock is not so appropriate an expression in this case as capital. Stock is a more general term, and may be defined to be, all the material possessions of a country, or all its actual wealth, whatever may be its destination, while capital is that particular part of these possessions, or of this accumulated wealth, which is destined to be employed with a view to profit in the production and distribution of future wealth. They are often, however, used indiscriminately, and perhaps no great error may arise from it; but it may be useful to recollect, that all stock is not, properly speaking, capital, though all capital is stock; and consequently that capital may increase by an alteration in the proportion of that part of the whole stock which is employed productively, while the whole quantity of the stock, or the wealth of a country may remain at first the same.

The profits of capital consist of the difference between the value of a commodity produced, and the value of the advances necessary to produce it, and these advances consist of accumulations generally made up of wages, rents, taxes, interest, and profits.

The rate of profits is the proportion which the difference between the value of the commodity produced, and the value of the advances necessary to produce it, bears to the value of the advances. When the value of the product is great compared with the value of the advances, the excess being considerable, the rate of profits will be high. When the value of the product exceeds but little the value of the advances, the difference being small, the rate of profits will be low.

The varying rates of profit, therefore, obviously depend upon the causes which alter the proportions between the value of the advances necessary to production, and the value of the product obtained.

Profits, as we all know, are practically estimated by the money prices of the products compared with the money prices of the advances; and as money for the short periods during which mercantile transactions last, is universally considered as measuring value and not quantity, it follows, that profits, as it has been stated, are always practically estimated by the values of the products compared with the values of the advances, and not by their relative quantities. It would be impossible indeed to compare them as to quantity, because the advances necessary to produce commodities, are never all of the same kind as the commodities produced; and when they are not the same, their *quantities* do not admit of a comparison. We cannot compare shoes or cloth with corn or labour in regard to quantity.

It is of so much importance to be fully aware of the necessity of estimating both the advances and the returns of the capitalist in *value* and not in *quantity*, that it may be worth while to illustrate the difference in the results of the two modes of proceeding.

Of all the articles obtained by human industry, there is not one in which so great a part of the advances is identical with the produce as in the cultivation of corn. Let us consider what practically takes place in the production of this most important commodity.

The farmer practically pays his labourers in money. Let us suppose that this money, with the other money outgoings amounts to £200, that in the year in which the advance is made it will purchase 100 quarters of wheat, the price of wheat being £2 a quarter, and that the rate of profits is 20 per cent, in which case the return must be 120 quarters, or 20 per cent. in quantity. Now if in the next year there should be a scanty crop, yielding only 100 quarters instead of 120, then in reference to quantity there will be absolutely no excess in the returns, as compared with the outgoings, and the capitalist would have actually nothing to live upon. But would he really be so destitute? Far from it. He might perhaps be better off, instead of worse off than usual. Profits, as I have before stated, are always practically estimated by value, not quantity; and the real question is about the *price* of the produce compared with the *price* of the advances, and not the excess of the returns in wheat above the advances in wheat. Most happily for society such is the nature of things, that a diminution in the quantity of an article, other circumstances being the same, raises its price; and the diminution of one sixth in the supply of corn would probably raise it considerably more than one fifth. Taking the rise, however, only at one fifth, its value in money would be 48*s*. the quarter, and the sale of 83⅓ quarters would replace the capital expended, and leave 20 per cent. profit to the capitalist, that is, would leave as great a profit to the capitalist when the product in wheat was only equal to the advances in wheat, as when the product in wheat was 20 per cent. greater.

On the other hand, if the cultivator advanced capital of the value of £200 in rather a scarce year, when the price of wheat was 48*s*. the quarter, the advances in wheat would be represented by 83⅓ quarters, and if after harvest the produce were 120 quarters, in an estimate by quantity he would appear to gain 45 per cent.; but as his gains would really be estimated by value not quantity, and the price of wheat would have fallen from 48*s*. to 40*s*., it would take a hundred quarters of corn to replace the £200 advanced, and the produce being 120 quarters, profits would be only 20 per cent. instead of 45 per cent.

It appears, therefore, that if the profits of the cultivator were estimated by quantity they might vary between nothing and 45 per cent. at the very time when estimated by price or value, as they always are practically, the cultivator was in each year making a regular profit of 20 per cent.

In the above cases, I have supposed the price of the whole produce, and the rate of profits to remain the same; but if the price of the whole produce determined by the state of the supply compared with the demand, ceased to be to the prices of the advances in the proportion of 120 to 100, profits would either rise or fall. If the price of the whole produce should advance, that is, if the whole produce, whether consisting of 100 quarters or 120 quarters, should sell for £260 instead of £240, it is obvious that a smaller proportion of the whole value would be sufficient to replace the £200 advanced, and profits would be 30 per cent., instead of 20 per cent.*

On the other hand, if the price of the whole produce, whether great or small, were to fall, owing to the state of the supply compared with the demand, and instead of selling for £240, were to sell for £220, a larger proportion of the whole produce would be necessary to replace the capital of the £200 advanced, and profits would fall from 20 per cent., to 10 per cent.

It may be said, perhaps, that these variations in the quantity of produce are only temporary, and that it is the average excess which is referred to, and not the variations of that excess occasioned by the seasons. It may be observed in answer, that, as it is universally allowed that the prices of the farmer's whole crop never rises in proportion to its abundance, and never falls in proportion to its deficiency, it is certain, that the average excess of value would not be the same as the average excess of produce.

Corn, on account of its being the main support of

* It happens not very unfrequently, that the rise in the price of agricultural produce greatly exceeds this. Mr. Tooke in his *Details of the High and Low Prices*, supposes that, owing to a rise in the price of wheat from about 48*s*. a quarter to 75*s*. in 1795 and 1796, with a rise of other agricultural produce nearly in proportion, the farmers and landlords, after an allowance made for every probable deduction, must have divided between them a net additional profit of 12 to 14 millions per annum, and a still greater profit in 1800 and 1801, pp. 303 and 305, 2nd edit.

the labourer, is the only object in the production of which a comparison may be instituted between the quantity advanced and the quantity produced; yet even here we have found that the cause which determines profits is their relative values, and not their relative quantities.

In manufacturing and mercantile employments, there is no approach towards a possibility of comparing the advances with the products in regard to quantity. However, the powers of production in manufactures may increase, a nearly proportionate fall in the value of the produce determined by the state of the demand and supply prevents any permanent change in the division of produce, and consequently, leaves the capitalist in a short time with the same or nearly the same rate of profits. The workman receives a larger quantity of what he produces, but the same value; and his condition will be benefitted, chiefly in proportion to the utility of the article to him as a consumer. This is equally true in regard to mercantile products, cheapened by facility of transport, or the discovery of more abundant sources of foreign supply.

It is clear therefore, that profits are invariably measured by value, and never by quantity.

Now, it has been shown in the second chapter of this work, that the values of any commodities, or of the mass of commodities are always determined by the state of the supply compared with the demand; and that their values may be measured by the quantity of standard labour which they will command. It is also obvious from what has been said, that during the short periods which usually intervene between the advances of capital and the returns of produce, they may both be estimated correctly in money. In the employment of capital therefore, in any business, the advances, whether increasing or diminishing in value, may be known and measured beforehand, while the value of the product, and the proportion of that value which goes to replace the advances remains to be ascertained when the produce is sold.

The varying rate of profits therefore, in the production of every commodity depends upon the excess of its value when sold above the known value of the advances, determined in all cases by the state of the supply and the demand.

This is a universal proposition, equally applicable whether profits are affected by temporary or by more permanent causes, whether the productive powers of labour are great or small, increasing, stationary, or diminishing.

And it will be found, that this proposition is essentially the same as the proposition which states, that profits depend upon the proportion of the value of the whole produce, which goes to pay the wages of the labour employed to obtain it.*

The truth of this proposition is quite obvious in the cases where only immediate labour and the profits upon it are concerned. If a hundred pounds be expended in immediate labour, and the returns come in at the end of the year, and sell for £110, £120, or £130, it is evident that in each case the profits will be determined by the proportion of the value of the whole produce which is required to pay the labour employed.

If the value of the produce in the market be £110, the proportion required to pay the labourers will be $\frac{10}{11}$ of the value of the produce, and profits will be ten per cent. If the value of the produce be £120, the proportion required to pay the labour employed will be $\frac{10}{12}$, and profits will be twenty per cent. If the value of the produce be £130, the proportion required to pay the labour advanced will be $\frac{10}{13}$, and profits will be thirty per cent.

But it will be asked, how are we to compare the value of the produce with the labour required to obtain it, when the advances of the capitalist do not consist of labour alone.

In cases of this kind, the following very simple mode

* This, though rather differently worded, is Mr. Ricardo's proposition, but he has applied it incorrectly, as will be seen in a subsequent section.

of proceeding presents itself. It will be allowed that the capitalist generally expects an equal profit upon all the parts of the capital which he advances. Let us suppose that a certain portion of the value of his advances, one-fourth for instance, consists of the wages of immediate labour, and three-fourths consist of accumulated labour and profits, with any additions which may arise from rents, taxes, or other outgoings. In this case one-fourth of the value of the produce obtained replaces with its proportionate profit that part of his capital which has been employed in the payment of immediate labour; and the other three-fourths replace with the remaining profit all his other advances: and thus it will be strictly true that the profits of the capitalist will vary with the varying value of this one-fourth of the produce compared with the quantity of labour employed; or, in other words, that profits depend on the proportion of the value of the produce which goes to pay the labour which has been employed.

As an instance let us suppose that a farmer employs in the cultivation of a certain portion of land £2000, £1500 of which he expends in seed, keep of horses, wear and tear of his fixed capital, interest upon his fixed and circulating capitals, rent, tithes, taxes, &c. and £500 upon immediate labour; and that the returns obtained at the end of the year are worth £2400. It is obvious that the value required to replace the advances being £2000 the farmer's profits will be £400, or twenty per cent. And it is equally obvious that if we took one-fourth of the value of the produce, namely £600, and compared it with the amount paid in the wages of immediate labour, the result would shew exactly the same rate of profits.

There is no case however complicated which may not be easily solved in a similar manner.

When it is said that profits depend upon the division of the produce between the labourer and the capitalist, it is not of course meant to exclude the labourers and capitalists who have furnished those large portions of the advances which do not consist of the wages of immediate labour; and we must either trace accurately the proportions of accumulated labour and accumulated profits in these advances, which it is not always easy to do, or adopt the mode above suggested, which gives at once the proportion of the produce which goes to pay the wages of the immediate labour employed. The result is exactly the same as if we had measured the whole advances in standard labour, and had estimated the rate of profits by the excess of the value of the produce above what was required to pay the wages of that quantity of labour.

The reader will be aware that if we reckon the value of the fixed capital employed as a part of the advances, we must reckon the remaining value of such capital at the end of the year as a part of the annual returns. Without a correction of this kind it would appear that in those departments of industry in which the greatest quantity of fixed capital had been applied, the value of the capital compared with the value of the produce had been the greatest, from which it would seem to follow that the rate of profits had been the lowest; but though the capitalist naturally considers the whole of what he employs in production as capital advanced; yet in reality his annual advances consist only of his circulating capital, the wear and tear of his fixed capital with the interest upon it, and the interest of that part of his circulating capital which consists of the money employed in making his annual payments as they are called for.

The following is a statement in the first Report of the Factory Commissioners, (page 34) in which another class of advances under the head of contingencies is added:

Capital sunk in building and machinery £10,000
Floating capital 7,000

£500	Interest at 5 per cent. on £10,000 fixed capital.
350	Ditto on floating capital.
150	Rents, taxes, and rates.
650	Sinking Fund of $6\frac{1}{2}$ per cent. for wear and tear of the fixed capital.
£1,650	

£1,650	
1,100	Contingencies, carriage, coal, oil, &c.
2,750	
2,600	Wages and salaries.
£5,350	

Spun 363,000 *lbs.* Twist, Value £16,000.
Raw cotton required about 400,000 at 6*d*.

Equal to	£10,000	
Expenses	5,350	
	15,350	Value when sold, £16,000.

Profit 650 or about 4.2 on the advance of £15,350.

The wages of the operatives or of the immediate labour employed in the production of the twist, form about one-sixth of the advances, and the comparison of these advances with one-sixth of the value of the produce will clearly indicate the *rate* of profit upon the whole of the advances.

In drawing the particular attention of the reader to the profits, which may be said to belong to the immediate labour employed in any production, it is by no means intended to propose a better mode of ascertaining profits than the ordinary one of comparing the annual money advances, with the annual money returns. The object is to show, that the two modes always accord, (except in the rare case of a change in the price of labour or alteration in the value of money during the interval which elapses between the advances and returns); and whether we take the most simple case, where the advances consist of immediate labour alone, or the most complex one, where but a small part only of the advances consists of immediate labour, it will always be found true that profits vary according to the proportion of the value of the whole produce which goes to pay the wages of the labour employed to obtain it.

SECTION II.—*Of the limiting Principle of Profits.*

IT has been stated in the preceding section, that the varying rate of profits depends upon the causes which alter the proportion between the value of the advances necessary to production, and the value of the produce obtained.

The two main causes which affect these proportions, are, the productiveness, or unproductiveness of the last capitals employed upon the land, by which a smaller, or a greater proportion of the value of the produce is capable of supporting the labourers employed. This may be called the *limiting* principle of profits. And, secondly, the varying value of the produce of the same quantity of labour occasioned by the accidental or ordinary state of the demand and supply, by which a greater or smaller proportion of that produce falls to the share of the labourers employed. This may be called the *regulating* principle of profits, this second cause is constantly modifying the first, but it will be desirable to consider them separately.

If then we suppose the first cause to operate singly, and the corn wages of the individual labourer to be always the same, the whole skill in agriculture remained unchanged, and there were no taxes nor any means of obtaining corn from foreign countries, the rate of profits must regularly fall, as the society advanced, and as it became necessary to resort to inferior machines which required more labour to put in action.

It would signify little, in this case, whether the last land taken into cultivation for food had yielded a rent in its uncultivated state. It is certain that the landlord would not allow it to be cultivated, unless he could, at the least, obtain the same rent for it as before. This must be considered as an absolute condition on the worst lands taken into cultivation in an improved country. After this payment was made, the remainder of the produce would be divided almost entirely between the capitalists and the labourers, and it is evident that if the number of labourers necessary to obtain a given produce were continually increasing, and the corn wages of each labourer remained the same, the portion destined to the payment of labour would be continually encroaching upon the portion destined to the payment of profits; and the rate of profits would of course continue regularly diminishing till, from the want of power or will to save, the progress of accumulation had ceased.

In this case, and supposing an equal demand for all the parts of the same produce,* it is obvious that the profits of capital in agriculture would be in proportion to the fertility of the last land taken into cultivation, or to the amount of the produce obtained by a given quantity of labour. And as profits in the same country tend to an equality, the general rate of profits would follow the same course.

But a moment's consideration will shew us, that the supposition here made of a constant uniformity in the corn wages of labour is not only contrary to the actual state of things, but involves a contradiction.

The progress of population is almost exclusively regulated by the quantity of the necessaries of life actually awarded to the labourer; and if from the first he had no more than sufficient to keep up the actual population, the labouring classes could not in-

* It is necessary to qualify the position in this way, because, with regard to the main products of agriculture, it might easily happen that all the parts were not of the same value. If a farmer cultivated his lands by means of domestics living in his house whom he found in food and clothing, his advances might always be nearly the same in quantity and of the same high value in use; but in the case of a glut from the shutting up of an accustomed market, or a season of unusul abundance, a part of the crop might be of no value either in use or exchange, and his profits could by no means be determined, by the excess of the *quantity* produced, above the advances necessary to produce it, as before shewn, page 264.

crease, nor would there be any occasion for the progressive cultivation of poorer land. On the other hand, if the corn wages of labour were such as to admit of and encourage a considerable increase of population, and yet were always to remain the same, it would involve the contradiction of a continued increase of population at the same rate after the accumulation of capital, and the means of supporting such an increase had entirely ceased.

We cannot then make the supposition of a *natural* and *constant* rate of corn wages. And if we cannot fix the wages of labour estimated in necessaries, they must evidently vary with the progress of the funds destined for the maintenance of labour, compared with the supply of labour.

We may, however, if we please, suppose a uniform progress of capital and population, by which is not meant in the present case the same *rate* of progress permanently, which is impossible; but a uniform progress towards the greatest practicable amount, without temporary accelerations or retardations. And before we proceed to the actual state of things, it may be curious to consider in what manner profits would be affected under these circumstances.

At the commencement of the cultivation of a fertile country by civilized colonists, and while rich land was in great plenty, a small portion only of the value of the produce would be paid in the form of rent. The productiveness of labour being great, if nearly the whole were divided between wages and profits, the labourers might obtain a large quantity of produce, while a sufficient *proportion* of the whole might be left to yield large profits, and wages and profits would both be high at the same time.*

As the society continued to increase, if the territory were limited, or the soil of different qualities, it is quite obvious that the productive powers of labour as

* The reader will recollect that wages always refer to quantity, unless otherwise particularly expressed, and profits to proportion.

applied to the cultivation of land must gradually diminish; and as a given quantity of labour would yield a smaller and smaller return, there would evidently be a less and less produce to be divided between labour and profits.

If, as the powers of labour diminished, the physical wants of the labourer were also to diminish in the same proportion, then the same *share* of the whole produce might be left to the capitalist, and the *rate* of profits would not necessarily fall. But the physical wants of the labourer remain always the same; and though in the progress of society, from the increasing scarcity of provisions compared with labour, these wants are in general less fully supplied, and the corn wages of labour gradually fall; yet it is clear that there is a limit, and probably at no great distance, which cannot be passed. The command of a certain quantity of food is absolutely necessary to the labourer in order to support himself, and such a family as will maintain merely a stationary population. Consequently, if poorer lands which required more labour were successively taken into cultivation, it would not be possible for the corn wages of each individual labourer to be diminished in proportion to the diminished produce; a greater *proportion* of the whole would necessarily go to pay the wages of labour; and the rate of profits would continue regularly falling till the accumulation of capital had ceased.

Such would be the necessary course of profits and wages in the progressive accumulation of capital, as applied to the progressive cultivation of new and less fertile land, or the further improvement of what had before been cultivated; and on the supposition here made, the rates both of profits and of corn wages would be highest at first, and would regularly and gradually diminish together, till they both came to a stand at the same period, and the demand for an increase of produce ceased to be effective.

In the mean time, it will be asked, what becomes of the profits of capital employed in manufactures and commerce, a species of industry not like that employed upon the land, where the productive powers of labour necessarily diminish; but where these powers not only do not necessarily diminish, but very often greatly increase?

In the cultivation of land, the cause of the *necessary* diminution of profits is the diminution in the quantity of produce obtained by the same quantity of labour. In manufactures and commerce, it is the fall in the exchangeable value of the same amount of produce.

The labour required to produce corn, has a constant tendency to increase from inevitable physical causes, while the labour required to produce manufactures and articles of commerce sometimes greatly diminishes, sometimes remains stationary, and at all events increases much slower than the labour required to produce corn. When, therefore, profits fall in agriculture it becomes obviously more advantageous to employ capital in manufactures and commerce than on the land; and capital will in consequence be so employed till a fall has taken place in manufactures and commercial products from their comparative abundance. But it has been shown that the value of the same quantity of labour will always remain the same; and it is evident, that if the products fall in value, while the quantity of the labour, or the value of the capital required to produce them, remain the same, profits must fall. It is farther evident, that this fall must necessarily go on, till profits in manufactures and commerce have been reduced nearly to a level with those in agriculture. And thus it appears that in the progress of improvement, as poorer and poorer land is taken into cultivation, the general rate of profits must be limited by the powers of the soil last cultivated. If the last land taken into cultivation will only yield a certain excess of value above the lowest value of the capital necessary to produce it, it is obvious that profits, generally, cannot possibly be higher than this excess will allow. In the ascending scale, this is a barrier which cannot be passed. But limitation is essentially different from regulation. In the descending scale, while the land is still fertile profits may be lower in any degree. There is here no controlling necessity which determines the rate of profits; and below the highest limit which the actual state of the land will allow, ample scope is left for the operation of the regulating principle.

SECTION III.—*Of the regulating Principle of Profits.*

THE second cause which affects profits, is the varying value of the produce of the same quantity of labour on the same value of capital, determined by the state of the demand and supply. This may be called the regulating principle of profits, as within the extreme limits prescribed by the state of the land, all the variations of profits, whether temporary or durable, are regulated by it.

Such variations in the value of produce are occasioned principally by the abundance or scantiness of capital, including the funds for the maintenance of labour, as compared with the labour which it employs.

This is obviously a cause which, by awarding a greater or a smaller *proportion* of the produce to the labourer, must have a powerful influence on profits; and if considerable variations were to take place in the supplies of capital and produce and the supplies of labour, in a rich and unexhausted soil, the same effects might be produced on profits as by the operation of the first cause, and in a much shorter time.

In order to see more clearly the powerful effects of the second cause on profits, let us consider it for a moment as operating alone; and suppose, that while the capital and produce of a country continued increasing, its population were checked and kept short of the demand for it, by some miraculous influence. Under these circumstances, a gradation would take place in the proportion which capital and produce would bear to labour, and we should see in consequence a similar gradation take place in the rate of profits.

As capital and produce increased faster than labour, the profits of capital would fall, and if a progressive increase of capital and produce were to take place, while the population, by some hidden cause, were prevented from keeping pace with it, notwithstanding the fertility of the soil and the plenty of food, then profits would be gradually reduced, until, by successive reductions, the power and will to accumulate had ceased to operate; and this state of things might take place rapidly, if a great proportion of those who were engaged in personal services were rapidly converted by saving into productive labourers.

Profits in this case would experience the same kind of progressive diminution as they would by the progressive accumulation of capital in the present state of things; but rent and wages would be very differently affected. From what has before been stated on the subject of rent, the amount of it in such a country could not be great. According to the supposition, the progress of the population is retarded, and the number of labourers is limited, while land of considerable fertility remains uncultivated. The demand for fertile land therefore, compared with the supply, would be comparatively inconsiderable; and in reference to the whole of the national produce, the portion which would consist of rent would depend mainly upon the gradations of more fertile land which had been cultivated before the population had come to a stop, and upon the value of the produce to be derived from the land that was not cultivated.

With regard to wages they would continue progressively to rise, in necessaries, conveniences, and luxuries, so as to place the labourer in a condition continually and in all respects improving, as long as capital continued to increase.

In short, of the three great portions into which the

mass of produce is divided, rent, profits, and wages, the two first would be low, because both the supply of land and the supply of capital would be abundant compared with the demand; while the wages of labour would be very high, because the funds for the maintenance of labour would be in great abundance compared with the supply of labourers; and thus the value of each would be regulated by the great principle of demand and supply.

If, instead of supposing the population to be checked by some peculiar influence, we make the more natural supposition of a limited territory, with all the land of nearly equal quality, and of such great fertility as to admit of very little capital being laid out upon it, the effects upon the profits of capital would be just the same as in the last instance, though they would be very different on rents and wages. After all the land had been cultivated, and no more capital could be employed on it, there cannot be a doubt that rents would be extremely high and profits and wages very low. The competition of increasing capital in manufactures and commerce would reduce the rate of profits, while the principle of population would continue to augment the number of the labouring classes, till their corn wages were so low as to check their further increase. It is probable that, owing to the assumed fertility of all the soil and the great proportion of persons which might be employed in manufactures and commerce, the exports would be great and the value of money very low. The money price of corn and money wages would perhaps be as high as if the cost of the whole produce in labour had been double or treble; food would then be a strict monopoly; rents would rise to an extraordinary height without any assistance from poor lands, and the gradations of soil; and profits might fall to the point only just sufficient to keep up the actual capital without any additional labour being necessary to procure the food of the labourer.

The effects which would obviously result from the

two suppositions just made, clearly shew that the increasing quantity of labour required for the successive cultivation of poorer land is not theoretically necessary to a fall of profits from the highest rate to the lowest.

The former of these two suppositions further shews the great power possessed by the labouring classes of society, if they chose to exercise it. The comparative check to population, which was considered as occasioned by some miraculous influence, might in reality be effected by the prudence of the poor; and it would unquestionably be followed by the result described. It may naturally appear hard to the labouring classes that, of the vast mass of productions obtained from the land, the capital, and the labour of the country, so small a quantity should fall to the share of each individual. But the quantity is at present determined, and must always in future be determined, by the inevitable laws of supply and demand. If the market were comparatively understocked with labour, the landlords and capitalists would be obliged to give a larger quantity of produce to each workman. But with an abundant supply of labour, such a quantity, for a permanence, is an absolute impossibility. The rich have neither the power, nor can it be expected that they should all have the will, to keep the market understocked with labour. Yet every effort to ameliorate the lot of the poor generally, that has not this tendency, is perfectly futile and childish. It is quite obvious therefore, that the knowledge and prudence of the poor themselves, are absolutely the *only* means by which any general and permanent improvement in their condition can be effected. They are really the arbiters of their own destiny; and what others can do for them, is like the dust of the balance compared with what they can do for themselves. These truths are so important to the happiness of the great mass of society, that every opportunity should be taken of repeating them.

But, independent of any peculiar efforts of prudence on the part of the labouring classes, it appears from experience that while the productive powers of labour remain nearly the same, the supplies of labour and the supplies of capital and produce do not always keep pace with each other. Practically, they are often separated at some distance, and for a considerable period; and sometimes population increases faster than capital and produce, and at other times capital and produce increase faster than population.

It is obvious, for instance, that from the very nature of population, and the time required to bring full-grown labourers into the market, a sudden increase of capital and produce cannot effect a proportionate supply of labour in less than sixteen or eighteen years. On the other hand, when capital and produce are nearly stationary from the want of will to accumulate, it is well known that population in general is apt to increase faster than the produce which is to support it, till the wages of labour are reduced to that standard which, with the actual habits of the country, are no more than sufficient to maintain a stationary population.

These periods, in which population and produce do not keep pace with each other, are evidently of sufficient extent, essentially to alter the proportion which goes to pay the wages of labour; and consequently, to influence essentially the rate of profits.

So entirely, indeed, does the rate of profits depend on the division of the produce, occasioned by the state of the supply and the demand, that in comparing two countries together, the rate of profits will sometimes be found the lowest in that country, in which the productiveness of labour on the land is the greatest.

In Poland, and some other parts of Europe, where capital is scarce, profits are said to be higher than in America; yet it is probable that the last land taken into cultivation in America is much richer than the last land taken into cultivation in Poland. But in America the labourer earns perhaps the value of eighteen or twenty quarters of wheat in the year; in Poland only the value of eight or nine quarters of rye. This difference in the division of the produce, must make a great difference in the rate of profits; yet the causes which determine this division, far from being of so temporary a nature that they may be safely overlooked, might operate most powerfully for a great length of time. Such is the extent of America, that the corn wages of its labour may not essentially fall for a long term of years; and the effects of a scanty but stationary capital on an overflowing but stationary population might last for ever.

In dwelling thus upon the powerful effects which must inevitably be produced by the proportion which capital and produce bear to labour, and upon the necessity of giving adequate weight to the principle of demand and supply, or competition, in every explanation of the circumstances which determine profits, it is not meant to underrate the importance of that cause which depends upon the diminishing productiveness of labour on the last land taken into cultivation. This cause is indeed of such a nature, that, if its action goes on, it must finally overwhelm every other. Yet, still an attempt to estimate the rate of profits in any country for ten or twenty years together by a reference to this cause alone, would lead to the greatest practical errors.

The value of the government long annuities has a natural and constant tendency to diminish as they approach towards the term for which they were granted; yet it is well known, that out of the comparatively short term of 90 years, so large a proportion as twenty, has sometimes elapsed not only without any diminution, but with an actual increase of their value. When, however, they approach near to the term at which they expire, they must necessarily so diminish in value on this account alone, that no demand arising from plenty of money could possibly keep up their price. In the same manner, when cultivation is pushed to its extreme practical limits, that is, when the labour of a man upon the last land taken into cultivation will scarcely do more than support such a family as is necessary to maintain a stationary population, it is evident that no other cause or causes can prevent profits from sinking to the lowest rate required to maintain the actual capital. But though this principle is finally of the very greatest power, yet its progress is extremely slow and gradual; and while it is proceeding with scarcely perceptible steps to its final destination, the second cause is producing effects which entirely overcome it, and often for twenty or thirty, or even 100 years together, make the rate of profits take a course absolutely different from what it ought to be according to the first cause.

SECTION IV.—*Of Profits as affected by the Causes practically in operation.*

WE come now to the consideration of the various causes which may influence profits in the actual state of things, particularly in this country. And here it is evident that we shall have in operation both the causes already stated, with others which disturb and modify them.

In the progressive cultivation of poor land, occasioned by the increase of capital and population, profits as far as they depend upon natural fertility, will regularly fall; but if at the same time improvements in agriculture are taking place, they may certainly be such as, for a considerable period, not only to prevent profits from falling, but to allow of a rise. To what extent, and for what length of time, this circumstance might interrupt the progressive fall of profits occasioned by the necessity of taking poorer land into cultivation, without such improvements, it is not easy to say; but, as it is certain that in an extensive territory, consisting of soils not very different in their natural powers of production, the fall of profits arising from this cause would be slow, it is probable that for a considerable extent of time agricultural improvements, including of course the improved implements and machinery used in cultivation, as well as an improved system of cropping and managing the land, might more than balance it.

A second circumstance which would contribute to the same effect is, an increase of personal exertion among the labouring classes. This exertion is extremely different in different countries, and at different times in the same country. A day's labour of a Hindoo, or a South-American Indian, will not admit of a comparison with that of an Englishman; and it has even been said, that though the money price of day-labour in Ireland is little more than the half of what it is in England, yet that Irish labour is not really cheaper than English, although it is well known that Irish labourers when in this country, with good examples and adequate wages to stimulate them, will work as hard as their English companions.

This latter circumstance alone clearly shows how different may be the personal exertions of the labouring classes in the same country at different times; and how different therefore may be the products of a given number of days labour, as the society proceeds from the indolence of the savage to the activity of the civilized state. This activity indeed, within certain limits, appears almost always to come forward when it is most called for, that is, when there is much work to be done without a full supply of persons to do it. The personal exertions of the South American Indian, the Hindoo, the Polish boor, and the Irish agricultural labourer, may be very different indeed 500 years hence.

A third circumstance which has a considerable effect on profits, and not unfrequently occurs, is, the unequal rise of some parts of the farmer's capital, when the price of corn is raised by an increased demand. Under such a rise, (which if it continues is generally accompanied by an advanced price of standard labour, or a fall in the value of money,) the prices of many home commodities will be considerably modified for some time, by the unequal pressure of taxation, and the unequal rise in the prices of foreign commodities, and of the commodities worked up at home from foreign materials. The rise of corn and labour at home will not proportionally raise the price of such products; and as far as these products together with taxes, form a part of the farmer's capital, a smaller proportion of the produce, owing to its increased value, will replace it. This remark is applicable to leather, timber, soap, candles, cottons, woollens, &c. &c., all of which enter more or less into the capitals of the farmer, or the wages of the labourer, and are all influenced in their prices more or less by importation.

A fourth circumstance, which favours a rise of profits is a fall in the prices of some important manufactures, as compared with corn, owing to improvements in machinery. This state of things always allows of some diminution in the corn wages of labour without a proportionate diminution of the comforts of the labourer: and if the money price of the farmer's produce increases without a proportionate increase in the price of labour, and in the materials of which his advances consist, his profits must necessarily rise.

It appears then, that practically, and in the actual state of things, the physical necessity of a fall of profits in agriculture arising from the increasing quantity of labour required to produce the same quantity of food, may be so counteracted and overcome, for a considerable time by other causes, as to leave very great play to the influence of the competitions of capital.

The facts which support this conclusion are numerous and incontrovertible. It may be said, indeed, with truth that the different rates of profits during periods of peace and war, which are observed to take place in all countries, are chiefly attributable to the abundance or scarcity of capital and produce compared with the demand, and not to the varying productiveness of labour on the land. To the instances of this kind which have before been stated may be added the following one, which is so remarkably strong as to be alone almost decisive of the question, and having happened in our own country, is completely open to the most minute examination.

From the accession of George II. in 1727 to the commencement of the war in 1793, the interest of money was little more than 3 per cent. The public securities which had been reduced to 4 per cent. rose considerably after the reduction. According to Chalmers, the *natural* rate of interest ran steadily at 3 per cent.;* and it appears by a speech of Sir John Barnard's that the 3 per cent. stocks sold at a premium upon Change. In 1750, after the termination of the war, the 4 per cent. stocks were reduced to 3½, for seven years, and from that time to 3 per cent. permanently.†

Excluding then the interval of war, we have here a period of twenty-two years, during which the general rate of interest was between 3½ and 3 per cent.

The temporary variations in the value of government securities will not certainly at all times be a correct criterion of the rate of profits or even of the rate of interest; but when they remain nearly steady for some time together, they must be considered as a fair approximation to a correct measure of interest; and when the public creditors of a government consent to a great fall in the interest which they had before received, rather than be paid off, it is a most decisive proof of a great difficulty in the means of employing capital profitably, and consequently a most decisive proof of a low rate of profits.

After an interval of nearly seventy years from the

* Estimate of the strength of Great Britain, ch. vii. p. 115.
† Ibid. ch. vii. p. 120.

commencement of the period here noticed, and forty years from the end of it, during which a great accumulation of capital had taken place, and an unusual quantity of new land had been brought into cultivation, we find a period of twenty years succeed in which the average market rate of interest was rather above than below 5 per cent.; and we have certainly every reason to think, from the extraordinary rapidity with which capital was recovered, after it had been destroyed, that the rate of profits in general was quite in proportion to this high rate of interest.

The difficulty of borrowing on mortgage during a considerable part of the time is perfectly well known; and though the pressure of the public debt might naturally be supposed to create some alarm, and incline the owners of disposable funds to give a preference to landed security; yet it appears from the surveys of Arthur Young, that the number of years purchase given for land, was in 1811, $29\frac{1}{4}$, and forty years before, 32 or $32\frac{1}{2}$,*—the most decisive proof that can well be imagined of an increase in the profits of capital employed upon land.

The nature of these facts, and the state of things under which they took place, (in the one case, in a state of peace with a slack demand for capital and produce, and in the other, a state of war with an unusual demand for both,) obviously and clearly point to the *relative* redundancy or deficiency of capital and produce as their cause. And the question which now remains to be considered, is, whether the circumstances which have been stated in this section are sufficient to account theoretically for such a free operation of this principle, notwithstanding the progres-

* Annals of Agriculture, No. 270, pp. 96, and 97, and No. 271, p. 215. Mr. Young expresses considerable surprise at these results, and does not seem to be sufficiently aware, that the number of years purchase given for land has nothing to do with prices, but expresses the abundance or scarcity of moveable capital compared with the means of employing it.

sive accumulation of capital, and the progressive cultivation of fresh land, as to allow of low profits at an earlier period of this progress and higher profits at a later period. At all events, the facts must be accounted for, as they are so broad and glaring, and others of the same kind are in reality of such frequent recurrence, that they must be considered as at once decisive against any theory of profits which is inconsistent with them.

In the first period of the two which have been noticed it is known that the price of corn had fallen, and that the wages of labour had not only not fallen in proportion, but had been considered by some authorities as having risen. Adam Smith states the fall of corn and the rise of labour during the first sixty-four years of the last century as a sort of established fact;* but Arthur Young, in his very useful inquiries into the prices of corn and labour published in his Annals of Agriculture, seems to think that the fact is not well authenticated, and is inconsistent with the apparently slack demand for labour and produce, and comparatively slow progress of population, which took place during the period in question.† Allowing, however, even a stationary price of labour, with a falling price of corn, not arising from improvements, and the fall of agricultural profits is at once accounted for. Such a state of prices might alone be much more than sufficient to counteract the effects arising from the circumstance of pretty good land being yet uncultivated. When we add, that the other outgoings belonging to the farmers' capital, such as leather, iron, timber, &c. &c., are supposed to have risen while the price of his main produce was falling, we can be at no loss to account for a low rate of agricultural profits, notwithstanding the unexhausted state of the country. And as to the low rate of mercantile and manufacturing

* Wealth of Nations, Book I. ch. xi. p. 309, 313, 6th edit.

† Annals of Agriculture, No. 270, p. 89.

profits, that would be accounted for at once by the increase of mercantile and manufactured products compared with the demand for them, and their consequent diminished prices in relation to labour.

In the subsequent period, from 1793 to 1813, it is probable that all the circumstances noticed in this section concurred to give room for the operation of that principle which depends upon the demand compared with the supply of capital.

In the first place, there can be no doubt of the improvements in agriculture which were going forwards during these twenty years, both in reference to the general management of the land, and the instruments which are connected with cultivation, or which in any way tend to facilitate the bringing of raw produce to market. 2dly, the increasing practice of task-work during these twenty years, together with the increasing employment of women and children, unquestionably occasioned a great increase of personal exertion; and more work was done by the same number of persons and families than before.

If to these two causes of the increased productiveness of the powers of labour we add a fall in the prices of manufactures from improved machinery, and a rise in the price of corn from increased demand, unaccompanied by a proportionate rise of most foreign, and many home commodities, the effect of taking poorer land into cultivation is so likely to be counterbalanced under such circumstances, that in the actual state of many countries, or in their probable state for some centuries to come, we may fairly lay our account to such a result when the occasion calls for it.

I should feel no doubt, for instance, of an increase in the rate of profits in this country for twenty years together, at the beginning of the twentieth century, compared with the twenty years which are now coming on; provided this near period were a period of profound tranquillity and peace and abundant capital, and the future period were a period in which capital was scanty in proportion to the demand for it owing to a war, attended by the circumstances of an increasing trade, and an increasing demand for agricultural produce similar to those which were experienced from 1793 to 1813.

But if this be so, and past experience justifies it, it follows, that in the actual state of things in most countries of the world, and within limited periods of moderate extent, the rate of profits will practically depend more upon the causes which affect the relative abundance or scarcity of capital, and the demand for produce compared with the supply, than on the fertility of the last land taken into cultivation. And consequently, to dwell on this latter point as the sole, or even the main cause which determines profits, must lead to the most erroneous conclusions. Adam Smith, in stating the cause of the fall of profits, has omitted this point, and in so doing has omitted a most important consideration; but in dwelling solely upon the abundance and competition of capital, he is practically much nearer the truth* than those who dwell almost exclusively on the quality of the last land taken into cultivation.

In individual cases, the illustration of this principle is constantly before our eyes. If a capital of a hundred pounds be expended in producing twelve hundred yards of calico, which sell for £120, profits will be 20 per cent. On the other hand, if they sell for £110, profits will be only 10 per cent.; and whether they sell for £110 or £120 will be determined by the state of the supply compared with the demand. The money wages of labour and the value of money may remain the same; but a different proportion of the produce is required to replace the capital:† in the

* It ought to be allowed that Adam Smith, in speaking of the effects of accumulation and competition on profits, naturally means to refer to a limited territory, a limited population, and a limited demand; but accumulation of capital under these circumstances involves every cause that can affect profits.

† The reader is aware of the corrections to be made for fixed capital.

first case a thousand yards are required, in the second nearly eleven hundred. It is evident however that the increase in the quantity of produce required to replace the capital is the *consequence*, not the *cause* of the fall of profits. The cause is the fall in the value of the produce of the same quantity of labour, or the same value of capital.

If instead of supposing that the same quantity of produce is obtained by the same value of capital, and sells at various prices, we suppose that the quantity produced and the prices at which it sells are both variable, which is the actual state of things, as profits depend upon *proportion* not quantity, it will be still true that profits will be determined by the proportion of the value of the produce which goes to replace the capital, whether the quantity remaining for profits be one hundred yards or four hundred yards, whether the labour employed on the land becomes less productive or more productive.

It will be said, perhaps, and truly, that the ordinary prices of commodities are not determined by the accidental state of the supply compared with the demand, but by the ordinary costs of production; but ordinary profits are one of the necessary conditions of the continued supply of commodities, and consequently one of the elements of their ordinary cost to the consumer; and this element is specifically determined by the ordinary state of the supply compared with the demand of the produce of the same value of capital. If the outlay of £100 for a year will obtain a produce which, on an average of ten or twelve years, sells for £120, the ordinary rate of profits will be 20 per cent. If at a future time the produce of the same value of outlay sells on an average during a similar period for £110, the ordinary rate of profits will be 10 per cent. The proportion of the produce which goes to replace the capital will in the latter case be $\frac{10}{11}$ instead of $\frac{10}{12}$, and it is obvious that this increased proportion of the same produce which is required to replace the capital, is specifically occasioned by a fall in the value of the produce of the same capital.

It appears therefore that whether we refer to immediate or to ordinary profits, they must always depend upon the different values of the produce of the same value of capital determined by the state of the supply, immediate or ordinary, compared with the demand. And if labour be the measure of value which I trust has been shewn, this is the same as saying that profits are determined by the proportion of the value of the produce which goes to pay the labour which has obtained it; and it follows as a direct consequence that profits never fall but when the value of the produce of the same quantity of labour falls, and never rise but when the value of the produce of the same quan tity of labour rises.*

SECTION V.—*Remarks on Mr. Ricardo's Theory of Profits.*

ACCORDING to Mr. Ricardo profits are regulated by wages, and are high or low in proportion as wages are low or high; † or as he has expressed himself more fully in another part of his chapter on profits,

"In all countries, and at all times, profits depend upon the quantity of labour requisite to provide necessaries for the labourers on that land, or with that capital which yields no rent."‡

* It is to be observed, that the various causes which practically affect profits, and which the author has enumerated in this section, are all reducible to one or the other of the two grand distinctions which are treated of in the two foregoing sections.—For instance, agricultural improvements, or increased personal exertions on the part of the labourer, whereby a larger produce is obtained with the same amount of labour, clearly belong to what he has denominated the *limiting* principle of profits, whilst the various circumstances which affect the value of the same quantity of produce, the labour employed being also the same, belong to the *regulating* principle of profits.—*Ed.*

† Principles of Political Economy, ch. vi. p. 108, 3rd edit.

‡ Id. p. 128.

It is here understood, that there are no other advances except those of wages; and, under these circumstances, the necessaries required to pay ten labourers must have required fewer than ten labourers to produce them, or there would have been no profits. It is further obvious that the profits upon the produce necessary to pay the wages of ten labourers must depend upon the difference between the whole produce, and that portion of it which is required to pay the number of labourers, whether nine, eight, seven, or any other proportion actually employed to produce the wages of the whole ten.

Mr. Ricardo's proposition therefore will be found to be essentially the same as if he had said that profits are determined by the proportion of the produce which goes to pay the wages of the labour which obtained it. And so far this theory is quite correct. But in its application he combines with it two assumptions, which being unfounded renders it as a whole essentially erroneous. He assumes,*

1st. That the commodities which have cost in their production the same quantity of labour will on an average always be of the same value. And

2ndly. That the value of the same quantity of labour varies in proportion to the share of the produce which goes to pay the labourer; and the varying value of this labour being thus taken out of the *supposed* constant value of the produce obtained by them, the remainder determines the rate of profits.

If these assumptions were well founded the theory would be correct. But it has been shewn, in the 4th section of the 2nd chapter, that commodities which have cost in their production the same quantity of labour, or the same value of capital, are subject to great variations of value, owing to the varying rate and varying quantity of profits which must be added to the quantity of accumulated and immediate labour employed upon them, in order to make up their value.

* Principles of Political Economy, ch. vi. p. 111, 3rd edit.

And it has further been shewn in the 6th section of the same chapter that, however variable may be the *quantity* or proportion of produce awarded to each labourer, the value of that quantity or proportion will always be the same.

It is clear then that profits must be regulated upon a principle essentially different from that stated by Mr. Ricardo, and that instead of being determined by the varying value of a certain quantity of labour employed, compared with the given value of the commodity produced, they will be determined by the *varying* value of the commodity produced compared with the *given* value of the certain quantity of labour employed.

This conclusion will appear strikingly obvious, if we adopt that supposition respecting the mode of procuring the precious metals which would certainly maintain them most strictly of the same value, that is, if we suppose them to be procured by a uniform quantity of unassisted labour without any advances in the shape of capital beyond the necessaries of a single day. That the precious metals would in this case retain, more completely than in any other, the same value cannot be denied, as the quantity of labour actually employed in their production, and the quantity of labour they would command would be the same. But in this case, as was before stated, the money price of labour must remain permanently the same. We cannot however for a moment imagine that this impossibility of a rise or fall in the money price of labour could in any respect impede or interrupt the natural career of profits. The continued accumulation of capital and increasing difficulty of procuring subsistence would unquestionably lower profits. All commodities, in the production of which the same quantity of labour continued to be employed, but with the assistance of capitals of various kinds and amount, would fall in price, and just in proportion to the degree in which the price of the commodity had before been affected by profits; and with regard to corn, in the production of which more labour would be necessary, this article would rise in money price just to that point which would so reduce corn wages as to retard the progress of population in proportion to the diminution of effectual demand; and thus all the effects upon profits, attributed by Mr. Ricardo to a rise of money wages, would take place while money wages and the value of money remained precisely the same. It is obvious that, in this case, profits can only be regulated by the principle of competition, or of demand and supply, which would determine the degree in which the prices of commodities would fall; and their prices, compared with the uniform price of labour, would regulate the rate of profits.

If however instead of supposing gold to be obtained by immediate labour alone in the way here stated, we suppose with Mr. Ricardo that it is obtained by fixed and circulating capitals in certain proportions, it will be found (as we have before intimated) that the state of prices and the rise of labour, contemplated by him in the progress of cultivation, are owing to a *fall* in the value of money, and not to a *rise* in the value of labour.

As a further illustration of this point so essential to a just theory of profits, let us suppose a country supplied with gold by a mine of its own, from which the same quantity of metal could always be obtained by the same quantity of labour with the same value of other capital; and further let us suppose, that at a particular period the accumulation of capital was increasing faster than the effectual demand for the produce at its former price; under these circumstances, let us consider what would be the consequences on the prices of commodities and labour. It is obvious that all those commodities which continued to be obtained by the same quantity of labour with the same value of other capital would fall in value from the abundance of the supply; and gold among the rest becoming more abundant, a different division of the produce would take place between the labourers and the capitalists; a smaller proportion of it would go to pay profits, and a larger proportion to pay wages. Profits therefore would fall, and the money wages of labour would rise. And the question is whether the rise in the money wages of labour ought to be considered as a rise in the *value* of labour, or a fall in the *value* of money. Mr. Ricardo considers it a rise in the *value* of labour, and has founded all his calculations in his chapters on rent, wages, and profits, on this assumption. If indeed the value of the produce of the same quantity of labour, or of labour and capital,* were to remain the same, which is what he supposes, then it would be quite true that if a larger proportion of this produce went to pay the wages of labour, the value of labour would rise. But if the value of the produce falls, then the circumstance of a larger proportion of the produce going to pay the wages of labour by no means implies that the value of labour has risen. It only implies that the labourer receives a larger quantity of an article which has fallen in value. And that in the present case the article has fallen in value may with certainty be inferred both from the state of the supply compared with the demand, and the elementary costs of its production. It has been assumed that the supply is comparatively more abundant than before, on account of the increase of capital, although the productiveness of labour has remained the same. This must necessarily occasion a fall of profits, and this fall will be permanent if the same competition of capital continues. But if the *rate of profits* has fallen the elementary costs of production have fallen. In this case, the conditions of the supply of a certain quantity of

* Mr. Ricardo often uses the terms *quantity of labour*, and *quantity of labour and capital*, to express the same thing. Generally, when on the subject of profits, he means the *quantity of labour and capital*, although it must be allowed that machinery and materials of different kinds cannot be estimated and compared by quantity. The true condensed expressions in regard to the advances on which profits are estimated must be (as it has appeared) either the *quantity of labour*, or the *value of the capital*. They are equivalent, and give the same results.

gold are the advance of the same quantity of labour, with the same value of other capital, as before, *and a less* remuneration for profits. Consequently the elementary cost of gold to the purchaser is less than before.

If it be said, as Mr. Ricardo says, that a greater quantity of labour is required to produce the corn which pays the wages of the labourer, this may be conceded; but as a proportionate fall of profits is found to have taken place, the diminution of the element of profits balances * the increase of the element of labour, leaving the *value* of labour the same as before, while its increased price is occasioned by the fall in the value of money. And that the value of money must have fallen is further evident from the conclusions of Mr. Ricardo himself, quite independently of the measure which I have applied to it. According to his theory the prices of manufactured commodities, which have not been produced by improved machinery, will, in the progress of cultivation, remain nearly the same, while labour and all raw products will rise. If therefore we measure the value of money by its general power of purchasing, its fall is decidedly established. Of a certain mass of objects it purchases the same quantity as before; of a much larger mass of objects it purchases a smaller quantity.

If then in the system of Mr. Ricardo commodities obtained by the same quantity of labour *appear* to be of the same value, it is only because he has adopted as his measure a money, which from the nature of its composition as consisting in part of profits, necessarily varies with the variations in the values of the very commodities which it is intended to measure.

But in reference to the great limiting principle, which in his system is the only one which regulates profits, namely the increasing difficulty of procuring food from the soil, it merely in fact determines the

* This balance necessarily takes place, as we have said, in the *elementary cost* of the varying wages of a given number of men, which always remains the same.

range of possible profits; how high they may by possibility rise, and how low they may by possibility fall. It is indeed always ready to act; and, if not overcome by countervailing facilities, will necessarily lower the rate of profits on the land, from which it will be extended to all other departments of industry. But even then it always operates according to the laws of demand and supply and competition.

The specific reason why profits must fall as the land becomes more and more exhausted is, that from the intrinsic nature of necessaries, and of the soil from which they are procured, the demand for them and their price cannot possibly go on increasing in proportion to the expense of producing them. Though the value of a given quantity of produce rises on account of the increased quantity of labour required to obtain it, yet the value of the diminished produce of the *same* quantity of labour, or its efficiency in setting fresh labourers to work necessarily falls from the state of the demand and supply. The boundary to the further value of and effectual demand for corn, lies clear and distinct before us. Putting importation out of the question, it is precisely when the produce of the last land taken into cultivation will but just replace the capital and support the population employed in cultivating it. Profits must then be at their lowest theoretical limit. In their progress towards this point, the continued accumulation of capital will always have a *tendency* to lower them; and at no one period can they ever be higher than the state of the land, under all the circumstances, will admit.

They may be much lower, however, as was before stated, from an abundant supply of capital compared with the demand for produce, while the soil is still rich. Practically they are very rarely so high as the actual state of the land combined with the smallest possible quantity of food awarded to the labourer would admit of; and very rarely so low as not to allow the means of further accumulation.

What would be the effects upon the profits of stock of any given increase of capital, or even of any given increase of the labour necessary to produce a certain quantity of corn, it would be quite impossible to say before hand.* In the case of a mere increase of capital, however large, it has appeared that circumstances might occur to prevent any fall of profits for a great length of time. And, even in the case of an increase in the quantity of labour necessary to produce corn, it would depend entirely upon the principles of demand and supply and competition, whether the increase in the price of corn would be such as to throw *almost the whole* of the increased difficulty of production upon the labourer, or upon the capitalist, or again such as to divide the loss more equally between them, which is what generally happens.

No theory of profits therefore can approach towards correctness, which attempts to get rid of the principle of demand and supply and competition.

* It has sometimes been said that profits depend entirely upon the productiveness of labour. If by productiveness of labour be meant what the words usually mean, and what they certainly ought to mean, namely the *quantity* of produce obtained by a given quantity of labour, every day's experience shews that the statement is quite unfounded. If the words be intended to mean productiveness of *value* then no doubt profits depend upon the productiveness of labour. This truth is involved in the very definition of profits, namely the excess of the value of the produce above the value of the advances, or of a given quantity of labour advanced. It is exactly what has been here inculcated, but the usual and correct meaning of terms must not be changed on particular occasions.

CHAPTER VI.

OF THE DISTINCTION BETWEEN WEALTH AND VALUE.

It has been justly stated by Adam Smith that a man is rich or poor according to the degree in which he can afford to enjoy the necessaries, conveniences, and luxuries of human life. And it follows from this definition that, if the bounty of nature furnished all the necessaries, conveniences and luxuries of life to every inhabitant of a country in the fullest measure of proportion to his wishes, such a country would be in the highest degree wealthy, without possessing any thing which would have exchangeable value, or could command a single hour's labour.

In this state of things, undoubtedly, wealth has nothing to do with exchangeable value. But as this is not the actual state of things, nor likely to be so at any future time; as the bounty of nature furnishes but few of the necessaries, conveniences and luxuries of life to man without the aid of his own exertions; and as the great practical stimulus to exertion is the desire to possess what can only be possessed by means of some labour or sacrifice, it will be found that, in the real state in which man is placed on earth, wealth and exchangeable value, though still by no means the same, are in many points nearly connected.

In considering the different quantities of the same commodity which, under different circumstances, have the same exchangeable value, the distinction is indeed perfectly obvious. Stockings do not lose half their power of contributing to the comfort and convenience of the wearer, because by improved machinery they can be made at half the price, or their exchangeable value be reduced one half. It will be readily allowed that the man who has two pairs of stockings of the same quality instead of one pair, possesses, as far as stockings are concerned, a double portion of the conveniences of life.

Yet even in this case he is not *in all respects* doubly rich. If, indeed, he means to use them himself, he may have twice as much wealth, though this has been denied by some writers, but if he means to exchange them for other commodities, he certainly has not; as one pair of stockings, under certain circumstances, may command more labour and other commodities than two or even three pairs after very great improvements have been made in the machinery used in producing them. In all cases however of this description, the nature of the difference between wealth and value is sufficiently marked.

But when we come to compare objects of different kinds, there is no other way of estimating the degree of wealth which the possession and enjoyment of them confer on the owner, than by the estimation in which they are respectively held, evinced by their respective exchangeable values. If one man has a certain quantity of tobacco, and another a certain quantity of muslin, we can only determine which of the two is the richer by ascertaining their respective command of labour, money, or some other third commodity in the market. And even if one country exports corn, and imports lace and cambrics, notwithstanding that corn has a more marked and definite value in use than any other commodity, the estimate must be formed exactly in the same way. Luxuries are a part of wealth as well as necessaries. The country would not have received lace and cambrics in exchange for its corn unless its wealth, or its necessaries, conveniences and luxuries taken together, had been increased by such exchange; and this increase of wealth cannot possibly be measured in any other way than by the increase of value so occasioned, founded upon the circumstance that the commodities received are more wanted and held in higher estimation than those which were sent away.

The wealth of a country, however, it will be allowed, does not always increase in proportion to the increase of value; because an increase of value may sometimes take place under an actual diminution of commodities; but neither does it increase in proportion to the mere quantity of what comes under the denomination of wealth, because the various articles of which this quantity is composed may not be so proportioned to the wants and powers of the society as to give them their proper value. The most useful commodity, in respect of its qualities, if it be absolutely in excess, not only loses its exchangeable value, but its power of supplying the wants of the society to the extent of its quantity, and part of it therefore loses its quality of wealth. If the roads and canals of England were suddenly broken up and destroyed, so as to prevent all passage and interchange of goods, there would at first be no diminution of commodities, but there would be immediately a most alarming diminution both of value and wealth. A great quantity of goods would at once lose their value by becoming utterly useless; and though others would rise in particular places, yet from the want of power to purchase in those districts, the rise would by no means compensate for the fall. The whole exchangeable value of the produce estimated in labour, or money, would be greatly diminished; and it is quite obvious that the wealth of the society would be most essentially impaired; that is, its wants would not be in any degree so well supplied as before.

It appears then that the wealth of a country depends partly upon the quantity of produce obtained by its labour, and partly upon such an adaptation of this quantity to the wants and powers of the existing population as is calculated to give it value. Nothing can be more certain than that it is not determined by either of them alone.

But where wealth and value are perhaps the most nearly connected, is in the necessity of the latter to the production of the former. In the actual state of things, no considerable quantity of wealth can be obtained except by considerable exertions; and unless the value which an individual or the society places on the object, when obtained, fully compensates the sacrifice which has been made to obtain it, such wealth will not be produced in future. If labour alone be concerned in its production, as in shrimping, in the collection of hurts and wild strawberries, and some other exertions of mere manual labour, it is obvious that this wealth will not be collected, nor will be used to supply any of the wants of the society, unless its value when collected will, at the least, command as much labour as the collection of it has cost.

If the nature of the object to be obtained requires advances in the shape of capital, as in the vast majority of instances, then by whomsoever this capital is furnished, whether by the labourers themselves or by others, the commodity will not be produced, unless the estimation in which it is held by the society or its intrinsic value in exchange be such, as not only to replace all the advances of labour and other articles which have been made for its attainment, but likewise to pay the usual profits upon those advances; or, in other words, to command an additional quantity of labour, equal to those profits.

It is obviously therefore the value set upon commodities,—it is the sacrifice of labour or of labours worth which people are willing to make in order to obtain them, that in the actual state of things may be said to be *almost the sole cause* of the existence of wealth; and this value is founded on the wants of mankind, and the adaptation of particular commodities to supply these wants, independently of the actual quantity of labour which these commodities may have cost in their collection or production. It is this value which is not only the great stimulus to the production of all kinds of wealth, but the great regulator of the forms and relative quantities in which it shall exist. No species of wealth can be brought to market for a continuance, unless some part of the society sets a value upon it equal to its natural or necessary price, and is both able and willing to make a sacrifice to this extent in order to obtain it. A tax will entirely put an end to the production of a commodity, if no one of the society is disposed to value it at a price equal to the new conditions of its supply. And on the other hand, commodities will be continually increased in quantity so long as the demands of those, who are able and willing to give a value for them equal to this price, continue to increase.

In short, the market prices of commodities are the immediate causes of all the great movements of society in the production of wealth, and these market prices (when the relation of money to labour is known,) always express clearly and unequivocally the exchangeable values of commodities arising from intrinsic causes at the time and place in which they are exchanged, and differ only from the natural and necessary prices, as the *actual* state of the demand and supply, with regard to any particular article, may differ from its *ordinary* and *average* state.

Mr. Ricardo was, I believe, the first writer of note, who took pains to make a marked distinction between wealth and value; and in this, he appears to me to have rendered an unquestionable service to the science of political economy: but owing to the peculiar view which he took of exchangeable value as depending exclusively upon the quantity of labour actually employed in production, he has made the distinction much broader than it really is.

If the great measure of the exchangeable value of a commodity were what he has represented it to be, value would depend exclusively upon difficulty of production, and its power of measuring wealth would be extremely imperfect: while, if the great measure of the value of a commodity is, as I have endeavoured to shew, the quantity of labour which it will command, such a measure will be found to be very much more comprehensive, and to make much nearer approaches to a measure of wealth. It may indeed safely be said that though wealth and value rarely go on together at an even pace ; yet that when a just view is taken of the mass of value in any country, all the general causes of a permanent nature which are most effective in the production of wealth will be found also the most effective in the production of value; and in reference to the whole produce of a country, quantity seldom fails to increase value, except in those temporary cases of a general glut, in which it must be allowed that even the wealth of a country is far from being proportioned to the increased quantity of the commodities it has produced.

It would certainly be desirable to be able to form some estimate of the wealth of different nations with a view to the comparison of them with each other. An attempt to do this by estimating the *quantity* of their respective produce without reference to its value would be perfectly futile, as it is obvious, that nothing could be inferred by comparing the quantity of wine in France with the quantity of tallow in Russia, or the quantity of tin in England with the quantity of raw cotton in the United States.

On the other hand, if we were to take as our measure of wealth, that measure of value which is determined by the quantity of immediate and accumulated labour, actually worked up in commodities, we should be but little better off, as all the wealth derived from superior fertility of soil, peculiar products, and the great mass of profits arising from fixed and circulating capitals would at once be left out in the computation.

But the case would be very different, if we were to take as a rough measure of the wealth of a country the quantity of the standard labour of that country which its whole produce would command, or exchange for. This measure would embrace all the advantages derived by different countries from their peculiar products, the superior fertility of their soil either natural or acquired, and the mass of their profits occasioned either by the general *rate* of profits, or by the amount of their fixed and circulating capitals, &c. The quantity of standard labour which the whole yearly produce would exchange for, according to the actual money prices of labour and commodities at the time might be considered as an approximating estimate of the gross annual revenue of the country, while the excess of this value above the immediate and accumulated labour advanced in producing it, would be an approximating estimate of what has sometimes been called its neat revenue, or the mass of rents, profits and taxes derived from these advances.

Different countries tried in this way by the value of their produce, would in general answer very nearly to the estimates which would be formed of their relative wealth, by the most careful and intelligent practical observations.

An agricultural country, with a bad soil and the great mass of the population employed on the land would be universally considered as poor; and tried by the test proposed the value of its produce would in the first place appear to be small compared with its extent of territory; and secondly, the quantity of standard labour which it would command would not much exceed the quantity of labour employed in production.

A country almost entirely agricultural, yet possessing a rich soil would appear to have a greater gross revenue, and a greater population on the same extent of territory than the country before described; and further, it would be observed to possess a great body of wealthy landed proprietors maintaining numerous menial servants, and retainers; while the sovereign would probably be rich and powerful, as the state would certainly have the means of keeping up a large military force in proportion to its size. It would be distinguished by the comparative large amount of its neat produce, and the great excess of the quantity of standard labour, which its produce would command, compared with the quantity which had been actually employed in obtaining that produce.

Countries almost exclusively manufacturing and commercial, are generally small in extent, and would generally be observed to possess a large amount of produce and population in a comparatively small compass; but that appearance of wealth and neat produce which shews itself in leisure, would be but little seen; and the test proposed would exactly show this result. By this test the wealth of the country would appear to be very great compared with its extent of territory: but it would appear at the same time that the quantity of standard labour which the value of the produce would command, would not so much exceed the quantity of labour which it had actually employed, as in the second case comsidered.

If, as a fourth case, we suppose a large country with a very rich soil well cultivated, and at the same time highly commercial and manufacturing, such a country would to the eye of every observer exhibit all the conceivable appearances of wealth, large landed fortunes, large mercantile and manufacturing fortunes, considerable leisure, great public establishments, a great public revenue, &c. &c.; and tried by the test proposed, it would undoubtedly measure very rich. On account of the small size of those states which depend almost entirely on commerce and manufactures, and consist chiefly of towns, it is probable that it would not contain so great a produce and population in so small a compass as states similar to those of Holland, Hamburgh and Venice, but it would be richer compared with the population. If, owing to the fertility of its soil and the skill with which it was worked, a small proportion of the people were employed upon it, and the tastes of the society were such as to encourage material conveniences and luxuries rather than menial service, the great mass of these objects combined with the raw produce, particularly under the employment of much fixed capital and improved machinery, might be of unusually high value compared with the population. It is indeed conceivable that under such circumstances the value of the whole produce might be such as to command the labour of 3 or 4 times the number of families in the country actually engaged in productive labour, estimated according to the usual earnings of agricultural families at the time.*

It will be readily understood that the labour which commodities will command or purchase, is used entirely as a measure, and has little more relation to the actual quantity of labour employed in the country, than a thousand feet in length has to the number of foot rules existing in the town where the length may be measured.

Neither is it intended to be stated that a measure of value can measure satisfactorily all the variations in wealth. There are some points where it must be allowed to fail. In the first place it does not express correctly the wealth of the labouring classes of society, which is a very important deficiency. Secondly, as it does not notice the relative value of the precious metals, it does not express the superior power which the labour of one country may possess in commanding the labour and wealth of another. Thirdly, it does not sufficiently mark the degree of wealth in luxuries and conveniences derived from skill and machinery. Whether with a view to the first of these circumstances, it might be useful in an estimate of wealth, to take a mean between corn and labour, instead of the measure of value-labour; and with a view to the second and in some degree to the third, to refer in part to foreign labour instead of domestic labour exclusively, may be fairly a subject of consideration.† Perhaps by so doing, facility and simplicity might be lost, without gaining a sufficient advantage in point of accuracy. But whether a measure of value can be made a measure of wealth or not, it must be

* The estimate here made must of course be quite conjectural; but if the soil were very fertile, and a large part of the value of the mercantile and manufacturing products of the profits of fixed capital, the conjecture is probably not beyond the truth. In England at present the value of the annual produce would purchase the labour of double the number of families actually existing in the country, if paid at the price of common agricultural labour.

† This is what I did in my former edition of this work.

allowed that no approximation towards a measure of wealth can be formed without a reference to value, and that when a just view of value is taken, it is found to have so intimate a connection with wealth, in many points, that the measure of it, without further modification, may be practically of use, in enabling us to form a judgment of the wealth of different nations which we may wish to compare with each other; and we shall be little liable to be led into any essential error by the use of this measure, as we know beforehand the points in which its accuracy is the most likely to fail, and are consequently enabled to make proper allowances.*

* In comparing the wealth of the United States of America with almost any other country, we should underrate her wealth, unless we made an allowance both for the large quantity of corn awarded to the labourer and the high money price of labour, or low value of money, which enables the American labourer to command so much foreign produce.

In comparing England with the countries on the continent an allowance for the lower value of money would be sufficient.

BOOK II.

CHAPTER I.

ON THE PROGRESS OF WEALTH.

SECTION I.—*Statement of the particular Object of Inquiry.*

THERE is scarcely any inquiry more curious, or, from its importance, more worthy of attention, than that which traces the causes which practically check the progress of wealth in different countries, and stop it, or make it proceed very slowly, while the power of production remains comparatively undiminished, or at least would furnish the means of a great and abundant increase of produce and population.

In a former work * I endeavoured to trace the causes which practically keep down the population of a country to the level of its actual supplies. It is now my object to shew what are the causes which chiefly influence these supplies, or call the powers of production forth into the shape of increasing wealth.

Among the primary and most important causes which influence the wealth of nations, must unquestionably be placed, those which come under the head of politics and morals. Security of property, without a certain degree of which, there can be no encouragement to individual industry, depends mainly upon the political constitution of a country, the excellence of its laws and the manner in which they are adminis-

* Essay on the Principle of Population.

tered. And those habits which are the most favourable to regular exertions as well as to general rectitude of character, and are consequently most favourable to the production and maintenance of wealth, depend chiefly upon the same causes, combined with moral and religious instruction. It is not however my intention at present to enter fully into these causes, important and effective as they are; but to confine myself chiefly to the more immediate and proximate causes of increasing wealth, whether they may have their origin in these political and moral sources, or in any others more specifically and directly within the province of political economy.

It is obviously true that there are many countries, not essentially different either in the degree of security which they afford to property, or in the moral and religious instruction received by the people, which yet, with nearly equal natural capabilities, make a very different progress in wealth. It is the principal object of the present inquiry to explain this; and to furnish some solution of certain phenomena frequently obtruded upon our attention, whenever we take a view of the different states of Europe, or of the world; namely, countries with great powers of production comparatively poor, and countries with small powers of production comparatively rich.

If the actual riches of a country not subject to repeated violences and a frequent destruction of produce, be not after a certain period in some degree proportioned to its power of producing riches, this deficiency must have arisen from the want of an adequate stimulus to continued production. The practical question then for our consideration is, what are the most immediate and effective stimulants to the continued creation and progress of wealth.

Section II.—*Of the Increase of Population considered as a Stimulus to the continued Increase of Wealth.*

Many writers have been of opinion that an increase of population is the sole stimulus necessary to the increase of wealth, because population, being the great source of consumption, must in their opinion necessarily keep up the demand for an increase of produce, which will naturally be followed by a continued increase of supply.

That a continued increase of population is a powerful and necessary element of increasing demand, will be most readily allowed; but that the increase of population alone, or, more properly speaking, the pressure of the population hard against the limits of subsistence, does not furnish an effective stimulus to the continued increase of wealth, is not only evident in theory, but is confirmed by universal experience. If want alone, or the desire of the labouring classes to possess the necessaries and conveniences of life, were a sufficient stimulus to production, there is no state in Europe, or in the world, which would have found any other practical limit to its wealth than its power to produce; and the earth would probably before this period have contained, at the very least, ten times as many inhabitants as are supported on its surface at present.

But those who are acquainted with the nature of effectual demand, will be fully aware that, where the right of private property is established, and the wants of society are supplied by industry and barter, the desire of any individual to possess the necessaries, conveniences and luxuries of life, however intense, will avail nothing towards their production, if there be no where a reciprocal demand for something which he possesses. A man whose only possession is his labour has, or has not, an effective demand for produce according as his labour is, or is not, in demand by those who have the disposal of produce. And no productive labour can ever be in demand with a view to profit unless the produce when obtained is of greater value than the labour which obtained it. No fresh hands can be employed in any sort of industry merely in consequence of the demand for its produce occasioned by the persons employed. No farmer will take the trouble of superintending the labour of ten additional men merely because his whole produce will then sell in the market at an advanced price just equal to what he had paid his additional labourers. There must be something in the previous state of the demand and supply of the commodity in question, or in its price, antecedent to and independent of the demand occasioned by the new labourers, in order to warrant the employment of an additional number of people in its production.

It will be said perhaps that the increase of population will lower wages, and, by thus diminishing the costs of production, will increase the profits of the capitalists and the encouragement to produce. Some temporary effect of this kind may no doubt take place, but it is evidently very strictly limited. The fall of real wages cannot go on beyond a certain point without not only stopping the progress of the population but making it even retrograde; and before this point is reached, the increase of produce occasioned by the labour of the additional number of persons will have so lowered its value, and reduced profits, as to determine the capitalist to employ less labour. Though the producers of necessaries might certainly be able in this case to obtain the funds required for the support of a greater number of labourers; yet if the effectual demand for necessaries were fully supplied, and an adequate taste for unproductive consumption, or personal services had not been established, no motive of interest could induce the producers to make an effectual demand for this greater number of labourers.

It is obvious then in theory that an increase of population, when an additional quantity of labour is not required, will soon be checked by want of employment and the scanty support of those employed, and will not furnish the required stimulus to an increase of wealth proportioned to the power of production.

But, if any doubts should remain with respect to the *theory* on the subject, they will surely be dissipated by a reference to *experience*. It is scarcely possible to cast our eyes on any nation of the world without seeing a striking confirmation of what has been advanced. Almost universally, the actual wealth of all the states with which we are acquainted is very far short of their powers of production; and among those states, the slowest progress in wealth is often made where the stimulus arising from population alone is the greatest, that is, where the population presses the hardest against the actual limits of subsistence. It is quite evident that the only fair way, indeed the only way, by which we can judge of the practical effect of population alone as a stimulus to wealth, is to refer to those countries where, from the excess of population above the funds applied to the maintenance of labour, the stimulus of want is the greatest. And if in these countries, which still have great powers of production, the progress of wealth is very slow, we have certainly all the evidence which experience can possibly give us, that population alone cannot create an effective demand for wealth.

To suppose a great and continued increase of population is to beg the question. We may as well suppose at once an increase of wealth; because such an increase of population cannot take place without a proportionate or nearly proportionate increase of wealth. The question really is, whether encouragements to population, or even the natural tendency of population to increase beyond the funds destined for its maintenance, will, or will not, alone furnish an adequate stimulus to the increase of wealth. And this question, Spain, Portugal, Poland, Hungary, Turkey, and many other countries in Europe, together with nearly the whole of Asia and Africa, and the greatest part of America, distinctly answer in the negative.

SECTION III.—*Of Accumulation, or the Saving from Revenue to add to Capital, considered as a Stimulus to the Increase of Wealth.*

THOSE who reject mere population as an adequate stimulus to the increase of wealth, are generally disposed to make every thing depend upon accumulation. It is certainly true that no permanent and continued increase of wealth can take place without a continued increase of capital; and I cannot agree with Lord Lauderdale in thinking that this increase can be effected in any other way than by saving from the stock which might have been destined for immediate consumption, and adding it to that which is to yield a profit; or in other words, by the conversion of revenue into capital.*

But we have yet to inquire what is the state of things which generally disposes a nation to accumulate; and further, what is the state of things which tends to make that accumulation the most effective, and lead to a further and continued increase of capital and wealth.

It is undoubtedly possible by parsimony to devote at once a much larger share than usual of the produce of any country to the maintenance of productive la-

* See Lord Lauderdale's Chapter on Parsimony, in his Inquiry into the Nature and Origin of Public Wealth, ch. iv, p. 198, 2d edit. Lord Lauderdale appears to have gone as much too far in deprecating accumulation, as some other writers in recommending it. This tendency to extremes is one of the great sources of error in political economy, where so much depends upon proportions.

bour; and suppose this to be done, it is quite true that the labourers so employed are consumers as well as those engaged in personal services, and that as far as the labourers are concerned, there would be no diminution of consumption or demand. But it has already been shewn that the consumption and demand occasioned by the workmen employed in productive labour can never *alone* furnish a motive to the accumulation and employment of capital; and with regard to the capitalists themselves, together with the landlords and other rich persons, they have, by the supposition, agreed to be parsimonious, and by depriving themselves of their usual conveniencies and luxuries to save from their revenue and add to their capital. Under these circumstances, it is impossible that the increased quantity of commodities, obtained by the increased number of productive labourers, should find purchasers, without such a fall of price as would probably sink their value below that of the outlay, or, at least, so reduce profits as very greatly to diminish both the power and the will to save.

It has been thought by some very able writers, that although there may easily be a glut of particular commodities, there cannot possibly be a glut of commodities in general; because, according to their view of the subject, commodities being always exchanged for commodities, one half will furnish a market for the other half, and production being thus the sole source of demand, an excess in the supply of one article merely proves a deficiency in the supply of some other, and a general excess is impossible. M. Say, in his distinguished work on political economy, has indeed gone so far as to state that the consumption of a commodity by taking it out of the market diminishes demand, and the production of a commodity porportionably increases it.

This doctrine, however, as generally applied, appears to me to be utterly unfounded, and completely to contradict the great principles which regulate supply and demand.

It is by no means true, as a matter of fact, that commodities are always exchanged for commodities. An immense mass of commodities is exchanged directly, either for productive labour, or personal services: and it is quite obvious, that this mass of commodities, compared with the labour with which it is to be exchanged, may fall in value from a glut just as any one commodity falls in value from an excess of supply, compared either with labour or money.

In the case supposed there would evidently be an unusual quantity of commodities of all kinds in the market, owing to those who had been before engaged in personal services having been converted, by the accumulation of capital, into productive labourers; while the number of labourers altogether being the same, and the power and will to purchase for consumption among landlords and capitalists being by supposition diminished, commodities would necessarily fall in value compared with labour, so as very greatly to lower profits, and to check for a time further production. But this is precisely what is meant by the term glut, which, in this case, is evidently general not partial.

M. Say, Mr. Mill,* and Mr. Ricardo, the principal authors of these new doctrines, appear to me to have fallen into some fundamental errors in the view which they have taken of this subject.

In the first place, they have considered commodities as if they were so many mathematical figures, or arithmetical characters, the relations of which were to

* Mr. Mill, in a reply to Mr. Spence, published in 1808, has laid down very broadly the doctrine that commodities are only purchased by commodities, and that one half of them must always furnish a market for the other half. The same doctrine appears to be adopted in its fullest extent by the author of an able and useful article on the Corn Laws, in the supplement to the Encyclopædia Britannica, which has been referred to a previous chapter. These writers do not seem to be aware of what is unquestionably true, that demand is always determined by *value*, and supply by *quantity*. Two bushels of wheat are double the quantity of one in regard to supply; but in numerous cases, two bushels will not make so great a demand as one bushel.

be compared, instead of articles of consumption, which must of course be referred to the numbers and wants of the consumers.

If commodities were only to be compared and exchanged with each other, then indeed it would be true that, if they were all increased in their proper proportions to any extent, they would continue to bear among themselves the same relative value; but, if we compare them, as we certainly ought to do, with the means of producing them, and with the numbers and wants of the consumers, then a great increase of produce with comparatively stationary numbers or with wants diminished by parsimony, must necessarily occasion a great fall of value estimated in labour, so that the same produce, though it might have *cost* the same quantity of labour as before, would no longer *command* the same quantity; and both the power of accumulation and the motive to accumulate would be strongly checked.

It is asserted that effectual demand is nothing more than the offering of one commodity in exchange for another which has cost the same quantity of labour. But is this all that is necessary to effectual demand? Though each commodity may have cost the same quantity of labour in its production, and they may be exactly equivalent to each other in exchange, yet why may not both be so plentiful as not to command more labour, than they have cost, that is, to yield no profit, and in this case, would the demand for them be effectual? Would it be such as to encourage their continued production? Unquestionably not. Their relation to each other may not have changed; but their relation to the wants of the society, and their relation to labour, may have experienced a most important change.*

* The variations which take place in the *general* rate of profits being common to all commodities, will not of course affect their *relative* values; that is, whether commodities *universally* rise to a higher price, or sink to a lower one, or even fall below their cost, they will continue to bear the same proportion to each other

It will be readily allowed that a new commodity thrown into the market, which, in proportion to the labour employed upon it, is of higher exchangeable value than usual, is precisely calculated to increase demand; because it implies, not a mere increase of quantity, but an increase of value owing to a better adaptation of the produce to the tastes, wants and consumption of the society. But to fabricate or procure commodities of this kind is the grand difficulty; and they certainly do not naturally and necessarily follow an accumulation of capital and increase of commodities, most particularly when such accumulation and increase have been occasioned by economy of consumption, or a discouragement to the indulgence of those tastes and wants, which are the very elements of demand and of value.

Mr. Ricardo, though he maintains as a general position that capital cannot be redundant, is obliged to make the following concession. He says, "There is only one case, and that will be temporary, in which the accumulation of capital with a low price of food

as they did before. But no one would ever think of saying, that the demand for them (in the ordinary sense of the word) was the same in both cases. When, therefore, Mr. Mill explains the equality of demand and supply to consist in this;—"that goods which have been produced by a certain quantity of labour, exchange for goods which have been produced by an equal quantity of labour," (Elements of Polit. Econ. 3rd edit. p. 239.) he uses the term *demand* in a sense quite different from that which is usually meant by it. The demand and supply, as he understands them, may be equal to each other, when, owing to a general slackness of trade, the mass of goods are selling at a price very much below their ordinary costs of production; or when, in consequence of unusual briskness, they are selling very much above their costs; that is, when, according to Adam Smith, and to the accustomed language of society, the supply would be said, either greatly to exceed the demand, or to fall considerably short of it.

Throughout the chapter from which the foregoing passage is taken, Mr. Mill uses the term *demand*, as if it were synonymous with *extent of consumption*. By an increase or diminution of the demand, he means to refer simply to the greater or less quantity of goods bought or sold. What is usually meant by it, is, the rise or fall in the value of any given quantity of them.

An error, not to the same extent, but somewhat similar in kind, may be attended with a fall of profits; and that is, when the funds for the maintenance of labour increase much more rapidly than population;—wages will then be high and profits low. If every man were to forego the use of luxuries and be intent only on accumulation, a quantity of necessaries might be produced for which there could not be any immediate consumption. Of commodities so limited in number, there might undoubtedly be an universal glut; and consequently there might neither be demand for an additional quantity of such commodities, nor profits on the employment of more capital. If men ceased to consume, they would cease to produce." Mr. Ricardo then adds, "This admission does not impugn the general principle."* In this last remark I can by no means agree with him. It appears to me most completely to impugn the general principle. Even if we suppose with Mr. Ricardo, what is not true, that an increase of population would certainly remedy the evil; yet as from the nature of a population, an increase of labourers cannot be brought into the market, in consequence of

pervades the writings of Col. Torrens.—He represents *effectual and profitable demand* as consisting in the power of exchanging commodities for a *greater* quantity of the ingredients of capital than have been expended in their production. (Essay on Wealth, p. 360.) This view of demand, though nearer to the truth than the foregoing one, is nevertheless incorrect. The chief ingredients of capital, and frequently by far the largest, are food and clothing; and this Col. Torrens admits, since he represents the costs of production, as consisting in the advance of a given number of quarters of corn and suits of clothing. Now, although a man should sell his commodity for more corn and clothing than it has cost him, he may, notwithstanding, find himself in this predicament, that, the corn and clothing when obtained, may not, owing to a change in their relation to labour, command the services of the same number of men as were employed in the production of the commodity for which they have been exchanged; in which case the *apparent* profit would be greatly reduced, or might even disappear altogether. It is then in vain for us to measure the demand for a commodity by the quantity of any other commodity which can be had in exchange for it, since we must at last resort to labour as the only standard of the real value of every thing, and of the effectual demand for it.—*Ed.*

* Princ. of Polit. Econ. ch. xxi. p. 343, 3rd edit.

a particular demand, till after the lapse of sixteen or eighteen years, and the conversion of revenue into capital by saving, may take place much more rapidly; a country is always liable to an increase in the quantity of the funds for the maintenance of labour faster than the increase of population. But if, whenever this occurs, there may be an universal glut of commodities, how can it be maintained, as a general position, that capital is never redundant; and that because commodities may retain the same relative values, a glut can only be partial, not general?

Another fundamental error into which the writers above-mentioned and their followers appear to have fallen is, the not taking into consideration the influence of so general and important a principle in human nature, as indolence or love of ease.

It has been supposed * that, if a certain number of farmers and a certain number of manufacturers had been exchanging their surplus food and clothing with each other, and their powers of production were suddenly so increased that both parties could, with the same labour, produce luxuries in addition to what they had before obtained, there could be no sort of difficulty with regard to demand, as part of the luxuries which the farmer produced would be exchanged against part of the luxuries produced by the manufacturer; and the only result would be, the happy one of both parties being better supplied and having more enjoyments.

But in this intercourse of mutual gratifications, two things are taken for granted, which are the very points in dispute. It is taken for granted that luxuries are always preferred to indolence, and that an adequate proportion of the profits of each party is consumed as revenue. What would be the effect of a desire to save under such circumstances, shall be considered presently. The effect of a preference of indolence to luxuries would evidently be to occasion a want of de-

* Edinburgh Review, No. LXIV. p. 471.

mand for the returns of the increased powers of production supposed, and to throw labourers out of employment. The cultivator, being now enabled to obtain the necessaries and conveniences to which he had been accustomed, with less toil and trouble, and his tastes for ribands, lace and velvet not being fully formed, might be very likely to indulge himself in indolence, and employ less labour on the land; while the manufacturer, finding his velvets rather heavy of sale, would be led to discontinue their manufacture, and to fall almost necessarily into the same indolent system as the farmer. That an efficient taste for luxuries and conveniences, that is, such a taste as will properly stimulate industry, instead of being ready to appear at the moment it is required, is a plant of slow growth, the history of human society sufficiently shows; and that it is a most important error to take for granted, that mankind will produce and consume all that they have the power to produce and consume, and will never prefer indolence to the rewards of industry, will sufficiently appear from a slight review of some of the nations with which we are acquainted. But I shall have occasion for a review of this kind in the next section; and to this I refer the reader.

It has been said, that it is specifically the deficiency of production on the part of the indolent, which occasions the want of demand for the products of the industrious; and that, if the idle were made to produce, the surplus would disappear. But this remark is evidently beside the question.* The real question is, whether under the actual habits and tastes of the society, any number of persons who might be inclined to save and produce, if they suited their produce to

* This answer of the author will hardly be thought satisfactory. For if the allegation set up be a *true* one, it certainly falls within the limits of the question. The proper answer is, that it is *not a true* one. If the idle were to produce, it could only be by means of a larger accumulation, that is, of the conversion of more *revenue* into *capital*. But this, though it might make some alteration in the channels of demand, could not possibly increase the sum total of the demand. *Ed.*

these habits and tastes, would be secure of finding such a demand for all they could bring into the market as to prevent the possibility of what is called a glut, or a great fall of profits in a large mass of commodities. What might happen under different tastes and habits is entirely a different question.

It has also been said, that there is never an indisposition to consume, that the indisposition is to produce. Yet, what is the disposition of those master manufacturers, and merchants who produce very largely and consume sparingly? Is their will to purchase commodities for their consumption proportioned to their power? Does not the use which they make of their capital clearly show that their will is to produce, not to consume? and in fact, if there were not in every country some who were indisposed to consume to the value of what they produced, how could the national capital ever be increased?

A third very serious error of the writers above referred to, and practically the most important of the three, consists in supposing that accumulation ensures demand; or that the consumption of the labourers employed by those whose object is to save, will create such an effectual demand for commodities as to encourage a continued increase of produce.

Mr. Ricardo observes, that "If £10,000 were given to a man having £100,000 per annum, he would not lock it up in a chest, but would either increase his expenses by £10,000, employ it himself productively, or lend it to some other person for that purpose; in either case demand would be increased, although it would be for different objects. If he increased his expenses, his effectual demand might probably be for buildings, furniture, or some such enjoyment. If he employed his £10,000 productively, his effectual demand would be for food, clothing, and raw materials, which might set new labourers to work. But still it would be *demand*."*

* Prin. of Polit. Econ. ch. xxi. p. 361, 2nd edit.

Upon this principle it is supposed that if the richer portion of society were to forego their accustomed conveniences and luxuries with a view to accumulation, the only effect would be a direction of nearly the whole capital of the country to the production of necessaries, which would lead to a great increase of cultivation and population. But this is precisely the case in which Mr. Ricardo distinctly allows that there might be a universal glut; for there would undoubtedly be more necessaries produced than would be sufficient for the existing demand. This state of things could not, however, continue; since, owing to the fall which would take place, cultivation would be checked, and accumulation be arrested in its progress.

It is therefore obvious that without an expenditure which will encourage commerce, manufactures, and personal services, the possessors of land would have no sufficient stimulus to cultivate well; and a country such as our own, which had been rich and populous, would, with too parsimonious habits, infallibly become poor and comparatively unpeopled.

This reasoning will obviously apply to the case noticed before. While the farmers were disposed to consume the luxuries produced by the manufacturers, and the manufacturers those produced by the farmers, all would go on smoothly; but if either one or both of the parties were disposed to save largely, with a view of bettering their condition, and providing for their families in future, the state of things would be very different. The farmer, instead of indulging himself in ribands, lace, and velvets,* would be disposed to be satisfied with more simple clothing, but by this economy he would disable the manufacturer from purchasing the same amount of his produce; and for the returns of so much labour employed upon the land, and all greatly increased in productive power, there would evidently be no market. The manufacturer, in like manner, instead of indulg-

* Edinburgh Review, No. lxiv. p. 471.

ing himself in sugar, grapes, and tobacco, might be disposed to save with a view to the future, but would be totally unable to do so, owing to the parsimony of the farmers and the want of demand for manufactures.*

An accumulation, to a certain extent, of common food and common clothing might take place on both sides; but the amount must necessarily be extremely confined. It would be no sort of use to the farmer to go on cultivating his land with a view merely to give food and clothing to his labourers. He would be doing nothing either for himself or family, if he neither consumed the surplus of what they produced himself, nor could realize it in a shape that might be transmitted to his descendants. If he were a tenant, such additional care and labour would be entirely thrown away; and if he were a landlord, and were determined, without reference to markets, to cultivate his estate in such a way as to make it yield the greatest neat surplus with a view to the future, it is quite cer-

* Theoretical writers in Political Economy, from the fear of appearing to attach too much importance to money, have perhaps been too apt to throw it out of their consideration in their reasonings. It is an abstract truth that we want commodities, not money. But, in reality, no commodity for which it is possible to sell our goods at once, can be an adequate substitute for a circulating medium, and enable us in the same manner to provide for children, to purchase an estate, or to command labour and provisions a year or two hence. A circulating medium is absolutely necessary to any considerable saving; and even the manufacturer would get on but slowly, if he were obliged to accumulate in kind all the wages of his workmen. We cannot therefore be surprised at his wanting money rather than other goods; and, in civilized countries, we may be quite sure that if the farmer or manufacturer cannot sell his products so as to give him a profit estimated in money, his industry will immediately slacken. The circulating medium bears so important a part in the distribution of wealth, and the encouragement of industry, that it is hardly ever safe to set it aside in our reasonings, and all attempts at illustration, by supposing advances of a certain quantity of corn and clothing, instead of a certain quantity of money, which every year practically represents a variable quantity of corn, cannot fail to lead us wrong.

tain that the large portion of this surplus which was not required either for his home consumption, or to purchase clothing for himself and his labourers, would be absolutely wasted. If he did not choose to use it in the purchase of luxuries or the maintenance of personal services, it might as well be thrown into the sea. To save it, that is to use it in employing more labourers upon the land, would be to impoverish both himself and his family, and render it impossible at a future time to obtain a large disposeable produce from his land, without retracing his steps and dismissing half his labourers, who might starve when their labour was no longer wanted.

It would be still more useless to the manufacturers to go on producing clothing beyond what was wanted by the agriculturists and themselves. Their numbers indeed would entirely depend upon the demands of the agriculturists, as they would have no means of purchasing subsistence, but in proportion as there was a reciprocal want of their manufactures. The population required to provide simple clothing for such a society with the assistance of good machinery would be inconsiderable, and would absorb but a small portion of the proper surplus of rich and well cultivated land. There would evidently therefore be a general want of demand, both for produce and population; and while it is quite certain that an adequate passion for consumption may fully keep up the proper proportion between supply and demand, whatever may be the powers of production, it appears to be quite as certain that an inordinate passion for accumulation must inevitably lead to a supply of commodities beyond what the structure and habits of such a society will permit to be profitably consumed.*

But if this be so, surely it is a most important error

* The reader must already know, that I do not share in the apprehensions of Mr. Owen about the permanent effects of machinery. But I am decidedly of opinion, that on this point he has the best of the argument with those who think that accumulation ensures effectual demand.

to couple the passion for expenditure and the passion for accumulation together, as if they were of the same nature; and to consider the demand for the food and clothing of the labourer, who is to be employed productively, as securing such a general demand for commodities and such a rate of profits for the capital employed in producing them, as will adequately call forth the powers of the soil, and the ingenuity of man in procuring the greatest quantity both of raw and manufactured produce.

If, in the process of saving, all that was lost by the capitalist was gained by the labourer, the check to the progress of wealth would be but temporary, as stated by Mr. Ricardo; and the consequences need not be apprehended. But if the conversion of revenue into capital pushed beyond a certain point must, by diminishing the effectual demand for produce, throw the labouring classes out of employment, it is obvious that the adoption of parsimonious habits beyond a certain point, may be accompanied by the most distressing effects at first, and by a marked depression of wealth and population afterwards.

It is not, of course, meant to be stated that parsimony, or even a temporary diminution of consumption,* is not often in the highest degree useful, and sometimes absolutely necessary to the progress of wealth. A state may certainly be ruined by extravagance; and a diminution of the actual expenditure may not only be necessary on this account, but when the capital of a country is deficient, compared with the demand for its products, a temporary economy of consumption is required, in order to provide that supply of capital which can alone furnish the means of an increased consumption in future. All that is contended for is, that no nation can *possibly* grow rich by an accumulation of capital, arising from a permanent diminution of consumption; because such accu-

* Parsimony, or the conversion of revenue into capital, may take place without any diminution of consumption, if the revenue increases first.

mulation being beyond what is wanted in order to supply the effectual demand for produce, a part of it would very soon lose both its use and its value, and cease to possess the character of wealth.

The laws which regulate the rate of profits and the progress of capital, bear a very striking and singular resemblance to the laws which regulate the rate of wages and the progress of population.

Mr. Ricardo has very clearly shewn that the rate of profits must diminish, and the progress of accumulation be finally stopped, under the most favourable circumstances, by the increasing difficulty of procuring the food of the labourer. I, in like manner, endeavoured to shew in my Essay on the Principle of Population that, under circumstances the most favourable to cultivation which could possibly be supposed to operate in the actual state of the earth, the real wages of the labourer would gradually become more scanty, and the progress of population be finally stopped by the increasing difficulty of procuring the means of subsistence.

But Mr. Ricardo has not been satisfied with proving the position just stated. He has not been satisfied with shewing that the difficulty of procuring the food of the labourer is the only *absolutely necessary* cause of the fall of profits, in which I am ready fully and entirely to agree with him: but he has gone on to say, that there is *no other cause* of the fall of profits in the actual state of things that has any degree of permanence.* In this latter statement he appears to me to have fallen into precisely the same kind of error as I should have fallen into, if, after having shewn that the unrestricted power of population was beyond comparison greater than the power of the earth to produce food under the most favourable circumstances possible, I had allowed that population could not be redundant unless the powers of the earth

* By this expression I mean such a degree of permanence as to be called the ordinary rate of profits.

to keep up with the progress of population had been tried to the uttermost. But I all along said, that population might be redundant, and greatly redundant, compared with the demand for it and the actual means of supporting it, although it might most properly be considered as deficient, and greatly deficient, compared with the extent of territory, and the powers of such territory to produce additional means of subsistence; that, in such cases, notwithstanding the acknowledged deficiency of population, and the obvious desirableness of having it greatly increased, it was useless and foolish directly to encourage the birth of more children, as the effect of such encouragement, without a demand for labour and the means of paying it properly, could only be increased misery and mortality with little or no final increase of population.

Now the same kind of reasoning ought, I think, to be applied to the rate of profits and the progress of capital. Fully acknowledging that there is hardly a country in the four quarters of the globe where capital is not deficient, and in most of them very greatly deficient, compared with the territory and even the number of people; and fully allowing at the same time the extreme desirableness of an increase of capital, I should say that, where the state of the demand for commodities was such as to afford much less than ordinary profits to the producer, and the capitalists were at a loss where and how to employ their capitals to advantage, the saving from revenue to add still more to these capitals would only tend prematurely to diminish the motive to accumulation, and still further to distress the capitalists, with little increase of a wholesome and effective capital.

What is wanted in both these cases, prior to the increase of capital and population, is an effectual demand for commodities, that is, a demand by those who are able and willing to pay an adequate price for them; and though high profits are not followed by an increase of capital, so certainly as high wages are by an increase of population, yet it will be found that they are so followed more generally than they appear to be, because, in many countries, profits are often thought to be high, owing to the high interest of money, when they are really low; and because, universally, risk in employing capital has precisely the same effect in diminishing the motive to accumulate and the reward of accumulation, as low profits. At the same time it will be allowed that determined extravagance, and a determined indisposition to save, may keep profits permanently high. The most powerful stimulants may, under peculiar circumstances, be resisted; yet still it will not cease to be true that the natural and legitimate encouragement to the increase of capital is that increase of the power and will to save which is held out by certain and steady profits; and under circumstances in any degree similar, such increase of power and will to save must almost always be accompanied by a proportionate increase of capital.

One of the most striking instances of the truth of this remark, and a further proof of a singular resemblance in the laws that regulate the increase of capital and of population, is to be found in the rapidity with which the loss of capital is recovered during a war which does not interrupt commerce. The loans to government convert capital into revenue, and increase demand at the same time that they at first diminish the means of supply.* The necessary consequence must be an increase of profits. This naturally increases both the power and the reward of accumulation; and if only the same habits of saving prevail among the capitalists as before, the recovery of the lost stock must be rapid, just for the same kind of

* Capital is withdrawn only from those employments where it can best be spared. It is hardly ever withdrawn from agriculture. Nothing is more common, as I have stated in the Chapter on Rent, than increased profits, not only without any capital being withdrawn from the land, but under a continual addition to it. Mr. Ricardo's assumption of constant prices would make it absolutely impossible to account theoretically for things as they are. If capital were considered as not within the pale of demand and

reason that the recovery of population is so rapid after some great mortality.

It is now fully acknowledged that it would be a gross error in the latter case, to imagine that, without the previous diminution of the population, the same rate of increase would still have taken place; because it is precisely the high wages occasioned by the demand for labour, which produce the effect of so rapid an increase of population. On the same principle it appears to me as gross an error to suppose that, without the previous loss of capital and an increased demand for produce occasioned by the expenditure in question, capital should be as rapidly accumulated; because it is precisely the high profits of stock occasioned by the demand for commodities, and the consequent demand for the means of producing them, which at once give the power and the will to accumulate.

Though it may be allowed therefore that the laws which regulate the increase of capital are not quite so distinct as those which regulate the increase of population, yet they are certainly just of the same kind; and it is equally vain, with a view to the permanent increase of wealth, to continue converting revenue into capital, when there is no adequate demand for the products of such capital, as to continue encouraging marriage and the birth of children without a demand for labour and an increase of the funds for its maintenance.

supply, the very familiar event of the rapid recovery of capital would be quite inexplicable. The amount of capital employed on the land during the revolutionary war, was prodigiously increased owing to the great increase of profits; and although many merchants and manufacturers were occasionally subjected to great losses, yet the high rate of profits generally seemed more than to balance them; and there cannot be a doubt of the increase both of mercantile and manufacturing capitals.

SECTION IV.—*Of the Fertility of the Soil, considered as a Stimulus to the continued Increase of Wealth.*

IN speaking of the fertility of the soil as not affording with certainty an adequate stimulus to the continued increase of wealth, it must always be recollected that a fertile soil gives at once the greatest natural capability of wealth that a country can possibly possess. When the deficient wealth of such a country is mentioned, it is not intended to speak positively, but comparatively, that is with reference to its natural capabilities; and so understood, the proposition will be liable to few or no exceptions. Perhaps, indeed, it may be said that no instance has occurred, in modern times, of a large and very fertile country having made full use of its natural resources; while there have been many instances of small and unfertile states having accumulated within their narrow limits, by means of foreign commerce, an amount of wealth very greatly exceeding what could be expected from their physical capabilities.

If a small body of people were possessed of a rich and extensive inland territory, divided into large portions, and not favourably situated with respect to markets, a very long period might elapse before the state became wealthy and populous, notwithstanding the fertility of the soil and the consequent facility of production. The nature of such a soil would make it yield a profit or rent to the owner in its uncultivated state. He would set a value therefore upon his property, as a source of profit as well as of power and amusement; and though it was capable of yielding much more raw produce than he and his immediate dependents could consume, he would by no means be disposed to allow others to seize on it, and divide it at their pleasure. He would probably let out considerable portions of it for small rents. But the tenants of these portions, if there were no foreign vent for the raw produce, and the commodities which contribute to the conveniences and luxuries of life were but little known, would have but small incitement to call forth the resources of his land, and give encouragement to a rapid increase of population. By employing ten families he might perhaps, owing to the richness of the soil, obtain food for fifty; but he would find no proportionate market for this additional food, and would be soon sensible that he had wasted his time and attention in superintending the labour of so many persons. He would be disposed therefore to employ a smaller number; or if, from motives of humanity, or any other reason, he was induced to keep more than were necessary for the supply of the market, upon the supposition of their being tolerably industrious, he would be quite indifferent to their industry, and his labourers would naturally acquire the most indolent habits. Such habits would probably be generated both in the masters and servants by such circumstances, and when generated, a considerable time and considerable stimulants are necessary to get rid of them.

It has been said, that those who have food and necessaries at their disposal will not be long in want of workmen, who will put them in possession of some of the objects most useful and desirable to them.* But this appears to be directly contradicted by experience. If the establishment, extension, and refinement of domestic manufactures were so easy a matter, our ancestors would not have remained for many hundred years so ill supplied with them, and been obliged to expend the main part of their raw produce in the support of idle retainers. They might be very ready, when they had the opportunity, to exchange their surplus raw produce for the foreign commodities with which they were acquainted, and which they had learnt to estimate. But it would be a very diffe-

* Ricardo's Princ. of Polit. Econ. ch. xxi. p. 342, 3rd edit.

rent thing, and very ill suited to their habits and degree of information, to employ their power of commanding labour in setting up manufactures on their own estates. Though the land might be rich, it might not suit the production of the materials most wanted; and the necessary machinery, the necessary skill in using it, and the necessary intelligence and activity of superintendance, would all unavoidably be deficient at first, and under the circumstances supposed, must be of very slow growth; so that after those ruder and more indispensable articles were supplied, which are always wanted and produced in an early stage of society, it is natural enough that a great lord should prefer distinguishing himself by a few splendid foreign commodities, if he could get them, and a great number of retainers, than by a large quantity of clumsy manufactures, which involved great trouble of superintendance.

It is certainly true, however, taking as an instanee an individual workman, and supposing him to possess a given degree of industry and skill, that the less time he is employed in procuring food, the more time will he be able to devote to the procuring of conveniences and luxuries; but to apply this truth to whole nations, and to infer that the greater is the facility of procuring food, the more abundantly will the people be supplied with conveniences and luxuries would be one among the many rash and false conclusions which are often made in the application of a proposition without due attention to all the parts of the premises on which it rests. In the present case, all depends upon the supposition of a given degree of industry and skill, and the encouragement to employ them. But if, after the necessaries of life were obtained, the workman should consider indolence as a greater luxury than those which he was likely to procure by further labour, the proposition would at once cease to be true. And as a matter of fact, confirmed by all the accounts we have of nations, in the different stages of their progress, it must be allowed that this choice seems to be very general in the early periods of society, and by no means uncommon in the most improved states.

Few indeed and scanty would be the portion of conveniences and luxuries found in society, if those who are the main instruments of their production had no stronger motives for their exertions than the desire of enjoying them. It is the want of *necessaries* which mainly stimulates the labouring classes to produce luxuries; and were this stimulus removed or greatly weakened, so that the necessaries of life could be obtained with very little labour, instead of more time being devoted to the production of conveniences, there is every reason to think that less time would be so devoted.

At an early period of cultivation, when only rich soils are worked, as the quantity of corn is the greatest, compared with the quantity of labour required to produce it, we might expect to find a small portion of the population engaged in agriculture, and a large portion engaged in administering to the other wants of the society. And there can be little doubt that this is the state of things which we really should see, were it true, that if the means of maintaining labour be found, there can be no difficulty in making it produce objects of adequate value; or that when food can be obtained with facility, more time will be devoted to the production of conveniences and luxuries. But in examining the state of unimproved countries, what do we really see?—almost invariably, a much larger proportion of the whole people employed on the land than in those countries where the increase of population has occasioned the necessity of resorting to poor soils; and less time instead of more time devoted to the production of conveniences and luxuries.

Of the great landed nations of Europe, and indeed of the world, England, with hardly an exception, is supposed to have pushed its cultivation the farthest; and though the natural qualities of its whole soil by no means stand very high in the scale of comparative richness, there is a smaller proportion of the people employed in agriculture, and a greater proportion employed in the production of conveniences and luxuries, or living on monied incomes, than in any other agricultural country of the world. According to a calculation of Susmilch, in which he enumerates the different proportions of people in different states, who live in towns, and are not employed in agriculture, the highest is that of three to seven, or three living in towns to seven in the country ;* whereas in England the proportion of those engaged in manufactures and commerce, and other employments not connected with the land, compared with those engaged in agriculture is as much as three to two.†

This is a very extraordinary fact, and affords a striking proof how very dangerous it is, in political economy, to draw conclusions from the physical quality of the materials which are acted upon, without reference to the moral as well as the physical qualities of the agents.

It is undoubtedly a physical quality of very rich land, if worked by people possessing a given degree of industry and skill, to yield a large quantity of produce, compared with the number of hands employed; but, if the facility of production which rich land gives has the effect, under certain circumstances, of preventing the growth of industry and skill, the land may become practically less productive, compared with the number of persons employed upon it, than if it were not distinguished for its richness.

Upon the same principle, the man who can procure the necessary food for his family, by two days labour in the week, has the physical power of working much longer to procure conveniences and luxuries, than the man who must employ four days in procuring food ;

* Susmilch, vol. iii. p. 60. Essay on Population, vol. i. p. 459. edit. 5th. In foreign states very few persons live in the country who are not engaged in agriculture ; but it is not so in England.

† Population Abstracts, 1811.

but if the facility of getting food creates habits of indolence, this indolence may make him prefer the luxury of doing little or nothing, to the luxury of possessing conveniences and comforts ; and in this case, he may devote less time to the working for conveniences and comforts, and be more scantily provided with them than if he had been obliged to employ more industry in procuring food.

Among the crowd of countries which tend more or less to illustrate and confirm by their present state the truth of these positions, none perhaps will do it more strikingly than the Spanish dominions in America, of which M. Humboldt has given so valuable an account.

Speaking of the different plants which are cultivated in New Spain, he says of the banana, " Je doute qu'il existe une autre plante sur le globe qui, sur un si petit espace de terrain, puisse produire une masse de substance nourrissante aussi considérable."* He calculates in another place more particularly, that " dans un pays éminemment fertile un demi hectare, ou un arpent légal cultivé en bananes de la grande espèce, peut nourrir plus de cinquantes individus, tandis qu'en Europe le même arpent ne donneroit par an, en supposant le huitième grain, que 576 kilogrammes de farine de froment, quantité qui n'est pas suffisante pour la subsistance de deux individus : aussi rien ne frappe plus l'Européen récemment arrivé dans la zone torride que l'extrême petitesse des terrains cultivés autour d'une cabane qui renferme une famille nombreuse d'indigènes."†

It appears further, that the banana is cultivated with a very trifling quantity of labour, and " se perpétue sans que l'homme y mette d'autre soin que de couper les tiges dont le fruit a mûri, et de donner à la terre une ou deux fois par an un léger labeur en piochant autour des racines."‡

* Essai Politique sur la Nouvelle Espagne, tom. iii. l. iv. c. ix. p. 28.

† Id. p. 36.

‡ Id. p. 28.

What immense powers of production are here described! What resources for unbounded wealth, if effectively called into action? Yet what is the actual state of things in this fertile region. M. Humboldt says, " On entend souvent répéter dans les colonies Espagnoles, que les habitans de la région chaude (tierra caliente) ne pourront sortir de l'état d'apathie dans lequel ils sont plongés depuis des siècles, que lorsqu'une *cedule royale* ordonnera la destruction des bananiers. Le remède est violent; et ceux qui le proposent avec tant de chaleur ne déploient généralement pas plus d'activité que le bas-peuple qu'ils veulent forcer au travail en augmentant la masse de ses besoins. Il faut espérer que l'industrie fera des progrès parmi les Mexicains sans qu'on emploie des moyens de destruction. En considérant d'ailleurs la facilité avec laquelle l'homme se nourrit dans un climat où croissent les bananiers, on ne doit pas s'étonner que dans la région equinoctiale du nouveau continent la civilisation ait commencé dans les montagnes, sur un sol moins fertile, sous un ciel moins favorable au développement des êtres organisés où le besoin même réveille l'industrie.

" Au pied de la Cordillère dans les vallées humides des Intendances de Vera-Cruz, de Valladolid, ou de Guadalaxara, un homme qui employe seulement deux jours de la semaine à un travail peu pénible peut fournir de la subsistance à une famille entière." *

It appears then, that the extreme fertility of these countries, instead of affording an adequate stimulus to a rapid increase of wealth and population, has produced, under the actual circumstances in which they have been placed, a degree of indolence which has kept them poor and thinly peopled after the lapse of ages. Though the labouring classes have such ample time to work for conveniences and comforts, they are almost destitute of them. And, even in the necessary article of food, their indolence and improvidence pre-

* Humboldt's Nouvelle Espagne, tom. iii. l. iv. c. ix. p. 38.

vent them from adopting those measures which would secure them against the effects of unfavourable seasons. M. Humboldt states that famines are common to almost all the equinoctial regions; and observes that, " sous la zone torride, où une main bienfaisante semble avoir répandu le germe de l'abondance, l'homme insouciant et phlegmatique éprouve périodiquement un manque de nourriture que l'industrie des peuples cultivés éloigne des régions les plus stériles du Nord." *

It is possible, however, that the heat of the climate in these lower regions of New Spain, and an inferior degree of healthiness compared with the higher regions, though by no means such as to preclude a full population, may have assisted in keeping them poor and thinly peopled. But when we ascend the Cordilleras, to climates which seem to be the finest in the world, the scene which presents itself is not essentially different.

The chief food of the lower classes of the inhabitants on the elevated plains of the Cordilleras, is maize; and maize, though not so productive, compared with the labour employed upon it, as the banana, exceeds very greatly in productiveness the grains of Europe, and even of the United States. Humboldt states, that " La fécondité du *thaolli*, ou maïs Mexicain, est au-delà de tout ce que l'on peut imaginer en Europe. La plante, favorisée par de fortes chaleurs et par beaucoup d'humidité, aquiert une hauteur de deux à trois mètres. Dans les belles plaines qui s'étendent depuis San Juan del Rio à Quiretaro, par exemple, dans les terres de la grande métairie de l'Esperanza, un fanègue de maïs en produit quelquefois huit cents; des terreins fertiles en donnent, année commune, trois à quatre cents. Dans les environs de Valladolid on regarde comme mauvaise une récolte qui ne donne que 130 ou 150 fois la semence. Là où le sol est le plus stérile, on compte

* Id. tom. i. l. ii. c. v. p. 358.

encore soixante ou quatre-vingt grains. On croit qu'en général le produit du maïs peut être évalué dans la région equinoctiale du royaume de la Nouvelle Espagne à cent cinquante pour un."*

This great fertility produces, as might be expected, its natural effect of making the maintenance of a family in ordinary times extremely easy.

In the town of Mexico itself, where provisions are very considerably dearer than in the country, on account of the badness of the roads, and the expense of carriage, the very dregs of the people are, according to Humboldt, able to earn their maintenance by only one or two days' labour in the week.† "Les rues de Mexico fourmillent de vingt à trent mille malheureux (*Saragates Guachinangos*), dont la plûpart passent la nuit à la belle étoile, et s'étendent le jour au soleil, le corps tout nu enveloppé dans une couverture de flanelle. Cette lie du peuple, Indiens et Metis, présentent beaucoup d'analogie avec les Lazaronis de Naples. Paresseux, insoucians, sobres comme eux, les Guachinangos n'ont cependant aucune férocité dans le caractère; ils ne demandent jamais l'aumône: s'ils travaillent un ou deux jours par semaine, ils gagnent ce qu'il leur faut pour acheter du pulque, ou de ces canards qui couvrent les lagunes Mexicaines, et que l'on rôtit dans leur propre graisse."

But this picture of poverty is not confined to the dregs of the inhabitants of a large town. "Les Indiens Mexicains, en les considérant en masse, présentent le tableau d'une grande misère. Relégués dans les terres les moins fertiles; indolens par caractère, et plus encore par suite de leur situation politique, les natifs ne vivent qu'au jour le jour."‡

With these habits they are little likely to make provision against the occasional failures in the crops of maize, to which these crops are peculiarly liable;

* Essai Politique sur la Nouvelle Espagne, tom. iii. l. iv. c. ix. p. 56.

† Nouvelle Espagne, tom. ii. l. ii. c. vii. p. 37.

‡ Tom i. l. ii. c. vi. p. 429.

and consequently, when such failures take place, they are exposed to extreme distress. Speaking generally of the immediate obstacles to the progress of population in New Spain, Humboldt seems to consider famine and the diseases which it produces, as the most cruel and destructive of all. "Les Indiens Américains," (he says) "comme les habitans de l'Indostan, sont accoutumés à se contenter de la moindre quantité d'alimens qu'exige le besoin de la vie; ils augmentent en nombre sans que l'accroissement des moyens de subsistance soit proportionel à cette augmentation de population. Indolens par caractère, et surtout à cause de la position dans laquelle ils se trouvent sous un beau climat, sur un sol généralement fertile, les indigènes ne cultivent en maïs, en pommes de terre, et en froment que ce qu'il leur faut pour leur propre nourriture, ou tout au plus ce que requiert la consommation des villes et celle des mines les plus voisines." And further on, he says, "le manque de proportion qui existe entre les progrès de la population et l'accroissement de la quantité d'alimens produite par la culture, renouvelle le spectacle affligeant de la famine chaque fois qu'une grande sécheresse ou quelque autre cause locale a gâté la récolte du maïs."*

These accounts strikingly shew the indolence and improvidence which prevail among the people. Such habits must necessarily act as formidable obstacles in the way of a rapid increase of wealth and population. Where they have been once fully established, they are not likely to change, except gradually and slowly under a course of powerful and effective stimulants. And while the extreme inequality of landed property continues, and no sufficient vent is found for the raw produce in foreign commerce, these stimulants will be furnished very slowly and inadequately.

That the indolence of the natives is greatly aggravated by their political situation, cannot for a moment be doubted; but that, in spite of this situation, it

* Nouvelle Espagne, tom. i. liv. ii. c. v. pp. 355 et 356.

yields in a great measure to the usual excitements is sufficiently proved by the rapid cultivation which takes place in the neighbourhood of a new mine, where an animated and effective demand is created for labour and produce. "Bientôt le besoin réveille l'industrie; on commence à labourer le sol dans les ravins, et sur les pentes des montagnes voisines, par tout où le roc est couvert de terreau: des fermes s'établissent dans le voisinage de la mine: la cherté des vivres, le prix considérable auquel la concurrence des acheteurs maintient tous les produits de l'agriculture, dédommagent le cultivateur des privations aux-quelles l'expose la vie pénible des montagnes."*

When these are the effects of a really brisk demand for produce and labour, we cannot be at a loss for the main cause of the slow cultivation which has taken place over the greatest part of the country. Except in the neighbourhood of the mines and near the great towns, the effective demand for produce is not such as to induce the great proprietors to bring their immense tracts of land properly into cultivation: and the population, which, as we have seen, presses hard at times against the limits of subsistence, evidently exceeds in general the demand for labour, or the number of persons which the country can employ with regularity and constancy in the actual state of its agriculture and manufactures.

In the midst of an abundance of fertile land, it appears that the natives are often very scantily supplied with it. They would gladly cultivate portions of the extensive districts held by the great proprietors, and could not fail of thus deriving an ample subsistence for themselves and families; but in the actual state of the demand for produce in many parts of the country, and in the actual state of the ignorance and indolence of the natives, such tenants might not be able to pay a rent equal to what the land would yield in its uncultivated state, andin this case they would

* Nouvelle Espagne, tom. iii. liv. iv. c. ix. p. 12.

seldom be allowed to intrude upon such domains; and thus lands which might be made capable of supporting thousands of people, may be left to support a few hundreds of cattle.

Speaking of a part of the Intendency of Vera Cruz, Humboldt says, "Aujourd'hui des espaces de plusieurs lieues carrées sont occupés par deux ou trois cabanes, autour desquelles errent des bœufs à demi-sauvages. Un petit nombre de familles puissantes, et qui vivent sur le plateau central, possèdent la plus grande partie du littoral des Intendances de Vera Cruz, et de San Luis Potosi. Aucune loi agraire ne force ces riches propriétaires de vendre leurs majorats, s'ils persistent à ne pas vouloir défricher eux-mêmes des terres immenses qui en dépendent." *

Among proprietors of this description, caprice and indolence might often prevent many from cultivating their lands. Generally, however, it might be expected, that these tendencies would yield, at least in a considerable degree, to the more steady influence of self-interest. But a vicious division of territory prevents the motive of interest from operating so strongly as it ought to do in the extension of cultivation. Without sufficient foreign commerce to give value to the raw produce of the land; and before the general introduction of manufactures had opened channels for domestic industry, the demand of the great proprietors for labour would be very soon supplied; and beyond this, the labouring classes would have nothing to give them for the use of their lands. Though the landholders might have ample power to support an extended population on their estates, the very slender increase of enjoyments, if any, which they might derive from it, would rarely be sufficient to overcome their natural indolence, or overbalance the possible inconveniences or trouble that might attend the proceeding. Of that encouragement to the increase of population, which arises from the division and sub-

* Nouvelle Espagne, tom ii. l. iii. c. viii. p. 342.

division of land as new families are brought into being, the country is deprived by the original state of property, and the feudal customs and habits which it necessarily tends to generate. And under these circumstances, if a comparative deficiency of commerce and manufactures, which great inequality of property tends rather to perpetuate than to correct, prevents the growth of that demand for labour and produce, which can alone remedy the discouragement to population occasioned by this inequality, it is obvious that Spanish America may remain for ages thinly peopled and poor, compared with her natural resources.

And so, in fact, she has remained. For though the increase of population and wealth has been considerable, particularly of late years, since the trade with the mother-country has been more open, yet altogether it has been far short of what it would have been, even under a Spanish government, if the riches of the soil had been called forth by a better division of landed property, or a greater and more constant demand for raw produce.

Humboldt observes that "Les personnes qui ont réfléchi sérieusement sur la richesse du sol Mexicain savent que, par le moyen d'une culture plus soignée, et sans supposer des travaux extraordinaires pour l'irrigation des champs, la portion de terrain déjà défriché pourroit fournir de la subsistance pour une population huit à dix fois plus nombreuse." He then adds, very justly, "Si les plaines fertiles d'Atalisco, de Cholula et de Puebla ne produisent pas des récoltes plus abondantes, la cause principale doit être cherchée dans le manque des consommateurs, et dans les entraves que les inégalités du sol opposent au commerce intérieur des grains, surtout à leur transport vers les côtes qui sont baignées par la mer des Antilles."* In the actual state of these districts, the main and immediate cause which retards their cultivation is indeed the want of consumers, that is, the want of

* Tom. iii. l. iv. c. ix. p. 89.

power to sell the produce at such a price as will at once encourage good cultivation, and enable the farmers to give the landlords something that they want, for the use of their land. And nothing is so likely to prevent this price from being obtained, as any obstacles natural or artificial to internal and external commerce.

That the slow progress of New Spain in wealth and population, compared with its prodigious resources, has been more owing to want of demand than want of capital, may fairly be inferred from the actual state of its capital, which, according to Humboldt, is rather redundant than deficient. Speaking of the cultivation of sugar, which he thinks might be successfully carried on in New Spain, he says, "La Nouvelle Espagne, outre l'avantage de sa population, en a encore un autre très important, celui d'une masse énorme de capitaux amoncelés chez les propriétaires des mines ou entre les mains de négocians qui se sont retirés du commerce."*

Altogether the state of New Spain, as described by Humboldt, clearly shews—

1st. That the power of supporting labour may exist to a much greater extent than the will.

2dly. That the time employed in working for conveniences and luxuries is not always great in proportion as the time employed in working for food is small.

3dly. That the deficient wealth of a fertile country may be more owing to want of demand than want of capital.

And, in general, that fertility of soil alone is not an adequate stimulus to the continued increase of wealth.

It is not necessary, however, to go so far as the Spanish dominions in America, to illustrate these propositions. The state of the mother-country itself, and of most of the countries of Europe, would furnish the

* Tom. iii. l. iv. c. x. p. 178.

same conclusions. We need not indeed go farther than Ireland to see a confirmation of them to a very considerable extent.

The cultivation of the potatoe, and its adoption as the general food of the lower classes of the people in Ireland, has rendered the land and labour necessary to maintain a family, unusually small, compared with most of the countries of Europe. The consequence of this facility of production, unaccompanied by such a train of fortunate circumstances as would give it full effect in the increase of wealth, is a state of things resembling, in many respects, countries less advanced in civilization and improvement.

The prominent feature of Ireland is, the power which it possesses and actually exercises, of supporting a much greater population than it can employ, and the natural and necessary effect of this state of things, is the very general prevalence of habits of indolence. The landed proprietors and principal tenants being possessed of food and necessaries, or at least of the ready means of procuring them, have found workmen in abundance at their command; but these workmen not finding sufficient employment in the farms on which they had settled, have rarely been able to put their landlords in possession of the objects "most useful and most desirable" to them. Sometimes, indeed, from the competition for land occasioned by an overflowing population, very high rents have been given for small portions of ground fit for the growth of potatoes; but as the power of paying such rents must depend, in a considerable degree, upon the power of getting work, the number of families upon an estate, who can pay high money rents, must have an obvious limit. This limit, there is reason to believe, has been often found in the inability of the Irish cotter to pay the rent which he had contracted for; and it is generally understood that the most intelligent Irish landlords, influenced both by motives of humanity and interest, are now endeavouring to check the progress of that redundant population upon their estates, which, while it generates an excessive degree of poverty and misery as well as indolence, seldom makes up to the employer, in the lowness of wages, for the additional number of hands which he is obliged to hire, or call upon for their appointed service in labour. He is now generally aware that a smaller number of more industrious labourers would enable him to raise a larger produce for the consumption of towns and manufacturers, and at the same time that they would thus contribute more largely to the general wealth of the country, would be in a more happy condition themselves, and enable him to derive a larger and more certain rent from his estates.

The indolence of the country-labourers in Ireland has been universally remarked. And whether this arises from there being really little for them to do in the actual state of things,* or from a natural tendency to idleness, not to be overcome by ordinary stimulants; it is equally true that the large portion of time of which they have the command, beyond what is employed in providing themselves with necessaries, does not certainly produce the effect of making them abound in conveniences and luxuries. The poor clothing and worse lodging of the Irish peasant are as well known as the spare time which it might be expected would be the means of furnishing him amply with all kinds of conveniences.

In defence, however, of the Irish peasant, it may be truly said, that in the state or society in which he has been placed, he has not had a fair trial; he has not been subjected to the ordinary stimulants which produce industrious habits. In almost every part of the island, particularly in the south and west, the popu-

* In applying labour as a rough measure of wealth, or in measuring value in Ireland we must remember, as before intimated, that we must take the price of the labour which is actually, and with average constancy engaged, and not the price at which it may be occasionally offered by a half employed population. The caution which Adam Smith has given about the labour of cotters, already referred to in this work, must be particularly attended to.

lation of the country districts is greater than the actual business to be done on the land can employ. If the people, therefore, were ever so industriously inclined, it is not possible for them all to get regular employment in the occupations which belong to the soil. In the more hilly parts of the country which are devoted chiefly to pasture, this impossibility is more particularly striking. A small farm among the Kerry mountains may support perhaps a large family, among whom are a number of grown-up sons; but the business to be done upon the farm is a mere trifle. The greatest part of it falls to the share of the women. What remains for the men cannot occupy them for a number of hours equal to a single day in the week; and the consequence is, they are generally seen loitering about, as if time was absolutely of no value to them.

They might, one should suppose, with all this leisure, employ themselves in building better houses, or at least in improving them, and keeping them neat and clean. But with regard to the first, some difficulties may occur in procuring materials; and with regard to the second, it appears from experience, that the object is either not understood, or not considered as worth the trouble it would cost.

They might also, one should suppose, grow or purchase the raw materials of clothing, and work them up at home; and this in fact is really done to a certain extent. Most of the linen and wollen they wear is prepared by themselves. But the raw materials, when not of home growth, cannot be purchased without great difficulty, on account of the low money prices of labour; and in preparing them for wear, the temptations to indolence will generally be too powerful for human weakness, when the question is merely about a work which may be deferred or neglected, with no other effect than that of being obliged to wear old clothes a little longer, where it can be done certainly without any violation of the customs of the country.

If the Irish peasant could find such a market for the result of his in-door occupations as would give him constant employment at a fair money price, his habits might soon change; but it may be doubted whether any large body of people in any country ever acquired regular and industrious habits, where they were unable to get regular and constant work, and when, to keep themselves constantly and beneficially employed, it was necessary to exercise a great degree of providence, energy, and self-command.

It may be said, perhaps, that it is capital alone which is wanted in Ireland, and that if this want were supplied, all her people might be easily employed. That one of the greatest wants of Ireland is capital will be readily allowed; but I conceive it would be a very great mistake to suppose that the importation of a large quantity of capital, if it could be effected, would at once accomplish the object required, and create a quantity of wealth proportioned to the labour which seems ready to be employed in its production. The amount of capital which could be laid out in Ireland in preparing goods for foreign sale, must evidently depend upon the state of foreign markets; and the amount that could be employed in domestic manufactures, must as evidently depend upon the domestic demand. An attempt to force a foreign market by means of capital, must necessarily occasion a premature fall of profits, and might, after great losses, be quite ineffectual; and with regard to the domestic demand, while the habits of the great mass of the people are such as they are at present, it must be quite inadequate to take off the products of any considerable mass of new capital. In a country, where the necessary food is obtained with so little labour, and the population is still equal or nearly equal to the produce, it is perhaps impossible that the time not devoted to the production of food should create a proportionate quantity of wealth, without a very decided taste for conveniences and luxuries among the lower classes of society, and such a power of purchasing as would occasion an effective demand for them. But it is well known, that the taste of the Irish peasant for articles of this description is yet to be formed. His wants are few, and these wants he is in the habit of supplying principally at home. Owing to the cheapness of the potatoe, which forms the principal food of the lower classes of the people, his money wages are low; and the portion which remains, after providing absolute necessaries, will go but a very little way in the purchase of conveniences. All these circumstances are most unfavourable to the increase of wealth derived from manufactures destined for home consumption. But the tastes and habits of a large body of people are extremely slow in changing; and in the mean time the application of capital in larger quantities than was suited to the progress of the change, would certainly fail to yield such profits as would encourage its continued accumulation and application in the same way. In general it may be said that demand is quite as necessary to the increase of capital as the increase of capital is to demand. They mutually act upon and encourage each other, and neither of them can proceed with vigour if the other be left far behind.

In the actual state of Ireland, I am inclined to believe, that the check which the progress of her manufactures has received, has been as much owing to a want of demand as a want of capital. Her peculiar distress upon the termination of the late war had unquestionably this origin, whatever might have been the subsequent destruction of capital. And the great checks to her manufactures formerly were the unjust and impolitic restrictions imposed by England which prevented, or circumscribed the demand for them.

There is indeed in Ireland a fatal deficiency in one of the greatest sources of prosperity, the perfect security of property; and till this defect is remedied, it is not easy to so pronounce upon the degree in which the redundant capital of England would flow into Ireland with the best effect. Such a change could not fail to produce a great increase in the effectual demand for capital, as well as its supply; but in the actual state of things, there is reason to think that advances of capital have sometimes been made with little beneficial result. A certain definite assistance in particular establishments, or in facilitating the communications between one part of the country and another, may be given by government with advantage; but any thing approaching to a forced supply of capital with a view to the general employment of the people in the extension of cultivation, would infallibly create an unnatural demand for labour which could not be maintained, would tend to paralyse individual efforts, and terminate in increased poverty and distress among the labouring classes.

The state of Ireland in respect to the time and labour necessary to the production of her food is such, that her capabilities for manufacturing and commercial wealth are prodigious. If under a state of things where all kinds of property were secure an improved system of agriculture were to raise the food and raw materials required for the population with the smallest quantity of labour necessary to do it in the best manner, and the remainder of the people, instead of loitering about upon the land, were engaged in manufactures and commerce carried on in great and flourishing towns, Ireland would be beyond comparison richer than England. This is what is wanted to give full scope to her great natural resources; and to attain this state of things an immense capital is undoubtedly required; but it can only be employed to advantage as it is gradually called for; and a premature supply of it would be much less beneficial and less permanent in its effects, than such a change in the tastes and habits of the lower classes of people, such an alteration in the mode of paying their labour and such an improvement in the structure* of the

* There is nothing so favourable to effectual demand as a large proportion of the middle classes of society.

whole society as would give both the lower and middle classes a greater will and power to purchase domestic manufactures and foreign commodities.

The state of Ireland then may be said to lead to nearly the same conclusions as that of New Spain, and to shew—

That the power of employing labour on the part of landholders may often exist to a much greater extent than the will;

That the necessity on the part of labourers of employing only a small portion of time in producing food does not always occasion the employment of a greater portion of time in procuring conveniences and luxuries;

That the deficiency of wealth in a fertile country may be more owing to want of demand than to want of capital;

And, in general, that the fertility of the soil alone is not an adequate stimulus to the permanent increase of wealth.

SECTION V.—*Of Inventions to save Labour, considered as a Stimulus to the continued Increase of Wealth.*

INVENTIONS to save labour seldom take place to any considerable extent, except when there is a decided demand for them. They are the natural consequence of improvement and civilization, and, in their more perfect forms, generally come in aid of the failing powers of production on the land. The fertility of the soil, being a gift of nature, exists whether it is wanted or not; and must often therefore exceed for many hundred years the power of fully using it. Inventions, which substitute machinery for manual exertions, being the result of the ingenuity of man, and called forth by his wants, will, as might be expected, seldom exceed those wants.

But the same law applies to both. They both

come under the head of facilities of production; and in both cases a full use cannot be made of this facility, unless the power of supply which it furnishes be accompanied by an adequate extension of the market.

When a machine is invented, which, by saving labour, will bring goods into the market at a much cheaper rate than before, the most usual effect is such an extension of the demand for the commodity, by its being brought within the power of a much greater number of purchasers, that the value of the whole mass of goods made by the new machinery greatly exceeds their former value; and, notwithstanding the saving of labour, more hands, instead of fewer, are required in the manufacture.

This effect has been very strikingly exemplified in the cotton machinery of this country. The consumption of cotton goods has been so greatly extended both at home and abroad, on account of their cheapness, that the value of the whole of the cotton goods and twist now made exceeds, beyond comparison, their former value; while the rapidly increasing population of the towns of Manchester, Glasgow, &c. during the last thirty years, amply testifies that, with a few temporary exceptions, the demand for the labour concerned in the cotton manufactures, in spite of the machinery used, has been increasing very greatly.

When the introduction of machinery has this effect, it is not easy to appreciate its enriching power, or its tendency to increase both the value and quantity of domestic and foreign commodities.

When however the commodity to which machinery is applied is not of such a nature that its consumption can extend with its cheapness, the increase of wealth derived from it is neither so great nor so certain. Still however it may be highly beneficial; but the extent of this benefit* depends upon circumstances.

* Considering the manner in which I have expressed myself here, it appears to me not a little extraordinary that I should sometimes have been classed with Mr. Sismondi as an enemy to machinery. If the reader will direct his attention to what I have

Let us suppose a number of capitalists in the habit of employing £20,000 each for labour, in a manufacture of limited consumption, and that machines were introduced which, by the saving of labour, would enable them to supply the actual demand for the commodity with capitals of ten thousand pounds each in the purchase of labour, instead of twenty. There would, in this case, be a certain number of ten thousand pounds, and the men employed by these capitals, thrown out of employment. On the other hand, there would be a portion of revenue set free for the purchase of fresh commodities; and this demand would undoubtedly be of the greatest advantage in encouraging the employment of the vacant capitals in other directions. At the same time it must be recollected that this demand would not be a new one, and, even when fully supplied, could only replace the diminution of capital and profits in one department, occasioned by the employment of so many ten thousands, instead of twenty thousands. But in withdrawing capital, a part of which must necessarily be fixed, from one employment and placing it in another, there is almost always a considerable loss. The uselessness of the old fixed capital would be at once a loss of revenue to the amount of the former interest and profits upon it. Even if the whole of the remainder could be immediately employed, it would probably be less in value: and on the whole, unless more menial servants were used, many persons would be thrown out of work; and thus the power of the whole capital and revenue to command the same quantity of labour would evidently depend upon the contingency of the vacant capitals being withdrawn *undiminished* from their old occupations, and finding

said, I think he must allow that it is hardly possible to say more with truth. To maintain that the *same extent* of benefit will result in all cases, and that there never can be the least difficulty in finding new employments for capital at the same profits, does appear to me, I own, an assertion equally contradicted by all just theory, and universal experience.

immediately equivalent employment in others. But this assumed facility of finding immediate employment for fresh capital in new occupations with undiminished profits, appears to me to be contradicted by general experience; and the supposition here made must be allowed to present a case essentially distinct from that where, as in most of our great manufactures, the extension of demand, owing to the cheapness occasioned by machinery, has greatly increased the whole value as well as the whole quantity of the produce.

If, in order to try the principle, we were to push it farther, and to suppose that, without any extension of the foreign market for our goods, we could by means of machinery obtain all the commodities at present obtained at home, with one third of the labour now applied, is it in any degree probable that the mass of vacant capitals could be advantageously employed, or that the mass of labourers thrown out of work could find the means of commanding an adequate share of the national produce? If there were other foreign trades which, by means of the capital and labour thrown out of employment, might be greatly extended, the case would be at once quite altered, and the returns of such trades might furnish stimulants sufficient to keep up the value of the national income. But, if only an increase of domestic commodities could be obtained, there is every reason to fear that the exertions of industry would slacken. The peasant, who might be induced to labour an additional number of hours for tea or tobacco, might prefer indolence to a new coat. The tenant or small owner of land, who could obtain the common conveniences and luxuries of life at one third of their former price, might not labour so hard to procure the same amount of surplus produce from the land. And the trader or merchant, who would continue in his business in order to be able to drink and give his guests claret and champagne, might think an addition of homely commodities by no means worth the trouble of so much constant attention.

It has been said that, when there is an income ready for the demand, it is impossible that there should be any difficulty in the employment of labour and capital to supply it, as the owner of such an income, rather than not spend it, would purchase a table or chair that had cost the labour of a hundred men for a year. This may be true, in cases of fixed monied revenues, obtained by inheritance, or with little or no trouble. We well know that some of the Roman nobles, who obtained their immense wealth chiefly by the expeditious mode of plunder, sometimes gave the most enormous prices for fancied luxuries. A feather will weigh down a scale when there is nothing in the opposite one. But where the amount of the revenues of a country depend, in a considerable degree, upon the exertion of labour, activity and attention, there must be something in the commodities to be obtained sufficiently desirable to balance this exertion, or the exertion will cease. And experience amply shews, by the number of persons who daily leave off business, when they might certainly have continued to improve their fortunes, that most men place some limits, however variable, to the quantity of conveniences and luxuries which they will labour for; and that very few indeed would attend a counting-house six or eight hours a day, in order to purchase commodities which have no other merit than the quantity of labour which has been employed upon them.

Still however it is true that, when a great revenue has once been created in a country, in the shape of a large mass of rents, profits and wages, a considerable resistance will be made to any essential fall in its value. It is a very just remark of Hume,* that when the affairs of a society are brought to this situation; that is, when, by means of foreign trade, it has acquired the tastes necessary to give value to a great quantity of labour not employed upon actual necessaries, it may lose most of this trade, and yet continue

* Essays, vol. i. p. 293.

great and powerful, on account of the extraordinary efforts which would be made by the spare capital and ingenuity of the country to refine home manufactures, in order to supply the tastes already formed, and the incomes already created. But if we were to allow that the revenue of such a nation might, in this way, by possibility be maintained, there is little chance of its increasing; and it is almost certain that it would not have reached the same amount, without the market occasioned by foreign commerce.

Of this I think we shall be convinced, if, in our own country, we look at the quantity of goods which we export chiefly in consequence of our machinery, and consider the nature of the returns obtained for them. In the accounts of the year ended the 5th of January, 1818, it appears that the exports of three articles alone in which machinery is used—cottons, woollen and hardware, including steel goods, &c. are valued at above 29 millions. And among the most prominent articles of the imports of the same year, we find coffee, indigo, sugar, tea, silks, tobacco, wines, and cotton-wool, amounting in value altogether to above 18 millions out of thirty! Now I would ask how we should have obtained these valuable imports, if the foreign markets for our cottons, woollens, and hardware had not been extended with the use of machinery? And further, where we could have found substitutes at home for such imports, which would have been likely to have produced the same effects, in stimulating the cultivation of the land, the accumulation of capital, and the increase of population? And when to these considerations we add the fortunes which have been made in these manufactures, the market for which has been continually extending, and continually requiring more capital and more people to be employed in them; and contrast with this state of things the constant necessity of looking out for new modes of employing the same capital and the same people, a portion of which would be thrown out of their old occupations by every new invention;—we must be convinced that the state of this country would have been totally different from what it is, and that it would not certainly have acquired the same revenue in rents, profits and wages, if the same ingenuity had been exercised in the invention of machinery, without the same extension of the market for the commodities produced.

It may justly be doubted, whether, at the present moment, upon the supposition of our foreign intercourse being interrupted, we should be likely to find efficient substitutes for teas, coffee, sugar, wines, silks, indigo, cottons, &c. so as to keep up the value of our present revenue; but it cannot well be doubted, that if, from the time of Edward the First, and setting out with the actual division of landed property which then prevailed, the foreign vent for our commodities had remained stationary, our revenue from the land alone would not have approached to what it is at present, and still less, the revenue from trade and manufactures.

Even under the actual division of the landed property in Europe, which is very much better than it was 500 years ago, most of the states of which it is composed would be comparatively unpeopled, if it were not for trade and manufactures. Without the excitements arising from the results of this sort of industry, no sufficient motives could be presented to great landholders either to divide their estates by sale, or to take care that they were well cultivated.

According to Adam Smith, the most important manufactures of the northern and western parts of Europe were established either in imitation of foreign articles, the tastes for which had been already formed by a previous foreign trade, or by the gradual refinement of domestic commodities till they were fit for exportation.* In the first case, the very origin of the manufacture is made to depend upon a previous extension of market, and the importation of foreign ar-

* Wealth of Nations, Vol. ii. B. iii. ch. iii. p. 115. 6th edit.

ticles, and in the second case, the main object and use of refining the domestic commodities in an inland country, appears to be the fitting them for an extensive market, without which the local advantages enjoyed would be in a great measure lost.

In carrying on the late war, we were powerfully assisted by our steam-engines, which enabled us to command a prodigious quantity of foreign produce and foreign labour. But how would their efficacy have been weakened if we could not have exported our cottons, cloths and hardware?

If the mines of America could be successfully worked by machinery, and the King of Spain's tax could be increased at will, so as to make the most of this advantage, what a vast revenue might they not be made to afford him! But it is obvious that the effects of such machinery would sink into insignificance, if the market for the precious metals were confined to the adjacent countries, and the principal effect of it was to throw capital and labour out of employment.

In the actual state of things in this country, the population and wealth of Manchester, Glasgow, Leeds, &c. have been greatly increasing; because, on account of the extending demand for their goods, more people have been continually required to work them up; but if a much smaller number of people had been required, on account of a saving of labour from machinery, without an adequate extension of the market, it is obvious that these towns would have been poorer, and more thinly peopled. To what extent the spare capital and labour thrown out of employment in one district would have enriched others, it is impossible to say; and on this subject any assertion may be made, as we cannot be set right by an appeal to facts. But I would ask, whether there are any grounds in the slightest degree plausible for saying, that not only the capital spared at any time from these manufactures would be preserved and employed elsewhere; but that it would be employed as profitably, and create as much exchangeable value in other places as it would have done in Manchester and Glasgow, with an extending market? In short, are there any plausible grounds whatever for stating that, if the twenty millions worth of cottons which we now export, were entirely stopped, either by successful foreign competition or positive prohibitions, we should have no difficulty in finding employment for our capital and labour equally advantageous to individuals in point of profit, and equally enriching to the country with respect to the exchangeable value of its revenue?

Unquestionably any country is entitled to consume all that it produces, however great in quantity; and every man in health has the *power* of applying his mind and body to productive labour for ten or twelve hours of the day. But these are dry assertions, which do not necessarily involve any practical consequences relating to the increase of wealth. If we could not export our cottons, it is quite certain that, though we might have the power, we should not have the will, to consume them all ourselves at such prices as would pay the producers. The quantity produced therefore would be very greatly diminished; and the maintenance of our national wealth and revenue would depend upon the circumstance whether the capital thrown out of the cotton trade could be so applied as to produce commodities which would be estimated as highly and consumed as eagerly as the foreign goods before imported. There is no magic in foreign markets. The final demand and consumption must always be at home; and if goods could be produced at home, which would excite people to work as many hours in the day, would communicate the same enjoyments, and create a consumption of the same *value*, foreign markets would be useless. We know however from experience, that very few countries are capable of producing commodities of the same efficacy, in this respect, as those which may be obtained by a trade to various climates and soils. Without such a trade, and with a great increase in the power of production, there is no inconsiderable danger that industry, consumption, and exchangeable value would diminish; and this danger would most unquestionably be realized if the cheapness of domestic commodities occasioned by machinery, were to lead to increased saving rather than to increased expenditure.

But it is known that facilities of production have the strongest tendency to open markets, both at home and abroad. In the actual state of things therefore, there are great advantages to be looked forward to, and little reason to apprehend any permanent evil from the increase of machinery. The presumption always is, that it will lead to a great extension both of wealth and value. But still we must allow that the pre-eminent advantages derived from the substitution of machinery for manual labour, depend upon the extension of the market for the commodities produced, and the increased stimulus given to consumption; and that, without this extension of market and increase of consumption, they must be in a considerable degree diminished. Like the fertility of land, the invention of good machinery confers a prodigious power of production. But neither of these great powers can be called fully into action, if the situation and circumstances, or the habits and tastes of the society prevent the opening of a sufficient market, and an adequate increase of consumption.

The three great causes most favourable to production are, accumulation of capital, fertility of soil, and inventions to save labour. They all act in the same direction; and as they all tend to facilitate supply, without reference to demand, it is not probable that they should either separately or conjointly afford an adequate stimulus to the continued increase of wealth.

Section VI.—*Of the Necessity of a Union of the Powers of Production with the Means of Distribution, in order to ensure a continued Increase of Wealth.*

We have seen that the powers of production, to whatever extent they may exist, are not alone sufficient to secure the creation of a proportionate degree of wealth. Something else seems to be necessary in order to call these powers fully into action. This is an effectual and unchecked demand for all that is produced. And what appears to contribute most to the attainment of this object, is, such a distribution of produce, and such an adaptation of this produce to the wants of those who are to consume it, as constantly to increase the exchangeable value of the whole mass. In a former section, relating to the distinction between wealth and value, it was observed, that where wealth and value are perhaps most nearly connected, is in the general necessity of the latter as a stimulus to the production of the former. Unless the estimation in which an object is held, or the value which an individual, or the society places on it when obtained, adequately compensates the sacrifice which has been made to obtain it, such wealth will not be produced in future.

In individual cases, the power of producing particular commodities is called into action, in proportion to the intensity of effectual demand for them; and the greatest stimulus to their increase, independent of improved facilities of production, is a high market price, or an increase of their exchangeable value, before a greater value of capital has been employed upon them.

In the same manner, the greatest stimulus to the continued production of commodities, taken altogether, is an increase in the exchangeable value of the whole mass, before a greater value of capital has been employed upon them.

It has been stated in a preceding section, that if all

the roads and canals of the country were broken up, and the means of distributing its produce were essentially impeded, the whole value of the produce would greatly fall; indeed, it is obvious that if it were so distributed as not to be suited to the wants, tastes, and powers of the actual population in different situations, its value might sink to such a degree as to be comparatively quite inconsiderable. Upon the same principle, if the means of distributing the produce of the country were still further facilitated, and if the adaptation of it to the wants and powers of the consumers were more complete than at present, and better fitted to inspire new tastes, there can be no doubt that a great increase in the value of the whole produce would follow; first, in the shape of increased profits, and then of increased quantity, without a proportionate fall of value.

But to illustrate the power of distribution in increasing the mass of exchangeable value, we need only refer to experience. Before the introduction of good roads and of canals in England, the prices of produce in many country districts were extremely low compared with the same kind of produce in the London markets. After the means of distribution were facilitated, the price of country produce in the country, and of some sorts of London produce in London, which were sent into the country in exchange for it, rose; and rose in a greater degree than the country produce fell in the London markets, or the London produce fell in the country markets; and consequently the value of the whole produce, or the supply of London and the country together, was increased; and while encouragement was thus given to the employment of a greater quantity of capital by the extension of demand, the temporary rise of profits, occasioned by this extension, would greatly contribute to furnish the additional capital and produce required. It has never, I believe, occurred, that the better distribution of the commodities of a country occasioned by improved facilities of communication has failed to increase the value as well as the quantity of the whole produce.

In estimating an increase in the value of the whole produce, bullion, our most common measure of value, might, in general, and for short periods, be safely referred to; and though abstractedly considered, wealth is nearly independent of money; yet in the actual state of the relations of the different countries of the world with each other, it rarely happens that any great increase or decrease in the bullion value of all the commodities of a country takes place, without an increase or decrease of demand for commodities, compared with the supply of them.

It happens however, undoubtedly that in reference to periods of some length, the value of bullion alters, not only generally, but in particular countries; and it is not meant to be said that a country cannot be stimulated to an increase of wealth after a fall has taken place in the money-price of all its commodities. When, therefore, there is any doubt, in regard to a change in the value of money we must refer to that standard, the utility and comparative correctness of which I have endeavoured to establish; and in reference to which Adam Smith himself, says, "Labour, be it remembered, and not any particular commodity or set of commodities, is the real measure of the value both of silver and of all other commodities."*

General wealth, like particular portions of it, will always follow effectual demand. Whenever there is a great demand for commodities, that is, whenever the whole mass will command a greater quantity of standard labour than before, without any greater value of capital having been required to produce them, there is the same kind of reason for expecting a general increase of commodities, as there is for expecting an increase of particular commodities when their market-prices rise; without a corresponding rise in their money-cost of production. And on the other

* Book I. ch. xi.

hand, whenever the produce of a country estimated in the labour which it will command falls in value, while the same value of advances is continued, the power and will to set labourers to work will be diminished and the increase of produce must, for a time, be checked.

Mr. Ricardo, in his chapter on Value and Riches, has stated that "a certain quantity of clothes and provisions will maintain and employ the same number of men, and will therefore procure the same quantity of work to be done, whether they be produced by the labour of a hundred or of two hundred men; but they will be of twice the value, if two hundred have been employed in their production."* But, even taking his own peculiar estimate of value, this statement would never be true. The clothes and provisions which had cost only one hundred days' labour would never, but in the most unnatural state of things, be able to procure the same quantity of work to be done as if they had cost two hundred days' labour. To suppose it, is to suppose that profits are at cent. per cent., and that the price of labour, estimated in necessaries, is the same at all times and in all countries, and does not depend upon the plenty or scarcity of necessaries compared with labour, a supposition contradicted by universal experience. Nine quarters of wheat will perhaps command a year's labour in England; but eighteen quarters will hardly procure the same quantity of work to be done in America. And the great variety of corn wages in different countries at the same time, and in the same country at different times shows most clearly that it is not the *quantity* of necessaries, but their *value* which determines their efficiency in setting labourers to work, and that whatever increases their value will at the same time increase their efficiency, and whatever diminishes their value will diminish it.

Nor is the remark less applicable to those articles

* Princ. of Polit. Econ. ch. xx. p. 349.

which are denominated luxuries, than it is to the necessaries of life, for although such commodities do not in kind form any part of the funds which are destined for the maintenance of ordinary labour, yet an increase in their value gives to those who produce them a greater command over those funds, which form the most stimulus to an increase of their quantity. In every case, therefore, a continued increase in the value of the whole produce estimated in labour seems to be necessary to a continued and unchecked increase of wealth; because without such an increase of value it is obvious that no fresh labour can be set in motion. And in order to support this value it is necessary that an effective distribution of the produce should take place, and a due proportion be maintained between the objects to be consumed and the number, wants, and powers of the consumers, or, in other words, between the supply of commodities and the demand for them.

It has already been shown that the value of the whole produce cannot be maintained in the case of a rapid accumulation of capital occasioned by an actual and continued diminution in the expenditure and consumption of the higher classes of society in the form of revenue.* Yet it will be most readily allowed that the saving from revenue to add to capital is an absolutely necessary step in the progress of wealth. How then is this saving to take place without producing the diminution of value apprehended?

It may take place, and practically almost always does take place, in consequence of a previous increase in the value of the national revenue, in which case a saving may be effected, not only without any diminution of demand and consumption, but under an actual increase of demand, consumption and value during every part of the process. And it is in fact this previous increase in the value of the national revenue which both gives the great stimulus to accumulation,

* Sect. III. of this chapter.

and makes that accumulation effective in the continued production of wealth.

M. Sismondi, in his late work, speaking of the limits of accumulation, observes, "On ne fait jamais après tout qu'échanger la totalité de la production de l'année contre la totalité de la production de l'année précédente."* If this were really the case, it would be difficult to say how the value of the national produce could ever be increased. But in fact a great increase of productions may immediately find an adequate market, and experience consequently a great increase of exchangeable value, if they are so well distributed and so well adapted to the tastes and wants of the society as to excite the desire of making an adequate sacrifice in order to procure and consume them. In fact, such an increase of value always really takes place on occasion of an increased foreign demand for commodities; and unquestionably a similar increase of value would take place in the case of such

* Nouveaux Principes d'Economie Politique, tom, i. p. 120. I agree with M. Sismondi in some of his principles respecting consumption and demand; but I do not think that the view which he takes of the formation of national revenue, on which all increase of consumption and demand depends, is just; and I can by no means go with him in the fears which he expresses about machinery, and still less in the opinion which he holds respecting the necessity of a frequent interference on the part of government to protect individuals, and classes, from the consequences of competition. With regard to population, he has misunderstood my work more than I could have expected from so able and distinguished a writer. He says, that my reasoning is completely sophistical, because I have compared the *virtual* increase of population with the *positive* increase of food. But surely I have compared the *virtual* increase of population with the *virtual* increase of food; and the *positive* increase of population with the *positive* increase of food; and the greater part of my book is taken up with the latter comparison. Practically M. Sismondi goes much farther than I do in his apprehensions of a redundant population, and proposes to repress it by all sorts of strange means. I never have recommended, nor ever shall, any other means than those of explaining to the labouring classes the manner in which their interests are affected, by too great an increase of their numbers, and of removing or weakening the positive laws which tend to discourage habits of prudence and foresight.

a production and distribution of domestic commodities as better to suit the tastes and desires of the domestic consumers.

The fortune of a country, though necessarily made more slow, is made in the same way as the fortunes of individuals in trade are generally made,—by *savings*, certainly; but by savings which are furnished from increased gains, and by no means involve a diminished expenditure on objects of luxury and enjoyment.

Many a merchant has made a large fortune although, during the acquisition of this fortune, there was perhaps hardly a single year in which he did not rather increase than diminish his expenditure in objects of luxury, enjoyment, and liberality. The amount of capital in this country is immense, and it certainly received very great additions during the last forty years; but on looking back, few traces are to be found of a diminished expenditure in the shape of revenue. If some such traces however are to be found, they will be found in exact conformity to the theory here laid down; they will be found during a period, when, from particular circumstances, the value of the national produce was not maintained, and there was in consequence a diminution of the power of expenditure, and a comparative check to the production of wealth.

Perhaps it will be said, that to lay so much stress on distribution, and to measure the increase of demand by the increase of the exchangeable value of the whole produce, is to exalt the gross revenue at the expense of the neat revenue of a country, and to favour that system of cultivation and manufacturing which employs on each object the greatest number of hands. But I have already shewn that the saving of labour, and the increase of skill, both in agricultural and manufacturing industry, by enabling a country to push its cultivation over poorer lands, without diminution of profits, and to extend far and wide the markets for its manufactures, must tend to increase the exchangeable value of the whole; and there cannot be a doubt that in this country they must have been the main sources of that rapid and astonishing increase in the value of the national wealth, which has taken place during the last thirty or forty years.

To dwell therefore mainly on the gross revenue of a country rather than on its neat revenue is in no respect to under-rate the prodigious advantage derived from skill and machinery, but merely to give that importance to the value of the whole produce to which it is so justly entitled. No description of national wealth, which refers only to neat revenue, can ever be in any degree satisfactory. The economists destroyed the practical utility of their works by referring exclusively to the neat produce of the land. And the writers who make wealth consist of rents and profits, to the exclusion of wages, commit an error exactly of the same kind though less in degree. Those who live upon the wages of labour, including of course those engaged in personal services, receive and expend much the greatest part of the annual produce, pay a very considerable sum in taxes for the maintenance of the government, and form by far the largest portion of its physical force. Under the prevalence of habits of prudence, the whole of this vast mass might be nearly as happy as the individuals of the other two classes, and probably a greater number of them, though not a greater proportion of them, happier. In every point of view therefore, both in reference to that part of the annual produce which falls to their share, and the means of health and happiness which it may be presumed to communicate, those who live on the wages of labour must be considered as the most important portion of the society; and any definition of wealth which should involve such a diminution of their numbers, as to require for the supply of the whole population a smaller annual produce, must necessarily be erroneous.

In the First Chapter of this Work, having defined wealth to be "the material objects which are necessary, useful, and agreeable to mankind," I stated as a consequence that a country was rich or poor according to the abundance or scantiness in which these objects were supplied, compared with the extent of territory. It will be readily allowed that this definition does not include the question of what may be called the amount of disposable produce, or the fund for taxation; it is nevertheless a much more correct definition of the wealth of a country than any that should refer to this disposable part alone in the sense understood, either by the French economists, who confine it to neat rent, or by Mr. Ricardo who confines it to rents and profits. What should we say of the wealth of this country, if it were possible that its rents and profits could remain the same, while its population and produce were reduced two-thirds? Certainly it would be much poorer according to the above definition; and surely there are not many that would dissent from such a conclusion.

That it would be desirable, in a definition of national wealth, to include the consideration of disposable produce, as well as of actual quantity and value, cannot be doubted; but such a definition seems to be in its nature impossible, because in each individual case it must depend upon opinion, what increase of disposable produce should be accounted equivalent to a given diminution of gross produce.

We must content ourselves therefore with referring generally to the amount and value of national produce; and it may be subsequently stated as a separate, though very important consideration, that particular countries, with the same amount and value of produce, have a larger or smaller proportion of that produce disposable. In this respect, no doubt, a country with a fertile territory will have a prodigious advantage over those whose wealth depends almost entirely on manufactures. With the same population, the same rate of profits and wages, and the same amount and value of produce, the landed nation would have a much larger portion of its wealth disposable, or in other words, a larger proportion of its population might enjoy leisure, or be engaged in personal services without prejudice to its wealth.

Fortunately, it happens but seldom that we have to determine the amount of advantage or disadvantage occasioned by the increase of the neat, at the expense of the gross revenue. The interest of individual capitalists uniformly prompts them to the saving of labour, in whatever business they are engaged; and both theory and experience combine to shew that their successful efforts in this direction, by increasing the powers of production, afford the means of increasing, in the greatest practicable degree, the amount and value of the gross produce,* provided always that such a distribution and consumption of the increased supply of commodities takes place as constantly to increase their exchangeable value.

The reader will be aware, from what has been said in this section, that in dwelling on the importance of distribution as a main cause of the immediate progress of wealth, I by no means confine the terms to that process which in reference to commodities in ordinary use, prevents cottons which are *not* wanted from being

* From what has been here said, the reader will see that I can by no means agree with Mr. Ricardo, in his chapter *On Gross and Net Revenue*. I should not hesitate a moment in saying, that a country with a neat revenue from rents and profits, consisting of food and clothing for five millions of men, would be decidedly richer and more powerful, if such neat revenue were obtained from seven millions of men, rather than five, supposing them to be equally well supported. The whole produce would be greater; and the additional two millions of labourers would some of them unquestionably have a part of their wages disposable. I agree, however, with Mr. Ricardo, in approving all saving of labour and inventions in machinery; but it is because I think that their tendency is to increase the gross produce and to make room for a larger population and a larger capital. If the saving of labour were to be accompanied by the effects stated in Mr. Ricardo's instance, I should agree with M. Sismondi and Mr. Owen in deprecating it as a great misfortune.

Mr. Ricardo, in his last edition, allows in a note that he has perhaps expressed himself too strongly on this subject, and that the labourer may have some portion of the net produce of the country; but he has not altered the text.

brought into the market, instead of woollens which *are* wanted. The persevering production of cottons, when very much larger profits might be made by producing woollens is too gross an error not to be soon corrected in any country, and least of all in such a country as this. The distribution, which I mean, is not so readily accomplished. It is that which effects the best adaptation of the supplies of produce, both in quantity and quality, to the actual tastes and wants of the consumers, and creates new tastes and wants by means of greater facilities of intercourse. Such a distribution by new commodities from foreign countries, by the growth of large towns in agriculture, involving, by the increase of the middle classes of society, a gradual improvement in the structure of the society, is of slow and difficult accomplishment. To increase indeed, the proportion of the demand to the supply without a diminution of the produce is no easy task. We may know, that the opening of new channels of trade, and the extension of markets both at home and abroad will give us what we want; but these are objects which it is rarely in the power of a people or a government to accomplish at will.

In general, an increase of produce and an increase of value go on together; and this is that natural and healthy state of things, which is most favourable to the progress of wealth. An increase in the quantity of produce depends chiefly upon the power of production, and an increase in the value of produce upon its distribution. Production and distribution are the two grand elements of wealth, which, combined in their due proportions, are capable of carrying the riches and population of the earth in no great length of time to the utmost limits of its possible resources; but which taken separately, or combined in undue proportions, produce only, after the lapse of many thousand years, the scanty riches and scanty population, which are at present scattered over the face of the globe.

SECTION VII.—*Of the Distribution occasioned by the Division of landed Property considered as the Means of increasing the exchangeable Value of the whole Produce.*

THE causes most favourable to that increase of value which depends upon distribution are, 1st, the division of landed property; 2dly, internal and external commerce; 3dly, the maintenance of an adequate proportion of the society employed in personal services, or otherwise entitled to make a demand for material products without contributing directly to their supply.

In the first settlement and colonization of new countries, an easy division and subdivision of the land is a point of the very highest importance. Without a facility of obtaining land in small portions by those who have accumulated small capitals, and of new proprietors settling upon the soil, as new families branch off from the parent stocks, no adequate effect can be given to the principle of population. This facility of settling upon the soil, as the population increases, is still more imperiously necessary in inland countries, which are not favourably situated for external and internal commerce. Countries of this description, if, from the laws and customs relating to landed property, great difficulties are thrown in the way of its distribution, may remain for ages very scantily peoplèd, in spite of the principle of population; while the easy division and subdivision of the land as new families arise to be provided for, might, with comparatively little commerce, furnish an effective demand for population, and create a produce which would have no inconsiderable value in exchange. Such a country would probably have a small neat produce compared with its gross produce; it would also be greatly deficient in the amount of its manufactures and mercantile products; yet still its actual produce and population might be respectable; and for the increase of exchangeable value which had produced these effects, it would be mainly indebted to that distribution of the produce which had arisen from the easy division of land.

The rapid increase of the United States of America, taken as a whole, has undoubtedly been aided very greatly by foreign commerce, and by the power of selling raw produce, obtained with little labour, for European commodities of a kind which, if made at home, would have cost much labour. But the cultivation of a great part of the interior territory has depended essentially upon the easy division of landed property. The facility with which even common workmen, if they were industrious and economical for some years, could become new settlers and small proprietors of land, has given prodigious effect to that high money price of labour, which could not have taken place without foreign commerce: and together they have occasioned yearly that extraordinary increase of exchangeable value, which has so distinguished the progress of the establishments in North America, compared with any others with which we are acquainted.

Over almost all Europe a most unequal and vicious division of landed property was established by conquest on the breaking up of the Western Roman Empire, and subsequently during the feudal times. In some states the laws, which protected and perpetuated this division, have been greatly weakened, and by the aids of commerce and manufactures have been rendered comparatively inefficient. But in others these laws still remain in great force, and throw very great obstacles in the way of increasing wealth and population. A very large proprietor, surrounded by very poor peasants, presents a distribution of property most unfavourable to effectual demand.

Adam Smith has well described the slack kind of cultivation which was likely to take place, and did in fact take place, among the great proprietors of the middle ages. But not only were they bad cultivators and improvers; and for a time perhaps deficient in a proper taste for manufactured products; yet, even if they had possessed these tastes in the degree found to prevail at present, their inconsiderable numbers would have prevented their demand from producing any important mass of such wealth. We hear of great splendour among princes and nobles in every period of history. The difficulty was not so much to inspire the rich with a love of finery, as to break down their immense properties, and to create a greater number of demanders in the middle ranks of life who were able and willing to purchase the results of productive labour. This, it is obvious, could only be effected very gradually. That the increasing love of finery assisted considerably in accomplishing this object is highly probable; but these tastes alone, unaccompanied by a better distribution of property in other respects, would have been quite inefficient. The possessor of numerous estates, after he had furnished his mansion or castle splendidly, and provided himself with handsome clothes and handsome carriages, would not change them all every two months, merely because he had the power of doing it. Instead of indulging in such useless and troublesome changes, he would be more likely to keep a number of servants and idle dependants, to take lower rents with a view of having a greater command over his tenants, and perhaps to sacrifice the produce of a considerable portion of his land in order to encourage more game, and to indulge, with more effect and less interruption, in the pleasures of the chase. Thirty or forty proprietors, with incomes answering to between one thousand and five thousand a year, would create a much more effectual demand for the necessaries, conveniences, and luxuries of life, than a single proprietor possessing a hundred thousand a year.

It is physically possible indeed for a nation, with a comparatively small body of very rich proprietors, and a large body of very poor workmen, to push both the produce of the land and of manufactures to the greatest extent, that the resources and ingenuity of the country would admit. But, in order to do this, we must suppose a passion among the rich for the consumption of manufactures, and the results of productive labour, much more excessive than has ever been witnessed in human society. And the consequence is, that no instance has ever been known of a country which has pushed its natural resources to a great extent, with a small proportionate body of persons of property, however rich and luxurious they might be. Practically it has always been found that the excessive wealth of the few is in no respect equivalent, with regard to effectual demand, to the more moderate wealth of the many. A large body of manufacturers and merchants can only find a market for their commodities among a numerous class of consumers below the rank of the great proprietors of land. And experience shews us that manufacturing wealth is at once the consequence of a better distribution of property, and the cause of further improvements in such distribution, by the increase in the proportion of the middle classes of society, which the growth of manufacturing and mercantile capital cannot fail to create.

But though it be true that the division of landed property, and the diffusion of manufacturing and mercantile capital to a certain extent, are of the utmost importance to the increase of wealth; yet it is equally true that, beyond a certain extent, they would impede the progress of wealth as much as they had before accelerated it. There is a certain elevation at which the projectile will go the farthest: but if it be directed either higher or lower, it will fall short. With a comparatively small proportion of rich proprietors, who would prefer menial servants, retainers and territorial influence to an excessive quantity of manufactured and mercantile products, the power among capitalists of supplying the results of productive labour would be much greater than the will to consume them, and the progress of wealth would be checked by the want of effectual demand.* With an excessive proportion of small proprietors both of land and of capital, all great improvements on the land, all great enterprizes in commerce and manufactures, and most of the wonders described by Adam Smith, as resulting from the division of labour, would be at an end; and the progress of wealth would be checked by a failure in the powers of supply.

It will be found, I believe, true that all the great results in political economy, respecting wealth, depend upon *proportions*;† and it is from overlooking this most important truth, that so many errors have prevailed in the prediction of consequences; that nations have sometimes been enriched when it was expected that they would be impoverished, and impoverished when it was expected that they would be enriched;‡ and that such contradictory opinions have occasionally prevailed respecting the most effective encouragements to the increase of wealth. But there is no part of the whole subject, where the efficacy of proportions in the production of wealth is so strikingly exemplified, as in the division of landed and other property; and where it is so very obvious that a division to a certain extent must be beneficial, and beyond a certain extent prejudicial to the increase of wealth.

On the effects of a great sub-division of property, a fearful experiment is now making in France. The law of succession in that country allows but a small

* It is perhaps just possible to conceive a passion for menial service, which would stimulate landlords to cultivate lands in the best way, in order to support the greatest quantity of such attendants. This would be the same thing as the passion for population adverted to in a former section. Such a passion, to the extent here supposed, may be *possible*; but scarcely any supposition can be less probable.

† It is not, however, in political economy alone that so much depends upon proportions, but throughout the whole range of nature and art.

‡ This was strikingly illustrated in the predictions, during the late war, of the abundant wealth which would be the immediate result of a peace.

portion of a father's property to be disposed of by will, and the rest is equally divided among all the children without distinction of age or sex.

This law has not yet prevailed long enough to shew what its effects are likely to be on the national wealth and prosperity. If the state of property in France appears at present to be favourable to industry and demand, no inference can thence be drawn that it will be favourable in future. It is universally allowed that a division of property to a certain extent is extremely desirable; and so many traces yet remain almost all over Europe of the vast landed possessions which have descended from the feudal times, that there are not many states in which such a law as that of France might not be of use, with a view to wealth, for a certain number of years. But if such a law were to continue permanently to regulate the descent of property in France; if no modes of evading it should be invented, and if its effects should not be weakened by the operation of an extraordinary degree of prudence in marriage, which prudence such a law would certainly tend to discourage, there is every reason to believe that the country, at the end of a century, will be quite as remarkable for its extraordinary poverty and distress, as for its unusual equality of property. The owners of the minute divisions of landed property will be, as they always are, peculiarly without resource, and must perish in great numbers in every scarcity. Very few will be rich except those who receive salaries from the government.

In this state of things, with little or none of the natural influence of property to check at once the power of the crown and the violence of the people, it is not possible to conceive that such a mixed government as France has now established can be maintained. Nor can I think that a state of things, in which there would be so much poverty, could be favourable to the existence and duration of a republic. And when, in addition to this, we consider how extremely difficult it is, under any circumstances, to establish a well-constituted republic, and how dreadfully the chances are against its continuance, as the experience of all history shews; it is not too much to say, that no well-grounded hope could be entertained of the permanent prevalence of such a form of government.

But the state of property above described would be the very soil for a military despotism. If the government did not adopt the Eastern mode of considering itself as sole territorial proprietor, it might at least take a hint from the Economists, and declare itself co-proprietor with the landlords, and from this source, (which might still be a fertile one, though the landlords, on account of their numbers, might be poor,) together with a few other taxes, the army might easily be made the richest part of the society; and it would then possess an overwhelming influence, which, in such a state of things, nothing could oppose. The despot might now and then be changed, as under the Roman emperors, by the Prætorian guards; but the despotism would certainly rest upon very solid foundations.

It is hardly necessary to enter into the question, whether the wealth of the British empire would be essentially increased by that division of landed property which would be occasioned by the abolition of the law of primogeniture, and the power of entail, without any interference with testamentary dispositions. It is generally acknowledged that the country, in its actual state and under its actual laws, presents a picture of greater wealth, especially when compared with its natural resources, than any large territorial state of modern times. By the natural extinction of some great families, and the natural imprudence of some others, but, above all, by the extraordinary growth of manufactures and commerce, the immense landed properties which formerly prevailed all over the country have been in a great degree broken down, notwithstanding the law of primogeniture. And the few which remain may perhaps be of use in furnishing motives to the merchant and master-manufacturer, to continue the exercise of their skill and powers till they have acquired large capitals, and are able to contend in wealth with the great landlords. If, from the abolition of the law of primogeniture, the landed fortunes were all very inconsiderable, it is not probable that there would be many large capitals among merchants; and, in this case, much productive power would unquestionably be lost.

But however this may be, it is certain, that a very large body of what may be called the middle classes of society has been established in this country; while the law of primogeniture, by forcing the younger sons of the nobility and great landed proprietors into the higher divisions of these classes, has, for all practical purposes, annihilated the distinctions founded on rank and birth, and opened the fairest *arena* for the contests of personal merit in all the avenues to wealth and honours. It is probable that the obligation generally imposed upon younger sons to be the founders of their own fortunes, has infused a greater degree of energy and activity into professional and commercial exertions than would have taken place if property in land had been more equally divided. Altogether, the country possesses a very large class of effective demanders, who derive their power of purchasing from the various professions, from commerce, from manufactures, from wholesale and retail trade, from salaries of different kinds, and from the interest of public and private debts; and these demanders are likely, perhaps, to acquire tastes more favourable to the encouragement of wealth than the owners of small properties on the land.

Under these circumstances, which, to the extent in which they prevail, it must be allowed are almost peculiar to this country, it might be rash to conclude that the nation would be richer if the law of primogeniture were abolished. But even if we were able to determine the question in the affirmative, it would by no means determine the policy of such a change. In all cases of this kind there are higher considerations to be attended to than those which relate to mere wealth.

It is an historical truth which cannot for a moment be disputed, that the first formation, and subsequent preservation and improvement, of our present constitution, and of the liberties and privileges which have so long distinguished Englishmen, are mainly due to a landed aristocracy. And we are certainly not yet warranted by any experience to conclude that without an aristocracy, which cannot certainly be supported in an effective state but by the law of primogeniture, the constitution so established can be in future maintained. If then we set a value upon the British Constitution; if we think that, whatever may be its theoretical imperfections, it has practically given a better government, and more liberty to a greater mass of people for a longer time than any which history records, it would be most unwise to venture upon any such change as would risk the whole structure, and throw us upon a wide sea of experiment, where the chances are so dreadfully against our attaining the object of our search.*

* This was written in 1820. Imperious circumstances have since brought on a reform of a more sudden and extensive nature than prudence would have perhaps suggested, if the time and the circumstances could have been commanded. Yet it must be allowed, that all which has been done, is to bring the practical working of the constitution nearer to its theory. And there is every reason to believe, that a great majority of the middle classes of society, among whom the elective franchise has been principally extended, must soon see that their own interests, and the interests and happiness of those who are dependent upon them, will be most essentially injured by any proceedings which tend to encourage turbulence and shake the security of property. If they become adequately sensible of this most unquestionable truth, and act accordingly, there is no doubt that the removal of those unsightly blots, of those handles, which, with a fair show of reason, might at any time be laid hold of to excite discontents and to stir up the people, will place the British Constitution upon a much broader and more solid base than ever.

It is not perhaps easy to say to what extent the abolition of the law of primogeniture and entails would divide the landed property of this country. If the power of testamentary bequest were left untouched, it is possible that past habits might still keep many estates together for a time; but the probabilities are, that by degrees a considerable subdivision of land would take place; and if there were few estates of above a thousand a year, the mercantile classes would either be induced to moderate their exertions in the acquisition of wealth, from the absence of the motive of competition with the landlords, as I stated above; or, if the merchants and manufacturers were still to acquire great wealth, excited either by a competition with each other or by political ambition, they would be the only persons who could possess great influence in the state; and the government of the country would fall almost wholly into their hands. In neither case, probably, could our present constitution be maintained. In the first, where the property of individuals would be so inconsiderable, and so equal, the tendencies would be either to democracy or military despotism, with the chances greatly in favour of the latter. And in the second case, whatever might be the form of government, the merchants and manufacturers would have the greatest influence in its councils; and it is justly observed by Adam Smith, that the interests of these classes do not always prepare them to give the most salutary advice.

Although therefore it be true that a better distribution of landed property might exist than that which actually prevails in this country at present; and although it be also true, that to make it better, the distribution should be more equal; yet it may by no means be wise to abolish the law of primogeniture, which would be likely to lead to a subdivision of land greater probably than would be favourable even to the wealth of the country; and greater certainly than would be consistent with those higher interests, which relate to the protection of a people equally from the tyranny of despotic rulers, and the fury of a despotic mob.

But, whatever conduct the wisdom and policy of a legislature may dictate respecting the laws of succession, the principle will still be true, that the division of landed property is one of the great means of the distribution of wealth, which tends to keep up and increase its exchangeable value, and to encourage further production; and that the distribution so occasioned will, as it extends, continue to produce a more favourable effect on wealth, till it meets its antagonist principle, and begins to interfere with the power of production. This will take place sooner or later, according to circumstances, depending chiefly upon the activity of foreign and domestic commerce, and the mass of effective demanders besides the landlords. If the demand be great, independently of the land, a slight diminution in the power of production may turn the scale; and any change which is unfavourable to accumulation, enterprize, and the division of labour, will be unfavourable to the progress of wealth. But if the country be ill situated for foreign commerce, and its tastes, habits, and internal communications be such as not to encourage an active home trade, nothing can occasion an adequate demand for produce, but an easy subdivision of landed property; and without such a subdivision, a country with great natural resources might slumber for ages with an uncultivated soil, and a scanty yet starving population.

SECTION VIII.—*Of the Distribution occasioned by Commerce, internal and external, considered as the Means of increasing the exchangeable Value of Produce.*

THE second main cause favourable to that increase of exchangeable value, which depends upon distribution, is internal and external commerce.

Every exchange which takes place in a country,

effects a distribution of its produce better adapted to the wants of the society. It is with regard to both parties concerned, an exchange of what is wanted less for what is wanted more, and must therefore raise the value of both the products. If two districts, one of which possessed a rich copper mine, and the other a rich tin mine, had always been separated by an impassable river or mountain, there can be no doubt that on the opening of a communication, a greater demand would take place, and a greater price be given both for tin and copper; and this greater price of both metals, though it might only be temporary, would alone go a great way towards furnishing the additional capital wanted to supply the additional demand; and the capitals of both districts, and the products of both mines, would be increased both in quantity and value to a degree which could not have taken place without this new distribution of the produce, or some event equivalent to it.

The French Economists, in their endeavours to prove the unproductive nature of trade, always insisted that the effect of it was merely to equalize prices, which were in some places too high and in others too low, but in their amount the same as they would be after the exchange had taken place. This position must be considered as unfounded, and capable of being contradicted by incontrovertible facts. The increase of price at first, from the extension of the market, is unquestionable. And when to this we add the effect occasioned by the demand for further produce, and the means thus afforded of rapid accumulation for the supply of this demand, it is impossible to doubt for a moment the direct tendency of all internal trade to increase both the quantity and value of the national produce.

If indeed it did not tend to increase the value of the national produce, it would not be carried on. It is out of this increase that the merchants concerned are paid; and if some London goods are not more valued in Glasgow than in London, and some Glasgow goods more valued in London than in Glasgow, the merchants who exchange the articles in which these towns trade, would neither be doing themselves any good, nor any one else. It is a mere futile process to exchange one set of commodities for another, if the parties, after this new distribution of goods has taken place, are not better off than they were before. The giving one article for another has nothing to do with effectual demand, unless the commodity received so far exceeds in value the labour employed on the commodity parted with, as to yield adequate profits to the capitalists concerned, and to give them both the power and the will to set fresh labour to work in the same trade.

It has been said that the industry of a country is measured by the extent of its capital, and that the manner in which this capital is employed, though it may make some difference to the enjoyment of the inhabitants, makes very little in the *value* of the national revenue. This would be true on one supposition, and on one supposition only; namely that the inhabitants could be persuaded to estimate their confined productions just as highly, to be as eager to obtain and consume them, and as willing to work hard for them, and to make great sacrifices for them, as for the commodities which they obtain from a distance. But are we at liberty to make such a supposition? It is specifically to overcome the want of eagerness to purchase domestic commodities that the merchant exchanges them for others more in request. Could we but so alter the wants and tastes of the people of Glasgow as to make them estimate as highly the profusion of cotton goods which they produce, as any articles which they could receive in return for them under a prosperous trade, we should hear no more of their distresses. It may be allowed that the quantity of productive industry maintained in a country is nearly proportioned to the quantity of capital employed; but the value of the revenue will be greater or less, according to the market prices of the commodities produced. These market prices must obviously depend upon the interchange of goods; and consequently the value of the revenue, and the power and will to increase it, must depend upon that distribution of commodities which best adapts them to the wants and tastes of the society.

The whole produce of a nation may be said to have a market price in money and labour. When this market price is high, that is, when the prices of commodities rise so as to command a greater excess of labour above what they had cost in production than before, while the same capital and number of people had been employed upon them, it is evident that more fresh labour will be set in motion every year, and the increase of wealth will be certain and rapid. On the other hand, when the market prices of commodities are such as to be able to command very little more labour than the production of them has cost, it is as evident that the national wealth will proceed very slowly, or perhaps be quite stationary.

In the distribution of commodities, the circulating medium of every country bears a most important part; and, as I intimated before in a note, we are much more likely to obscure our reasonings than to render them clearer, by throwing it out of our consideration. It is not easy indeed, without reference to a circulating medium, to ascertain whether the commodities of a country are so distributed as to give them their proper value.

It may be said, perhaps, that if the funds for the maintenance of labour are at any time in unusual abundance, it may fairly be presumed that they will be able to command a more than usual quantity of labour. But they certainly will not be able to command more labour, nor even so much, if the distribution of them be defective; and in a country which has a circulating medium, the specific proof of the distribution being defective is, that the whole produce does not exchange for so large an amount of circulating medium as before, and that consequently the producers have been obliged to sell at a great diminution of money profits, or a positive money loss.

From the harvest of 1815 to the harvest of 1816, there cannot be a doubt that the funds for the maintenance of labour in this country were unusually abundant. Corn was particularly plentiful, and no other necessaries were deficient; yet it is an acknowledged fact, that great numbers were thrown out of employment, partly from the want of power, and partly from the want of will to employ the same quantity of labour as before. How is this fact to be accounted for? It would certainly not be easy to explain it without referring to a circulating medium. But the moment we refer to a circulating medium, the theory of the fact observed becomes perfectly clear. It is acknowledged that there was a fall in the money value of the raw produce, to the amount of nearly one third. But if the farmer sold his produce for only two thirds of the price at which he had before sold it, while the money price of labour had not fallen, it is evident that he would be quite unable to command the same quantity of labour, and to employ the same quantity of capital on his farm as he did the year before. And when afterwards a great fall of money prices took place in almost all manufactured products, occasioned in a considerable degree by this previous fall of raw produce, it is as evident that if the price of labour had not fallen, or not in proportion, so large a quantity of produce would be required to pay the labourer, that the manufacturers would be unable to employ the same number of workmen as before. In the midst of the plenty of necessaries, these two important classes of society would really have their power of employing labour diminished, while all those who possessed fixed incomes would have their power of employing labour increased, with very little chance of an increase of will to extend their demand in proportion; and the general result would resemble the effects of that partial distribution of products which would arise from the interruption of accustomed communications. The same quantity of commodities might be produced for a short time; but the distribution not being such as to proportion the supply in each quarter to the demand, the whole would fall in exchangeable value, and a decided check to production would be experienced in reference to the whole country. It follows, that the labouring classes of society may be thrown out of work in the midst of an abundance of necessaries, if these necessaries are not in the hands of those who are at the same time both able and willing to employ an adequate quantity of labour.

As long as this fall in the money price of produce continues to diminish the power of commanding labour, a discouragement to production must obviously continue; and if, after labour has adjusted itself to the new level of prices, the permanent distribution of the produce and the permanent tastes and habits of the people should not be favourable to an adequate degree of effectual consumption, the clearest principles of political economy shew that the profits of stock might be lower for any length of time than the state of the land rendered necessary; and that the retarded rate of production might be as permanent as the faulty distribution of the produce and the unfavourable tastes and habits which had occasioned it.

It is scarcely possible for any essential changes to take place in the value of the circulating medium of a country without occasioning an alteration in the distribution of its produce. The imprudent use of paper money must be allowed to be the principal cause of these changes. But even without a paper currency, or with one always maintaining the same value as bullion, every country is liable to changes in the value of its produce, compared with its money; and as such changes must have a great effect on the distribution of produce, partly temporary and partly permanent, a determination to reason on these subjects, without taking into account the effects of so powerful an agent, would be purposely to shut our eyes to the truth. Referring therefore ultimately to the command over labour as the best practical measure of the value of the whole produce, it will be useful to refer previously to its bullion value, in order to ascertain whether the distribution of the produce is such as to enable it to command labour in proportion to the increase of its quantity. If the bullion value of a country's products so increases as to command yearly an increased quantity of labour without a fall of profits, we may feel pretty well assured that it is proceeding without check in wealth and prosperity. But, if there is merely an increase of commodities, it is impossible to say, without further inquiry, that they may not be so distributed as to retard, instead of promote, the further progress of national wealth.

It has been fully stated and allowed, that a period of comparative stagnation must finally arrive in every country from the difficulty of procuring subsistence. But a deficiency of effectual demand has often occasioned a similar stagnation at an early period of a nation's progress. No country with a very confined market, internal as well as external, has ever been able to accumulate a large capital, because such a market prevents the formation of those wants and tastes, and that desire to consume, which are absolutely necessary to keep up the market prices of commodities, and prevent the fall of profits. The distribution of commodities occasioned by internal trade is the first step towards any considerable increase of wealth and capital; and if no exchanges could have taken place in this country, at a greater distance than five miles, it is probable that not a fifth part of our present capital could have been employed before the effective encouragement to accumulation and the further progress of wealth had nearly ceased.

The motives which urge individuals to engage in foreign commerce are precisely the same as those which lead to the interchange of goods between the more distant parts of the same country, namely, a desire to increase or keep up the market prices of the local products; and the increase of profits thus made by the individual, or the prevention of that fall of profits which would have taken place if the capital had been employed at home, must be considered as a comparative increase in the value of the national produce.

Mr. Ricardo begins his Chapter on Foreign Trade by stating that " No extension of foreign trade will immediately increase the amount of value in a country although it will very powerfully contribute to increase the mass of commodities, and therefore the sum of enjoyments." This statement is quite consistent with his peculiar view of value, as depending solely upon the labour which a commodity has cost. However abundant may be the returns of the merchant, or however greatly they may exceed his exports in value according to the common acceptation of the term, it is certain that the labour employed in procuring these exports will at first remain the same. But, as it is so glaring and undeniable a fact that the returns from an unusually favourable trade will exchange for an unusual quantity of money, labour and domestic commodities; as this increased power of commanding money, labour and commodities is in reality what is meant by the merchant when he talks of the extension of the foreign market and a favourable trade, and as it is known that such a state of things often lasts a sufficient time to produce the most important results, it must be allowed that the statement is quite incorrect.

Undoubtedly, as Mr. Ricardo observes, the interest of the merchant is no way affected by importing fifty pipes of wine instead of twenty-five, if the fifty pipes be not of greater value. Profits, as I have shown, are always estimated by value, not by quantity. The specific object which the merchant has in view when he engages in foreign commerce, is to obtain returns for his capital of greater *value* than if he had employed it at home; and in all cases of a favourable foreign trade from extending markets, this is specifically what he obtains.

But Mr. Ricardo thinks that value cannot increase in one department of produce without its being diminished in some other.* This again may be true according to his view of value, but is utterly unfounded according to that more enlarged view of exchangeable value which is established and confirmed by experience. If any foreign power were to send to a particular merchant commodities of a new description which would sell in the London market for fifty thousand pounds, the wealth of such merchant would be increased to that extent; and who, I would ask, would be the poorer for it? It is no doubt true that the purchasers of these commodities may be obliged to forego the use of some of the articles which they had before been in the habit of buying,† and so far in some quarters demand may be diminished; but, to counterbalance this diminution, the enriched merchant will become a purchaser of additional goods to the amount perhaps of the whole fifty thousand pounds, and thus prevent any general fall in the value of the native produce consumed in the country, while the value of the foreign produce so consumed has increased to the amount of the whole of the new produce imported. I see no difference between a present from abroad, and the unusual profits of a new foreign trade, in their effects upon the wealth of a state. They are equally calculated to increase the

* It appears to me that if the two first sentences in Mr. Ricardo's Chapter on Foreign Trade were well founded, there would be no intercourse between nations.

† This, however, will not necessarily happen. The greater temptation offered to consumption may induce some persons to spend what they otherwise would have saved, and in many cases the wealth of the country, instead of suffering by this change, will gain by it. The increased consumption, as far as it goes, will occasion an increase of market prices and profits, and this increase of profits will soon restore the capital which for a short time had been diverted from its destined office.

wealth of the community, by an increase both of the quantity and *value* of the produce obtained.

It may perhaps be thought that the *money* value of the whole produce cannot be increased without an importation of money. But, in fact, a successful extension of foreign trade is exactly that state of things which most directly leads to the importation of bullion.* For what is it that the merchant exporter specifically considers as a successful extension of foreign commerce in dealing with civilized nations? Undoubtedly, the power of selling his exports abroad for a greater value than usual, estimated in bullion; and of course, if the goods which he would import

* The importation of bullion is not necessary to a rise of prices; for, there is no necessary connection between a given quantity of money and a given scale of prices.—If a certain quantity of money be exchanged for a certain quantity of goods, their price is of course represented by that money; but if the money is exchanged for *one half* only of the goods at a time, the *whole* quantity of goods will be worth *twice* the money; and if the money be exchanged for one *third* the goods at a time, their total price will be equal to *three* times the amount of the money. The quantity of goods, and the quantity of money may therefore remain the same, and prices may rise or fall notwithstanding.

This is fully exemplified by what occurs when there is a deficiency or an excess of any one commodity which is of very extensive consumption.—Take corn as an instance.—The total *money* value of a scanty crop is known to be much *more*, and the total *money* value of a super-abundant crop much *less*, than that of an ordinary crop, while the prices of other things remain the same. In this case, it is obvious, that the price of the whole produce, agricultural and manufactured together, (or its value estimated in money) will be either greater or less than ordinary, even though there shall be no greater or less quantity of money in circulation. And this is very easily explained. Those who have to pay dearer or cheaper for their corn, have no doubt *less* or *more* to spend on other things. But, to counterbalance this, the farmers means of purchasing other things are *increased* or *diminished* in the very same proportion. If I have a commodity, which, from being in great request, rises fron £10 to £20, the purchaser must forego his demand for other things to the extent of £20 instead of £10; but my demand for other things is increased from £10 to £20. All this may take place, and indeed is constantly taking place, without a shilling being added to the circulation.—*Ed.*

in return will not sell at home so much higher as to warrant their importation, a part of the returns will finally be imported in money. But if on the whole trade only such an amount be imported as shall bear the same proportion to the returns in goods as the whole of the currency of the country does to the whole of its produce, it is obvious that no difficulty whatever can occur in the circulation of the commodities of the country at their former prices, with the single exception of those articles with which the foreign goods might directly enter into competition, which in this case would never be sufficient to prevent a general increase of value in the whole produce.

I most distinctly therefore differ from Mr. Ricardo in the conclusion *implied* in the following passage. "In all cases the demand for foreign and home commodities together, as far as regards value, is limited by the revenue and capital of the country. If one increases, the other must diminish."* It appears to me that in almost every case of successful foreign trade, it is a matter of unquestionable fact that the demand for foreign and home commodities taken together decidedly increases; and that the increase in the value of foreign produce does not occasion a proportionate diminution in the value of home produce.

I would still however allow that the demand for foreign and home commodities together is limited by the value of the revenue and capital of the country; but, according to my view of the subject, the national revenue, which consists of the sum of rents, profits, and wages, is at once decidedly *increased* by the increased profits of the foreign merchant, without a proportionate diminution of revenue in any other quarter; whereas Mr. Ricardo is evidently of opinion that, though the abundance of commodities is increased, the revenue of the country, as far as regards value, *remains the same.*

* Princ. of Polit. Econ. ch. vii. p. 138, 2nd edit.

It will readily be allowed that an increase in the *quantity* of commodities is one of the most desirable effects of foreign commerce; but I wish particularly to press on the attention of the reader that in almost all cases, another most important effect accompanies it, namely, an increase in the amount of exchangeable value. And that this latter effect is so necessary, in order to create a continued stimulus to productive industry, and keep up an abundant supply of commodities, that in the few cases in which it does not take place, a stagnation in the demand for labour is immediately perceptible, and the progress of wealth is checked. An extension of foreign commerce, according to the view which Mr. Ricardo takes of it, would, in my opinion, place us frequently in the situation in which this country was in the early part of 1816, when a sudden abundance and cheapness of corn and other commodities, from a great supply meeting a deficient demand, so diminished the value of the income of the country, that it could no longer command the same quantity of labour at the same price; the consequence of which was that, in the midst of plenty, thousands were thrown out of employment—a most painful but almost unavoidable preliminary to a fall in the money wages of labour, which it is obvious could alone enable the general income of the country to employ the same number of labourers as before, and, after a period of severe check to the increase of wealth, to recommence a progressive movement.

Mr. Ricardo always seems to think that it is quite the same to the labourer, whether he is able to command more of the necessaries of life by a rise in the money price of labour, or by a fall in the money price of provisions; but these two events, though apparently similar in their effects, may be, and in general are, most essentially different. An increase in the money wages of labour, generally implies such a distribution of the actual wealth as to give it an increasing value, to ensure full employment to all the labouring classes, and to create a demand for further produce, and for the capital which is to obtain it. In short, it is the infallible sign of health and prosperity. Whereas a general fall in the money price of necessaries often arises from so defective a distribution of the produce of the country, that the general amount of its value cannot be kept up; in which case, under the most favourable circumstances, a temporary period of want of employment and distress is unavoidable; and in many cases, (as may be too frequently observed in surveying the different countries of the globe,) this fall in the money price of necessaries is the accompaniment of a permanent want of employment and the most abject poverty, in consequence of a retrograde and permanently diminished wealth.

The reader will be fully aware that a great fall in the price of particular commodities, either from improved machinery or foreign commerce, is perfectly compatible with a continued and great increase, not only in the exchangeable value of the whole produce of the country, but even in the exchangeable value of the whole produce of these particular articles themselves. It has been already stated that the whole value of the cottons produced in this country has been prodigiously increased, notwithstanding the great fall in their price. The same may be said of teas, sugars, and many other articles, although when they were first imported, their prices were greatly higher than at present; and there can be little doubt, that if we were to attempt to make our own wines by means of hot-houses, they would altogether be worth much less money, and would give encouragement to much less industry that at present.

The causes of an increase in the effectual demand for particular commodities are of very easy explanation; but it has been considered, and with reason, as not very easy to explain the cause of that general briskness of demand which is sometimes so very sensibly felt throughout a whole country, and is so strikingly contrasted with the feeling which gives rise to the expression of trade being universally very dead.

As the specific and immediate cause of this general increase of effective demand, I should decidedly point to such a distribution of the produce, and such an adaptation of it to the wants and tastes of the society as will give the money price for which it sells an increased command of labour before more labour has been employed on its production; and I am inclined to think that, if this test be applied to all the striking cases that have occurred, it will rarely or never be found to fail.

It cannot for a moment be doubted, for instance, that the annual increase of the produce of the United States of America, estimated either in bullion or in labour, has been greater than that of any country we are acquainted with, and that this has been greatly owing to their foreign commerce, which, notwithstanding their facility of production, has given a value to their corn and raw produce nearly equal to what they bear in many of the countries of Europe, and has consequently given to them a power of commanding the produce and labour of other countries which is quite extraordinary when compared with the quantity of labour which they have employed. It can as little be doubted that in this country, from 1793 to 1814, the whole exchangeable value of the produce, estimated either in labour, or in bullion, was greatly augmented every year. In this increase of value, as well as of riches, the extension of our foreign commerce has been considered, almost without a dissentient opinion, as a most powerful agent; and certainly till 1815, no appearances seemed to indicate, that the increasing value of our imports had the slightest tendency to diminish the value of our domestic produce. They both increased, together, and increased greatly, estimated either in bullion or labour.

But while in every country to which it seems possible to refer, an increase of value will be found to accompany increasing prosperity and riches, I believe that no single instance can be produced of a country engaged in a successful commerce, and exhibiting an increasing plenty of commodities, where the value of the whole produce estimated in labour, was retrograde or even stationary. And of the two ways in which capital may be accumulated, as stated by Mr. Ricardo in his chapter on Foreign Commerce, namely *increase of revenue* from increased profits, or a *diminished expenditure* arising from cheap commodities,* it will be found that the latter never has been, nor ever will be, experienced as an effective stimulus to the permanent and continued production of increasing wealth.

It is the natural tendency of foreign trade, (as of all sorts of exchanges by which a distribution is effected better suited to the wants of society,) *immediately* to increase the value of that part of the national revenue which consists of profits, without a proportionate diminution elsewhere. It is precisely this *immediate* increase of national income arising from the exchange of what is of less value in the country, for what is of more value, that furnishes both the power and will to employ more labour, and occasions the animated demand for labour, produce and capital, which is a striking and almost universal accompaniment of successful foreign commerce; whereas, a mere abundance of commodities falling very greatly in value compared with labour, though it may be called an actual increase of wealth, would obviously at first diminish the power of employing the same number of workmen, and a temporary glut and general deficiency of demand could not fail to ensue in labour, in produce, and in capital, attended with the usual distress which a glut must necessarily occasion.

Mr. Ricardo always views foreign trade in the light of means of obtaining *cheaper* commodities. But this is only looking to one half of its advantages, and I am strongly disposed to think, not the larger half. In our own commerce at least, this part of the trade is comparatively inconsiderable. The great mass of our

* Princ. of Pol. Econ. ch. vii. p. 132, 2d edit.

imports consists of articles as to which there can be no kind of question about their comparative cheapness, as raised abroad or at home. If we could not import from foreign countries our silk, cotton and indigo, our tea, sugar, coffee and tobacco, our port, sherry, claret and champagne, our almonds, raisins, oranges and lemons, our various spices and our various drugs, with many other articles peculiar to foreign climates, it is quite certain that we should not have them at all. To estimate the advantage derived from their importation by their cheapness, compared with the quantity of labour and other advances which they would have cost, if we had attempted to raise them at home, would be perfectly preposterous. In reality, no such attempt would have been thought of. If we could by possibility have made fine claret at ten pounds a bottle, few or none would have drunk it; and the actual quantity of labour and other advances employed in obtaining these foreign commodities is at present beyond comparison greater than it would have been if we had not imported them.

We must evidently therefore estimate the advantage which we derive from such a trade upon a very different principle. This is the simple and obvious one often adverted to as the foundation of every act of barter, whether foreign or domestic, namely, the increased value which results from exchanging what is wanted less for what is wanted more. After we had, by our exports of home commodities, obtained in return all the foreign articles above-mentioned, we might be very much puzzled to say whether we had increased or decreased the *quantity* of our commodities, but we should feel quite certain that the new distribution of produce which had taken place, by giving us commodities much better suited to our wants and tastes than those which had been sent away, had decidedly increased the exchangeable value of our possessions, our means of enjoyment, and our wealth.

Taking therefore a very different view of the effects of foreign commerce on exchangeable value from Mr. Ricardo, I should bring forward the extension of markets as being, in its general tendency, pre-eminently favourable to that increase of value and wealth which arises from distribution.

Section IX.—*Of the Distribution occasioned by personal services and unproductive Consumers, considered as the Means of increasing the exchangeable Value of the whole Produce.*

The third main cause which tends to keep up and increase the value of produce by favouring its distribution is the employment of individuals in personal services, or the maintenance of an adequate proportion of consumers not directly productive of material objects.

It has been already shewn that, under a rapid accumulation of capital, or in other words, a rapid conversion of persons engaged in personal services into productive labourers, the demand, compared with the supply of material products, would prematurely fail, and the motive to further accumulation be checked, before it was checked by the exhaustion of the land. It follows that, without supposing the productive classes to consume much more than they are found to do by experience, particularly when they are rapidly saving from revenue to add to their capitals, it is necessary that a country with great powers of production should possess a body of consumers who are not themselves engaged in production.

In the fertility of the soil, in the powers of man to apply machinery as a substitute for labour, and in the motives to exertion under a system of private property, the laws of nature have provided for the leisure or personal services of a certain portion of society; and if this beneficent offer be not accepted by an adequate number of individuals, not only will a positive good, which might have been so attained, be lost, but the rest of the society, so far from being benefited by such self-denial, will be decidedly injured by it.

What the proportion is between the productive labourers and those engaged in personal services, which affords the greatest encouragement to the continued increase of wealth, it has before been said that the resources of political economy are unequal to determine. It must depend upon a great variety of circumstances, particularly upon the fertility of the soil and the progress of invention in machinery. A fertile soil and an ingenious people can not only support without injury a considerable proportion of consumers not directly productive of material wealth, but may absolutely require such a body of demanders, in order to give effect to the powers of production. While, with a poor soil and a people of little ingenuity, an attempt to support such a body would throw land out of cultivation, and lead infallibly to impoverishment and ruin.

Another cause, which makes it impossible to say what proportion of consumers directly productive to those not directly productive is most favourable to the increase of wealth, is the difference in the degree of consumption which may prevail among the producers themselves.

Perhaps it will be said that there can be no occasion for unproductive consumers, if a consumption sufficient to keep up the value of the produce takes place among those who are engaged in production.

With regard to the capitalists who are so engaged, they have certainly the power of consuming their profits, or the revenue which they make by the employment of their capitals; and if they were to consume it, with the exception of what could be beneficially added to their capitals, so as to provide in the best way both for an increased production and increased consumption, there might be little occasion for unproductive consumers. But such consumption is not consistent with the actual habits of the generality of capitalists. The great object of their lives is to save a fortune, both because it is their duty to make a provision for their families, and because they cannot spend an income with so much comfort to themselves, while they are obliged perhaps to attend a counting-house for seven or eight hours a day.

It has been laid down as a sort of axiom among some writers that the wants of mankind may be considered as at all times commensurate with their powers; but this position is not always true, even in those cases where a fortune comes without trouble; and in reference to the great mass of capitalists, it is completely contradicted by experience. Almost all merchants and manufacturers save, in prosperous times, much more rapidly than it would be possible for the national capital to increase, so as to keep up the value of the produce. But if this be true of them as a body, taken one with another, it is quite obvious that, with their actual habits, they could not afford an adequate market to each other by exchanging their several products.

There must therefore be a considerable class of persons who have both the will and power to consume more material wealth than they produce, or the mercantile classes could not continue profitably to produce so much more than they consume. In this class the landlords no doubt stand pre-eminent; but if they were not assisted by the great mass of individuals engaged in personal services, whom they maintain, their own consumption would of itself be insufficient to keep up and increase the value of the produce, and enable the increase of its quantity more than to counterbalance the fall of its price. Nor could the capitalists in that case continue with effect the same habits of saving. The deficiency in the value of what they produced would necessarily make them either consume more, or produce less; and when the mere pleasure of present expenditure, without the accompaniments of an improved local situation and an advance in rank, is put in opposition to the continued labour of attending to business during the greatest part of the day, the probability is that a considerable body of them will be induced to prefer the latter alternative, and produce less. But if, in order to balance the demand and supply, a permanent diminution of production takes place, rather than an increase of effective consumption, the whole of the national wealth, which consists of what is produced and consumed, will be decidedly diminished.

Mr. Ricardo frequently speaks, as if saving were an end instead of a means. Yet even with regard to individuals, where this view of the subject is nearest the truth, it must be allowed that the final object in saving is expenditure and enjoyment. But, in reference to national wealth, it can never be considered either immediately or permanently in any other light than as a means. If however commodities are already so plentiful that an adequate portion of them is not profitably consumed, to save capital can only be still further to increase the plenty of commodities, and still further to lower already low profits, which can be comparatively of little use.

National saving, therefore, considered as the means of increased production, is confined within much narrower limits than individual saving. While some individuals continue to spend, other individuals may continue to save to a very great extent; but the national saving, in reference to the whole mass of producers and consumers, must necessarily be limited by the amount which can be advantageously employed in supplying the demand for produce; and to create this demand, there must be an adequate and effective consumption either among the producers themselves, or other classes of consumers.

Adam Smith has observed "that the desire of food is limited in every man by the narrow capacity of the human stomach; but the desire of the conveniences and ornaments of building, dress, equipage, and household furniture, seems to have no limit or certain boundary." That it has no *certain* boundary is unquestionably true; that it has no limit must be allowed to be too strong an expression, when we consider how it will be practically limited by the countervailing luxury of indolence, or by the general desire of mankind to better their condition, and make a provision for a family; a principle which, as Adam Smith himself states, is on the whole stronger than the principle which prompts to expense.* But surely it is a glaring misapplication of this statement in any sense in which it can be reasonably understood, to say, that there is no limit to the saving and employment of capital except the difficulty of procuring food. It is to found a doctrine upon the *unlimited* desire of mankind to consume; then to suppose this desire *limited* in order to save capital, and thus completely alter the premises, and yet still to maintain that the doctrine is true. Let a sufficient consumption always take place, whether by the producers or others, to keep up and increase the exchangeable value of the whole produce; and I am perfectly ready to allow that, to the employment of a national capital, increasing only at such a rate, there is no other limit than that which bounds the power of maintaining population. But it appears to me perfectly clear in theory, and universally confirmed by experience, that the employment of capital may, and in fact often does, find a limit, long before there is any real difficulty in procuring the means of subsistence; and that both capital and population may be at the same time, and for a period of considerable length, redundant, compared with the effectual demand for produce.

Of the wants of mankind in general, it may be further observed, that it is a partial and narrow view

* Wealth of Nations, vol. ii. b. ii. ch. ii. p. 19, 6th edit.

of the subject, to consider only the propensity to spend what is actually possessed. It forms but a very small part of the question to determine that if a man has a hundred thousand a year, he will not decline the offer of ten thousand more; or to lay down generally that mankind are never disposed to refuse the means of increased power and enjoyment. The main part of the question respecting the wants of mankind, relates to their power of calling forth the exertions necessary to acquire the means of expenditure. It is unquestionably true that wealth produces wants; but it is a still more important truth, that wants produce wealth. Each cause acts and re-acts upon the other, but the order, both of precedence and of importance, is with the wants which stimulate to industry; and with regard to these, it appears that, instead of being always ready to second the physical powers of man, they require for their developement "all appliances and means to boot." The greatest of all difficulties in converting uncivilized and thinly peopled countries into civilized and populous ones, is to inspire them with the wants best calculated to excite their exertions in the production of wealth. One of the greatest benefits which foreign commerce confers, and the reason why it has always appeared an almost necessary ingredient in the progress of wealth, is, its tendency to inspire new wants, to form new tastes, and to furnish fresh motives for industry. Even civilized and improved countries cannot afford to lose any of these motives. It is not the most pleasant employment to spend eight hours a day in a counting-house. Nor will it be submitted to after the common necessaries and conveniences of life are attained, unless adequate motives are presented to the mind of the man of business. Among these motives is undoubtedly the desire of advancing his rank, and contending with the landlords in the enjoyment of leisure, as well as of foreign and domestic luxuries.

But the desire to realize a fortune as a permanent

provision for a family is perhaps the most general motive for the continued exertions of those whose incomes depend upon their own personal skill and efforts. Whatever may be said of the virtue of parsimony or saving, as a *public* duty, there cannot be a doubt that it is, in numberless cases, a most sacred and binding *private* duty; and were this legitimate and praiseworthy motive to persevering industry in any degree weakened, it is impossible that the wealth and prosperity of the country should not most materially suffer. But if, from the want of other effective consumers, the capitalists were obliged to consume all that could not be advantageously added to the national capital, under such circumstances the motives which support them in their daily tasks must essentially be weakened, and the same powers of production would not be called forth.

It has appeared then that, in the ordinary state of society, the master producers and capitalists, though they may have the power, have not the will, to consume in the shape of revenue to the necessary extent. And with regard to their workmen, it must be allowed that, if they possessed the will, they have not the power. It is indeed most important to observe that no power of consumption on the part of the labouring classes can ever, according to the common motives which influence mankind, alone furnish an encouragement to the employment of capital. No one will ever employ capital merely for the sake of the demand occasioned by those who work for him. Unless they produce an excess of value above what they consume, which he either wants himself in kind, or which he can advantageously exchange for something which he desires, either for present or future use, it is quite obvious that his capital will not be employed in maintaining them. When indeed this further value is created and affords a sufficient excitement to the saving and employment of capital, then certainly the power of consumption possessed by the workmen will greatly add to the whole national demand, and make room for the employment of a much greater capital.

It is most desirable that the labouring classes should be well paid, for a much more important reason than any that can relate to wealth; namely, the happiness of the great mass of society. But as a great increase of consumption among the working classes must greatly increase the cost of production, it must lower profits, and diminish or destroy the motive to accumulate, before agriculture, manufactures, and commerce have reached any considerable degree of prosperity. If each labourer were actually to consume double the quantity of corn which he does at present, such a demand, instead of giving a stimulus to wealth, would unquestionably throw a great quantity of land out of cultivation, and greatly diminish both internal and external commerce.*

It may be thought perhaps that the landlords could not fail to supply any deficiency of demand and consumption among the producers, and that between them there would be little chance of any approach towards redundancy of capital. What might be the result of the most favourable distribution of landed property it is not easy to say from experience; but experience certainly tells us that, under the distribution of land which actually takes place in most of the countries in Europe, the demands of the landlords, added to those of the producers, have not always been found sufficient to prevent any difficulty in the employment of capital. In the instance alluded to in a former chapter, which occurred in this country in the middle of last century, there must have been a considerable difficulty in finding employment for capital, or the national creditors would rather

* The demand created by the productive labourer himself can never be an *adequate* demand, because it does not go to the full extent of what he produces. If it did, there would be no profit, consequently no motive to employ him. The very existence of a profit upon any commodity presupposes a demand *exterior* to that of the labour which has produced it. *Ed.*

have been paid off than have submitted to a reduction of interest from 4 per cent. to 3½, and afterwards to 3. And that this fall in the rate of interest and profits arose from a redundancy of capital and a want of demand for produce, rather than from the difficulty of production on the land, is fully evinced by the low price of corn at the time, and the very different state of interest and profits which has occurred since.

A similar instance took place in Italy in 1685, when, upon the Pope's reducing the interest of his debts from 4 to 3 per cent., the value of the principal rose afterwards to 112; and yet the Pope's territories have at no time been so cultivated as to occasion such a low rate of interest and profits from the difficulty of procuring the food of the labourer. Under a more favourable distribution of property, there cannot be a doubt that such a demand for produce, agricultural, manufacturing, and mercantile, might have been created, as to have prevented for many many years the interest of money from falling below 3 per cent. In both these cases, the demands of the landlords were added to those of the productive classes.

But if the master-producers, from the laudable desire they feel of bettering their condition, and providing for a family, do not consume their revenue sufficiently to give an adequate stimulus to the increase of wealth; if the working producers, by increasing their consumption, supposing them to have the means of so doing, would impede the growth of wealth more by diminishing the power of production, than they could encourage it by increasing the demand for produce; and if the expenditure of the landlords, in addition to the expenditure of the two preceding classes, be found insufficient to keep up and increase the value of that which is produced, where are we to look for the consumption required but among the unproductive labourers of Adam Smith?

Every society must have a body of persons engaged in personal services of various kinds; as every society, besides the menial servants required, must have statesmen to govern it, soldiers to defend it, judges and lawyers to administer justice and protect the rights of individuals, physicians and surgeons to cure diseases and heal wounds, and a body of clergy to instruct the ignorant, and administer the consolations of religion. No civilized state has ever been known to exist without a certain portion of all these classes of society in addition to those who are directly employed in production. To a certain extent therefore they appear to be absolutely necessary. But it is perhaps one of the most important practical questions that can possibly be brought under our view, whether, however necessary and desirable they may be, they must be considered as detracting so much from the material products of a country, and its power of supporting an extended population; or whether they furnish fresh motives to production, and tend to push the wealth of a country farther than it would go without them.

The solution of this question evidently depends, first, upon the solution of the main practical question, whether the capital of a country can or cannot be redundant; that is, whether the motive to accumulate may be checked or destroyed by the want of effective demand long before it is checked by the difficulty of procuring the subsistence of the labourer. And secondly, whether, allowing the *possibility* of such a redundance, there is sufficient reason to believe that, under the actual habits of mankind, it is a probable occurrence.

In the Chapter on Profits, but more particularly in the Third Section of the present Chapter, where I have considered the effect of accumulation as a stimulus to the increase of wealth, I trust that the first of these questions has been satisfactorily answered. And in the present Section it has been shewn that the actual habits and practice of the productive classes, in the most improved societies, do not lead them to consume as revenue so large a proportion of what they produce, even though assisted by the landlords, as to prevent their finding frequent difficulties in the employment of their capitals. We may conclude therefore, with little danger of error, that such a body of persons as I have described is not only necessary to the government, protection, health, and instruction of a country, but is also necessary to call forth those exertions which are required to give full play to its physical resources.

With respect to those persons who are not employed in the production or distribution of material objects, it is obvious that such as are paid voluntarily by individuals, will be the most likely to be useful in exciting industry, and the least likely to be prejudicial by interfering with the costs of production. It may be presumed that a person will not take a menial servant, unless he can afford to pay him; and that he is as likely to be excited to industry by the prospect of this indulgence, as by the prospect of buying ribands and laces.

It is also very important to observe, that menial servants are absolutely necessary to make the resources of the higher and middle classes of society efficient in the demand for material products. No persons possessing incomes above five hundred pounds a year, would be inclined to have such houses, furniture, clothes, carriages and horses, and such eatables and drinkables in their houses as they have at present, if they were obliged to sweep their own rooms, brush and wash their own furniture and clothes, clean their own carriages and horses, and had none but themselves to make a demand for eatables and drinkables. And it is farther to be remarked, that all personal services paid voluntarily, whether of a menial or intellectual kind, are essentially distinct from the labour necessary to production. They are paid from revenue, not from capital. They have no tendency to increase cost and lower profits. On the contrary, while they leave the cost of production, as far as regards the quantities of labour required to obtain any particular commodities the same as before, they increase profits by occasioning a more brisk demand for material products, as compared with the supply of them.

Yet to shew how frequently the doctrine of proportions meets us at every turn, and how much the wealth of nations depends upon the relation of parts, rather than on any positive rule respecting the advantages of productive labour as compared with personal services, it may be worth while to remind the reader that, though the employment of a number of persons in menial service, varying with the neat revenue of the society, is in every respect desirable, there could hardly be a taste more unfavourable to the progress of wealth than a strong preference of menial service and ill accommodated followers to material products. We may, however, safely trust to the inclinations of individuals in this respect; and it will be allowed generally, that there is little difficulty in reference to those classes which are supported voluntarily, though there may be much with regard to those which must be supported by taxation.

With regard to these latter classes, such as statesmen, soldiers, sailors, and those who live upon the interest of a national debt, it cannot be denied that they contribute powerfully to distribution and demand; they frequently occasion a division of property more favourable to the progress of wealth than would otherwise have taken place; they ensure that effective consumption which is necessary to give the proper stimulus to production; and the desire to pay a tax, and yet enjoy the same means of gratification, must often operate to excite the exertions of industry quite as effectually as the desire to pay a lawyer or physician. Yet to counterbalance these advantages, which so far are unquestionable, it must be acknowledged that injudicious taxation might stop the increase of wealth at almost any period of its progress, early or late;* and that the most judicious taxation might ultimately be so heavy as to clog all the channels of foreign and domestic trade, and almost prevent the possibility of accumulation.

The effect therefore on national wealth of those classes of unproductive consumers which are supported by taxation, must be very various in different countries, and must depend entirely upon the powers of production, and upon the manner in which the taxes are raised in each country. As great powers of production are neither likely to be called into action, or, when once in action, kept in activity without a great effective consumption, I feel very little doubt that instances have practically occurred of national wealth being decidedly stimulated by the consumption of those who have been supported by taxes. Yet taxation is a stimulus so liable in every way to abuse, and it is so absolutely necessary for the general interests of society to consider private property as sacred, that no one would think of trusting to any government the means of making a different distribution of wealth, with a view to the general good. But when, either from necessity or error, a different distribution has taken place, and the evil, as far as it regards private property, has actually been committed, it may not be wise to attempt, at the expense of a great temporary sacrifice, a sudden return to the former distribution, without very fully considering whether, if it were effected, it would be really advantageous; that is, whether, in the actual circumstances of the country, with

* The effect of obliging a cultivator of a certain portion of rich land to maintain two men and two horses for the state, might in some cases only induce him to cultivate more, and create more wealth than he otherwise would have done, while it might leave him personally as rich as before, and the nation richer; but if the same obligation were to be imposed on the cultivator of an equal quantity of poor land, the property might be rendered at once not worth working, and the desertion of it would be the natural consequence. An indiscriminate and heavy tax on gross produce might immediately scatter desolation over a country, capable, under a better system, of producing considerable wealth.

reference to its powers of production, more would not be lost by the want of effectual demand than gained by the diminution of taxation.

If there could be no sort of difficulty in finding profitable employment for any amount of capital, provided labour were sufficiently abundant, the way to national wealth, though it might not always be easy, would be quite straight, and our only object need be to save from revenue, and repress unproductive consumers. But, if it has appeared that the greatest powers of production are rendered comparatively useless without effectual consumption,* and that a proper distribution of the produce is as necessary to the continued increase of wealth as the means of producing it, it follows that, in cases of this kind, the question depends upon proportions; and it would be the height of rashness to determine, under all circumstances, that the sudden diminution of a national debt and the removal of taxation must necessarily tend to increase the national wealth, and provide employment for the labouring classes.

I am very far, however, from being insensible to the evils of a great national debt. Though, in many respects, it may be a useful instrument of distribution, it must be allowed to be a very cumbersome and very dangerous instrument. In the first place, the revenue necessary to pay the interest of such a debt can only be raised by taxation; and, as this taxation, if pushed to any considerable extent, can hardly fail of interfering with the powers of production, there is always danger of impairing one element of wealth, while we are improving another. A second important objection to a large national debt, is the feeling which prevails so very generally among all those not immediately concerned in it, and consequently among the great mass of the population, that they would be im-

* By *effectual* consumption is meant, a consumption by those who are able and willing to pay such a price for produce, as will *effect* the continuation of its supply without a fall of profits not required by the state of the land.

mediately and greatly relieved by its extinction; and, whether this impression be well founded or not, it cannot exist without rendering the interest paid for it in some degree insecure, and exposing a country to the risk of a great convulsion of property, particularly as it prevents any economy of expenditure which is practicable, from affording such a relief from taxation, as will tell upon the feelings of the people. A third objection to such a debt is, that it greatly aggravates the evils arising from changes in the value of money. When the currency falls in value, the annuitants, as owners of fixed incomes, are most unjustly deprived of their proper share of the national produce; when the currency rises in value, the pressure of the taxation necessary to pay the interests of the debt, may become suddenly so heavy as greatly to distress the productive classes;* and this kind of sudden pressure must very much enhance the insecurity of property vested in public funds.

On these and other accounts it would be desirable gradually to diminish the debt, and more especially to discourage the growth of it in future, even though it were allowed that its past effects had been favourable to wealth, and that the advantageous distribution of produce which it had occasioned, had, under the actual circumstances, more than counterbalanced the obstructions which it might have given to commerce.

On the whole it may be observed, that the specific use of a body of unproductive consumers, is to give

* In a country with a large public debt, there is no duty which ought to be held more sacred on the part of the administrators of the government than to prevent any variations of the currency beyond those which necessarily belong to the varying value of the precious metals. I am fully aware of the temporary advantages which may be derived from a fall in the value of money; and perhaps it may be true that a part of the distress during the last year, though I believe but a small part, was occasioned by the measure lately adopted, for the restoration of the currency to its just value. But some such measure was indispensably necessary; and Mr. Ricardo deserves the thanks of his country for having suggested one which has rendered the transition more easy than could reasonably have been expected. This was written in 1820.

encouragement to wealth by maintaining such a balance between produce and consumption as will give the greatest exchangeable value to the results of the national industry. If such consumers were to predominate, the comparatively small quantity of material products brought to market would keep down the value of the whole produce, from the deficiency of quantity. If, on the other hand, the productive classes were in excess, the value of the whole produce would fall from excess of supply. There is therefore a certain proportion between the two which will yield the greatest value, and command for a continuance the greatest quantity of labour; and we may safely conclude that, among the causes necessary to that distribution, which tends to keep up and increase the exchangeable value of the whole produce, we must place the maintenance of a certain body of consumers who are not themselves engaged in the immediate production of material objects. This body, considered as a stimulus to wealth, should vary in different countries, and at different times, according to the powers of production; and the most favourable result evidently depends upon their numbers being best suited to the natural resources of the soil, and the skill, and acquired tastes of the people.

SECTION X.—*Application of some of the preceding Principles to the Distresses of the Labouring Classes since* 1815, *with General Observations.*

IT has been said that the distresses of the labouring classes since 1815 are owing to a deficient capital, which is evidently unable to employ all that are in want of work.

That the capital of the country does not bear an adequate proportion to the population; that the capital and revenue together do not bear so great a proportion as they did before 1815; and that such a disproportion will at once account for very great distress among the labouring classes, I am most ready to allow. But it is a very different thing to allow that the capital is deficient compared with the population; and to allow that it is deficient compared with the demand for it, and the demand for the commodities procured by it.* The two cases are very frequently confounded, because they both produce distress among the labouring classes; but they are essentially distinct. They are attended with some very different symptoms, and require to be treated in a very different manner.

If one fourth of the capital of a country were suddenly destroyed, or entirely transferred to a different part of the world, without any other cause occurring of a diminished demand for commodities, this scantiness of capital would certainly occasion great inconvenience to consumers, and great distress among the working classes; but it would be attended with great advantages to the remaining capitalists. Commodities, in general, would be scarce, and bear a high price on account of the deficiency in the means of producing them. Nothing would be so easy as to find a profitable employment for capital; but it would by no means be easy to find capital for the number of employments in which it was deficient; and consequently the rate of profits would be very high. In this state of things there would be an immediate and pressing demand for capital, on account of there being an immediate and pressing demand for commodities; and the obvious remedy would be, the supply of the demand in the only way in which it could take place, namely, by saving from revenue to add to capital. This supply of capital would, as I have before stated, take place just upon the same principle as a supply of population would

* It is a contradiction in terms, to say that labour is redundant compared with capital, and that capital is at the same time redundant compared with labour:—but it is no contradiction in terms to say that both labourers and capital may be redundant, compared with the means of employing them profitably. I have never maintained the former position, though I have been charged with so doing; but the latter has been so fully established by experience, that I am surprized at the pertinacity with which theoretical writers continue to refuse their assent to it.

follow a great destruction of people on the supposition of there being an immediate and pressing want of labour evinced by the high real wages given to the labourer.

On the other hand, if the capital of the country were diminished by the failure of demand in some large branches of trade, which had before been very prosperous, and absorbed a great quantity of stock; or even if, while capital were suddenly destroyed, the revenue of the landlords was diminished in a greater proportion owing to peculiar circumstances, the state of things, with the exception of the distresses of the poor, would be almost exactly reversed. The remaining capitalists would be in no respect benefited by events which had diminished demand in a still greater proportion than they had diminished the supply. Commodities would be every where cheap. Capital would be seeking employment, but would not easily find it; and the profits of stock would be low. There would be no pressing and immediate demand for capital, because there would be no pressing and immediate demand for commodities; and, under these circumstances, the saving from revenue to add to capital, instead of affording the remedy required, would only aggravate the distresses of the capitalists, and fill the stream of capital which was flowing out of the country. The distresses of the capitalists would be aggravated, just upon the same principle as the distresses of the labouring classes would be aggravated if they were encouraged to marry and increase, after a considerable destruction of people, although accompanied by a still greater destruction of capital which had kept the wages of labour very low. There might certainly be a great deficiency of population, compared with the territory and powers of the country, and it might be very desirable that it should be greater; but if the wages of labour were still low, notwithstanding the diminution of people, to encourage the birth of more children would be to encourage misery and mortality rather than population.

Now I would ask, to which of these two suppositions does the present state of this country* bear the nearest resemblance? Surely to the latter. That a great loss of capital has lately been sustained, is unquestionable. During nearly the whole of the war, owing to the union of great powers of production with a great effectual consumption and demand, the prodigious destruction of capital by the government was much more than recovered. To doubt this would be to shut our eyes to the comparative state of the country in 1792 and 1813. The two last years of the war were, however, years of extraordinary expense, and being followed immediately by a period marked by a very unusual stagnation of effectual demand, the destruction of capital which took place in those years was not probably recovered. But this stagnation itself was much more disastrous in its effects upon the national capital, and still more upon the national revenue, than any previous destruction of stock. It commenced certainly with the extraordinary fall in the value of the raw produce of the land, to the amount, it has been supposed, of nearly one third. When this fall had diminished the capitals of the farmers, and still more the revenues both of landlords and farmers, and of all those who were otherwise connected with the land, their power of purchasing manufactures and foreign products was of necessity greatly diminished. The failure of home demand filled the warehouses of the manufacturers with unsold goods, which urged them to export more largely at all risks. But this excessive exportation glutted all the foreign markets, and prevented the merchants from receiving adequate returns; while, from the diminution of the home revenues, aggravated by a sudden and extraordinary contraction of the currency, even the comparatively scanty returns obtained from abroad found a very insufficient domestic demand, and the profits and consequent expenditure of merchants and manufac-

* This was written in 1820.

turers were proportionably lowered. While these unfavourable changes were taking place in rents and profits, the powerful stimulus which had been given to population by the continued demand for labour during the war, occasioned the pouring in of fresh supplies of labour, which, aided by the disbanded soldiers and sailors, and the failure of demand arising from the losses of the farmers and merchants, reduced generally both wages and profits, and left the country with a greatly diminished capital and revenue;—not merely in proportion to the alteration of the value of the currency, but in reference to the bullion value of its produce, and the command of this bullion value over labour, at the price at which it was actually employed. For the four or five years since the war, on account of the change in the distribution of the national produce, and the want of effectual consumption and demand occasioned by it, a check has been given to the rate of production, and the population, under its former impulse, has increased, not only faster than the demand for labour, but faster than the actual produce; yet this produce, though deficient, compared with the population, is redundant, compared with the effectual demand for it and the revenue which is to purchase it. Though labour is cheap, there is neither the power nor the will to employ it all; because not only has the capital of the country diminished, compared with the number of labourers, but, owing to the diminished revenues of the country, the commodities which those labourers would produce are not in such request as to ensure tolerable profits to the reduced capital.

But when profits are low and uncertain, when capitalists are quite at a loss where they can safely employ their capitals, and when on these accounts capital is flowing out of the country; in short, when all the evidence which the nature of the subject admits, distinctly proves that there is no effective demand for capital at home, is it not contrary to the general principles of political economy, is it not a vain and fruitless opposition to that first, greatest, and most universal of all its principles, the principle of supply and demand, to recommend saving, and the conversion of more revenue into capital? Is it not just the same sort of thing as to recommend marriage when people are starving and emigrating?

I am fully aware that the low profits of stock, and the difficulty of finding employment for it, which I consider as an unequivocal proof that the immediate want of the country is not capital, has been attributed to other causes; but to whatever causes they may be attributed, an increase in the proportion of capital to revenue must aggravate them. With regard to these causes, such as the cultivation of our poor soils, our restrictions upon commerce, and our weight of taxation, I find it very difficult to admit a theory of our distresses so inconsistent with the theory of our comparative prosperity. While the greatest quantity of our poor lands were in cultivation; while there were more than usual restrictions upon our commerce, and very little corn was imported; and while taxation was at its height, the country confessedly increased in wealth with a rapidity never known before. Since some of our poorest lands have been thrown out of cultivation; since the peace has removed many of the restrictions upon our commerce, and, notwithstanding our corn laws, we have imported a great quantity of corn; and since seventeen millions of taxes have been taken off from the people, we have experienced the greatest degree of distress, both among capitalists and labourers.

I am very far indeed from meaning to infer from these striking facts that restrictions upon commerce and heavy taxation are beneficial to a country. But the facts certainly show that, whatever may be the future effect of the causes above alluded to in checking the progress of our wealth, we must look elsewhere for the immediate sources of our present distresses. How far our artificial system, and particularly the changes in the value of our currency operating upon a large national debt, may have aggravated the evils we have experienced, it would be extremely difficult to say. But I feel perfectly convinced that a very considerable portion of these evils might be experienced by a nation without poor land in cultivation, without taxes, and without any fresh restrictions on trade.

If a large country, of considerable fertility, and sufficient inland communications, were surrounded by an impassable wall, we all agree that it might be tolerably rich, though not so rich as if it enjoyed the benefit of foreign commerce. Now, supposing such a country gradually to indulge in a considerable consumption, to call forth and employ a great quantity of ingenuity in production, and to save only yearly that portion of its revenue which it could most advantageously add to its capital, expending the rest in consumable commodities and personal services, it might evidently, under such a balance of produce and consumption, be increasing in wealth and population with considerable rapidity. But if, upon the principle laid down by M. Say, that the consumption of a commodity is a diminution of demand, the society were greatly and generally to slacken their consumption, and add to their capitals, there cannot be the least doubt, on the principle of demand and supply, that the profits of capitalists would soon be greatly reduced, though there were no poor land in cultivation; and the population would be thrown out of work and would be starving, although without a single tax, or any restrictions on trade.

The state of Europe and America may perhaps be said, in some points, to resemble the case here supposed; and the stagnation which has been so generally felt and complained of since the war, appears to me inexplicable upon the principles of those who think that the power of production is the only element of wealth, and, who consequently infer that if the means of production be increased, wealth will certainly increase in proportion. Now it is unquestionable that the means of production were increased by the cessation of war, and that more people and more capital were ready to be employed in productive labour; but notwithstanding this obvious increase in the means of production, we hear every where of difficulties and distresses, instead of ease and plenty. In the United States of America in particular, a country of extraordinary physical resources, the difficulties which have been experienced are very striking, and such certainly as could hardly have been expected. These difficulties, at least, cannot be attributed to the cultivation of poor land, restrictions upon commerce, and excess of taxation. Altogether the state of the commercial world, since the war, clearly shows that something else is necessary to the continued increase of wealth besides an increase in the means of producing.

That the transition from war to peace, of which so much has been said, is a main cause of the effects observed, will be readily allowed, but not as the operation is usually explained. It is generally said that there has not been time to transfer capital from the employments where it is redundant to those where it is deficient, and thus to restore the proper equilibrium. But such a transfer could hardly require so much time as has now elapsed since the war; and I would ask, where are the under-stocked employments, which, according to this theory, ought to be numerous, and fully capable of absorbing all the redundant capital, which is confessedly glutting the markets of Europe in so many different branches of trade? It is well known by the owners of floating capital, that none such are now to be found; and if the transition in question is to account for what has happened, it must have produced some other effects besides that which arises from the difficulty of moving capital. This I conceive to be a diminution of the demand compared with the supply of produce. The necessary changes in the channels of trade would be effected in a year or two; but the general diminution of demand, compared with the supply occasioned by the transition from such a war to a peace, may last for a very considerable time. The returned taxes, and the excess of individual gains above expenditure, which were so largely used as revenue during the war, are now in part, and probably in no inconsiderable part, saved. I cannot doubt, for instance, that in our own country very many persons have taken the opportunity of saving a part of their returned property-tax, particularly those who have only life-incomes, and who, contrary to the principles of just taxation, had been assessed at the same rate with those whose incomes were derived from realized property. This saving is quite natural and proper, and forms no just argument against the removal of the tax; but still it contributes to explain the cause of the diminished demand for commodities, compared with their supply since the war. If some of the principal governments concerned spent the taxes which they raised in a manner to create a greater and more certain demand for labour and commodities, particularly the former, than the present owners of them, and if this difference of expenditure be of a nature to last for some time, we cannot be surprised at the duration of the effects arising from the transition from war to peace.

The changes, however, which have taken place so generally must have operated very differently upon the different countries of the commercial world, according to the different circumstances in which they were placed; and it will be found generally, as the principles which have been laid down would lead us to expect, that those states which have suffered the most by the war have suffered the least by the peace. In the countries where a great pressure has fallen upon moderate or scanty powers of production, it is hardly possible to suppose that their wealth should not have been stopped in its progress during the war, or perhaps rendered positively retrograde. Such countries must have found relief from a state of things, which now allows them to accumulate capital, without which no state can permanently increase in wealth. But in those countries, where the pressure of the war found great powers of production, and seemed to create greater; where accumulation, instead of being checked, was accelerated, and where the vast consumption of commodities was followed by supplies which occasioned a more rapid increase of wealth than before, the effect of peace would be very different. In such countries it is natural to suppose that a great diminution of the demand compared with the supply, would decidedly check the progress of wealth, and occasion very general and severe distress, both to capitalists and the labouring classes. England and America come the nearest to the countries of this latter description. They suffered the least by the war, or rather were enriched by it, and they are now suffering the most by the peace.

It is certainly a very unfortunate circumstance that any period should ever have occurred in which peace should appear to have been, in so marked a manner, connected with distress; but it should always be recollected that it was owing to the very peculiar circumstances attending the late war that the contrast has been so striking. In the American and former wars it was very different; and, if the same exertions had been attempted, without the same powers of supporting them, that is, without the command of the greatest part of the commerce of the world, and a more rapid and successful progress in the use of machinery than was ever before known, we might have been in a state to have felt the greatest relief at the cessation of hostilities. When Hume and Adam Smith prophesied that a little increase of national debt beyond the then amount of it, would probably occasion bankruptcy; the main cause of their error was the very natural one, of not being able to see the vast increase of productive power to which the nation would subsequently attain. An expenditure, which would have absolutely crushed the country in 1770, might be little more than what was necessary to call forth its prodigious powers of production in 1816. But just in proportion to this power of production, and to the facility with which a vast consumption could be supplied, consistently with a rapid accumulation of capital, would be the distress felt by capitalists and labourers upon any great and sudden diminution of expenditure.

On this account there is reason to doubt the policy of raising the supplies of a long and expensive war within the year, a policy which has been recommended by very able writers. If the country were poor, such a system of taxation might completely keep down its efforts. It might every year positively diminish its capital, and render it every year more ruinous to furnish the same supplies; till the country would be obliged to submit to its enemies from the absolute inability of continuing to oppose them with effect. On the other hand, if the country were rich, and had great powers of production, which were likely to be still further called forth by the stimulus of a great effective consumption, it might be able to pay the heavy taxes imposed upon it, out of its revenue, and yet find the means of adequate accumulation; but if this process were to last for any time, and the habits of the people were accommodated to this scale of public and private expenditure, it is scarcely possible to doubt that, at the end of the war, when so large a mass of taxes would at once be restored to the payers of them, the just balance of produce and consumption would be completely destroyed, and a period would ensue, longer or shorter, according to circumstances, in which a very great stagnation would be felt in every branch of productive industry, attended by its usual concomitant general distress. The evil occasioned by imposing a tax is very rarely compensated by the taking it off. We should constantly keep in mind that the tendency to expenditure in individuals has most formidable antagonists in the love of indolence, and in the desire of saving, in order to better their condition and provide for a family; and that all theories founded upon the assumption that mankind always produce and consume as much as they have the power to produce and consume, are founded upon a want of knowledge of the human character and of the motives by which it is usually influenced.

It will be said, perhaps, that as the capital of the country compared with its population has been diminished since the war, partly by the unrecovered destruction which it sustained during the last two years of the contest, and still more by the sudden want of demand which occurred on its termination; how is the lost capital ever to be recovered, except by accumulation? Now it is perfectly true that the recovery and increase of our capital can take place in no other way than by accumulation. But in looking to this most desirable object, it is absolutely necessary that we should listen to the dictates of those great general laws which seldom fail to direct us in the right course. If population were ever so deficient in a state compared with its territory, yet, if the wages of labour still continued very scanty, and the people were emigrating, the great general laws of demand and supply would instruct us that some previous change in the state of things was necessary, before we ought to wish for an increased proportion of marriages, which in fact, under the actual circumstances, would not accomplish the object aimed at. In the same manner, if a portion of our capital be destroyed, and yet the profits of the remainder are low, and accompanied with frequent losses, and a tendency to emigrate, surely the great general laws of demand and supply cannot more clearly shew us that something else is wanted before we can accumulate with effect.

What is now wanted in this country is an increased national revenue,—an increase in the exchangeable value of the whole produce estimated in bullion,—and in the command of this bullion over labour. When we have attained this, which can only be attained by increased and steady profits, we may then begin again to accumulate, and our accumulation will then be effectual. But if, instead of saving from increased profits, we save from diminished expenditure; if, at the very time that the supply of commodities compared with the demand for them, clearly admonishes us that the proportion of capital to revenue is already too great, we go on saving from our revenue to add still further to our capital, all general principles concur in shewing that we must of necessity be aggravating instead of alleviating our distresses.

But how, it will be asked, are we to obtain this increase of revenue? What steps are we to take in order to raise the exchangeable value of the whole produce, and prepare the way for the future saving which is acknowledged to be necessary? These questions I have endeavoured to answer in the latter Sections of this very long Chapter *On the immediate Causes of the Progress of Wealth*, where it has appeared that a union of the means of distribution with the powers of production is absolutely necessary to create an adequate stimulus to the continued increase of wealth; and that the three causes, which, by favouring distribution, tend most to keep up and increase the exchangeable value of the whole produce, are, the division of landed property, the extension of domestic and foreign trade, and the maintenance of such a proportion of unproductive consumers as is best adapted to the powers of production.

The mention of these causes is alone sufficient to shew that they are much less within our immediate controul than the common process of accumulation. If it were true that, in order to employ all that are out of work, and to create at the same time a sufficient market for what they produce, it is only necessary that a little more should be saved from the revenue and added to the capital of the country, I am fully persuaded that this species of charity would not want contributors, and that a change would soon be wrought in the condition of the labouring classes. But when we know, both from theory and experience, that this proceeding will not afford the relief sought for, and are referred to an increase in the exchangeable value of the whole produce as the only cause which can restore a healthy and effective demand for labour, it must be allowed that we may be at a loss with respect to the first steps which it would be advisable to take, in order to accomplish what we wish.

Still, however, it is of the utmost importance to know the immediate object which ought to be aimed at; that if we can do but little actually to forward it, we may not, from ignorance, do much to retard it. With regard to the first main cause which I have mentioned, as tending to increase the exchangeable value of the national produce, namely the division of landed property, I have given my reasons for thinking that, in the actual and peculiar state of this country, the abolition of the law of primogeniture would produce more evil than good; and there is no other way in which a different division of land could be effected, consistently with an adequate respect for the great fundamental law of property, on which all progress in civilization, improvement, and wealth, must ever depend. But if the *distribution* of wealth to a certain extent be one of the main causes of its increase, while it is unadvisable directly to interfere with the present division of land in this country, it may justly become a question, whether the evils attendant on the national debt are not more than counterbalanced by the distribution of property and increase of the middle classes of society, which it must necessarily create; and whether by saving, in order to pay it off, we are not submitting to a painful sacrifice, which, if it attains its object, whatever other good it may effect, will leave us with a much less favourable distribution of wealth? By greatly reducing the national debt, if we are able to accomplish it, we may place ourselves perhaps in a more safe position, and this no doubt is a most important consideration; but grievously will those be disappointed who think that, either by greatly reducing or at once destroying it, we can enrich ourselves, and employ all our labouring classes.

With regard to the second main cause of an increase in the exchangeable value of the whole produce—namely, the extension of domestic and foreign trade, it is well known that we can by no means command either of these at pleasure, but we may do much to impede both. We cannot indeed reasonably attribute any sudden deficiency of trade to causes which have been of long duration; yet there can be little doubt that our commerce has been much impaired by unnecessary restraints, and that much benefit might be derived from the removal of them. While it is necessary to raise a large sum by taxation for the expenses of the government and the payment of the interest of the national debt, it would by no means be advisable to neglect so fair and fruitful a resource as the customs. In regulating these taxes, it is also natural that those foreign commodities should be taxed the highest, which are either of the same kind as the native commodities which have been taxed, or such as, for special reasons of health, happiness, or safety, it is desirable to grow largely at home. But there seems to be no reason for the absolute prohibition of any commodities whatever; and there is little doubt that, upon this principle, a much greater freedom might be given to foreign commerce, at the same time that a greater revenue might be derived from the customs. I have already stated, in more places than one, why, under all the circumstances of the case, I think it desirable that we should permanently grow nearly our own consumption of corn. But I see no sufficient cause why we should permanently prefer the wines of Portugal and the silks of London to the wines and silks of France. For the same reason that more British capital and labour is even now employed in purchasing claret than would be employed in attempting to make it at home, we might fairly expect that, in the case of an extended trade with France, more British capital would be employed in purchasing the wines and silks of France, than is now employed in purchasing the wines of Portugal and making the silks of Spitalfields and Derby.

At the same time it should be remarked that, in looking forward to changes of this kind, it is always incumbent upon us, particularly in the actual situation of our people, to attend to the wise caution suggested by Adam Smith. Fully convinced of the benefits of unrestrained trade, he observes, that, "The case in which it may sometimes be a matter of deliberation how far, and in what manner, it is proper to restore the free importation of foreign goods, after it has been for some time interrupted, is, when particular manufactures, by means of high duties and prohibitions upon all foreign goods which can come into competition with them, have been so far extended as to employ a great multitude of hands. Humanity may in this case require that the freedom of trade should be restored only by slow gradations, and with a good deal of reserve and circumspection. Were these high duties and prohibitions taken away all at once, cheaper foreign goods of the same kind might be poured so fast into the home market as to deprive all at once many thousands of their ordinary employment and means of subsistence."* The caution here given by Adam Smith certainly applies in a very marked manner to the silk trade; and, however desirable it may be (and it is so most unquestionably) to open the trade with France, a sudden and incautious admission of a large quantity of French silks would tend to aggravate, instead of to relieve the present distresses of our working classes.

In all cases where, under peculiar circumstances, the distress of the country would be aggravated by the opening of certain trades, which had before been subject to restrictions, the exchangeable value of the whole produce estimated in labour, would for a time

* Wealth of Nations, Book iv. ch. vii. p. 202, 6th edit.

be diminished. But, in general, as I have endeavoured to shew in the 8th Section of this Chapter, the natural and permanent tendency of all extension of trade both domestic and foreign, is to increase the exchangeable value of the whole produce. This is more especially the case when, instead of changing the channels of commerce, we are able to make large and distinct additions to them. The good is then unalloyed by partial and temporary evil. This better distribution of the produce of the country, this better adaptation of it to the wants and tastes of the consumers, will at once give it a greater market value, and at once increase the national revenue, the rate of steady profits, and the wages of labour.

With regard to the third cause of an increase in the exchangeable value of the whole produce, the maintenance of unproductive consumers—though many have no power to be of use in this respect, others may do something; and it must certainly be advantageous that the truth, whatever it may be, relating to the effects of unproductive consumers, should be fully known, that we may not aim at what will obstruct the progress of wealth, and clamour at what is calculated to advance it. Whatever it may be thought advisable to do respecting the diminution of unproductive consumers, with a view to the placing ourselves in a safer position, we shall be led to proceed with more deliberation, if we are not hurried on by the impression that, by this diminution, we are affording immediate relief to the labouring classes.

It is also of importance to know that, in our endeavours to assist the working classes in a period like the present, it is desirable to employ them in those kinds of labour, the results of which do not come for sale into the market, such as roads and public works. The objection to employing a large sum in this way, raised by taxes, would not be its tendency to diminish the capital employed in productive labour; because this, to a certain extent, is exactly what is wanted; but it might, perhaps, have the effect of concealing too much the failure of the national demand for labour, and prevent the population from gradually accommodating itself to a reduced demand. This however might be, in a considerable degree, corrected by the wages given. And altogether I should say, that the employment of the poor in roads and public works, and a tendency among landlords and persons of property to build, to improve and beautify their grounds, and to employ workmen and menial servants, are the means most within our power and most directly calculated to remedy the evils arising from that disturbance in the balance of produce and consumption, which has been occasioned by the sudden conversion of soldiers, sailors, and various other classes which the war employed, into productive labourers.

If by the operation of these three causes, either separately or conjointly, we can make the supply and demand bear a more advantageous proportion to each other, so as to increase the exchangeable value of the whole produce, the rate of profits may then permanently rise as high as the quality of the soil in cultivation combined with the actual skill of the cultivators will allow, which is far from being the case at present. And as soon as the capitalists can begin to save from steady and improving profits, instead of from diminished expenditure, that is, as soon as the national revenue, estimated in bullion, and in the command of this bullion over labour, begins yearly and steadily to increase, we may then begin safely and effectively to recover our lost capital by the usual process of saving a portion of our increased revenue to add to it.

It is, I believe, the opinion of many persons, particularly among the mercantile classes, that nothing would so soon and so effectively increase the revenue and consumption of the country as a free issue of paper. But in holding this opinion, they have mistaken the nature of the great advantage which the national wealth may sometimes unquestionably derive from a fall in the value of the currency. The specific effect of this fall is to take away property from those who have fixed incomes, and give a greater command over the produce of the country to those who buy and sell. When the state of the national expenditure is such that there is a difficulty of supplying it, then whatever tends to throw a greater proportion of the produce into the hands of capitalists, as it must increase the power of production, must be just calculated to supply what is wanted. And, though the continuation of the act of restriction beyond the immediate necessity of the case, can hardly be considered in any other light than that as an act of positive injustice towards the possessors of fixed incomes; yet there is little doubt that the fall in the value of money, and the facility of credit which it occasioned, acting in the way described, must have contributed greatly to that rapid recovery of vast capital destroyed, which, in the same degree, never probably occurred in the history of any nation before.

But, if we were now to make similar issues of paper, the effect would be very different. Perhaps a sudden increase of currency and a new facility of borrowing might under any circumstances, give a temporary stimulus to trade, but it would only be temporary. Without a large expenditure on the part of the government, and a frequent conversion of capital into revenue, the great powers of production acquired by the capitalists, operating upon the diminished power of purchasing possessed by the owners of fixed incomes, could not fail to occasion a still greater glut of commodities than is felt at present; and experience has sufficiently shewn us, that paper cannot support prices under such circumstances. In the history of our paper transactions, it will be found that the abundance or scantiness of currency has generally followed and aggravated high or low prices, but seldom or never led them; and it is of the utmost importance to recollect that, at the end of the war, the prices failed before the contraction of the currency began. It was, in fact, the failure of the prices of agricultural produce, which destroyed the country banks, and shewed us the frail foundations on which the excess of our paper-currency rested. This sudden contraction no doubt aggravated very greatly the distresses of the merchants and of the country; and for this very reason we should use our utmost endeavours to avoid such an event in future; not, however, by vain efforts to keep up prices by forcible issues of paper, in defiance at once of the laws of justice and the great principles of supply and demand, but by the only effectual way, that of steadily maintaining our paper of the same value with the coin which it professes to represent, and subjecting it to no other fluctuations than those which belong to the precious metals.

In reference to the main doctrine inculcated in the latter part of this work, namely, that the progress of wealth depends upon proportions; it will be objected, perhaps, that it necessarily opens the way to differences of opinion relating to these proportions, and thus throws a kind of uncertainty over the science of political economy which was not supposed to belong to it. If, however, the doctrine should be found, upon sufficient examination, to be true; if it adequately accounts for things as they are, and explains consistently why frequent mistakes have been made respecting the future, it will be allowed that such objectors are answered. We cannot make a science more certain by our wishes or opinions; but we may obviously make it much more uncertain in its application, by believing it to be what it is not.

Though we cannot, however, lay down a certain rule for growing rich, and say that a nation will increase in wealth just in the degree in which it saves from its revenue, and adds to its capital: yet even in the most uncertain parts of the science, even in those parts which relate to the proportions of production and effective consumption, we are not left without guides; and if we attend to the great laws of demand and supply, they will generally direct us into the right course. It is justly observed by Mr. Ricardo that "the farmer and manufacturer can no more live without profit than the labourer without wages. Their motive for accumulation will diminish with every diminution of profit, and will cease altogether when their profits are so low as not to afford them an adequate compensation for their trouble, and the risk which they must necessarily encounter in employing their capital productively."* Mr. Ricardo applies this passage to the final and necessary fall of profits occasioned by the state of the land. I would apply it at all times, throughout all the variable periods which intervene between the first stage of cultivation and the last. Whenever capital increases too fast, the motive to accumulation diminishes, and there will be a natural tendency to spend more and save less. When profits rise, the motive to accumulation will increase, and there will be a tendency to spend a smaller proportion of the gains, and to save a greater. These tendencies, operating on individuals, direct them towards the just mean, which they would more frequently attain if they were not interrupted by bad laws or unwise exhortations. If every man who saves from his income is necessarily a friend to his country, it follows that all those who spend their incomes, though they may not be absolute enemies, like the spendthrift, must be considered as failing in the duty of benefiting their country, and employing the labouring classes, when it is in their power; and this cannot be an agreeable reflection to those whose scale of expenditure in their houses, furniture, carriages and table, would certainly admit of great retrenchment, with but little sacrifice of real comfort. But if, in reality, saving is a national benefit, or a national disadvantage, according to the circumstances of the period; and, if these circumstances are best declared by the rate of profits, surely it is a case in which individual interest needs no extraneous assistance.

* Princ. of Polit. Econ ch. vi. p. 127.

Saving, as I have before said, is, in numerous instances, a most sacred private duty. How far a just sense of this duty, together with the desire of bettering our condition so strongly implanted in the human breast, may sometimes, and in some states of society, occasion a greater tendency to parsimony than is consistent with the most effective encouragement to the growth of public wealth, it is difficult to say; but whether this tendency, if let alone, be ever too great or not, no one could think of interfering with it, even in its caprices. There is no reason, however, for giving an additional sanction to it, by calling it a public duty. The market for national capital will be supplied, like other markets, without the aid of patriotism. And in leaving the whole question of saving to the uninfluenced operation of individual interest and individual feelings, we shall best conform to that great principle of political economy laid down by Adam Smith, which teaches us a general maxim, liable to very few exceptions, that the wealth of nations is best secured by allowing every person, as long as he adheres to the rules of justice, to pursue his own interest in his own way.

Still it must be allowed that this very doctrine, and the main doctrines of the foregoing work, all tend to shew, as was stated in the Introduction, that the science of political ecomony bears a nearer resemblance to the sciences of morals and politics, than to the science of mathematics. But this truth, though it detracts from its certainty, does not detract from its importance. While the science of political economy involves some of the questions which have the nearest connection with the well-being of society, it must always be a subject of the highest interest. The study of it is calculated to be of great practical use, and to prevent much positive evil. And if its principles be carefully founded on an experience sufficiently extended, we have good reason to believe, from what they have already done, that, when properly applied, they will rarely disappoint our just expectations.

There is another objection which will probably be made to the doctrines of the latter part of this work, which I am more anxious to guard against. If the principles which I have laid down be true, it will certainly follow that the sudden removal of taxes will often be attended with very different effects, particularly to the labouring classes of society, from those which have been generally expected. And an inference may perhaps be drawn from this conclusion in favour of taxation. But the just inference from it is, that taxes should never be imposed, nor to a greater amount, than the necessity of the case justifies, and particularly that every effort should be made, consistently with national honour and security to prevent a scale of expenditure so great that it cannot proceed without ruin, and cannot be stopped without distress.

Even if it be allowed that the excitement of a prodigious public expenditure, and of the taxation necessary to support it, operating upon extraordinary powers of production, might, under peculiar circumstances, increase the wealth of a country in a greater degree than it otherwise would have increased; yet, as the greatest powers of production must finally be overcome by excessive borrowing, and as increased misery among the labouring classes must be the consequence, whether we go on or attempt to return, it would surely have been much better for the society if such wealth had never existed. It is like the unnatural strength occasioned by some violent stimulant, which, if not absolutely necessary, should be by all means avoided, on account of the exhaustion which is sure to follow it.

In the Essay on Population I have observed, that "In the whole compass of human events, I doubt if there be a more fruitful source of misery, or one more invariably productive of disastrous consequences, than a sudden start of population from two or three years of plenty, which must necessarily be repressed by the first return of scarcity, or even of average crops."*

* Vol. ii. p. 170. 4th edit.

The great demand for labour which took place during the war must have had an effect precisely of a similar kind, only aggravated by duration; and as this is a state of things which cannot in its nature continue, it is obviously the duty of all governments, if they have any regard for the happiness of their subjects, to avoid all wars and excessive expenditure as far as it is possible; but if war be unavoidable, so to regulate the necessary expenditure as to occasion the least pressure upon the people during the contest, and the least convulsion in the state of the demand at the termination of it. We may have good reason to lament that such taxation and consumption should ever have taken place, and that so great an impetus, which could only be temporary, should have been given to the wealth and population of the country; but it is a very different question, what is the best remedy now that the evil has been incurred? If the population had made a start during a few years of plenty, we should surely make great efforts to prevent, by importation, the misery which would be occasioned by the sudden return of average crops. If the human body had been subjected to a very powerful stimulus, we should surely be cautious not to remove it too suddenly. And, if the country had been unfortunately subjected to the excitement of a long continuance of excessive expenditure, it surely must be against all analogy and all general principles, to look for the immediate remedy of it in a great and sudden contraction of consumption.

There is every reason to believe that the working classes of society would be severely injured by attaining the object which they seem so ardently to wish for. To those who live upon fixed incomes, the relief from taxation is a great and unmixed good; to the mercantile and trading classes it is sometimes a good and sometimes an evil, according to circumstances; but to the working classes, no taking off of taxes, nor any degree of cheapness of corn, can compensate a want of demand for labour. If the general demand for labour fail, particularly if the failure be sudden, the labouring classes will be wretched in the midst of cheapness; if the demand for labour be considerable, they will be comparatively rich in the midst of dearness.*

To state these facts is not to favour taxes; but to give one of the strongest reasons against them; namely, that they are not only a great evil on their first imposition, but that the attempt to get rid of them afterwards, is often attended with fresh suffering. They are like those injudicious regulations of the mercantile system noticed by Adam Smith, which, though acknowledged to be pernicious, cannot be removed without producing a greater evil for an interval of considerable length.

Theoretical writers are too apt, in their calculations, to overlook these intervals; but eight or ten years, recurring not unfrequently, are serious spaces in human life. They amount to a serious sum of happiness or misery, according as they are prosperous or adverse, and leave the country in a very different state at their termination. In prosperous times the mercantile classes often realize fortunes, which go far towards securing them against the future; but unfortunately the working classes, though they share in the general prosperity, do not share in it so largely as in the general adversity. They may suffer the greatest distress in a period of low wages, but cannot be adequately compensated by a period of high wages. To them fluctuations must always bring more evil than good; and, with a view to the happiness of the great mass of society, it should be our object, as far as possible, to maintain peace, and an equable expenditure.

* When there is no demand for labour, however low the price of food may be, the labouring classes can only obtain it by charity.

THE END.

INDEX.